BEHIND THE BLACK ROBES
ROBES

Failed Justice

BARBARA C. JOHNSON

ISBN: 1-4392-4115-5
ISBN-13: 9781439241158
LCCN: 2009905286

Visit www.booksurge.com to order additional copies.

DEDICATION

This book would not exist were it not for the insolence of the judiciary to ignore the People's constitutional rights to due process and the equal protection of the laws—constitutional, statutory, or common law, rules, regulations.

There is nothing like motivation spurred by lawlessness, particularly by the judiciary, regardless of whether they are attached to state or federal judicial systems.

This book is therefore dedicated to each and every lawless judge named in this book. They should all be forthwith impeached without pension or health benefits. Each took an oath and did not abide by it.

There are 100s more across this nation. Readers should email me the names of their "favorite" judges and the reasons their judges should be on a list of judges to whom to dedicate a supplement to this book.

TABLE OF CONTENTS

PREFACE

Birds of a Feather Don't Stick Together

Impeach all the judges. Kill all the lawyers. Jail the conspirators. The Internet is ablaze with these cries. Why? Because people are losing their law cases without reasonable, common sense explanations.

This book attempts to provide those reasonable, common sense explanations. This book attempts to illustrate why we desperately need court reform in the United States. This book attempts to alert you to the tricks and traps for the unwary that the courts use to make your case fail.

The courts' reasons are many: They want to stem the flood of cases being filed. They want to stem the number of frivolous cases. They want to protect the interest of wealthy, vested entities, both natural— say, a politician's favorite friend—and unnatural—say, Big Pharma. They want to protect the revenue in the States' coffers.

In each case that does not settle, at least one party claims victory and at least one party claims defeat. Many who are defeated should not be defeated and many who win should not win. When does justice win? Not as often as it should. Why? This new millennium's system of American jurisprudence interferes with justice by both ignoring or mis-applying federal and state constitutions and statutes and relying in most instances on judge-made common law. When judges make new law, we say that the judges are operating by judicial fiat. And judicial fiat gives us surprises, surprises that cause cases to wind through the court systems, attorneys fees to rise, and your anxiety to increase . . . all torturously.

This book is also not a book of lawsuit tombstones. This book is not a book of an Al Qaeda type solution to the problem of the courts . . . although there would be millions of Hoorahs on our streets should the courts be the targets of alleged terrorists. This book is not espousing Thomas Jefferson's recommendation of a revolution every score of years.

A revolution is impossible. The major population centers are too far apart. The association of birds of a feather is inconvenient, if not

impossible. Even if gun laws were not strict in some of these population centers, the U.S. military would squash any revolutionaries with
ease. Even John Brown, were he not a-lying and a-spinning in his grave
today, would not try to revolt. Neither would Shays and his neighboring, armed farmers dare rebel as they did against crushing debt, taxes,
and debtors' courts and prison.\¹/

It is no longer a question of courage. Courage has become fool-
hardiness.

Well, enough is enough. It is time to reform our courts. And this
great need for court reform applies to both the federal court and the
50 state court systems.

I have found that the courts responsible for the greatest distress
are the family-law courts—a world in which judges enjoy far too much
power with far too little scrutiny—probate courts, appellate courts,
and any federal court when dealing with the Federal Civil Rights Act,
known as section 1983.\²/

Some of the causes of the distress are federal laws and the federal
bonuses given to each of the States annually. These include the bonuses
given for compliance and enforcement of the so-called domestic violence laws and guidelines, child-support laws and guidelines.\³/ They
have all arisen out of CAPTA, the Child Abuse Prevention and Treatment
Act,\⁴/ the result of the most lobbied bill in the history of our country.
Known also as the Mondale Act, CAPTA was allegedly well-intentioned
legislation. Senator Walter Mondale also used it to boost his candidacy in
the 1976 presidential campaign. However, incremental changes by federal and state legislatures, bureaucracies, and the judiciary have caused
CAPTA to stray seriously awry.

Some religious groups have put some blame onto the no-fault divorce laws. The paradigm shift in family values from the structured
roles in the 1950s to the anything goes in the 2000s may have something to do with these changes.

And the fathers' rights groups vociferously identify the Violence
Against Women Act (VAWA) as a primary cause of distress.

The impediments to finding relief from the legal nightmares un-
necessarily caused by the present justice system are the judges and the
unlawful judge-made doctrine of judicial immunity. Immunity comes
in several flavors, quasi, prosecutorial, qualified, and the most favorite,
absolute. Add to the equation the judicially created federal abstention
doctrines: Rooker-Feldman, Younger, Burford, and a few others. These

doctrines are often discussed in legal treatises under the sections on comity and federalism, but they are, in fact, judge-made legal prescriptions made to relieve the judiciary from being accountable for judicial decisions that favor ill-motivated political policies and designs. The legal treatises never mention the judicial goal of accommodating ill-motivated political decisions. If the treatises were to do so, the apparition of political and financial backing would become visible. So, instead, the treatises expound grandly that the abstention doctrines are necessary in order to save the judiciary from having to overwork because of frivolous cases.

A treasonous side-effect of the abstention doctrines is the disappearance of constitutional due process and equal protection. The cornerstone of due process is fundamental fairness, which arises **(1)** when you are given notice of why you are being served with a formal Complaint or of why you are being criminally charged and **(2)** when you are given an opportunity to be heard, that is, an opportunity to cross-examine your adversaries and to present your defenses.

A more grotesque side-effect has been the holocaust of the American family, the disappearance of fatherhood, the impotence of the American male, and the disparagement of the American boy.

One blatant example of the drifting away from our fundamental constitutional rights to due process and equal protections is the plight your lawyers are suffering. Some readers will not find this a sympathetic plight. That unfortunately is a mistake. There are some lawyers who fight like hell for their clients and their clients' constitutional rights, and when they do, the entities that regulate the practice of law act to suspend or disbar those lawyers, leaving fewer and fewer lawyers across this country to zealously represent clients.

The lawyers lose. Their potential clients—you—lose.

With only a few exceptions, the States' Rules of Professional Conduct do not provide constitutional protections in their attorney discipline systems. The ordinary lawyer who has crossed the line of challenging the judiciary because of erroneous rulings or final decision is then led to his or her slaughter without any opportunity to defend himself or herself from life-changing sanctions imposed by the regulatory entity—whether or not they have juridical power—or by the State's High Court.

The unlawful prosecutions of lawyers who exercise their First Amendment rights in order to protect their clients has reached endemic proportions, making it almost impossible for a potential client to find a lawyer willing to take his or her civil rights case or any other acrimonious case he or she might have and for which he or she is seeking legal representation.

I am one of those lawyers. In 2006, after practicing law for almost 19 years, I was disbarred after a three-year politically motivated fight following my run for governor on a platform of court reform and the abolishment of judicial immunity. I submit that there was retaliation against my practice with the growing popularity of my website, *http:// www.falseallegations.com,\5/* which contains pleadings that my website visitors can freely download and use as boilerplate for their own law suits and on which I criticize judges who deserve to be criticized and whose judicial appointments should never have occurred.

Despite my wrongful disbarment, my passion will not diminish until there is a metamorphosis of our current court system—now entrenched, ensconced, and elitist—into one that permits, promotes, and proudly extols the fundamentals of fairness, justice, transparency, consistency and common sense.

I hope you the reader joins me with your passion in the fight for court reform so that the public will be able to find relief from our federal and state courts.

Only then will the increasing volume of the Internet's blaze of these cries—*All the lawyers are thieves! All the judges are corrupt! The courts are corrupt. We are living in Amerika, not America*—be silenced.

INTRODUCTION

A Lawcase
A Game of Chess

A law case is like a game of chess. The game starts when someone says, Let's play! . . . and uses a Complaint to tell who the players are (the plaintiffs and defendants), the facts describing both the event(s) about which the plaintiff is unhappy and the actions for which the plaintiff seeks money from the defendants. In some legal actions, a plaintiff might seek only that a defendant be ordered to do or not do something.

You are the plaintiff if you are initiating a Complaint.

The defendant is the person you are suing.

Your facts are your men.

Your causes of action are your goals. Such goals are to prove that the defendant committed, for example, a violation of a contract, fraud, trespass of property, interference with parental or other civil rights.

Your strategy remains secret . . . and is slowly revealed in your oppositions to the defendants' motions and your surreplies to their replies.

You reveal only as much as necessary in your discovery motions and replies. The same rules apply if you must fight any counterclaims against you.

Each defendant must respond to the Complaint. There are two types of responses to a Complaint: a pleading called an Answer and one called a Motion to Dismiss. A defendant is more likely to serve you with a Motion to Dismiss and to file it in court before he or she serves you and files an Answer.\6/

Why? When a defendant files a Motion to Dismiss, he does not have to admit or deny any of the facts you have put in your Complaint. At this stage, the court will deem all the facts as you stated them in your Complaint as being true—whether or not they are. The defendant may, however, challenge your Complaint on legal grounds. Perhaps you waited too long after the fact to file a Complaint. Perhaps you do not have enough men, that is, facts, on your chess board, your Complaint. If his challenge is successful, your Complaint is dismissed. If the defendant's challenge is not successful, he must then and only then serve on you and file in court his Answer.

In his Answer, the defendant must write his "affirmative defenses," which are justified or justifiable excuses for the defendant's behavior.\7/ These are the arrows in the defendant's quiver of one his knights, perhaps. He has many arrows, which are called accord and satisfaction, arbitration and award, assumption of risk, contributory negligence, discharge in bankruptcy, duress, estoppel, failure of consideration, fraud, illegality, injury by fellow servant, laches, license, payment, release, *res judicata*, statute of frauds, statute of limitations, waiver, /and any other matter constituting an avoidance or affirmative defense.\8/ Some of these terms likely sound familiar to you. Since this book is not a law course, I'll not attempt to explain them here. If, however, you are acting or going to act pro se, you should consider searching for the unfamiliar terms on the Internet.

If a case is not dismissed, the parties enter the Discovery phase. The parties send each other Interrogatories and Requests for Production of Documents. These should not require explanation now. Your intuition should be sufficient. The rules of civil procedure dictate how long you have to respond to the Interrogatories and the Requests. In Massachusetts, parties must answer Interrogatories within 45 days and respond to Requests within 30 days. The timing in the Federal court differs slightly . . . and so does the number of Interrogatories that can be posed differ in the State and Federal court.

Because the profession of law has turned into a business like any other, and the quality of the lawyers practicing varies greatly, the Discovery phase of the action more than often becomes very contentious.

Some lawyers will file a Motion for Sanctions if a response arrives at their office a day late. This is stupid. Notwithstanding the foolishness, your lawyer must oppose that motion—and will charge you for the opposition—for there are some judges who will automatically allow a motion that is not opposed and there are some judges who will consider an opposition that is a day late as being late . . . and sanctionable. An order commanding you to pay your opponent's attorney's fees might be one such sanction. I cannot say with certitude because the rule, while not loosy-goosy, is a toothless tiger: judges rarely enforce it.

If judges did, of course, what the rules provide for, particularly the discovery rules, cases would take a much shorter time to resolve, there would be fewer hearings necessary, compelling compliance would shorten the length of time it takes to resolve a law case, and in the long run, your attorney's fees would be lower.

Reasonable lawyers will request opposing counsel to assent to an extension of, say, two weeks. A reasonable lawyer will assent, knowing that the business is sometimes so crazy—all kinds of emergencies, including but not limited to unexpected emergency motions, unexpected emergency hearings—that assenting to a two-week extension is a professional, courteous thing to do.

If and when the requests for extensions become repeated and unreasonable, then your lawyer can move for a motion to show cause or a motion to compel answers to the Interrogatories or responses to the Requests for the Production of Documents.

The longer the wait for responses to your discovery requests, the more likely sanctions will be awarded to you—the movant, the party who files the motion.

Caveat: Although it is not mandatory to oppose a motion, it is wise to oppose each motion. Sometimes the oppositions are so wild in their factual accounts or so unsupported by the law that it is necessary to file a Reply to the Opposition. And sometimes, the opponent will file a Surreply to your Reply.

This fighting can generate high bills for attorney's fees. Your lawyer might not be the lawyer responsible for the discovery fight, but he or she cannot sell you down the river by **not** filing the pleadings required by the fight. Your lawyer is then in a lose-lose situation unless you ultimately prevail on the case. It's one of those situations that causes the public to want to hang and quarter all the lawyers, whether or not the lawyer deserves such obloquy from you or the public.

After the Discovery phase, for which there is generally a time limit, the plaintiff can expect to receive a Motion for Summary Judgment from the one or more defendants.

A Motion for Summary Judgment can be likened to a trial on paper. Each party must write a list of Undisputed Facts and a list of Disputed

Facts. If there is a genuine issue of material fact [read, *disagreement about the fact that will convince a jury how to make the ultimate decision*; for example, not that the contract was violated but that it was *you* who violated the contract],\9/ the case must be given to a jury to decide. Therefore the movant—the party who writes the motion—will claim that all of the material facts are undisputed and therefore that there need be no jury trial. The party who is opposing the motion will claim that the material facts are disputed and that a jury must decide which facts are true.

"Joe American's 'day in court' has ended—so say the alarmists. Trials have 'vanished' as judges 'rush' to summary judgment in a desperate attempt to 'survive' oppressively crowded dockets. Moreover, the United States Supreme Court—far from respecting the Seventh Amendment jury-trial guarantee—has been complicit, enabling judges to take cases from juries. Its trilogy of decisions from 1986 offered a 'ceremonial crowning' to Federal Rule of Civil Procedure (FRCP) 56. Judges never looked back from the 'systemic sea change' that ensued. The alarmists, however, have been slow to support their hyperbole with proof."\10/

If the plaintiff's case survives a motion for summary judgment, the case can be expected to go to trial. However, the parties should be warned, a motion for summary judgment can be brought as often as a party wants to bring one. I had a case in which the movant brought such a motion six times, including midtrial *and* after trial, looking for the right judge, one who would allow it. I discuss this case, an interesting one, in Chapter 23.

If you are the plaintiff and the defendant loses his Motion for Summary Judgment, you are coming up to trial preparation. Make sure your men are ready. If they are, your discovery is complete: that is, your deposition transcripts have been reread, you have certified documents where necessary, you have your documents in binders (one for the court, one for the opponent, one for yourself with copies of the original documents, and one for yourself with the original documents you will give to the clerk when you offer them for evidence in the trial), you have your motions in limine ready to be argued in front of the judge, you have your Motion for Directed Verdict drafted, you have your list of witnesses ready.

If everything is ready and you know your case so well that it is in your gut, you are ready for CHECKMATE.

Chapter 1

Marriage and Divorce

"She got the ring, he got the finger."

Husbands are yelling, *Marriage is a contract. The marriage vows are the terms.\[11\]/ My wife filed for divorce. What happened "till death do us part"? She is the one who breached the contract. Why am I the one who is being penalized? How is it fair to punish me, the one who is not breaching the contract, and to reward her, the one who is?*

Well, laddies and lassies, the history of marriage and divorce is complicated. It is not at all what you think it is. Because this book is not intended to be a history of marriage and divorce, but simply a collection of anecdotes to call attention to *some* areas where problems develop once you are in the courtroom, I've skipped lots of the history and summarized only those parts that I believe are the most important to an understanding of marriage and divorce today.

The parts I skipped are essentially the steps it took for the law to develop from 1620, when the Pilgrims arrived at Plymouth (Remember Plymouth Rock!) and the only things around in Massachusetts were Indians, trees, grasses, corn, turkeys, and other wildlife. There were no legislatures, no courts, no executives. They were yet to be developed. As they developed, the people who reached these shores relied on the political structures at hand and gave the powers to decide marriage and divorce to those who were "handy" and gave them "handy" titles.

Let's begin with what we know. *Marriage* was a contract only between a man and woman. *Married* is a status.\[12\]/ *Divorce* has always been an action for the dissolution of a marriage. *Divorced* is a status.

In Massachusetts, the Pilgrims of Plymouth, who signed the Mayflower Compact in 1620 and were influenced by Dutch law, considered marriage a civil contract and not a sacrament, and "long before coming to Massachusetts had tried unsuccessfully to reform English law in order to liberalize divorce.

"[A] valid marriage could take place without a church ceremony, i.e. by the mere exchange of consent between the parties."\¹³/ (In fact, in 2003, the Court, in the case allowing same-sex marriages, went further: "No religious ceremony has ever been required to validate a Massachusetts marriage.")\¹⁴/ "Canon Law of the Roman Catholic Church did not require a marriage ceremony in the presence of a priest until the Council of Trent in 1563."\¹⁵/ And the Puritans of Massachusetts Bay Colony, however, between 1630 and 1692, did *not* allow religious marriages.

"Once the Massachusetts Bay Colony was established under their control they were free to permit divorce."\¹⁶/ "These early Massachusetts divorce cases generally resemble the kinds of marital problems which come before the courts today."\¹⁷/

"Because the common law courts in colonial Massachusetts could not grant domestic relations relief, and there were no ecclesiastical courts, the legislature and the governor's counsel were the forums in which our early law of marriage and divorce evolved."\¹⁸/

When the Provincial Charter ruled, between 1692 and 1780, almost a century, the solemnization of marriage was by statute and, for the first time, by ministers. The Provincial Charter of 1692 did not, however, "grant divorces at all, except during the period of turmoil brought on by the American Revolution when the royal governor had fled the state. This practical elimination of legislative power to grant divorces distinguished Massachusetts from other colonies because the practice of legislative divorces persisted into the 19th Century in most other states."\¹⁹/

It was not until 1753 that England mandated a ceremonial marriage.\²⁰/ Both the Pilgrims and the Puritans, however, required the announcement of the intent to marry [banns] and a marriage ceremony long before those requirements were adopted in England.\²¹/

Over time, divorce came slowly to be accepted in Massachusetts.\²²/ "[A] total of 38 annulments, separations and dissolutions were granted in Massachusetts Bay and Connecticut between 1760 and 1776."\²³/

In 1780, the Constitution for the Commonwealth of Massachusetts was ratified and contained a provision to transfer domestic relations jurisdiction to the judiciary.\²⁴/

"Massachusetts was the first common law jurisdiction to permit absolute divorce."\²⁵/ "In the mid-Atlantic and Southern colonies, where the influence of the Church of England was more pervasive than it was in New England, divorce was almost unknown."\[26]/

Males could marry at 14 and females, at 12. Clearly such ages comported with the ages of puberty. To the Puritans and Pilgrims, sexual intercourse with a 12-year-old female was neither pedophilia nor statutory rape, which was not yet on the books. Today, a 12-year-old female would be deemed a "victim" . . . whether or not she consented to the intercourse . . . and many will argue that a 12-year-old is too young to understand what consent is and therefore is, indeed, a victim. The 14-year-old male would be institutionalized in a facility for youths, if not treated as an adult and sentenced to prison for a term of years.

I must digress here for a moment to explain why there must be reform of the statutory rape statutes. Let's turn to D. Brock Hornby, Chief Justice of the United States District Court in Portland, Maine. Hornby, about six years ago, found 7-year-olds old enough to be deemed "domiciled" in Maine. *Background:* A temporary order allowed Mom to remove the children from Massachusetts to Maine. Dad opposed the move for many reasons (which are revealed in Chapter 6), and brought a diversity suit in federal court on behalf of the children. A diversity suit means that the plaintiffs must be from one State and the defendants must be from one or more other States. Here, the children, the plaintiffs, are from Massachusetts. Mom and grandpa, are from Maine.

Mom argued that she was a domiciliary\[27]/ of Maine, that she intended to remain in Maine, and therefore that the children were and wanted to be domiciliaries of Maine. Dad argued that the children were too young to decide to be domiciliaries of Maine. Justice Hornby concluded that given that Mom was a domiciliary of Maine, so were the 7-year-olds and that they could consent to staying in Maine.

This issue of "consent" is, therefore, in stark contrast with today's statutory rape statutes. Seven-year-old children, who do not even know what "domiciliary" means are determined old enough to give their consent to becoming domiciled in a State, but girls aged 12 cannot give consent to having "sex." Clearly, the arbitrary line for "consent" must be redrawn.

Now back to the subject of divorce.

A married woman could convey all her personal property to a trustee with instructions to gift over the property upon her death; the trustee was subject to be changed by appointment during her lifetime on giving written notice to the trustee.\28/ By using the trust, she could retain a beneficial interest during her life and avoid having her property go to her husband upon her death. Such a conveyance was not invalid if made for the purpose of preventing the husband of the donor from sharing in the distribution of the property on her death.\29/

After 1785 in Massachusetts, the wife could get her property restored when she obtained a divorce from the "bond of matrimony" on the grounds of incest and bigamy,\30/ and on proof of impotency and adultery.\31/ If the wife proved her husband to be an adulterer, she was entitled to all her property being restored to her and "to retain dower rights in the adulterous husband's property," and the court was empowered to allow alimony for her. \32/ If the husband proved the wife to be an adulteress, he was allowed to retain the estate of his adulterous wife. \33/

In 1995, Maine repealed the polygamy law, \34/ which voided marriage contracted while either of the parties has an undivorced, former wife or husband still living.

In 2008, in South Carolina, a wife was married twice. While married to her second husband, she sought and got an annulment of the first marriage. She then moved to dismiss her second husband's action for bigamy. "Wife could not assert her annulment to defeat Husband # 2's bigamy claim."\35/

Article 20, Par. 2 of the Arizona Constitution reads: "Polygamous or plural marriages, or polygamous cohabitation, are forever prohibited within this State."\36/

Once the court was established, the Massachusetts Supreme Judicial Court had jurisdiction over divorce and alimony. In 1877, the legislature repealed the statute allowing jury trials in domestic relations cases.\37/ In 1887, the Superior Court was given exclusive jurisdiction. In 1922, the Probate Court was given concurrent original jurisdiction with the Superior Court over divorce and actions to affirm or annul marriage.\38/

After divorce was authorized by statute, it was treated as an action at law (where one can demand a jury trial), not an action in equity (where one may not demand a jury trial), but the court sitting in a divorce case had equitable jurisdiction to the extent needed to resolve the case under applicable statutes.\39/ Around 100 years later, in 1986, exclusive original jurisdiction over actions for divorce and actions to annul or affirm marriage was given to the Probate & Family Court .\\[40]/\\[41]/

Although the current rules of procedure allow a jury to hear the facts when the facts are disputed, in today's practice in Massachusetts, *no one* ever gets a jury trial—despite the demand for one, despite an interlocutory appeal, despite an appeal from a final judgment. The courts want to control all facets of a case. The motive is money, the money that comes to the Commonwealth—and other States—as annual bonuses from the federal government: money for applying the child-support guidelines,\\[42]/ money for applying restraining orders as encouraged by the domestic violence legislation,\\[43]/ money for allowing the "taking" of children from biofamilies and putting them up for adoption.\\[44]/

Marriage is, however, still considered a contract. A Separation Agreement (a weird name for an agreement ending a marriage) that is not merged with the divorce judgment and retains its "independence" after divorce may be sued upon as a contract in the trial court (Superior Court), where judges—at least in Massachusetts—are more likely to know the law than those judges in family court, where some have only a miniscule amount of time, if any at all, practicing law prior to receiving their judgeship.

In a real sense, there are three partners to every civil marriage: two willing spouses and an approving State.\\[45]/ On marriage, the parties "assumed new relations to each other and to the State."\\[46]/ While only the parties can mutually assent to marriage, the terms of the marriage—who may marry and what obligations, benefits, and liabilities attach to civil marriage—are set by the Commonwealth.

Society in New York did not approve of divorce, so divorce actions were heard in criminal court until the Divorce Reform Law of 1966 became effective. Today, New York is the only State (or Commonwealth, such as Virginia, Pennsylvania, Massachusetts, and Kentucky)\\[47]/ that does not have a "No-Fault" divorce law.\\[48]/\\[49]/\\[50]/ In the other 49 States and Commonwealths, there is a divorce granted for each and every divorce complaint filed. The court does decide, however, who is awarded the judgment of divorce, the plaintiff or the defendant.

In Massachusetts, there are both fault and no-fault divorces and regardless of the type of divorce, a judgment of divorce is granted for each and every divorce complaint filed. A marriage in which one of the parties committed bigamy or polygamy is void *ab initio* or voidable and shall be annulled or judicially declared void.

The primary difference between the fault and no-fault divorce process: No-fault divorce requires both a signed statement and a dissolution agreement of the parties to accompany the filing of the complaint for divorce. A Fault divorce does not require a signed statement and a dissolution agreement of the parties to accompany the filing of the complaint for divorce.

What does a No-Fault law do? Billy Miller, an email aficionado, vigorously complains:

> Our family courts take control of your family, your time, your budget, and your actions toward each member of your family. Our family courts are also nearly all-powerful, unaccountable 'Star Chambers that openly reject due process, traditional legal rights, and the Constitution itself.
>
> Where family courts are courts of equity, not criminal courts, and most constitutional protections and procedures do not apply, severe and immediate changes are required.
>
> What difference does it make, as far as these protections and procedures are involved, whether a matter is civil or criminal? Is a person in civil court not equal, as a citizen, to a person in criminal court? Snipers, terrorists, murderers, rapists, pedophiles, drug dealers, sexual abusers, and other criminals receive more justice in the courtroom than do spouses who are fighting to keep their marriages and families together. Even Saddam Hussein received more justice than do American citizens who want to keep their marriage and family intact.
>
> Spouses who oppose the divorce often have taken from them not only their marriage and children, but also their houses, life savings, and future earnings. They may even be jailed if they resist the unwanted divorce—a FORCED DIVORCE.
>
> There is no defense against such a divorce.
>
> The issuance of an *ex parte* Protection Order, very often issued on the same day a divorce libel is filed, prevents any possibility of working through with the complaining spouse whatever problems have put the marriage at risk. Given

also both that the law only requires 180 days of separation before granting the divorce and that the Protective Order is left in place, any contact that might lead to reconciliation is also prevented.

Recently, many states have announced legislative "studies", introduced new legislation, or "amended" some of their "family law" system. Virtually all of it is akin to putting band-aids on a cancer patient. These committees consistently are composed of family court judges, family law attorneys, and caseworkers; and all are the very people whose greatest interest is in continuation of the *status quo*.\[51]/

In Massachusetts, there is little mentioned substantively re children in the statutory scheme for the dissolution of marriage or divorce.\[52]/ Children are but a possible byproduct of a marriage. Children are, of course, mentioned in the statutory scheme for actions involving out-of-wedlock relationships, for without children, there would be no need of the scheme. These children are euphemistically called "nonmarital children." The term "bastards" is a term of yesteryear kept pulsating in Charles Dickens' novels . . . and in a recent broadcast of Host Howie Carr's talk show when he was discussing the newborns of OctoMom, Nadya Suleman. Nonmarital children are to be treated the same as "marital children." And like the mothers of marital children, will OctoMom be suing for child support from the sperm donor—assuming she knows who he is?

The statutes give the courts authority to make orders relevant to the care and maintenance of the minor children but fail to say what defines care and maintenance. So what *is* proper care or proper maintenance? No authority states explicitly what it is. Instead, in divorce cases, the fathers argue implicitly that it is not the care and maintenance given by the mother who is on prescription or street drugs, or who is bipolar, or who has a borderline personality. Similarly, the mothers argue implicitly that it is not the care and maintenance that would be given by the father, who is abusive, yells, or spanks the children. (Love was blind when they married.)

Assuming that the husband or the wife can prove their accusations, there are vigorous controversies as to whether a bipolar and/or a borderline personality are real diseases, whether psychologists have some ulterior motive for making such diagnoses, whether these alleged diseases are treatable.

There is also a vigorous controversy as to what constitutes abuse. Is yelling abusive? I suppose it can be, but where is the bright line between yelling as a legitimate expression of human emotion and yelling that is frequent and excessive . . . and what is excessive? And spanking, where is the bright line between spanking on the bum for necessary discipline—Don't go near the stove. Don't play with the dials on the stove. Don't touch that, it's hot; you'll burn yourself.—and spanking that is corporal punishment? In Massachusetts, the court held that a divorcing father, a Woburn pastor, who beat his severely, physically disabled son with a belt to teach him to behave in school—although the child did not appear to have *mis*behaved in school—was not abusive.\[53]/

Assuming that the husband and/or the wife can prove their accusations, is it humanly possible for a judge to conclude that one or the other is not giving the children proper care? Of course not. This is why it is imperative that shared custody be a presumption at the beginning of the divorce. If the law makes it a rebuttable presumption, with *clear and convincing evidence,* then either parent may later seek a modification of the divorce court's judgment.

The Massachusetts divorce statute requires a judge to consider up to 31 factors when determining how to assign to either husband or wife the so-called marital assets. *See* the factors in the margin.\[54]/

How much time do you expect a court to take to determine with fairness how to split each of those items, 15 minutes, 15 hours, or 15 days? Clearly with the number of divorces filed these days, a judge does not have 15 days to devote to each case. And one of the primary incentives of a party is to finish the case as fast as possible and save as much money on legal fees as possible. Innocent people also believe that if they tell the truth, they will be believed . . . and it will not take long. So much for naïveté. And when the result issues from the court, a mixture of rolling or welled-up tears and anger become overwhelming. Knowledge of the law had been absent. Thinking had been waived. Rights were not preserved. Appeals had become impossible.

One must ask, Do domestic relations issues, in which emotions overrule reason, belong in a court? Are not these issues better dealt with by *proven neutral* mediators? *NOTE:* Neutrality is critical. Neutrality has been an issue when the court has appointed alleged neutrals, e.g., guardians *ad litem*, masters, psychologists, attorneys for the children, family service workers, mediators. Most—at least in Massachusetts—have been anything but neutral.\[55]/ So *bona fide* neutrality must be established. To do that, a reliable process for making that determination must first be established. There is not a moment in time or a dollar spent considering the need for court reform or considering how to design and accomplish that reform.

And in contrast with this nation's spending, aka stimulus bill, court reform would cost less than what is currently in any court's budget.

Property

Prior to the 1970s, except in the western and southwestern community-property States, the assignment of property interests in divorce cases was not possible. In the early 1970s, some States allowed courts to divide marital property. The Uniform Marriage and Divorce Act in 1973 encouraged other States to consider a statutory amendment to give the courts greater power to balance the financial interests of the divorcing couple more equitably. Today every State has some sort of property division statute.

In Massachusetts, the legislature enacted a statute empowering the courts to assign, at the time of the divorce or later, if not done at the divorce, all the property interests owned by the divorcing partners.

Prior to 1974, only child support and alimony or quasi-alimony were awarded upon divorce. Alimony, rooted in the statutory duty of spousal support, was the sole means by which a court could try to establish something close to economic equity of those divorcing couples who could not reach agreement on financial issues.

Also prior to 1974, the courts assigned property interests by awards similar to alimony in that they were, like alimony, based on need, but the courts could not provide a mechanism for considering items such as homemaker contributions to the marital partnership.

In 2006, the theme of the Massachusetts Bar Association's 16th Annual Family Law Conference was "Show Me the Money: Financial I$$ues in Family Law Practice." Of the five topics covered, the first was "Where's the Money? Finding Hidden Income and Assets."

Some assets are not so hidden: inheritances past, present, and future, which are split between the couple; retirement funds, pensions, lottery winnings, money damages from lawsuits sounding in torts. It's all up for grabs.\[56]/ Anything goes.

According to caselaw, or common law, property is to be distributed once, but, in fact, that notion does not always hold true.

Anecdote #1.

Abel and Mathilde Jones, both lawyers, were divorced about a decade ago. The Joneses have two children, of whom Wife has physical custody. (One, being physically abused by both his mother and his sister, was quite unhappy in that custody and looked forward to being put in the custody of his father.) Although the divorce judgment split the property 50-50, the wife was given exclusive possession of the home until the children no longer lived in it. The once-marital home was worth well over $600,000 at that time (in the late '90s).

After the divorce was final, the wife continued to remodel the house. It was not the type of home that would justify getting a spread in House Beautiful, but the wife had delusions of grandeur and tried to make the house match her delusions. Although the wife had a boyfriend who (an undertaker whose business was unaffected by the economy) gave her $20,000 for a new roof which was not yet necessary, she sought the money from her ex-husband to repay the boyfriend. She knew Abel did not have either the $20,000 for the roof or the other tens of thousands of dollars she spent on the house. So she devised a plan: she would go into court and ask that her ex-husband's potential reimbursement for her home-improvement expenditures be deducted from his interest in the real property.

Such a scheme had not been contemplated at the time of the divorce.

In the meantime, Abel was renting a walk-up apartment in a run-down building in Brookline. Fortunately his artistic talent and taste are impeccable so the interior was inviting, warm, spotless, and comforting to him and those visiting.

When post-trial financial matters began to consume more time than the original divorce proceedings, Abel approached me for representation. He had been living primarily off of partial disability insurance payments (approximately $38,000 a year), which he received after suffering a serious illness caused by a dangerous virus.

During the marriage, he and his Wife were law partners in downtown Boston. Since the divorce, both became solo practitioners. He practiced out of an office in his apartment. His earnings were *de minimus.* In contrast, Mathilde's law practice, relocated in Newton, had grown. She had grossed approximately $230,000 annually during the previous two years.

Despite the distinctive difference in earning power and income, Abel had been ordered to pay Mathilde child support to that extent where he had to use all his retirement funds to meet the excessive court orders and was in jeopardy of not being able to pay his own rent each month. So dire was his financial existence that he was plagued monthly by late charges and overdraft payments.

So Abel had filed for a modification of the child support. Mathilde had filed both a Complaint for Contempt and a motion for reimbursement of her expenditures for the home improvements. A hearing was granted. In lieu of immediate payment of the expenditures, Mathilde wanted to modify the allocation of the couple's equitable interests in the home.

On the day of the posttrial hearing, both Judge Edward Donnelly and Judge Dorothy Gibson were reviewing certified bank statements for the wife's personal and law-office accounts. (For a bizarre new administrative reason, half the hearing appeared in front of Donnelly and half in front of Gibson.)

Abel offered the bank statements as proof on both the child-support and home-improvement issues . . . as well as proof of his wife's interference with his disability payments and putting him at the brink of eviction.

That same day, Mathilde filed a motion to jail him for not reimbursing her for improvements she had made on their home. It was euphemistically a mean-spirited act with no justifiable basis.

That day, Judge Donnelly, who has quite a pleasant demeanor and appears to listen very well, said he would give us a decision by the end of that week. Fortunately, I was able to convince the disability payor to release Abel's check, and he had been able to convince the landlady to await his rent payment, so tragedy was avoided that month.

But there was still over his head contempt charges due to grossly inequitable past court orders. That he should have been required to pay the Wife child support when her income was between 400 and 500 percent greater than his was remarkable and smacked of the invidious gender discrimination by "Petticoat Judges"\57/ against men in the probate and family courts about which I have been so outspoken and the courts have tried so hard to hide.

That Abel was not awarded alimony because of his disability is unconscionable. Were he not male, an award of alimony of at least $2000 a week, given his ex-wife's proven gross annual income of approximately one-quarter million dollars, would have been instantly granted.

The anxiety caused Abel was considerable. I sought not only a timely resolution of the matters before Judges Donnelly and Gibson but also a fair one, one taking into consideration the wide disparity between the income of Mathilde and that of Abel.

Gibson (1) vacated—without notice to me—the mortgage Abel gave me for my fees and (2) allowed to Mathilde a $250,000 *ex parte* attachment on Abel's interest in the marital property. I jumped up and down and Gibson reduced the wife's attachment to $25,000. Amazingly the attachment was for *future* arrearages Abel might incur. I reported Gibson to the Commission on Judicial Conduct. The complaint was dismissed. Whether there was an investigation is unknown, for *secrecy* is the invisible middle name of the commission.

And Donnelly, calling Abel's disability "wages," assigned half of them to Mathilde, leaving her with over a *quarter million dollars annual income* and Abel with $19,200 *before* taxes. Abel reported Donnelly to the Commission on Judicial Conduct. The complaint was dismissed. Whether there was an investigation is unknown because of the *secrecy*.

Meanwhile, the couple's son wanted to live with his father. His mother's behavior was reprehensible. We worked on strategy for a while . . . and she relented.

Postscript.

Lots of delightful happenings arranged by Abel a few summers ago for his son, which included sending him to a special guitar school in California. The son then on his own volition went to live with Abel and began school (an excellent one) around the corner. He made friends immediately, had play dates, and the little girls in his class gave him their phone numbers!

The morning of the first night Mom was to have the son, she called Abel and said she wanted him to take the son. Apparently she had a date that night which was more important. Abel did not ask for a modification of child support, believing that Mom would nix the plan, since she really wants the money more than she wants the son.

Abel said, "Hey, the child support is ransom. It's actually costing me more because I'm naturally buying him food and supplies and so on. But my son is worth it!! I'm not going to let money stand in my way of getting his mother to go along with our plan."

Since then, another three years have passed. The son was put on Ritalin, which I believe altered him mind. The young teenager's mood, behavior, and attitude toward his father changed remarkably. Ultimately he was wooed back to living with his mom . . . and is again flunking school.

Although Abel is no longer renting an apartment in the environs of Boston, which he could not afford, he still pays child support out of his disability payments, leaving him with a little over $1600 a month and the wife with upwards of a quarter of million dollars per year. This is justice under Massachusetts Petticoat Judges.

How does one instill fairness into a judge? Is the lack of fairness a result of genetics, environment, the judicial culture—the Black Robe syndrome—or financial incentives from the federal annual bonuses?

How does one remove unfair judges from the bench? Certainly the Commission on Judicial Conduct will do nothing. That is a given. Impeachment? That will not happen unless—maybe—there is a front-page scandal and a trial. If the trial goes badly, there will be a last-minute voluntary settlement and retirement, so that the judge will retain his or her mammoth life-time pension. The only sure way is to elect judges.

Anecdote #2.

CaseyatBat had an attorney, JB. While Casey was in Arizona visiting his sister, JB stupidly stipulated to a receiver taking over CaseyatBat's highly successful cash auto-body business (half-a-million-dollars-a-month sales).

Judge Judith Dilday approved the receivership in Casey's absence. It was outrageous, despite Casey's attorney, JB, having stipulated to same.

Casey's wife, the Dingbat Wolverine, helped the receiver, and was allowed to take cash from the register each day. Tools, equipment, and inventory were sold off almost immediately, and the sale of the real property was in the offing. The fees to the receiver and *his* attorneys and an accountant and *his* attorney were extraordinary and unwarranted.

Between November 1995, when the order appointing a receiver issued, and January 1996, around which time I was retained, the business was raked and taken apart. It was next to being unsalvageable. Casey, who had built up the business on hard work and a shoestring, believed he could put it back together despite the devastation, provided the building and the land were not sold out from under him.

Incapable of wielding the power she has on the bench, Dilday would not vacate the receivership, and did not appear to understand the implications of what she had done and how her orders allowed an unconstitutional taking. It was rape by judicial order.

By the time I got on the case, because too much time had elapsed since Dilday allowed the receivership to file an interlocutory appeal, I moved for the court to vacate the receivership. I used a well-established but little-used doctrine that allows a judge on the same level to undo the offending order issued.\[58]/ I call it the "undo" doctrine.\[59]/ When Judge Edward Ginsberg refused to vacate the receivership and the order allowing the sale of the real property, he affirmed the rape-by-court.

A few years later, the couple's eldest child, a son, who had been left in the Dingbat Wolverine's custody, was arrested by a DEA SWAT team for distributing and selling drugs outside a school. According to the Boston Globe, he was sentenced to a term in federal prison.

Effect of divorce on men:– A Major Public Health Problem

A major public health problem today is the serious effect of separation and divorce on fathers. This problem has arisen out of the culture and gender wars that have plagued Americans for several decades, but the real victims are the children, whose chances of being abused or battered or becoming abusers, batterers, jailed, or pregnant go up significantly when their parents separate. The State spends millions of dollars annually on services for women going through a separation or divorce, but nothing for men in the same situation, despite the following serious problems:

Men going through separation or divorce are far more likely to experience acute health conditions, including infectious and parasitic diseases, respiratory illnesses, digestive illnesses, and severe injuries compared to those married, as well as higher levels of psychiatric disorders (depression), which can depress immune system function. Men are sometimes dangers to themselves and to their former partners at this time—men are eight times more likely to kill themselves or their former partners than at other times.

And many men get angry, as the "anonymous" Billy Miller wrote:

> People of integrity and courage will protect their families from robbers, rapists, and murderers, but they are prevented by the courts from protecting their marriage and family from the biggest robber, rapist, and murderer of all: divorce.
>
> Even though the marriage was "given" to two people to honor, according to state laws and subsequent court actions, it actually belongs to the quitter, to destroy any time they choose, without punishment, and with rewards. The state has nullified—stolen—the vows before they are spoken. The vows mean nothing to the state, nothing to the courts, and nothing to the abandoner/deserter.
>
> If businesses worked like divorce court, the buyer who defaults would be sheltered from responsibility, while the seller would be dragged into the court, threatened with the gravest of losses, asked for protection money, have his children stolen, as well as his property, his future income "garnished", and the money would be shared among the attorneys and the buyer who defaulted.

Judy Parejko, author of *Stolen Vows: The Illusion of No-Fault Divorce and the Rise of the American Divorce Industry,* agrees somewhat with Billy:

> Very few people truly grasp the nature of no-fault divorce, but one of the closest parallels I've found to describe how it was designed to work is the "takings doctrine" which has been in the news most recently due to a U. S. Supreme

> Court ruling. The "takings doctrine" means that a government body can use its power of eminent domain under some circumstances to take land from private citizens.
>
> The similarity to no-fault divorce is that the state has the power to "take" marriage through a court order (called a divorce decree) signed by the judge.

Some men—not all—lack parenting skills that they'll need to handle visitation or custody as a single parent. The States provide extensive support services specifically for women going through separation and divorce, but none for men, creating gender-based discrimination which *is* in violation of state and federal laws. (This is contrary to the law that requires colleges to spend equal amounts of money on women's sports as on men's sports.)

The lack of services for fathers is intolerable. Men of color are discriminated against as much because they are men as they are because of their color.

For these public health and legal reasons, the States urgently need programs to provide services to men going through a separation and divorce as follows: The legislatures should allocate funds for services targeted to men equal to the funds for services targeted to women. These services should include legal services for poor and rich men alike. United Way and other agencies that provide funding for gender-specific agencies should be required to fund agencies that provide services for men and women equally, to avoid violating antidiscrimination laws.

Unfortunately, with Joseph "Joe" Biden, the author of VAWA (*see* Chapter 7, *infra*), now Vice-President, it is highly unlikely that these urgent, exigent, critical services will be provided to men. The redundancy is necessary in this Age of Feminist Rebellion. The men need help and they are not getting it.

Instead, their reputations are being besmirched and their lives ruined. Given the absence of due process in the family courts, given the court orders devastating men financially, given the inevitability of criminal charges eventually arising out of restraining orders, also known as protection orders, the number of men who fear making a commitment is geometrically increasing and the number of men marrying is geometrically decreasing. Marriage is being avoided because it is cheaper in the long run to stay unmarried.

As a result, almost 40 percent of the children born in this country are being born out of wedlock. Although men still have to support the nonmarital children, their real property and business interests stay in their own name.

Of course, none of the latter is in the children's best interests, but the hysteria and all the pro-women legislation and societal attitudes have caused this terrible situation.

In the old days, farmers would call the "buck-f**k truck" for pro-creating a species. Nowadays, all that the modern women seem to want is to be near a sperm bank and to look forward to having a ready court-ordered supply of child-support money, which far too often exceeds the cost of supporting the child. Breeding children has become a business like any other. And not a not-for-profit business!

Mothers and grandmothers of male children, sisters, aunts, and especially second wives must unite and join the fight. Otherwise, we shall be unwilling witnesses to more devastation of humanity.

Chapter 2

Child Custody\\[60]/

For the Love of a Child

> "VAWA encourages women to make false allegations and then petition for full child custody and a denial of fathers' rights to see their own children. VAWA promotes the unrestrained use of restraining orders, which family courts issue on the woman's say-so."
>
> — Phyllis Schlafly, "Time to Defund Feminist Pork – the Hate-Men Law"

When child custody is disputed, it resembles the "war" against Iraq. Bomb dad away with shock and awe on Day 1 by filing with the Complaint for Divorce a motion for a restraining order, which immediately issues and commands dad out of the house, to not go near mom, and to not dare go near the children. It does not stop there. The so-called temporary order will show up when he police stop him for having a broken tail light. The order will show up if a potential employer performs a background check. If he is a police officer, he will have to turn in his weapon and he might lose his job. If he is a fireman, he might also lose his job because the chief might not want him going near a child . . . even if the child is trapped by fire and smoke. The bomb on dad's life was a direct hit.

The restraining order issues immediately because the "law" is a mutant and does not require dad to be told ahead of time that his rights are temporarily suspended.\\[61]/ He must be in court within 10 days to fight the *ex parte* order. If he is not there, the temporary order will be in place for one year. Depending on his financial condition, he will likely hire a lawyer to represent him at that hearing. Depending on the lawyer and how detailed dad's story is, it might cost dad $1500 to $3000 for representation on the restraining-order issue. Often when dad and his lawyer get to court, the hearing is continued to another date. The inefficiency or the court *and* the aggressiveness of mom and her lawyer increases the cost of dad's legal representation.

If dad hires a lawyer to represent him for the entire divorce and child custody,\[62]/ dad attorney's fees, depending on the lawyer chosen, will be anywhere from $10,000 to $250,000 . . . maybe even more. Dad will receive monthly invoices, stating both how much of his retainer has been consumed and when he must again put money into his account at the law firm. If he sees no progress, he will fire the first attorney and go to a second and maybe a third and maybe a fourth and maybe even a fifth and a sixth. Each time his retainer will be less because he has been searching for a "cheaper" attorney. There will always be an attorney who will take dad's last $3000 and then file a motion to withdraw because "Mr. Green" did not arrive as expected. Finally, dad, beat dead or plumb broke, will appear in court *pro se*, which means he is representing himself.

Dad will begin thinking there is a conspiracy between the lawyers and the judge or judges. When he finds men's groups on the Internet, he will be convinced such a conspiracy exists.

Do some of the lawyers know the judges? Sure. Do the lawyers have to pay the judges? No, although there might be a few who do. In fact, there is no need to conspire with a judge, for the state and federal laws are already pro-women and anti-men, and the federal government sends annual bonuses to provide the incentive to the States to apply the unconstitutional, discriminatory laws.\[63]/\[64]/

The incentive money the States receive for issuing restraining orders and enforcing domestic-violence guidelines is provided through the Violence Against Women Act (VAWA).\[65]/ In the opinions of many folks, including myself and other attorneys, the laws and programs arising out of VAWA are unconstitutional because they operate in the absence of due process and equal protection.

The domestic-violence statutes are used as a weapon in divorce when child custody is sought by men. There is more about the subject of domestic violence in chapter 7.

Shared Custody.

There is an ongoing dispute as to whether shared custody ought to be presumed at the beginning of a divorce case. Proponents insist that shared parenting is the only way for a child to have equal access to both of his or her parents and the only way for a parent to have equal access to his or her children. Each parent, wed or unwed, they say, must have 50 percent of physical custody of the children. Statistics comparing the futures of children living without the presence of a father and children living with the presence of a father are startling.

The reality is that, in 2005, in 85 percent of the divorce proceedings involving child custody, fathers who are fit to parent are relegated to little more than the status of a "visitor" in their children's lives. There are presently an estimated 40,000,000 American children that have suffered a parentectomy by being forcibly ripped from their fathers, who number approximately 25 million. Responsible for this familial disease is subsection 666 of Title 42 of the United States Code, which provides multi-millions of dollars in Federal grants to each of the States.\[66]/

The family is the very foundation of any stable and secure society. In the United States, that foundation is being increasingly undermined and destabilized by fathers being systematically ripped from the lives of their children and relegated to the status of visitor.

The court is by far even worse than the wives—or husbands—who alienate the children from the other parent and often use "the children do not want to see their father" as an excuse for not producing the children when it is dad's time to see or parent the children. The courts refuse to convict the mothers of contempt of a court order for "visitation" or "parenting time." The courts refuse to compel the mothers to produce the children. By so doing, the courts are aiding and abetting a revengeful woman to alienate the children from their dad. These events are often called "parental alienation."

Visitors are not in a position to impart core values to their children. The children are then positioned to acquire their values on the streets, where the values differ markedly from the values that can be imparted by a responsible, loving, caring parent. Street values can cost those kids their lives.

Denied sufficient time with their children, parent "visitors" are denied the opportunity to be a positive role model and mentor for their children to emulate. The children often emulate, instead, behaviors they view on television and on the local street corners. Often their peers are disturbed and angry.

Parent "visitors" who attempt to discipline their children are often unsuccessful because the word "abuse" has entered into society's vocabulary. To evade discipline, the child will threaten to make—and sometimes does make—a false accusation of abuse against the visiting parent. As a result, we often see children of divorce out of control.

"An estimated 40% of our nation's children are now living in homes without their own father. Most social problems are caused by kids who grow up in homes without their own fathers: drug abuse, illicit sexual activity, unwed pregnancies, youth suicide, high school dropouts, runaways, and crime."\[67]/ "Fatherless boys are 63 percent more likely to run away and 37 percent more likely to abuse drugs, and fatherless girls are twice as likely to get pregnant and 53 percent more likely to commit suicide. Fatherless boys and girls are twice as likely to drop out of high school twice as likely to end up in jail."\[68]/

The data demonstrate that children need both parents in their lives to prepare them for life in the real world. By 2007, in the U.S., approximately 28% of all the children, about 20 million of them, were raised in homes without a father present.\[69]/ In the 1960s, this was 6%, mostly due to the death of the father.\[70]/

Visitation Centers.

Almost invisible are the numerous visitation centers across the States. They shun publicity and the press does not seek them out. Funds for the Supervised Visitation Program arise under 42 U.S.C. §10420 (a).

The original intent of visitation centers was to provide a location for supervised visitation of children by abusive parents. Visitation centers charge $100 per hour or more for a father to visit with his children. If the father cannot afford to pay the money, then he isn't permitted to visit his kids.

Judges are requiring thousands of men to use visitation centers, even when the judge knows that the father is completely nonviolent. The visitation centers are private entities. From time to time, judges and district attorneys have a beneficial interest in those corporations.

They found them, they and their wives might sit on the boards of directors. (Such an example occurred in Brockton, Massachusetts, in the '80s and '90s.)

The danger of such intimate relationships is exemplified by a current action charging two Pennsylvania judges with taking $2.6 million in kickbacks for sending juveniles to privately run detention centers.

"Youngsters were brought before judges without a lawyer, given hearings that lasted only a minute or two, and then sent off to juvenile prison for months for minor offenses."\71/ One of the judges has pled guilty to fraud. To increase the amount of the payoffs, he trampled the constitutional rights of literally thousands of youngsters. He sent 25 percent of his juvenile defendants to the private detention centers, compared with a statewide rate of 10 percent.\72/ The second judge has remained silent.

Men have complained that they receive loathsome treatment at these visitation centers. Attendance is demeaning and insulting. Workers treat every man as if he were a diddler or a batterer. A man cannot even wipe a strand of hair out of his child's eye. One man described them as follows:

> "*There's no privacy. Every visit is supervised by a counselor from a battered woman's shelter. She writes down everything you say, and if you raise your voice, she writes down that you're violent. You can't hug your kids without her permission. If you say what she claims is the wrong thing, she reprimands you in front of your kids. They lecture you on parenting in front of the children. If you ever object, that's part of the validation that you're a violent person. If you tell your child to do something, she'll say to the child, 'You don't have to listen to him. You just have to listen to your mother.'*"

Each man must sign a contract with a visitation center before he is even permitted to use the center. I do not recommend signing these contracts. I recommend demanding both publication of the boards of directors and ownership of these centers and a financial accounting to substantiate the multibillion dollar industry which has grown up across the country, of which Massachusetts is still a part. I recommend two changes to visitation centers:

- Visitation centers should no longer charge fathers. With all the damage to society that fatherless children cause, it's unconscionable to charge a father $100 or more to visit his children for 45 minutes.

- To ease the cost to the state and to make the visitation centers more accommodating to fathers, fathers must be permitted to bring their own family members to supervise the visit, rather than having a hostile woman's shelter worker supervise the visit.

False Allegation Cases.

False allegation cases come in all flavors. Some arise out of marriages or intimate relationships gone sour. Some accuse a man of abusing the woman. Some accuse a man of child or sexual abuse, whether the child was hers, his, or theirs. Some accuse a woman of abuse. In fact, anyone may report so-called suspected abuse to the child services department or agency. Neighbors might report you, whether you are female or male, if your kids had an argument or scuffle and you stood up for your child. Your neighbor will have protection; his or her identity will be redacted from any child services report you are lucky to receive. Mandatory reporters must report suspected child or child sexual abuse. Designated mandatory reporters vary from State to State.

Department of Children and Families ["DCF"], formerly Department of Social Services ["DSS"], it is rumored, does one small thing correctly. It assigns more weight to reports when it knows who the accuser is than it does to anonymously filed reports. But it can still act on anonymous reports, which some Internet aficionados say is a hallmark of a police state.

In Massachusetts, there was even a bill to make lead inspectors mandatory reporters. Fortunately it did not pass. Can you imagine a poor woman who called for a lead inspection of the cheap apartment she is renting because she is worried about what appears to be old paint chips her toddler has chewed, and after the lead inspector finishes the inspection, he reports her for parental neglect? His reason is, the apartment is not as clean as he thinks it should be, or the kids are not allegedly "suitably dressed" . . . or anything from which the lead inspector can allege neglect. He does not consider that she might not have money to purchase cleaning products regularly or to buy the children new clothes.

The child service agency would then step in and bring an action against the mother and take the children from her and place them into foster care.

Anecdote #1.

Belinda and Tom had a medium-term marriage, a union out of which was born a beautiful little girl. The wife, well-educated and well-trained as a technician in the sciences, became obsessed with the notion that her husband was raping her. Having had a mother who was mentally ill on and off throughout his and his siblings lives and having learned from his devoted father great patience while dealing with his mother, Tom showed great patience with Belinda, too. Tom bought them a modest home with an extra room to use as a sewing room. Belinda loved to sew. As Belinda's obsession and alcoholism burgeoned, her sewing room became her bedroom.

Tom became the primary caregiver and homemaker: he prepared breakfast for the child while mommy slept her hangover off, came home from his work as a medical professional at lunch time to feed his beloved daughter, made the Sunday family dinners, did the laundry, the house-cleaning, and the shopping. After weekday suppers, he took the child with him to karate lessons at the YMCA, where the instructor had set aside a Kiddy's Korner to teach the youngsters karate as well. And Tom, of course, also took care of bathing the child. Belinda was useless as both a wife and a mother while she was drinking her six-pack.

At some point, Belinda began attending AA. Tom said, he was amazed. After her first AA meeting Belinda stopped drinking. She continued, however, to say he raped her. As soon as he opened the door after his work at the hospital, she would start ragging at him.

After a stint at pastoral couple's counseling for a short time, Belinda stopped attending because she felt the priest was not "on her side." Discounting Tom's willingness to help not only her but them, Belinda began attending a rape survivors' group. On her first visit, the intake worker told her to bring the child for an interview. Belinda did, and the intake worker, who had no credentials for evaluating children for abuse of any kind, told her—despite having absolutely no evidence—that the child, too, had been raped and immediately reported the alleged rape of the child services department. Ultimately, Belinda filed for divorce and on the first day moved for a restraining order commanding Tom to stay away from both Belinda and the child.

Tom was devastated. More religious than Belinda, he did not want a divorce. He also wanted a functional family in which their child could experience a happy childhood with all the benefits he could and was willing to provide.

Instead, he found himself defending a charge of rape of a minor in criminal court as well as defending against the divorce in family court. He then terminated his first counsel and came to me for representation. During that time, he had been allowed to phone the child one time per week. Belinda listened in on the extension. Both the child and Tom were aware of Belinda's "presence" during their conversations, but neither put up a fuss. Tom frequently sent little gifts to the child, for instance, a poster of her latest music idol, a special T-shirt, a book that they could "share" on the phone.

Fast forward about a year or year-and-a-half to the divorce trial. We had many witnesses: the chief doctor of Tom's unit, the karate instructor, Tom's father, and two magnificent experts—one a memory expert and one an expert on the penile plethysmograph (unfortunately, both experts are deceased now)—and, of course, Tom, as well as the child in the judge's chambers, which was non-intimidating with its mellow-colored Oriental rugs and historic fireplace. A transcriptionist was also present. Tom and Belinda and their counsel were not present. We were all allowed to read the immediate transcript and to write out new questions, if necessary, for the judge to ask of the child.

Over the five days of trial, the judge had opportunity to look at Belinda's bizarre demeanor and to listen to her guarded voice and monosyllabic speech, if any. In his decision, he declared Tom a "good man"—without that, Tom would have been terminated from his job—but the judge chose not to make a permanent custody decision until the criminal action had been resolved.

The first criminal trial ended up being declared a mistrial. Fast forward another few years until the second criminal trial. We believed the assistant district attorney was having difficulty getting the child to testify against Tom and needed time for further preparation. Belinda was as strange at the criminal trial as she was at the divorce trial. Within an hour, the jury came back with a verdict of Not Guilty.

Six weeks later, Tom married the woman he had met during the divorce proceedings. When his daughter phoned him, the woman answered the phone. His daughter asked him who the woman was, Was she the lady who sat behind you at the trial? Tom told her, Yes, and invited his daughter to the wedding. The child refused on the grounds that Mommy would be upset.

Lo those many years, Tom had not been able to be with his daughter but he had never lost hope and did not abandon her. He hung in there with his weekly phonecalls—albeit not private ones (Belinda never having stopped listening in)—and his non-ostentatious little gifts and tasteful greeting cards of all kinds.

Occasionally he saw her walking home from school. When her confirmation was upcoming, he asked me if he could go. I said, Sure. I did not know a judge who would deny him that pleasure. By this time, only the criminal trial remained pending. So he attended and proudly watched his little girl, but Belinda had been watching for him.

Within the week, the assistant D.A. had filed a motion for sanctions. For the hearing was one of the better judges, a decent man. He looked unbelievingly at the ADA for bringing such a motion and without hesitation after argument, denied it.

All that while, the restraining order was neither amended nor vacated, leaving a child in the custody of an unfit mother and depriving not only the father of a loving parent-child relationship with his daughter but also the child of a fit, caring, loving father.

As time went on, Tom's little girl grew up and eventually, of age, she went to live with Tom and his new wife. She is now 25.

Anecdote #2.

Robyn and Dick had a son—"Jamie"—born out of wedlock in 1985 in Massachusetts. They lived together while Robyn was pregnant and for a period thereafter until Dick decided he could no longer live with the volatile Robyn. She then moved with the child to her parents' home in Maine. Because Dick had bonded with Jamie, Dick, too, moved to Maine to be nearby Jamie. Once in Maine, Dick brought a paternity and custody action.

Dick got a temporary order from the State of Maine allowing him visitation with his child, but Dick wanted more visitation. Mediation was ordered to resolve his request. Robyn steadfastly refused to agree to more visitation. So she disappeared.

Ten months later, Dick found Robyn and their son in New Bedford, Massachusetts. So he, too, again moved, this time to New Bedford, again to be near Jamie and to facilitate any parenting time he could get. The Maine action was still pending. Maine never declined jurisdiction over him and Robyn. And no home-state hearing occurred in Massachusetts. So Dick immediately brought a paternity and custody action in Bristol County Probate & Family Court, resulting in the court ordering Dick to withdraw his case in Maine.

In the months that followed, Robyn and Dick drove together with Jamie from Massachusetts to Maine to participate in the court-ordered mediation and back again to Massachusetts. In March 1988, after a 3-hour-and-20-minute session, the mediation came to a stalemate.

Literally one day after the mediation stalemated as to the visitation issue, Robyn made an appointment with a community counselor, Eileen Kern, who shortly thereafter filed with the Department of Social Services ["DSS"] a report of suspected emotional, physical, and sexual abuse of the boy. Dick did not know that Kern reported anything to DSS.

In the meantime, notwithstanding the Maine temporary order for visitation, Robyn sought and obtained in Massachusetts an *ex parte*\[73]/ temporary restraining order against Dick from the District Court in New Bedford, Massachusetts.\[74]/ Suddenly he was not allowed to see Jamie. (But for two supervised visits with Jamie when he was around five years of age, Dick did not see his son again.)

DSS believed Kern, supported or substantiated the allegations, and opened a Care and Protection case in the local Juvenile Court.\[75]/ Shortly thereafter Kern recommended to Judge Ronald Harper that a sexual-abuse assessment be performed.

Although there was no "home state" hearing to determine which State—Maine or Massachusetts—had the authority to exercise jurisdiction, Judge Harper ordered an investigatory report by Christopher Salt, a licensed social worker, a Britisher.

After reading Salt's report, Dick was so traumatized by the false accusation of sexual abuse that he spontaneously lost his voice. Over the years, many diagnoses have been rendered: hyperfunctional voice disorder, maladaptive vocal and respiratory habits, vocal chord nodules....

Neither Dick nor his half-dozen prior attorneys got the DSS reports, unredacted or redacted, and Dick himself simply got a letter saying the accusation had been substantiated (now called "supported").

It was not until 1999, eleven years later, after Dick wrote the Attorney General's office as well as DSS, that Dick got his first copy of the 1988 DSS report . . . and that report was redacted.

Dick can still remember his tears when he could not articulate. He had to use his speech therapy exercises each day until this day, more than a dozen years later. He has never gotten over the pain of not seeing his son. The accusation of having abused him was the most horrifying thing in his life. Subsequently, Dick suffered a potpourri of physical and psychological symptomatologies: agoraphobia, depression, insomnia, headaches, nightmares, appetite loss, weight loss, inability to concentrate, loss of trust in public officials, the judiciary, and mental-health workers (which has been particularly distressful to him inasmuch as he has had to work in his professional capacity with them on a daily basis), and extreme mental distress and anxiety. To address these problems, he tried traditional and nontraditional medical treatment—everything from doctors through meditation.

The stress of hurdle-jumping from worker to worker, court hearing to court hearing, lawyer to lawyer, and being in the same place after all these years left Dick stunned, then enraged, and ultimately numbed. Six lawyers and thousands and thousands of dollars later, he was no further along than he was at the very beginning.

To this day, Dick has never seen any evidence of the basis or bases of the reports: no therapy notes, no progress/process notes. The only thing which was recognizable was the accumulative effect of the successive reports and opinions. The "system" was like a runaway train crushing him and his child in its path.

Dick tried repeatedly to no avail to get visitation or custody, but at no time was he afforded by either juvenile or probate court an evidentiary hearing or an opportunity to confront his accusers or to test the alleged evidence against him or, for that matter, to give testimony himself in either court.

The disparaging reports had further consequences on his life. Dick was injured beyond belief when he could no longer see or communicate with his son in any manner or at any time, or take him to visit with his family and friends on holidays and other special occasions. When his younger nieces and nephews were at the age when they asked, "Do you have any kids?" Dick said "Yes" and then they asked, "Where is he? When can we play with him?" Dick found those occasions, euphemistically, somewhat depressing.

And to this day Dick must confront doubt; for example, a woman Dick recently met asked, "Does your son ski?" Dick could only answer, "I don't know," and then inevitably he had to explain why he did not know. "It all started with a little Day-Glo dinosaur from a cold cereal box. . . . Oh, yes, and let's not forget Batman and Robin and Batmobile and the Batcave!" It's been a living nightmare.

Until a few years ago, when a meeting with his son was arranged by a drug dealer, Dick had last seen the boy when he was three years of age. His son had no independent memory of Dick. In fact, he thought that Dick was dead. How truthful could Deborah Wolf, the lawyer who had been appointed to represent his son, have been when she told the court about the child being in fear of his father? Not very, given that the boy believed Dick to be dead!

Dick came to me for representation sometime in 2000. By then, Jamie was 15. Dick had heard negative rumors about Robyn. He wanted custody of Jamie. On his behalf, I filed a Complaint for Modification of Child Custody. Because Robyn's address had been impounded, I moved to have the court serve the Complaint. That request was denied by Judge Elizabeth O'Neill LaStaiti for no valid reason. Of course, like most family-court judges, LaStaiti did not supply one, valid or not. Only very time-consuming, creative sleuthing on our own provided us Robyn's address. The time and effort it took to learn Robyn's address should not have been necessary. LaStaiti's denial was malicious and evil-spirited. Her action was an institutional response: support the female and get a federal monetary benefit for the court.

I amended the Complaint and inserted the new address which we had found. (See Amended Complaint for Modification Pursuant to Mass.R.Civ.P. 15(a), Drano #22, at *http://www.falseallegations.com/drano22-js-rgs.htm.*)

After we got the Amended Complaint served on Robyn under Rule 15, which allows amendment of a Complaint without needing to get permission if it is served prior to receiving a response from the opponent, we got a hearing in front of Judge Prudence M. McGregor.

Not only did the attorney for the boy argue when she had no standing to argue, Deborah Wolf also lied to the court when she claimed the boy was in fear of his biodad. Allegedly relying on Wolf's lies and incorrect legal arguments by Robyn's lawyer, but really relying on her instructions from the court to do that which would earn money from the feds, McGregor dismissed Dick's Complaint and left the case closed.

A few years later McGregor, laughing in the face of the law, released documents from the closed case on a motion by the Office of Bar Counsel. But for judges covering the butts of other judges, McGregor should have been impeached for depriving Dick of his rights and me of mine This was the second time that I experienced McGregor's bad acts. I knew, however, that she had been reprimanded by the judiciary for covering another judge's butt. That became public and is in the law books. Given my two experiences in front of her, it appears that she learned nothing with her brush with sanctions by the Commission on Judicial Conduct.\76/

Anecdote #3.

In anticipation of marriage, Harry gave Franny an engagement ring. Franny worked for a prescription pill distributor, Merck-Medco, which did not have security cameras in the room in which Franny filled prescriptions. Two for you, one for me. Well, not quite. The pills would slide down a chute. Some would roll onto the counter. Others would roll off the counter onto the floor. The prescription bottle would be weighed. Franny pocketed the pills that were within the acceptable margin of error. Occasionally she sold her extras to friends. She consumed the rest. She was hooked on prescription drugs. When Merck gave her a promotion to the job in which she had access to doctors' names and addresses, etcetera, she wrote a few prescriptions for herself.

Digression. Franny's prescription insurer was Merck-Medco. When I subpoenaed her account records, I found that Franny had had approximately 80 prescriptions filled within the year or so that she worked at Merck. With a handful of exceptions, all were for painkillers. And from one of the many subpoenaed medical records, we learned that Franny was seeking morphine. It was her favorite drug. Her second favorite was oxycontin with "APAP." With those records, the case was no longer a "he said/she said" case. It was a document case. **End of digression.**

Harry and Franny got pregnant. When Franny took pregnancy leave, she needed more pills. She was prepared. She visited doctors and to combat an assortment of pains, she got prescriptions for hydrocodone with acetaminophen, or acetaminophen with codeine, or Ultram. One suspicious nurse noted in the record that Franny wanted morphine. Ultram is not a narcotic but it is addictive. Around the same time, there was speculation that Ultram, too, would be put on the list of illegal drugs. Franny managed to convince a local doctor to give her a six-month supply of Ultram. She took them while she was pregnant.

Harry and Franny gave birth to a little girl, "Julianne." Franny kept Julianne strapped down in some kind of baby bouncer, unable to move her arms or legs. Tension grew between Harry and Franny over the baby's care. In September, Harry filed a paternity and custody action in the family court and when Franny's mother arrived from Florida, he sought and got a restraining order to keep Franny and the child in Massachusetts. That restraining order, issued by a local state district court, gave Harry custody of the child.

Almost simultaneously, when the child was around 6 weeks old, Franny left their house saying she was going shopping, but she never returned. Instead she headed secretly back to Florida to her mother's house with a few mysterious detours.

Throughout the Fall, there were court hearings in both States. In Massachusetts, neither the court nor the police enforced the restraining order against Franny, who was standing right there in front of them. Had Franny been a male, she would have been put immediately into jail and charged with criminal contempt and parental kidnapping. As a woman, she was Teflon-covered, thanks to then-Senator Joe Biden's law, the Violence Against Women Act, commonly known as VAWA, a law that allegedly protects women from abuse but does castrate men.

After the Florida judge spoke, as required by law, to the Massachusetts Judge Mary McCauley Manzi, Florida dismissed Franny's case, which she had brought after Harry had served papers on her.

Fast forwarding to the Spring. Harry, jeopardizing his ability to earn a living, had made several week-long trips to Florida throughout the Fall, Winter, and early Spring to see Julianne. Upset with what he saw, he pushed both in Florida and in Massachusetts for a medical evaluation of the child.

The Massachusetts court, after a hearing, held that Massachusetts was the child's home state and that it was exercising jurisdiction. It gave Harry visitation with the child in June, so that he could be present at the medical evaluation, and in August and October. In December, the child was to spend a month with Harry and his parents (they lived next door to one another).

In June, Julianne was 10 months old. She could not crawl, she could not sit up, she could not hold a bottle, she could not hold a cracker. By the end of the month, the Early Intervention team concluded her physical development was that of a 5-month-old. They set up a schedule for physical and occupational therapy for the child, which was to be assiduously followed.

During his week in Florida in June, Harry phoned to retain my services . . . after his mother had come to me for a thorough consultation.

In August, Harry saw Julianne and her condition had not changed. Franny had cancelled all the therapy but for two sessions. Notwithstanding that she was already in one of the primary vacation centers of the United States and had not been working, Franny had decided to vacation elsewhere. That vacation was, it is believed, was somewhere in New Jersey where there was a man of interest.

Franny was back in Florida in August when Harry was due in town, but she had cancelled Julianne's therapy sessions. Harry then had to fight to get the therapists to accept Julianne for therapy. He won. After he left for home, Franny cancelled therapy again.

When Harry flew into town on a Sunday for his October parenting time, he saw no improvement whatsoever in Julianne's condition. Worried that Julianne's arms and legs would atrophy, he took her on the next plane out to Massachusetts and planned to bring Julianne to Boston Children's Hospital first thing in the morning . . . which in fact he did. The hospital staff examined the child, sent Harry and the child to the therapeutic unit, and arranged for the child to visit with a doctor at Boston Floating Hospital who specialized in treating children adopted from places like Romania, where orphans and abandoned children are left almost untouched by human hands in cribs. The deleterious effects of such neglect has been proven.

On Tuesday, Harry surprised me by a visit with the child to my house so that I could see her condition with my own eyes. At 14 months of age, the child could still not crawl, not sit up on her own, not hold a bottle, not hold a graham cracker, not stand up, and did not smile or laugh or speak.

Because Harry was supposed to have been with the child in Florida, I thought it best to let Franny's Massachusetts attorney know that the child was safe and that Harry had set up several medical and therapeutic appointments for her. I also informed her of the names of the doctors seen and to be seen.

On Thursday, when Harry got home with the child, there were messages from various doctors cancelling the appointments. Franny's lawyer had phoned and threatened them with legal action were they to see Julianne. Harry, with the child, vanished.

Responding to a Short Order of Notice of Hearing on a Complaint for Contempt faxed to me by Franny's lawyer, I repeatedly phoned Harry and got no answer. I put the word out to a men's group for help. Three or four dozen men, holding shiny red and white placards reading Kangaroo Court (with a rendering of a stylized red kangaroo) on the top half and "Judge Puts Child in Harm's Way" on the bottom half, surrounded the court. With a few reporters and a few photographers present and the demonstrating men outside and a few men filling the pews in court, Judge Manzi did not hold the contempt hearing. I was able to swear truthfully that I did not know where Harry was, that I was faxed the notice of the hearing after he had vanished with the child, and that, as far as I knew, Harry had had no actual knowledge about the hearing on this date.

Manzi was taking no chances. She did not improperly close her court . . . which is often done by family-court judges. These were facts that she could not sweep under the proverbial rug or hide them in a folder locked away in her chamber as she has all-too often done, so I've been told by other attorneys over the years. Instead, she sent me, accompanied by a special master appointed *sua sponte* (when a judge acts spontaneously without any of the parties asking the judge to act in that way), into the court hallway to phone Harry. The judge had instructed the master to watch to make sure that I did phone Harry. I did phone and let the phone ring and ring and ring. Harry did not answer. She also had the police ride by, simultaneously with my phone call, Harry's house to check whether he and his vehicle were there.

We made the front page! One paper went with the headline, Did Dad Flee for Love of Child or for Hate of Mom?\[77]/

By the time Harry was found, five months later, Harry had provided the necessary therapy to Julianne. She smiled, she sang, she not only walked, she was able to run and play and ride on a swing. Harry had taken pictures! She was taking a nap when an Ada, Oklahoma SWAT team surrounded the house he had rented and arrested Harry.

The FBI had faked, literally, an arrest warrant. With the help of the National Center for Exploited and Missing Children, which is a shill for the Department of Justice, they publicized that Harry was unlawfully fleeing to avoid prosecution and that there was a federal warrant issued for his arrest. That was all untrue and was accomplished by the FBI agents' lying to enforcement authorities and to NCEMC and the companies which partnered with NCEMC—in particular, Wal-Mart, which hung WANTED posters in its stores.

To get a federal arrest warrant issued, there must be a State felony arrest warrant. There never was one. There was a State misdemeanor, not a felony, arrest warrant, which had been dubiously issued. There had been no order of custody that Harry had violated by taking the child.\[78]/ Because the FBI did not have a State felony arrest warrant, they could not lawfully apply for a federal arrest warrant in the U.S. District Court in Boston. The arrest warrant they had was a piece of paper unsigned by any judge or magistrate/judge. Interestingly, the FBI never showed that unsigned so-called warrant to the police in Massachusetts or in Oklahoma or anywhere else . . . or to me. Why? Because it was not real!

Remarkably Federal judges have written that warrants do not have to be signed to be enforceable. Take any paper in a pig pen and call it a federal warrant. It'll do.

After Harry's hair-raising arrest, Franny arrived in Oklahoma and Julianne was given to her.

Harry waived extradition and was brought back to Massachusetts in chains on a bus with dozens of other arrestees picked up and delivered to States south and west of Massachusetts. The trip "home" took about two weeks. The day after he reached his home court, Harry was arraigned, his parents put up the bail money, a year later he had a five-day trial, and after one hour, the jury found him Not Guilty.

But for one time for a few minutes, he has not seen Julianne again. But for a marriage to an old girl friend which has given him some pleasure, anger, anger, anger remains his mantra. But for the satisfaction and happiness in knowing he saved Julianne's muscles from atrophying, Harry's future remains a mystery.

Anecdote #4.

Wayne Cann divorced and happily remarried and had three more beautiful children, two young buys and one stepdaughter. His three bio-daughters were living primarily with their bio-mom and her boyfriend (Robert McDermott), but having shared custody of the girls, Wayne remained very close to them. The girls frequently told him of the verbal abuse and threats to them and their mom, Beth, by McDermott.

Wayne and McDermott also did not get along. Prior to McDermott moving in with Wayne's ex-wife and the children, one of their disputes ended up in Attleboro District Court in 2000. A jury found McDermott innocent of uttering threats to do bodily harm. A bit less than a year later, McDermott moved in with Beth and the three children.

At one point, Beth sought an abuse prevention (restraining order) order against her boyfriend McDermott, but she returned to court less than a month later to rescind the order.

Shortly afterward, two days after the middle child told her dad that McDermott "was acting funny and smelled of alcohol and pushed her hard enough to knock her off her feet" and that on many occasions she was frightened of him, Wayne went to family court to get emergency custody of his daughters.

Their mother, Beth, went to court and testified on behalf of McDermott. "Bob McDermott loves my girls and if I felt he was a threat to them in any way, he would not be in our lives," Beth wrote in December 2005. According to court records, she contended her husband, Wayne, was lying about McDermott's alleged drunken and abusive behavior toward the children.

Although the Sun Chronicle reported that Wayne "never followed through with his request for custody . . . because he felt the court would not grant him custody," the Boston Globe, reported: "In his effort to persuade a judge to grant him custody of his daughters, Cann cited McDermott's history of yelling and frightening the children and their mother, said Cann's mother-in-law, Gail Stanley. But he dropped the case when it appeared there was not enough evidence that McDermott posed a danger."\[79]/

Given that Judge Anthony R. Nesi was presiding over the motion, the real reason for not acting on it is unknown, but I'd speculate that Nesi repeatedly told Wayne that he did not have enough evidence to find in Wayne's favor.

About a year later, in the summer of 2007, McDermott fatally shot both Mother Beth and the family dog (Freedom), and then shot the youngest girl two times in the head and the middle girl one time in the head. Danielle said she had closed her eyes and was holding her dying mother when McDermott said, "Lights out, Danielle." Then he fled in Beth's car and shot himself on a commuter rail line track minutes before the train crushed him.

The oldest girl was in Florida for some special event. It was she who called her father to alert him that there was no one answering the phone at Mom's house and to ask him to go over and check it out. So Wayne and his wife went over and found the horror.

None of the medical professionals expected the girls to survive. They had been shot around 30 hours before being found. Miraculously they did survive. After intensive long-term care, the youngest survived but lost her sight in one eye, and the middle girl had suffered through more than a dozen surgeries, had to wear a brain helmet until the doctors could replace her forehead, and had to repeat her freshman year of high school. "That's okay, my cousin is in that class." Brave young teenagers.

Ironically Judge Nesi's son Ted wrote the Sun Chronicle story about Beth's funeral, but he never wrote that it was his father who did nothing about Wayne Cann's motion for emergency custody. This, of course, does not mean that had Wayne been given custody, McDermott would not have shot Beth or the children or the dog. What it does mean is that the court should not always believe the women who testify. They lie. Why did Judge Nesi not believe Wayne? Well, Wayne was a male and males are regularly discounted in family court. If the courts were to believe husbands and fathers in family court, the courts would not get the millions of dollars they have been getting for complying with the pro-feminist legislation pushed on our society by Joe Biden, unfortunately now Vice-President.

As it stands, Judge Anthony R. Nesi aided and abetted murder and attempted murders. Unfortunately Nesi is not the only criminal wearing Black Robes. Judicial immunity must be abolished. They must be made to answer for the crimes they have committed, crimes they would likely not have committed were they not to have a judge-made umbrella of protection from suit and liability.

Postscript.

After the tragedy, diverse local groups sent money they raised to a trust set up for the girl's medical and educational expenses. That money has not reached the girls or their dad and stepmom. Something has gone awry.

Apparently there are two major handlers of the funds raised via the many Cann Family Fund Raisers! The Spence Family, Beth's mom's family, controls the majority of the money. A group based out of Mansfield controls other monies.. These monies were to be used "for the girls" at the appropriate time for college, etc.

Chapter 3

Guardians *ad litem*

Arsenic in a Report

A guardian *ad litem*, GAL, is a man or woman appointed by the court to acquaint him- or herself with the father, mother, and children and whoever else is necessary to fill the picture the GAL is going to paint in a report for the appointing judge. The judge, at least, in Massachusetts, must fill out and sign a Reference of Appointment. The Reference should both specify the tasks the GAL is expected to complete and the date the GAL's report is due.

Each State has some rule that identifies the people who are allowed to be GALs. In Massachusetts, a GAL might be a a lawyer, a social worker, a psychologist. Rarely is a relative of the family being investigated chosen. In contrast, in Florida, other folks may be appointed as a GAL. The GAL program of Florida's Fifth Judicial Circuit has written: "Any person who has common sense and good judgment can be a Guardian Ad Litem! A GAL does not have to be a lawyer, counselor, therapist or parent, since he/she does not perform these roles for the child. A volunteer Guardian Ad Litem should be a person who has perhaps dealt with crisis in his/her own life, and is capable of helping a child in crisis." On my website at *http://www.falseallegations.com/guardian-ad-litem-standard.htm, see* more of what Florida's Fifth Judicial Circuit has to say about GALs.

Florida sounds great, but is it? Only Floridians know for sure.

All too often elsewhere, however, GALs are in the bag and often in the bag is an arsenic-filled report. One of my clients, Lucas Stockdale, and I were convinced that the GAL slipped into the proverbial bag with her toxins in June of 2000. Danger was on the horizon.

Digression. GALs have statutory immunity, meaning they, like the judges, are under the same umbrella of protection from suit and liability. So you have only two opportunities to interrogate the GAL: at a deposition or at trial.

I do not recommend deposing them. Why? Then they know what you want to know and will be inventing excuses prior to trial. They also want to be paid ahead of time for the deposition . . . about $2500 at the very least. The more evasive they are, the longer the depo will take, meaning the final bill will be higher. And if you do not pay him or her the final payment, the GAL will file a Complaint for Contempt and you might find yourself threatened with jail or on your way, handcuffed and shackled, to it.

You *DO*, however, want to try to get access to the GAL's entire file on the case. Then you'll know what is in it. Next you want get a set of copies of everything in the GAL's file.

If you do get it, and there is a good chance you will not, at least you will have a documentary record of your efforts to get it.

So your only *real* or realistic opportunity to interrogate the GAL is at trial, to which you must remember to subpoena the GAL *and* the GAL's entire file on the case, including his or her private notes on it.

If your spouse likes the GAL's arsenic-laden report, all your spouse must do is ask the courtroom clerk for the original report, which the GAL will have filed, and offer it into evidence at the trial. Your opportunity to question the GAL will have come and gone in your spouse's case. This is why I emphasize the importance of subpoenaing the GAL and his or her entire file to trial. Without that subpoena, the GAL will not be present for *you* to call to the witness stand in your case.

End of digression,

Back to the Stockdales: Primarily because the GAL, Barbara O'Brien Beardslee, would neither produce her file on the Stockdales during the discovery phase of the divorce proceedings nor allow us access to the file, and because Judge Nancy Mary Gould would not compel her to produce it, I had Beardslee on the stand for three and a half days during the trial before Judge Lisa A. Roberts, who had replaced Gould. It was show and tell time!

The first thing I did to prepare for trial was to follow a few gold-plated rules: Always examine the resumé of the GAL. It is likely she (or he) will have different versions of it. Check her courses of study and her certifications. She may not have the credentials she asserted she has. Review—again—the standards and guidelines she is to follow when doing her work. You will need this knowledge to prepare for the *voir dire*—a special hearing at which your opponent's counsel will request the court to declare the GAL an expert in clinical evaluation regarding custody and visitation issues.

In trying to establish that Beardslee, as an expert, had the proper education, training, and experience to make the determination on the issue of custody and visitation, we heard her say that there were no standards. She had only her own mental checklist. Everything she did was in her own head. She had been grandfathered into the profession because she had been in the business before 1981, when licensure came in. She took a test, but she didn't remember what it tested.

She wasn't able to name any course or any seminar that told her what criteria she was supposed to use when making a determination of custody or a recommendation of custody and visitation. She stated that there were no criteria. She was correct about that. We knew they did not exist.\[80]/ And she had no training; her psychoanalytic training was dealing with adults, not children. Not once did she identify when she learned or was trained to question children or anything about children.

But she had an opportunity to say what she learned through her education, training, and experience, and she did not. And she had an opportunity to say that a judge should carefully consider, during a proceeding, both the parents' recent positive gains, and historical evidence. But she didn't. Yet, as she did say, she's was a self-appointed expert.

It's a multibillion dollar business, this GAL industry. And the courts, given the explosion of divorce and out of-wedlock cases, have been abrogating their judicial responsibilities by delegating them to GALs.

I do not know the standards for GALs in States other than Massachusetts, but from the emails and phonecalls I have received from "out-of-towners," I suspect that lack of proper standards for GALs is a nationwide problem. So take care. Before you go asking for a GAL, check your State GAL statute, read some your State's caselaw, and get active on the Internet and inquire, inquire, and inquire. Do not forget to Google each GAL recommended for appointment to your case.

If the GAL is negligent or plainly incompetent, you cannot successfully sue her for the damages you suffer. Why? Because the GAL in most States, has immunity, which means the GAL may not be sued for liability, that is, for the damages you suffered.. Included in those damages are likely the $25,000 you had to expend for an attorney to represent you. It might also include the fees you were ordered to pay your spouse's counsel, too, and the GAL's fees. Say bye-bye to that money. You'll never see it again.

The bottom line in Massachusetts falls on the statute, which automatically admits into evidence the report(s) filed by the GAL. Those reports are filled with hearsay, much of it totem-pole hearsay. Totem-pole hearsay is when Tom said something to Dick who said something to Harry and Jane. The GAL insists that what Tommy, Dickie, and Harry said is true because Janie told her it was so. Remember the kids' parlor game at birthday parties. The last kid in line tells what he or she thnks the original statement—whispered by the first kid in line—was. Each kid has changed it a wee bit, so the first and last statements simply do not match. Those changes, even though just a wee bit at a time, *might* be significant to your case.

In the Stockdale case, Lucas, the dad, was the caregiver of the children, and mom was the breadwinner. She had a great professional position, for she was a very talented, intelligent young woman, but she came from an extremely dysfunctional biofamily. After Barbara O'Brien Beardslee filed her GAL report, mom suddenly became the primary caregiver, a pseudo caregiver because she still worked and farmed out the kids for someone else to take care of, rather than dad.

Beardslee should have included the history of Gloria's family, of her family's dysfunctionality. She could say, when doing a study of child custody and visitation, A, B, C, D are necessary. If there are allegations of any dysfunctionality, then F, G, H and I are necessary.

None of that came out. Beardslee had no guidelines, no checklists to use to help her do her work properly. Her checklist was in her head and it had never been tested. She was not an expert on anything. With statutory permission—that is, with permission of the legislators—judges abrogate their responsibility when they allow the hearsay to come in . . . and once a judge appoints a GAL, the statute makes it mandatory to admit the GAL's report. And Beardslee's two reports were whoppers.

The appellate courts have tried to soften the blow of mandatory admissibility of hearsay and totem-pole hearsay. In some cases, they have even applied the notion of due process and the Rules of Civil Procedure. One case held that it was error for the judge to rely solely on the report of the GAL.\[81]/ Another held that a judge may request a GAL to make a custodial recommendation, but the judge must also draw her own conclusions and make her decision independent of the guardian.\[82]/ A third case held that the judge "should draft his order from his own conclusions and not merely parrot the views or conclusory recommendations contained in an investigator's report."\[83]/

Arguing against the declaration of Beardslee as an expert, I told Lisa Roberts that she was going to have to make her own independent decision anyway. "You are more than capable—fortunately, I'm delighted—to make the decision. You don't need to listen to her. It'll be cumulative. You have to make your own independent decision . . . plus all she's going to offer you is hearsay, hearsay, and more hearsay.

"Now, Mr. Stockdale does not have the children because you precluded them from coming into court. So he's not going to be able to rebut what the GAL claims the children said. That is prejudicial.

"In *Adoption of Sean*,\[84]/ the judge's reliance upon the hearsay statements of the child contained in the guardian *ad litem*'s report, and the report of sexual abuse by her father, without conducting a hearing to determine the child's unavailability as a witness under the statute, denied the father the opportunity to rebut effectively this evidence.

"You are not allowing his tape of the children on the basis that they are not old enough to give consent [to being taped]. The children have not been allowed to come into court. So he would be highly prejudiced now for them to come in through the back door via Ms. Beardslee, because that's all she's going to offer. I've read all her hand notes, okay. That's all she's going to offer, what Gloria says, what the children said, allegedly, most of it through Gloria. She only saw the children a few times. She didn't build up any trust. She doesn't know the first thing about how to ask questions of the children. She didn't build any trust. She's going right at them within the first 20 minutes. She never met these kids before.

"And of course the last thing, of course, is the discrimination."

The court, Lisa Roberts, interrupted: "Wrap it up."

It would take more than "Wrap it up" to shut me up. I wanted to put my arguments on the record in case there was need to appeal the issue. "So there is nothing—not only would her testimony be incredible evidence of gender discrimination against my client, you'd be opening a can of worms. It would be cumulative, it would insult you, because you're perfectly capable of making an independent decision, I am convinced of that. It's full of hearsay. That's all she's going to offer is hearsay. She wasn't present at any of these things. Everything came to her after the fact. She was not a fact witness. She's absolutely not a fact witness.

"There are parental alienation problems here. They haven't surfaced entirely, but they're there, okay.

"Now, so there is no reason—the woman simply doesn't have the education. She simply doesn't. A few courses, a few seminars at her employer's, Children and the Law, does not an expert make. As you know very well, even a bar card doesn't make a lawyer, does not a lawyer make. There are more incompetent lawyers, and there are as many incompetent social workers acting as GALs.

"The standards just aren't there. The proper training is not there. Lawyers need more training as much as social workers need more training. Even I need more training. I'm humble enough to admit that. It hurts, but it's true.

"Now, there is nothing to be gained from her. What assistance is she really going to lend the court? That's the purpose of an expert. She doesn't have any assistance that she can lend the court. The court is much—is much more capable than the GAL. Where there is no assistance, there's no reason why the court cannot draw its own conclusions from the evidence it says is admissible.

"Where the court says the children aren't admissible, the court cannot allow the children's testimony to come in through the back door. That would be highly prejudicial to Mr. Stockdale. As the court in *Adoption of Sean* said, it would be denying him the opportunity to rebut effectively the evidence.

"All Ms. Beardslee would say, if I were to question her, is 'this is what the children said.' That is not going to be an effective cross-examination. It's not. It would be ludicrous.

"So on all those bases, that she doesn't have sufficient education on that particular subject. There are no guidelines to which she works. Her evidence would be strictly hearsay, nothing as a fact witness. And it would be highly discriminatory.

"And also, there is absolutely nothing that's reliable or valid in the way she can prove that her testimony would be reliable or valid. She's certainly not giving scientific evidence. It would never pass a Frye or a Daubert test. Just wouldn't do it. Wouldn't pass a Kumho test either, K U M H O.

"It wouldn't pass any of those tests. Your Honor, you don't need her. You truly don't need her."

THE COURT: "No one is more well aware than I of my authority and my obligation and my responsibility to make the final determination in this case with respect to custody and visitation. I have no intention of abrogating it to anyone.

"And there is no suggestion that by admitting the GAL report in this case or permitting this witness to testify as an expert, my obligation and authority will be delegated. It will not. The decision is mine. And I assure both of you that I will make it.

"Having said that, the case law that you have cited to me, ma'am, all have to do with just what I have said, that the final determination is mine. But none of that case law suggests that the report of a guardian *ad litem* on that issue is not admissible, nor has it suggested that the testimony of one who qualifies as an expert is not admissible.

"Your argument, ma'am, and I respect you for making it, has more to do with the weight of the testimony and the evidence than its admissibility. And I am capable of assessing the weight of evidence.

"The report of the guardian *ad litem* is admissible, and it may be admitted.

"This witness is qualified as an expert in the field of clinical or forensic child custody and visitation evaluations, and as a qualified expert, she will be entitled to testify, and the report may include her recommendations in that respect," the judge concluded. I was still unconvinced. There was no evidence whatsoever that Beardslee was ever trained in clinical or forensic child custody and visitation evaluations.

The judge continued defensively to reassure us. "Once again, I caution both of you, I understand those are recommendations. They are not the ultimate decision in this case. And I do not abrogate my authority to this witness or any other witness to make that determination."

"Well, Your Honor," I continued, "with all due respect, I do appreciate exactly what you've said, but you haven't addressed the primary issue that I have raised here also. And it is the discrimination, the fact that you have precluded the children from coming to court, you've precluded us from access—"

"Actually, ma'am, if you remember accurately, I deferred ruling on whether the children would come to this court until it was absolutely necessary for me to make that determination, because the very last thing I want to do is have two seven-year-olds come into this court and testify.

"And so at the conclusion of the other evidence, I will decide whether I need to have that evidence.

"I have not precluded your client from testifying with respect to the allegations he says the children made to him. He may testify to them.

"To the extent that the children spoke to the guardian *ad litem,* well, that is admissible hearsay under all of the tests, both under Chapter 215 Section 56A, the *Gilmore* and the *Jones* cases, and all of those following it. The GAL report may contain hearsay.

"To the extent that the GAL listened to a tape recording, if in fact she did—and I don't know that, because I have not yet seen or reviewed any report here—that testimony will be excluded, because the underlying evidence on the tape recording has been excluded. What was said on the tape recording is not admissible anywhere, anyhow, any time. The fact of the recording may be admitted, but what is derived from having listened to the tape recording, if that's the only source of information, because if this witness or any other one listened to a tape recording, that everyday is excluded. It has to be, because I've excluded the tape recording.

"Now, having said all that, I don't have a clue what the GAL report is going to tell me, because I've never looked at it.

"The GAL report is admissible, to the extent it does not include anything derived from listening to the tape recording. And this witness is qualified to testify as an expert in the area of forensic or clinical child custody and visitation evaluations. And I will take her recommendations, as I take any expert's recommendations, and give them the weight I think they should have, following direct and cross-examination."

Because I took the GAL over the coals, it helped on one hand, but no party, man or woman, should have to put that kind of effort to get over the power a GAL is given. The GAL statute must be changed. GALs must not be automatically considered experts. Nor should their reports be automatically entered into evidence. And judges should not leave matters to their discretion. To appeal based on an "abuse of discretion" is almost futile. It is *your* burden to prove that the judge abused his or her discretion. That is almost, if not absolutely, inpossible.

Because most legislators are political hacks or people who have never really worked for a living, they are not bright enough to write most of the legislation they have enacted. The GAL statute is a good example of legislative failure, badly in need of repeal and redrafting. Two good items to put in a new statute would be a statement of when a GAL appointment ends (e.g., ending at the filing of the requested report) and statement that a GAL is not entitled to absolute or qualified immunity even if appointed by a judge.

It simply is not good enough for a judge to say, "Go to it, GAL. Your ass is covered."

Tricks That Merrill, Judge Gould, and Beardslee Played.

In March 2000, Judge Gould appointed Beardslee as a GAL to investigate and make recommendations re child custody and visitation of the children. The GAL report was due within 90 days. Gould memorialized that order on a "Reference of Appointment," which should always be kept in the case file in the clerk's office.

Sometime in the Spring of 2000, Gloria's attorney, E. Chouteau Merrill contacted Beardslee and told her to add a recommendation that Gloria be allowed to relocate and remove the children to another State. That additional task was *not* added to the Reference of Appointment. Nor was a new Reference signed by Gould and added to the case file. Nor was Stockdale informed of wht Chouteau Merrill was doing.

Allegedly in June 2000, Chouteau filed a motion for relocation and removal of the children. (I say "allegedly" because the motion did not appear in the file passed over from Stockdale's previous lawyer to me when I took over the case in January 2001.)

At the end of July 2000, Beardslee filed her report. Although written nowhere, not in the GAL statute, not in any legal opinion, the scuttlebutt in the legal community believes that a GAL's appointment ends when the report is filed in the appointing court. In the report, Beardslee recommended that Gloria get sole legal and physical custody, that Stockdale get visitation with the children, and that Gloria be allowed to relocate and remove the children to another State.

On 8 August 2000, Gould allowed Gloria's motion. The existing law says if the nonmovant (the person who did not file the motion) does not consent to the removal, the nonmovant must be allowed an evidentiary hearing on the issue. Stockdale was not asked by anyone, particularly the judge, if he consented and was not given an evidentiary hearing. Simply put, Judge Gould did not allow Luke Stockdale to cross-examine Gloria or Beardslee.

That evidentiary hearing was critical for revealing Gloria's dysfunctional family. Stockdale had told Beardslee about Gloria's dysfunctional family at the top of their relationship, but Beardslee ignored the information he imparted to her. She never interviewed any of Gloria's family members.

Later, after asking his lawyer, Kevin Connelly, with the now-defunct famed family-law firm White, Inker, Aronson,\[85]/ what happened, Stockdale wanted an evidentiary hearing. Phone calls ensued. Jack Scully, Gould's right-hand man, her courtroom clerk, and an assistant register, phoned Chouteau and said, OK the hearing would take place but the parties would not be allowed to attend. (I found out about this when I subpoenaed to the trial Chouteau's bills to Gloria and saw the message on an entry for August 14th, 2000.)\[86]/ There was no entry on Kevin Connelly's bills that he received notice of the message from Chouteau or from Scully.

Amazing. A judge not allowing the parties of a divorce to attend a hearing in their own case! It simply did not make any sense that was acceptable. The unacceptable sense was that Gloria did not need to be in attendance, for clearly Chouteau had both the inside scoop as well as inside contact with Gould. Only Stockdale did not know. August 25th was the date of both the scheduled hearing and the Welcoming/Indoctrination day for the new kindergartners. Stockdale did not know about the scheduled hearing but did know about Indoctrination Day and did intend to make the trip to the distant school. On that same day, Chouteau was having a closed session in her own divorce action against Mark Salwasser in Gould's courtroom.

On August 25th, with only Chouteau and Connelly present for the proceeding in the *Stockdale* case, Gould allowed Gloria's motion to enroll the children in the out-of-state school. The egregious fraud being committed by Chouteau Merrill and the court is obvious. Gloria had not waited for the court order to enroll them. She and Luke were in the school that same day for the children's indoctrination. And, of course, Gloria and Chouteau knew in advance what Gould's decision was going to be.

On 15 November 2000, there was another proceeding scheduled for the *Stockdale* case. Stockdale, however, was not in court that day.

Connelly had told him he did not have to be there, but Connelly failed to tell Stockdale what was going to take place. A document entitled "Stipulation for Temporary Orders," signed by Chouteau on behalf of Gloria and by Connelly on behalf of Stockdale, was filed. The stipulation was the expansion of Beardslee's appointment to include removal. After the fact. Too late. Two lawyers and a family-court judge committing fraud. How surprising.

Another amazing order. Allowing Beardslee to recommend removal or not when she had already made the recommendation over three months earlier and the children had already been removed and enrolled in school. Retroactive justice! A farce. Pure farce.

On 19 March 2001, two months after I signed onto the case, a gay judge, Angela Ordonez (my understanding is that she is Polish but took the Spanish name from a distant relative so that she would be considered a two-fer, to wit, gay and Hispanic), stopped Stockdale's visitation (I prefer calling it "parenting time") with the children because he had taped the children.

The purpose of Luke Stockdale's tape was to record an answer from the children regarding a question the GAL Beardslee had asked him. When Stockdale asked the question, he was surprised by the answer: the children told of two sexually explicit events: one, that Gloria's father sodomized one of them and that the other saw Gloria having sexual ntercourse with a man named Steve. (The entire story is too complicated to describe it in this book.)

On 2 April 2001, two weeks after Stockdale brought the tape to court and was before Ordonez, Gloria's father showed up to get on the stand and testify that he did not sexually molest or sexually assault the children. On the stand, he admitted that his second daughter did not speak to him for 10 years—according to him—because of something that arose from the false memory syndrome. In layman's terms, that meant she, too, had accused her father of incest and thereafter avoided him for 10 years. Gloria's father also described himself as a man who retired too soon and spent his now-free time at recreation centers and parks. Judge Gould then remarkably found this accused pedophile to be "a pillar of the community."

In this book, one cannot get there from here. One can only wonder whether Gould also received some benefit from Gloria's father. It is not an extraordinary speculative thought: it is rumored that Nancy Mary Gould, while she was for 17 years an Assistant Register in Suffolk

County Probate & Family Court, was the mistress of the Joseph Warner, former Chief Judge of the Appeals Court. (I have no proof of this, but the rumor is widespread and decades old.) And mistresses, too, are known to enjoy collecting benefits.

Of course, Judge Gould was saved by the judge-made doctrine of immunity from prosecution and liability. A letter to her would also have been *verboten*.

So what could Stockdale do to get relief from the judicial wrongdoing. He sued under the Federal Civil Rights Act in October 2001. The case was dismissed, but did cause Gould's recusal from the case a few days after the Complaint was served upon her.

Prior to her appointment to a judgeship, Lisa Roberts, the replacement for Nancy Gould in the *Stockdale* case, was involved in a scandal that resulted in Judge Robert M. Ford retiring from the bench, in which it is revealed that seven members of Lisa's family received monetary compensation and that Lisa herself received $124,782 in addition to her pay as an Assistant Register in Norfolk County Probate & Famiy Court. See the *Ford/Roberts* case in note 87.\[87]/ See also the *Troy/Manzi* case in note 88.\[88]/

In June 2001, by which time she was no longer an appointed GAL on the case, Beardslee finally went to the home of Gloria's father, who is a multimillionaire. We believe that Beardslee went there to pick up a benefit for her anticipated testimony in the trial, which at that time Gloria believed was going to occur that month in front of Gould.

When, during the trial, a year later, I called Gould's judicial indiscretions to Roberts' attention, Roberts ignored both me and the law. Despite her tolerant demeanor in court, Roberts was an asp. Where Gould had hid in her chambers when controversy arose, Roberts welcomed controversy with a masque, in costume.

I challenged Beardslee's reports being admitted into evidence. "I know that she filed the report, that it's automatically accepted. I've seen it done time and time again. But the cases make clear that if a party is denied access and the opportunity to cross-examine the source of the hearsay information and the opportunity to rebut the evidence in it, his constitutional rights to due process have been violated. That is what Mr. Stockdale has not had.

"Then I do want to add that he has been deprived of his constitutional rights to due process by being not allowed to cross-examine the sources of the hearsay. Those reports are void *ab initio*. They are unlawful documents. He was not only unable to cross-examine, not given an opportunity in court, he was actually precluded from even going and deposing them."

THE COURT: It's great argument, but it's not an evidentiary objection. . . . I'm going to put you on a two-minute warning."

ME: I'm saying that every constitutional right, equal protection of the laws, due process is denied by these documents coming in. It's just the idea that the courts have said that hearsay is okay is frankly, in my estimation, unconstitutional. I may as well go on record on that.

THE COURT: You can take that up with the SJC.

Other Dirty Tricks by GALs.

Beardslee not only obfuscates, she files fraudulent reports to deceive the court. For instance, while her notes reveal that Stockdale told her that several of Gloria's nieces were badly injured (broken arm, broken leg) while in the care of their grandmother (Gloria's mother), Beardslee, knowing that Gloria would put the boys in her mother's care while Gloria was working, still recommended that Gloria be allowed to remove them to the other State. While in the care of Gloria's mother, Kirk cut a piece of his hand clean off between his thumb and index finger while cutting pineapple with a sharp knife, but Beardslee never put that into her report. She said she took that as an example of accidents that happen to kids and did not represent a pattern of neglect or flawed decision-making. While I agree that children are sometimes prone to accidents, how many such serious accidents within a short span of time are enough to induce one to look more closely at the caretaker?

While in her report, Beardslee wrote that Stockdale excessively spanked the boys, in her handwritten notes of 11 interviews with the boys, only once did they mention their father spanked them.

While Beardslee numbered 13 different dates when Gloria had committed contempt by not producing the children for dad's parenting time, Beardslee did not write about them in her reports. Beardslee defended her action by stating, "It occurred to me that if Mr. Stockdale had wanted to take some action regarding what he considered to be contempts, it would have been through his attorney and through the court and not through the GAL." The problem, she always acted in response to Gloria's complaints about Stockdale, but never in re-sponse to Stockdale's.

While Beardslee's handwritten notes reveal that the children re-peatedly told her that they missed their dad and love him, she failed to include that information in her report. Beardslee believed the chil-dren when it suited her agenda and did not believe them when it did not suit her agenda. For instance, Beardslee admitted that she did not write a report regarding the boys' wishes to see their dad as soon as possible. Asked during cross-examination whether there was a reason why not, Beardslee testified, "I didn't think that this represented any change in the boys' wishes." Ultimately, she admitted that not seeing their father was having a negative effect on the boys. One felt "unwor-thy." It did not bother her that Gloria did nothing about interfering with Stockdale's time with the children, and it did not bother her that she recommended that visitation between Lucas and the children be supervised, which is a heinous way to force a father see his children.

She, of course, had no basis for such cruelty. But she had been paid, hadn't she?

If a child has been sexually abused, an assessor or evaluator must prepare a safety plan with the child by having the child identify a per-son they felt comfortable to tell something to: a teacher, a neighbor, an adult friend, a father whom they trusted, a mother whom they may or may not have trusted. So I asked Beardslee, "You never asked Mikey and Kirk to identify a person to whom they could tell a problem, if they had one; isn't that true?" and she responded, "That's true." And she admitted twice that she never gave the children a safety plan, a plan which lets them know whom to tell when they have been sexually or physically abused.

And when Kirk told his dad that he had been sodomized by his ma-ternal grandfather, Gloria's father, Stockdale was but the messenger; so it would have been useless for Kirk to tell grandpa, "You sexually molested me, I don't like it?" Beardslee answered nothing, due to a sustained objection. I instead she claimed "a safety plan was not neces-sary for this child."

I took another tack: "Mr. Stockdale, at the outset of first meeting you, informed you of all his concerns about incest in Gloria's biologi-cal family. Did you believe him or not when he first came and told you that?"

"I didn't know whether to believe him or not."

"Isn't it true that when an accusation of alleged incest is made— Isn't it true that it is a good idea to check it out?"

"I would have done so, if I thought there was a threat to the boys."

"Did you believe Mr. Stockdale or not when he told you that there was possibly incest in Gloria's biological family, yes or no?" Beardslee did not reply.

"Who could Mikey and Kirk, at the time a little over five years old, who in their world of people that they knew, that they could trust, who could they have told that they were physically or sexually abused?" Again, Beardslee did not reply.

The Court, Roberts, stepped in: " Well, it may be inartful, but as I understand it, the question is, if these children—if this evaluator believed that these children were sexually abused, who in their world would she establish as the person to whom they would go in that safety plan—if she believed they were sexually abused." Beardslee still did not reply.

I changed the subject. "Isn't it true that when you were appointed to these people in March of the year 2000, the only fact that you absolutely knew was 100 percent true was that he was the father of the twins and that she was the mother of the twins?"

"That was the assumption I made."

"Wonderful. And isn't it true that you had no reason to believe that one was any more or less truthful than the other; isn't that true?"

"Yes."

"And isn't it also true that you had no reason to believe that he was lying any more than you had reason to believe that she was lying?"

"Yes."

"Okay. So when he came and told you that he was very concerned that there was sexual abuse, in fact, incest at her home with her sister and her father, that she had been brought up by her father, or lived a critical number of years, seven years or eight years with him, why didn't you believe him?" Beardslee did not reply. This was what was known early in the last century a "pregnant denial."

"But you were relying on a document written by an unknown person whom you've never met, never spoken to, never written to, never received anything from, to vouch for Gloria's honesty, isn't that true?"

"Yes."

"You asked for a psychological test to be done; isn't that true?

"And you told Doctor Duffly, don't bother. You didn't check it off as one of the things you even wanted to know about; isn't that true?"

"Didn't check off what?"

"On that request, 126-B, you didn't check off family history of psychosis, you didn't check off history of sexual abuse, you didn't check off history of physical abuse, you didn't check off family history of affective disorder. My God, she has six parents between her parents. You didn't look into all of this stuff with her. You weren't interested a damn in what her history was; isn't that true?"

"I was interested in her history as it related to the safety of the children.

"Is that a sufficient reason to have people spend $3,000 to get a test, to have it tested?"

"Do you know whether the MMPI tests for sexual difficulties?"

"No."

"Have you ever read anything regarding the MMPI?"

"No."

"Is that why you ignored putting anything that Doctor Duffly wrote about Gloria into your July 28, 2000 report?"

In answer to a later question, Beardslee replied, ". . . I continue to be puzzled as to why Mr. Stockdale has not continued to have contact with these boys despite the fact that the court has allowed him access."

"But only with a supervisor, which is insulting, demeaning, belittling, embarrassing and everything. And then [Gloria] pumps the supervisor, and she's had—— Do you know how many times she's tried to get him arrested?"

Clearly for a judge to abrogate to such a GAL as Barbara O'Brien Beardslee the responsibility to learn who the divorcing couple is and the dynamics of their relationship is absurd.

The problem is that most GALs do not differ from Beardslee: incompetent, uncaring, evasive, and probably on the take. And certainly none of them hesitates to bring contempt charges against the man who fails to pay the GAL's fee and certainly none of the judges hesitates to find the man guilty of contempt and throw him into jail.

I know of no women thrown into jail for not paying a GAL's fee,

Judges' Conspiracy

Massachusetts requires the Commonwealth to pay for the services of the guardians *ad litem,*\[89]/ but the judiciary has been ordering parties to pay. Some men who have refused have either been threatened with a decision adverse to them or have been handcuffed and thrown into a holding cell awaiting transportation to jail.

In Federal court, I sued a few of these judges for this very issue, . . . amongst others.\[90]/ As anticipated, the case was dismissed on the grounds of immunity. The primary judge was, however, either removed by a chief judge or removed herself from the case . . . within 5 days of being served with the Complaint.

Chapter 4

Child Support

With Pleasure or Punishment

> In 1984, Congress passed the Child
> Support Enforcement Amendment
> which required the states to adopt
> voluntary guidelines for child-support
> payments. In 1988, Congress passed
> the Family Support Act, which made the
> guidelines mandatory, along with criminal
> enforcement, and gave the states less
> than a year to comply.
>
> — Phyllis Schlafly, "Federal Incentives
> ake Children Fatherless"

Children, are they a gift, a reward, or an award?

During a divorce, a child basically has a huge price on his or her head: The child is typically worth hundreds of thousands of dollars in child support to the parent getting custody. There's no question that parents love their children, and would want custody irrespective of the amount of child support, but that such a huge amount of money comes with the child substantially distorts the child-custody problem.

Even worse, the child-support issue generates bitterness and hatred between the parents that lasts for decades and affects the children adversely.

Child support is the subject nationwide of the Child Support Guidelines, which were written by each State and then approved by the federal government. In Massachusetts, they are reviewed every four years. The Child Support Guidelines of many States must be changed. They are unfair. They are, in my opinion, unconstitutional. For instance, in some States.

- the guidelines attribute perquisite\[91]/ income to males,\[92]/ but not to females\[93]/

- the guidelines attribute earned income to the noncustodial parent, but not to the custodial female

- the guidelines are based on the income of the parents, not on the needs of the child.

- almost all the States require a vote by the legislature to enact child-support guidelines

- the guidelines do not consider the following items which the fathers also must usually pay:

  Alimony
  Expenses when children are with dad, Dad's living expenses
  Supervised visitation
  Fees for Wife's attorneys, children's attorney, Dad's attorney, special master, GAL, therapists, psychologist's or psychiatrist's fees
  Deposition transcripts
  Subpoena costs, service of process fees
  Insurance: Health, life, car
  Medical copayments, psychological tests
  Private school fees, summer camp, college tuition
  Social Security
  Taxes, federal, state, local, sales, excise

- where there is joint custody or shared parenting, the amount of child support is not proportionally divided

The guidelines do not attribute imputed income to males but judges do, and payment of a child-support order is enforced but a visitation order is not enforced.

The Massachusetts SJC has written, "Judges have considerable discretion under the guidelines, and the exercise of this discretion may result in a range of proposed support orders."\\[94]/ Given that an "abuse of discretion" is almost impossible to appeal successfully, this statement identifies a primary source of unfair child-support orders, as well as of male disgruntlement. In essence, the man becomes a wallet and often merely an occasional visitor in his child's life, and all too often the father does not get to spend any time at all with the children.

Then add to the mix the State's Department of Revenue, which has a contract with the Commonwealth for a piece of the action, like a collection agency: some for "you" (the Commonwealth) and some for "me" (the DoR) and *maybe* some for mom.

As of January 1, 2009, Massachusetts' child support guidelines called for payments amongst the highest in the United States: with the newly effective guidelines, support orders will increase anywhere between 20% and 300%. Under the new guidelines, if a man and a woman earn the same amount, the recipient will enjoy a standard of living almost *double* that of the payor.

Unlike Massachusetts, Georgia, during the last decade, ruled its Child Support Guidelines unconstitutional, and ordered that they be rewritten.

And "Minnesota launched a new child support formula last year, for the first time considering the income of both parents, not just the dad."\\[95]/ The alleged theory is that parents will be more likely to pay if support orders seem fairer. The change lines Minnesota up with 37 States that consider both incomes.\\[96]/

Not surprisingly the custodial parents, of whom nearly 90 percent are women, are unhappy. And, also not surprisingly, the fathers of the 255,000 children receiving support complain that the formula for calculating the child-support orders is based on unrealistic child-rearing expenses, resulting in child-support orders that are still too high.

Rather than basing the child support on the net income of the noncustodial parent (usually the dad) and the number of children, the new guidelines use the gross incomes of both parents, with deductions for parenting time and other child-rearing costs.\\[97]/ "It's all about lifestyle support, not the true cost of raising children. . . . And they [the court] are still calling parents voluntarily underemployed or unemployed, when they've simply just lost their jobs.' "\\[98]/

The working women in Minnesota are now making complaints similar to those of men in Massachusetts. The more hours they work to meet expenses, their child-support obligations also increase.

Initially, the new Minnesota law applied only to new support orders. Now it applies also to modifications of existing orders if the proposed modification can cause a change in the order of at least $75. One judge said, "It's simply too soon to tell if the new formula is an improvement."\99/

In sum, each State maintains statistics of when the guidelines are applied. When submitted to the federal government, those statistics constitute part of the basis upon which the State earns a considerable bonus that year from the federal government. (Title IV of the federal code explains when and for what the federal government hands bonuses to the States for items related to domestic relations.)\100/\101/

Phyllis Schlafly brilliantly summed up the history and consequences of the child-support laws.\102/ There is no sense for me to try and rewrite the Holy Grail. So here it is:

"In 1984, Congress passed the Child Support Enforcement Amendment which required the states to adopt voluntary guidelines for child-support payments. In 1988, Congress passed the Family Support Act, which made the guidelines mandatory, along with criminal enforcement, and gave the states less than a year to comply.

"The majority of states quickly adopted the model guidelines conveniently already written by an HHS consultant who was president of what was shortly to become one of the nation's largest private collection companies making its profits on the onerous guidelines that create arrearages.

"The 1988 law extended the guidelines to ALL child-support orders, even though the big majority of those families never had to interact with government in order to pay or receive child support. This massive expansion of federal control over private lives uses a Federal Case Registry to exercise surveillance over 19 million citizens whether or not they are behind in child-support payments.

"The states collect the child-support money and deposit it in a state fund, but the federal government pays most of the administrative costs and, therefore, dictates the way the system operates through mandates and financial incentives. The federal government pays 66 percent of the states' administrative overhead costs, 80 percent of computer and technology-enhancement costs, and 90 percent of DNA testing for paternity.

"In addition, the states share in a nearly-half-billion-dollar incentive reward pool based on whatever the state collects. The states can get a waiver to spend this bonus money anyway they choose.

"However, most of the child support owed by welfare-class fathers is uncollectible. Most are either unemployed or earn less than $10,000 per year.

"So, in order to cash in on federal bonus money, build their bureaucracies and brag about successful child-support enforcement, the states began bringing into the government system middle-class fathers with jobs who were never (and probably would never be) on welfare. These non-welfare families have grown to 83 percent of child-support cases and 92 percent of the money collected, creating a windfall of federal money flowing to the states.

"The federal incentives drive the system. The more divorces, and the higher the child-support guidelines are set and enforced (no matter how unreasonable), the more money the state bureaucracy collects from the feds.

"Follow the money. The less time that non-custodial parents (usually fathers) are permitted to be with their children, the more child support they must pay into the state fund, and the higher the federal bonus to the states for collecting the money.

"The states have powerful incentives to separate fathers from their children, to give near-total custody to mothers, to maintain the fathers' high-level support obligations even if their income is drastically reduced, and to hang onto the father's payments as long as possible before paying them out to the mothers. The General Accounting Office reported that in 2002 states were holding $657 million in UDC (Undistributed Child Support).

"Fatherless boys are 63 percent more likely to run away and 37 percent more likely to abuse drugs, and fatherless girls are twice as likely to get pregnant and 53 percent more likely to commit suicide. Fatherless boys and girls are twice as likely to drop out of high school twice as likely to end up in jail.

"We can no longer ignore how taxpayers' money is incentivizing divorce and creating fatherless children. Nor can we ignore the government's complicity in the predictable social costs that result from more than 17 million children growing up without their fathers."\[103]/

Controversy swirls, no matter from which angle you view child support.

After the economic stimulus checks\[104]/ began to be distributed in Spring 2008, the States unlawfully diverted the checks from their rightful owners, for *the owners had already paid taxes on that money.*\[105]/ How did this happen? The States submitted the names and Social Security numbers of allegedly deadbeat parents to the IRS, which crosschecked those names against the lists of taxpayers receiving stimulus checks and then sent the deadbeat parents' checks straight to state child support agencies."\106/ The question becomes: Did the IRS tell the States to submit the names and social security numbers or did the States somehow determine they would voluntarily submit the info? More likely the IRS ordered the States to submit the info.

According to the Treasury Department, more than 1.4 million checks were seized and a total of $831 million were collected by child support agencies nationwide.

The Massachusetts Department of Revenue's Child Support Enforcement Division intercepted $11.2 million from checks intended to reach more than 20,220 delinquent parents.\107/ "The extra cash increased child support collections to a record $554.3 million for the fiscal year that ended June 30, a $33 million jump over the previous year."\108/ "In California, $97.9 million was collected via 152,877 diverted checks, while Texas brought in $80.3 million from 132,144 payments. Rhode Island saw a $1.9 million boost from 3,465 diverted checks."\109/

Massachusetts deposited the intercepted checks and held them for 180 days to allow the parent to appeal. If the appeal is denied, the money will be turned over to the custodial parent (usually the mother) unless she has been on public assistance. If the appeal is allowed, the funds might go back to the state and federal government to reimburse the taxpayer.\110/

"Massachusetts added to the miniwindfall with a new program that crosschecks the names of delinquent parents with the state treasurer's abandoned property list. That generated $1.3 million. A second program targeting deadbeat parents' drivers licenses pulled in $35.9 million."\111/

Given that driver's licenses are not a luxury but a necessity, it is sheer insanity to pull driver's licenses. It is extremely regressive to pull a license which is needed to go to work to earn the money that the court has ordered.

Responding to the Globe article, Paul M. Clements, Senior Contributing Editor of "In Search of Fatherhood," a quarterly circulating across the USA and in several foreign countries, reacted to the revelation: "The States are double-dipping by taking the 'stimulus checks.' Those were tax rebate checks. Child support had already been deducted from the man's paycheck before those taxes were collected.

The States, therefore, were double dipping: deducting child support twice from the same income. This was not new income.

"Not only does each state receive an incentive payment from the federal government for collecting child support," he pointed out, "most states also charge the recipient for the money they get." His conclusion: "It is middle-class fathers who are being forced to pay support, in a Communistic 'transfer of wealth' scheme. No wonder there is so much opposition to shared physical custody. To keep the gravy train rolling, states separate fathers from their children, then separate them from their money. It costs taxpayers, and it costs children their emotional well-being."

At a symposium "Defining Marriage," Stephen Baskerville, an acclaimed author and college professor, angrily suggested, "Most States make a profit on their child-support program. States are free to spend this profit in any manner the State sees fit." In addition to charging penalties and interest, the States profit through receiving both federal payments based on the amount they collect and reimbursement from the feds of 66% of their operating costs and 90% of their computer costs."

In 2002, Baskerville told us, the federal government outlaid almost $3.5 billion. That year, Michigan collected over $200 million and California collected some $640 million. Clearly, the receipt of millions of dollars is the motive for courts to encourage divorce and fatherless children. Clearly, the receipt of millions of dollars is the motive for courts to order child-support payments at levels higher than needed to support the child or children involved.

"Isn't this a case of the States being penny-wise and pound foolish?" asks a critic. Of course, he suggests, the States are actually *losing* more money than they're taking in, given the hidden costs . . . such as the cost of enforcing the law against the delinquent offspring of failed marriages, the cost to the State of foreclosures. "Intact families are easily the most cost-effective way for the State to manage its citizens," he remarks, adding, "When families break up, there are many other ancillary costs to the general public."

The answer, in my opinion, depends upon where those monies appear on the books, whose books, which books, and who or which entity does the proper auditing. Those questions and their answers create a conundrum, one needing more facts to come up with the answer to the question whether the States are being penny-wise and pound foolish. For instance, law enforcement entities also receive annual bonuses from the federal government. Does that money cover their costs? Does the bonus money received from Washington exceed the revenue received from anger-management programs, from batterer programs, from supervision service centers, from shelter programs?

So insidious is the motive that Judy Parejko, in her recent book, *Stolen Vows: The Illusion of No-Fault Divorce and the Rise of the American Divorce Industry*, describes how government-funded marriage therapists may in fact work to undermine marriages.\[112]/

And consistent with the notion of keeping marriages broken rather than repairing them, there was in Massachusetts a seminar at which judges instructed attorneys how to find so-called "hidden assets." The Barnstable Bar Association made a party out of it at a luxury seaside resort in Chatham on Cape Cod.

Money, money, money, federal money provides the incentive for State courts to establish child-support obligations as high as possible without any consideration whatsoever as to whether the amount is appropriate.

As egregious, in California, in 2002, Governor Gray Davis vetoed a bill that would have exempted a man from paying child support if a DNA test showed he was not the child's biofather. Davis's motive: California would risk losing up to $40 million in federal funds.

In practice, if a male parent is behind on his child-support payments, he is first served with a Complaint for Contempt. That Complaint will have a hearing date on it. When he appears in court for the contempt hearing, he is then given the ultimatum to pay or to go to jail without passing **GO**. Depending on the judge, he might be given a chance to pay by a certain date, but most often the man is handcuffed and brought to the court's holding cell, from where he is allowed to call a friend or parent to cough up a loan so that he can avoid being transferred in handcuffs and ankle chains in a van to jail, another name for the outlawed debtors' prison.

Most disgusting is that the judges truly do not listen to any defenses the man might have—such as not having the money, because of his having been unemployed or having been ill—and even more disgusting is that the man is not given an evidentiary hearing. Due process and equal protection having long since disappeared from the courtroom.

The latter is caused by the Bradley Amendment, named after the former Sen. Bill Bradley (D) for New Jersey, which says that once a child-support obligation has been established, it cannot be retroactively reduced for any reason, ever, or be forgiven by a judge. Even the inability to pay while a man was ill or incapacitated for any reason, while a man was in the service, while a man was a prisoner of war or a prisoner in a civilian's jail, while a man had lost of job, or had no lawyer because he could not afford one does not count as acceptable excuse. Without doubt, the Bradley Amendment must be repealed.

Of course, once an innocent man is arrested for events beyond his control, the likelihood of any attempt to rehabilitate the marriage is nil. The marriage becomes like Humpty Dumpty: it can not be put back together again. It is unfortunate. Were a couple still together when a man lost his employment, the family would simply tighten their belts and live on a house painter's or a cabbies' salary and tips until the economy improved and the man managed to find reemployment at a salary close to or at his former healthy pay.

An Actual Pay or Go to Jail Story

Anecdote #1.

Defendant Jerry was divorced in New Jersey. His former wife, without a court order, removed their child to Virginia, where she works as an executive for the United States Department of Transportation. Jerry has not seen his child during the 14 years since his former wife removed the child.

Because of the loss of his business and medical problems—severe Type I diabetes, requiring an insulin pump inserted into his body, and causing both the loss of leg function and the loss of vision in one eye—Jerry has, since 1997, filed numerous motions for downward modification of his child-support order.

On or around July 2008, in the Family Court of the State of New York, Support Magistrate Cheryl Weir-Reeves, declining to consider any of Jerry's evidence regarding the loss of his business and the ability to earn because of the severe downturn in the markets over the past several years, denied or dismissed Jerry's latest petition for downward modification of child support.\[113]/

Weir-Reeves had found Jerry in willful violation of an 11-year-old New Jersey Order of Support, which had been registered in New York in 2006, and ordered him to pay in on or before October 3, 2008, both

$160.00 per week for child support and $23,040.78 toward the child-support arrearages of $97,412.27. If Jerry did not make his payment, he would, Weir-Reeves made it clear, be in criminal contempt and find himself imprisoned for 6 months.

Jerry contends (1) that because of his ex-wife's unilateral interference with his parental rights, he has unsuccessfully attempted to make contact and see his child for over 14 years, and is therefore absolved from any child-support obligation,\[114]/ (2) that terminating the court-ordered child-support obligation will not result in the child becoming a public charge, given that the ex-wife earns in excess of $100,000 annually and lives in a very nice house in a prestigious area outside of Washington, D.C.,\[115]/ and (3) that because the New Jersey child-support order was based on his ex-wife's proven false statements, he has been entitled to modifications as far back as 1997.

Jurisdiction is another problem that has been encountered in Jerry's case; in fact, it is frequently encountered in child-support and child-visitation cases. Inconsistencies created by State statutes and uniform laws are endemic,\[116]/ and they often create, as they did in Jerry's case, a Catch-22 situation.

For instance, in her July 2008 decision, Support Magistrate Weir-Reeves wrote that the court lacked jurisdiction to hear Jerry's downward modification petition . . . given that the order was entered in the State of New Jersey and registered for enforcement in New York. But New Jersey claimed the matter belongs in the New York courts since Jerry lives in New York. The New York courts said they have no jurisdiction and the matter should be addressed by the Virginia courts, where Jerry's ex-wife now resides.

The question becomes, Who is at fault? (a) the judges, (b) the legislatures, (c) the feds, or (d) all of the above? Clearly, the answer is (d). The federal incentives arising out of the Federal Child Support Enforcement law,\[117]/ without "strings attached" and based on the amount of child support awarded, enforced, and collected, is put into the state general treasury.\[118]/ The first items paid out of any state treasury are the pensions and salaries of state employees, including judges, magistrates, and legislators.\[119]/

Further, it is well-settled law that judges and magistrates must not sit on cases in which they have a financial interest in the outcome.\[120]/ Thus, where that conflict of interest exists, there is no decision regarding child support which is made by a neutral fact-finder, that is, a neutral judge. Where the existing federal laws enable that conflict, those laws are unconstitutional, the federal legislators are irresponsible in not repealing or amending those laws.

Moreover, where child support starts out as a purely civil debt and is converted along the way into a criminal matter, we must question, Isn't a defendant then entitled to his Miranda Rights, which inform him of his rights to remain silent—both testimonial and documentary silence?

Imputing income

Jerry is not alone. Courts regularly deny modifications of child-support awards. When men lose jobs, whether or not by any fault of their own, the courts impute income to them. For instance, if a man earned $70,000 as a system analyst or a programmer and then gets a job for $40,000 as a painter or a cab driver, simply so that he may earn a living, the court more often than not will say, You have shown you have the ability to earn $70,000, which is $30,000 more than you are currently earning, so you'd better get another job because this court is going to calculate the child-support order based on the "imputed" income of $70,000, your former salary.

You will never hear a court tell a wife that you used to earn $60,000 as a medical technician or as an office manager before you filed for divorce, your children are in college, so you'd better get re-employed so you, too, can contribute to their support. Teachers who stop teaching, nurses who stop nursing, accountants who stop accounting, technicians who stop technician-ing. The family courts are a woman's heaven and a man's hell.

Perquisite income

Upon divorce, the man often goes to live in his parent's home so that he can afford to pay his excessive child-support obligation. The rent that he would have to pay for his room and kitchen and bathroom rights if he were to rent the same from a stranger is considered "perquisite" income, income that is equal to the "free rent." The courts regularly add that perquisite income to the man's earned and unearned income.

I have never seen a court add perquisite income to a woman's earned and unearned income, the most common of which is the money she gets from a new live-in boyfriend or the spending money she gets from a new husband—the things she gets "free" from him that she would have to pay for if unmarried to him. As I said, the family courts are a woman's heaven and a man's hell. The concept of "fairness" is obsolete in family courts.

Morals and Money

A lawbook salesman and I were talking recently about the attorneys fees charged men for a divorce in which child custody is disputed. The big boys will get $100,000 to $250,000 for such a fight. I spoke of a renowned lawfirm's internal memo about the $5,000 left in one client's account; the memo concluded that they should be prepared to stop working on the case because the client had no more money. Given that the firm knew from the beginning how much money he had—$43,000—which they knew would not be enough to win the very acrimonious case, why did they take his money and the case?

The salesman said he had just had a conversation about the same subject with a divorce attorney. He asked the attorney that same question, Why did you take the case? The attorney's response was, Well if we didn't take his $40,000, someone else would have, so why not?

And then the court will order the husband to pay the wife's attorney's fees. Again I'll say it, The family courts are a woman's heaven and a man's hell.

Another Man's Struggle Against the Massachusetts Department of Revenue

Anecdote #2.

After receiving the Judgment for Divorce, Timothy received a DoR notice listing a weekly assignment of "$800" for child support and "$0" for alimony. He contacted DoR to correct them because it should have been $400 Child Support and $400 Alimony. They told Timothy, "It doesn't matter. Don't worry about it." He said, "No, I'd like it corrected and please send me a corrected copy." They never did.

Timothy suspected the DoR might be using the $800 figure for reporting to the Federal Government, thus scamming more Title IV-D money out of the dads and using the $400/$400 figures for internal accounting. Timothy is now waiting to hear from other dads to see if DoR is making similar so-called errors in other dads' cases.

Dealing with a Wildcat Judge: Randy Kaplan.

Anecdote #3.

Jimmy went to court *pro se* for a pretrial conference and a second issue of contempt for allegedly violating the April Job Seek order by not reporting every Monday to Cambridge to show that he had ten job interviews per week. He finally got a job in late July and has received at his place of employment a biweekly call from a probation officer requesting Jimmy to fax his paycheck receipt.

Even though Jimmy had been out of work and was in the court-ordered Job Seek program, he had also been ordered in April to pay $200 per month. Jimmy was going to make payments, but he did not know how to make the payments. He assumed "something" was mailed to his old address but no longer having a home of his own, he has been bouncing around from couch to couch at friend's and family's houses. Bottom line: In Concord (MA), when Jimmy next appeared in court, Judge Randy Kaplan had Jimmy arrested for 30 days because of the $1300 arrearage.

When they put Jimmy in the Concord tank, where the bailiffs were ridiculing and judging him for not paying his child support, Jimmy had in his wallet $850 cash. He had just cashed his biweekly paycheck and had planned on using it for a security deposit on an apartment he'd found the night before. *"The bailiffs all made fun of me,"* Jimmy wrote, *"for not telling the judge that I had that much money on me and that she would have accepted it versus the 1300."* He further said, *"I was never allowed to offer anything less, it was 1300 or jail at that minute."*

His father had to get a certified bank check for $1300 because the court would not let him use the cash he had with him.

"I was in jail by the way with attempted murderers, car thieves, heroid addicts, all kinds of criminals doing 2-10 years, learned A LOT! Even the COs in the jail area ridiculed me for not paying child support even though they

know nothing about what they're talking about. I'd say most men/fathers, even some in here, don't have a clue of the severity of the total screw job we as alienated parents really do get. The best part of the story is the security deposit money that I had in my wallet was NOT returned to me when I checked out of prison. It was confiscated and they told me they would mail me a check that would go in the mail today. so now I owe my father 1300 and don't even have my 852 in cash."\[121]/

Contempt for Nonpayment of Child Support and an Angry Man.

Anecdote #4.

"*I just left court and was found guilty of contempt also and sentenced to 60 days at the Worcester house of correction if I don't pay about $8,500 by 11/14. I am broke - primarily because of the illegal CS order which is under appeal and has ranged from 300% of my income to 50% when it should be 26%. The judge took every dime of my working capital in January and I have been unable to market my seminars since then.*

"*Mass. wants to collect all the money it orders and wants those orders higher every month.*

"*They get about $1 for every $3 in child support from the federal gov't. They KEEP all the interest and penalties on unpaid amounts.*

"*Research has shown that Sole Custody is Child Abuse. Yet judges award sole custody over 85% of the time making those family court judges the most prolific child abusers on the planet.*

"*The divorce system is a SCAM for lawyers to plunder the estates of divorcing couples using children as bait. Most of the family cou+rts operate unconstitutiionally for BILLIONS of dollars in federal kickbacks (under SSA Title IVd) and $50 BILLION in annual legal fees from custody battles that should almost never happen.*"\[122]/

The Angry Man is a man driven to irrationality and diarrhea of the fingers and mouth as a result of his anger. The significance, though, of his anger is that it is typical of the anger being experienced by other fathers whose children have been alienated by their former spouse or whose children have been parentectomized by a family court.

The Angry Man updated his message on a dads' listserv: "*Judge Roach in Worcester just dismissed my modification for CS adjustment also.*

The original order for CS was DOUBLED without notice, evidence or any CS guidelines worksheet EVER submitted (except by me that calculated less than 1/3 the order). Wife's attorney simply said 'we want more child support' and judge told me to shut up when I objected. These people just want as much money as they can steal."

If the Angry Man does not come up with $8500 by mid-November, he will go to jail for the third time for failure to pay child-support arrearages. Does he see his children? Now that is a foolish question. Of course not! The support order is regressive in that it has placed the beat-dead dad in a hole he is going to have a hard time climbing out of.

The federal child-support laws must be repealed or amended. Without those changes of federal law, the family courts will not be neutral, children will be parentectomized, and innocent dads will be imprisoned and made homeless. These results are not tolerable in our allegedly civilized society. And those judges and their flunkies must lose their judge-made immunity. If you and I are accountable for our conduct, they, too, must be made accountable.

In Massachusetts, immunity of officers and employees in all three branches of government is forbidden by article V of the Massachusetts Declaration of Rights. Unfortunately, the Massachusetts judges violate that provision of our Declaration of Rights on a daily basis.

Emancipation

Anecdote #5.

A child may be emancipated and unemancipated and re-emancipated and re-unemancipated. Watch for the games.

A dad who has been denied contact with his child does not know which college his child is attending, does not know whether the child has dropped out of that college or has joined the army or has married. And his ex-wife does not let the court know that there is a change in the status of the child.

Upon learning that his child has stopped attending college full time, is working, and is maintaining his own apartment, dad files a motion for emancipation of the child and the termination of the child-support order. Mother makes the child re-enroll in college, appears in court with the youngster, who is asked to flash his school ID card, and opposes the motion for emancipation of the child and the termination of child support. The judge allows the child to remain unemancipated and dad is not allowed restitution for the child support he rendered while the child was working and maintaining his own love pad. Two weeks later, the child has again dropped out of college, is again working, and returns to his love pad.

Upon learning from friends and assorted relatives that his second son dropped out of his engineering program, dad contacts the college and gets certified confirmation that his son has joined the air force. The young man's mother did not notify dad or the court when their son dropped out of school and joined the service. The mother can no longer assert that the son is unemancipated, but she opposes any restitution of the child support she had been receiving fraudulently since the son left school and joined the armed service. Title IV-D federal bonuses to the States once again motivate the judge to deny dad's motions. The denial once again deprives Dad of his constitutional right to the equal protection of the laws.

Nothing in the law provides for restitution either by the State or a mother. Nothing in the law requires mothers to report to the court or to the father that a child has finished or dropped out of college, is living on his or her own or with a friend, is working full-time, or has enlisted in a military service. The law must change.

Judge Judy Confirms That Child Support Is for Women's Pleasure and Men's Punishment

In her book *Don't Pee on My Leg and Tell Me It's Raining*, Judge Judy Sheindlin wrote:

> "American fathers are led down primrose path every day in our family courts, often with disastrous legal results. They wind up in the Land of Gender Bias, where they are systematically stripped of their rights, often without the slightest idea of why it is happening to them."
>
> "If you think the mother-father disparity is outrageous, consider the sexual abuse syndrome, and how it affects visitation and custody disputes. Here, the judicial impotence and chronic blindness to men's rights would appall you."

"Courts are supposed to approach cases of child custody, support payments, and visitation rights in what we call a gender-neutral posture. It sounds fair, and it is fair. But it is a myth. Judges are not enforcing these gender laws fairly, and few seem to care."

"We will see more of these problems until fathers organize to demand fairer treatment. So get it together dads: You have a legitimate legal beef and you need to make this a public issue. Right now the courts don't hear you."

The fathers *have* demanded fairer treatment from the courts and the revision of the VAWA laws, which encourage the discrimination against men in the courts by providing billions of dollars annually from the federal government to each and every State, but the media has not given sufficient coverage of the issue.

And now that Joe Biden, the granddaddy of VAWA, has become Vice-President, it is unlikely that the President will scratch out the VAWA/ Department of Justice annual federal bonuses when he performs promised line-item cuts.

Chapter 5

His, Hers, and Theirs! No, not Children, Property!

What's Mine is Mine and What's Yours is Mine
(and Financial Statements)

Property is another hot spot of divorce. In Massachusetts, not a community property State, property can be distributed only once by the court . . . unless there was fraud. The court allegedly learns of what those assets are on Financial Statements filed by the parties. The Financial Statement comes in two forms, a short form for those whose annual income is less then $75,000 and a long form for those whose annual income is or exceeds $75,000. These forms were revised in July 2007, so no case law has developed concerning them.

The short form has no space to write when the asset was obtained; in contrast, the long form asks specifically when the property was purchased. This distinction is provocative. The division of property is as important to folks with under $75,000 annual income as it is to those with or over $75,000 annual income.

Some questions posed: A guy inherits a house from his family. A few years later he marries. The deed stays in his name. Is that property part of the marital estate? If so, how is it divided and on what basis was the division?

A husband and wife purchase a property. He is the primary caregiver to the children. His wife is the breadwinner. There is no mortgage, just taxes and utilities to pay. While the children are in nursery school, the husband contributes his sweat into rehabilitating the property, e.g., installing new oak floors, new insulation, new walls, new baseboards, window and door trim. Is he entitled to some of the equity? If so, how much equity? And who gets possession of the property? Or must it be sold? If so, when?

A husband and his wife together purchase a home after they marry. Both were self-employed professionals and, in fact, professional partners. They are divorcing. They have two children. How is the property divided? Must the property be sold or must the property not be sold because the court does not want to make the children move until the youngest reaches 18 or is emancipated?

A husband purchases a home and puts the deed in his and his wife's names. He is the sole breadwinner. They have two children and are divorcing. Is she entitled to a share of the equity? How much? Must the home be sold or may the custodial parent stay in it until the youngest child reaches 18 or is emancipated?

Do any of these four couples own other real property? Do they have assets other than real property or real estate? Retirement plans, 401Ks, pension plans, stocks, bonds, gold coins, gold jewelry? Does the husband keep the dowry, the *proika*, or must he return it to her or her family? What if they are from a foreign land, such as India, where they were married, but they are divorcing here? Can one of them go back to India and start a divorce there, too? Which country's laws apply and to what?

A couple has real estate in one State. Although the mother is given the exclusive use and possession of the property, she, the custodial parent, moves with the children to a second State. What happens to the property? May the husband move into the now empty, once-upon-a-time marital home? If he does and the wife comes back for a visit, can she lawfully declare him a trespasser?

The answers to many of these questions can be found on the Financial Statements . . . but not easily. The courts are all over the place in answering them.

Let's start with te most basic of questions. One is asked by MikeC.

I have been divorced for 4 years and have managed to stay out of court somehow during that time. However, that might be about to end because my ex is starting to come at me for more money for college-related expenses.

My question revolves around the requirement to produce financial statements. If I contest her attempt to get money from me not because of inability to pay but because of the interpretation of the divorce decree combined with no related change in circumstances (for example, my daughter goes to the same college that she always has gone to), then I don't want to produce financial statements.

> *I keep hearing that financial statements are required virtually every time that you walk into a courtroom. Does anyone have any advice on fighting this requirement? Is this requirement codified anywhere? Has anyone ever refused to submit financial statements and what was the consequence if you did.*

No, Financial Statements are not required virtually every time that you walk into a courtroom. A Financial Statement need be filed **(1)** "within 45 days of the from the date of service of the summons or when the matter first becomes before the court,"\[123]/ **(2)** prior to a hearing on a motion for temporary orders or a pretrial conference,\[124]/ and **(3)** ten days after receiving a Request for a Financial Statement from your opponent.\[125]/ A second Request for a Financial Statement may not be made until 90 days after the first one is made.\[126]/

A Financial Statement must also be filed prior to any hearing of a *Complaint* for modification.\[127]/ [Note: Not a motion for modification but a Complaint for modification.]

Yes, I have refused on behalf of my clients on several occasions to submit a financial statement. Two of the times I refused and the consequences for doing so follow. In both cases, I was "successor counsel," which means a counsel representing the client *after* the client's previous lawyer quit or was terminated by the client.

Anecdote #1:

A little more about Samson and Delilah.

The previous November, the client had appeared *pro se* in Judge Catherine R. Sabaitis' court. The wife had come into court seeking payment from the husband of uninsured medical costs. The husband opposed the wife's motion because he had never been told about the medical services; he did not know whether they were for services to the wife, for whom he was no longer responsible, or for services to the children; he had never seen any bills for the alleged medical services. Sabaitis had allowed the wife's motion and ordered him to pay her the money, the total of which was $865.

His nonpayment provoked the wife into filing a Complaint for Contempt [Ch. 5]. The hearings on the contempt and the divorce trial were consolidated, meaning there would be one trial for both is-sues, the contempt and the divorce.

On my new client's behalf, I moved for the judge to vacate her No-vember order on the grounds that there was no documentary evidence presented, that there had been no testimony taken, that all the court heard was the argument by the wife's lawyer and a lawyer's argument is not evidence. In sum, the November hearing was unquestionably unfair and therefore violated my client's constitutional due process rights. "Fundamental fairness" is the cornerstone of constitutional due process.

Sabaitis denied my client's motion to vacate.

That motion hearing was followed immediately by the divorce trial. With well-hidden fury, I decided not to submit my client's Financial Statement. If the judge was not going to require the wife to proffer evidence, then I was not yet going to proffer any until I learned more of this judge.

During my cross-examination of the wife on her Financial State-ment, Judge Sabaitis, for instance, would not allow me to use certi-fied bank statements that had been admitted and marked as evidence. My client was entitled under constitutional due process to cross-exam-ine his wife on that Statement and to use admitted evidence as an aid during the cross-examination.

The issue I was working on was the wife's income, which the wife declared on her Financial Statement to be $1000 a month. I showed the wife the January bank statement and asked her the source of the $4000 deposit. Her lawyer objected and Sabaitis sustained. I objected to the judge's ruling. I then showed the wife the February bank state-ment and asked for the source of another sizable deposit. Again the wife's lawyer objected and Sabaitis sustained. After some legal argu-ments, I moved for a mistrial.

In the middle of this flurry of argument, the wife's lawyer noted that my client had not yet filed a Financial Statement for the trial. I argued that given that the court did not allow me to cross-examine on the wife's Financial Statement, I saw no point in filing my client's Fi-nancial Statement. The Statement was clearly meaningless, and given the arbitrary and capricious rulings and decisions by Sabaitis, filing his Financial Statement could have put my client in danger.

By then I was certain that if I objected to a question the wife's law-yer asked, Sabaitis would overrule my objection, but I was *un*certain why. Was I dealing with a judge who was discriminating against my client because he was a male or with a judge who was simply ignorant of the law? It probably did not matter which was the reason, the result was the same: her rulings were intolerable and my client was likely to continue to be screwed.

Having no rational response to my refusal to file my client's Statement, Sabaitis simply instructed her clerk to make a copy of the Financial Statement my client filed when he had the other lawyer, changed the DATE to the current date, and used the xeroxed copy of his signature. She did not ask him for, and I would not have allowed him anyway to sign, a sworn statement.\[128]/ I also refused to sign a certification *"that I have no knowledge that any of the information contained herein is false,"* on the grounds that it would be tantamount to unlawfully vouching. My signature was not a statutory requirement, it was simply a whim of some judges to put such a statement on the Financial Statement form.

Eventually I got the mistrial, but not until after I challenged the court again and again on both the issue of the fair market value of the marital home and the qualifications of the wife's so-called expert on real estate valuation. The man was not an appraiser, certified or otherwise. He knew, in my opinion, very little, if anything, about real estate appraising. He claimed he had been admitted as a real-estate expert in other trials, but could not identify the trials either by the parties' names or by docket numbers or by the courts or by the dates of the trials. Fa-ake!!

Throughout the two days of trial, Sabaitis repeatedly suspended the trial for a half-hour or more—not for the usual morning and afternoon breaks—but for what appeared to be phonecalls. Maybe she was seeking advice from some judge sitting at the end of a judge's 911 phone line. We never learned what her frequent interruptions were about. All we do know is that after one of them, she finally called a mistrial and recused herself from the case.

Anecdote #2.

Just after the New Millenium, the husband, Lucas, fired his attorney. In 2001, I took over the case. One of the primary issues was the valuation and distribution of the multiple real properties the couple owned. For this reason, I examined very closely the Financial Statements.

On the three or four Financial Statements filed in 2000, the wife, Gloria, wrote that the fair market value of a particular real property was $500,000. Her lawyer, E. Chouteau Merrill, before she became a judge, signed at the bottom of the statements that she had no knowledge that any of her client's responses were false. They could have been, of course. So the attorney's signature was tantamount to vouching, which is unlawful, but, as I have said, some judges decided to put it on the Financial Statement forms.

The property in which Lucas was adamant about keeping was the one Gloria had declared was worth $500,000. But that property was assessed at $192,000 and appraised (by an appraiser upon whom both parties had agreed) at $188,000, a few thousand dollars less than the assessed value.

Had that case settled before I took over and brought out the truth, the husband who wanted to keep that property, which he owned *before* marriage, Judge Nancy M. Gould would have accepted $500,000 as the value and would have made Lucas pay $250,000 to Gloria in order to buy her out. That's right, he would have had to pay his wife $250,000, half of an inflated value, rather than $94,000, half of the appraised value of the property. Another way of looking at those numbers reveals that the husband would have had to buy out the wife's half for $62,000 more than the value of the *entire* property. That was the danger and the *motive* of over-enhancing the fair market value on the Financial Statement.

When I brought this to Judge Gould's attention, Chouteau Merrill, the wife's lawyer, argued to the judge, who had been a First Assistant Register in that courthouse for 17 years and with whom it appeared that Chouteau had a pre-existing relationship, that the $500,000 was merely an estimate of what the fair market value was and therefore not a falsity.

True, but an estimate of fair market value must still be reasonable and not be a number submitted with bad faith and the intention to deceive. What was the methodology used to reach that estimate? For instance, an estimate based on expert judgment, sales in the area, existing tax valuations, and the adaptability of the land to better use. Here, at the time the $500,000 estimate was written on the Financial Statement, the assessment of the property was $188,000.

Judge Gould accepted Chouteau's explanation.

By the Fall of 2001, I sued Judge Gould in federal court for claims based on child-custody issues and the removal of the children to another State. Although that suit was dismissed on immunity grounds, Judge Gould was removed from the case within five days of being served with the Complaint. My putting the Complaint on my website\[129]/ might have fed into the decision to take Gould off the case . . . or for that matter for Gould's own decision to take herself off the case. (We don't know how that went down.)

By November 2001, Judge Gould was replaced by Judge Lisa A. Roberts.

Fast forward to the trial in 2002-2003. I had to cross-examine Gloria vigorously. She lied about everything. For instance, she lied about who paid the real-estate taxes on the so-called $500,000 property, and to support that lie, she produced a log that she purportedly wrote over a period of years. It took part of a day to break the "log" down line by line and finally get her admission that she wrote the entire so-called log in an afternoon or two.

She lied when she said her husband would not allow her to carry cash so she did not have cab money to take herself to the hospital when her labor pains began. The lie was proven by getting her to admit that she was in charge of check-writing for the couple, that her husband never made out checks, and that the bank she used was in the same building in which she was working as a lawyer when her labor pains had begun..

She lied on each and every Financial Statement: after she had moved to another State, she still reported expenses that were Massachusetts explicit: e.g., transportation (cabs) of children to school in Boston; an exercise club in Boston for herself.

Although Roberts should have but did not refer Gloria's alleged perjury to the District Attorney,\[130]/ Roberts did award Lucas 100 percent of the "$500,000" property and ordered the wife to deed over her interest to him. There was no mortgage on that property so that was not an issue. He still has that property.

I did not allow my client to file Financial Statements because of Gould's action re the fair market value. Roberts ignored the facts that my client did not file a new Financial Statement and that I did not sign any certification re a Financial Statement. I suggested, instead, that the judge change the date with certain corrections of assertions made by his first lawyer—who never asked my client for much info and filled out the Financial Statement on his own without allowing my client to review the filled-out Financial Statements.

My insistence on challenging potentially egregious judicial wrong-doing made me a bit notorious in the judicial community. Eventually, my aggressive stances on these issues fed *sub rosa* into my disbarment.

The ostensible reason for my disbarment was my criticism of judges. As the regulatory entity and high court of Massachusetts charged, my criticism of judges interfered with the administration of justice. By then, of course, I had sued four of them and then ran for governor on a platform of court reform and the abolishment of judicial and quasi-judicial immunity, and whenever appropriate, memorialized judicial wrongdoing on my website, *falseallegations.com*.

Chapter 6

Relocation and Child Removal Cases

*Genii, genii, come out of your bottle
and make my wish come true!*

More grief is suffered by the noncustodial parent, usually the father, when the child is removed to another State by the custodial parent, usually the mother. What adds to the grief is the inconsistency of the judicial decisions. Inconsistency is possible because of the nature of the guidelines (or "the standard"–in legal terms) the judges use to make their decisions. The inconsistency is, what we call in layman's terms, "double talk"!

The statutes are clear. The noncustodial parent must consent to the removal of the child(ren) to another State by the custodial parent. If the noncustodial parent does not consent to the removal, the court must give the noncustodial parent the opportunity to have an evidentiary hearing. An evidentiary hearing is a hearing at which people get on the witness stand, speak their piece, and are cross-examined by the opponent.

Because the statutes demand a statement of consent or an evidentiary hearing, one would think this happens. Not so! "Kidnapping by Kourt" is far more frequent.

Anecdote #1:

Gloria and Lucas "Luke" Stockdale.

Soon after Gloria filed for divorce and a restraining order against Lucas Stockdale, her lawyer, E. Chouteau Merrill,\131/ convinced Luke's first lawyer, Kevin Connelly, to agree to the appointment of a guardian *ad litem*, the afore-mentioned Barbara O'Brien Beardslee, a stiff-lipped woman who was contracting with Children & the Law, an entity associated in some mysterious way with Massachusetts General Hospital, and who was married to a psychiatrist at Boston's Children's Hospital.

Beardslee was appointed to investigate and report to the court her recommendation as to which parent should become the custodial parent. No more. No less. Beardslee's tasks were memorialized on a "reference of appointment" signed by the judge and placed in the Lukes' case file.

When Gloria wanted to relocate and take her and Luke's children with her to another State, Chouteau secretly contacted Beardslee and told her to add the recommendation that Gloria be allowed to remove the children to another State. Luke knew nothing about this until Beardslee filed her report.

Although Luke had not seen a motion by Gloria to relocate and remove the children, it suddenly appeared. And *voila!* Judge Nancy Mary Gould allowed it.

Despite the law providing that if consent is not given by the non-custodial parent, there must be an evidentiary hearing, Gould never asked if Luke consented and never gave Luke an evidentiary hearing.

This meant that Luke, who had been the caregiver to the children for the five years since their birth, missed his opportunity to question Beardslee about why she recommended that Gloria be the custodial parent and be allowed to take the twins and move to another State. Where Gloria had been making (in the year 2000) around $170,000 in her position as a lawyer in a prestigious Boston lawfirm, what was the "real advantage" of moving out of State with the children? Was not the real motive to spite Luke? If the court had been a fair one, the motive would have been seen to be *not* a sincere one. If the court and Beardslee had been bright, they would have listened and observed and come to understand that the little boys were like testosterone to Luke. By taking them away, they were attempting to castrate Luke and he would fight like hell for those kids.

And as far as the best interests of the children. That was a laugh. Gloria's biofamily was and had been for years dysfunctional. Her mother and father had been divorced. Her mother had sundry men, and her father was not only on his third marriage, he was believed to be a pedophile. And Gloria and the children were going to live in her bio-dad's home.

Luke stiffened and balked. Connelly, his lawyer at the time, asked for a hearing . . . even though the judge had already allowed Chouteau's motion for relocation. Gould had her courtroom clerk (really a First Assistant Register), Jack Scully, phone Chouteau and say, Yes, the judge will schedule a hearing but the parties are not allowed to attend.

(Chouteau then billed Gloria for taking that message, and when I sub-poenaed Chouteau's bills to trial, I found the entry on the bill and managed to get it admitted into evidence.) Insanity, on one hand, yes. But on the other, there was a backstory. Let's call it a C-plot.

Luke believed—and after I represented him, I came to the same conclusion—that Chouteau was friendly with Gould long before this case arose, that Gloria had Gould in the bag, that it did not matter that Gloria was not allowed at the evidentiary hearing for she knew in advance that Gould's decision would go her way. But it did mat-ter whether Luke was there, and he was not told of the hearing! In fact, the hearing was set for the same day that the children would be indoctrinated into the kindergarten. (We assume that Chouteau told Gould both when kindergartners' welcoming day would be held and that Luke was planning to attend so that he could meet the children's teachers. On that same day Chouteau would be divorced from Mark Salwasser in a closed session in Gould's courtroom.)

So, so much for "real advantage" and the "best interests of the chil-dren." How about a judge doing whatever she damn well wanted to do, regardless of the law?

When I took over at the top of 2001 and had been on the hunt for information as to what had happened, I filed several motions to get Gould to revisit the issues of custody and relocation and removal. Gould clammed up and would not hear those motions. I tried to get her also to recuse herself. That did not work It was just one more motion for which she did not want to hear legal or factual arguments, so she kept on setting and cancelling hearing dates on the recusal mo-tion. So I filed a petition for a writ of mandamus (a pleading filed in a State's highest court to get a lower-court judge to do what the judge is supposed to do). It was summarily dismissed.

The courts and I were at War.

By October 2001 I was fed up and sued Gould for acting outside the scope of her authority and three other judges (for diverse reasons, all exceptions to any possible immunity) in federal court. Although the case was dismissed on immunity grounds, Gould either took her-self off or was removed from the *Stockdale* case. (In retrospect, I be-lieve this is when I got on the High Court's not-too-peachy list and my Bar problems began.)

By November 2001, Judge Lisa A. Roberts replaced Gould on Luke and Gloria's divorce case. Roberts immediately denied hearing the motions re custody and removal upon which Gould had not acted. Those were any motions I filed before April 1st, 2001.

Anecdote #2.

Four years later, in *Dickenson v. Cogswell*,[132]/ the appeals court found that Pamela Dickenson's "sincere desire to follow" her new spouse, Mark Salwasser—Chouteau Merrill's former husband—was not a good reason for the move and was not in the best interests of her and Cogswell's child.

"A custodial parent may not remove a minor child from the Commonwealth without the consent of both parents, unless the [probate judge] *upon cause shown* otherwise orders,"[133]/ the panel in *Dickenson* wrote. "The words 'upon cause shown' mean only that removal must be in the best interests of the child."[134]/

"The first consideration in the process of determining the best interests of a child is whether there is a 'real advantage' to the move."[135]/ "This requires that the custodial parent establish 'a good, sincere reason for wanting to remove to another jurisdiction.'"[136]/. "Here, judges consider both 'the soundness of the reason for moving, and the presence or absence of a motive to deprive the noncustodial parent of reasonable visitation.'"[137]/ "The focus at this stage is on the reasoning of the custodial parent. If the custodial parent establishes a good, sincere reason for wanting to remove to another jurisdiction, none of the relevant factors becomes controlling in deciding the best interests of the child, but rather they must be considered collectively."[138]/ At this second stage "[e]very person, parent and child, has an interest to be considered."[139]/

Sounds wonderful, doesn't it? BUT, the appellate panel did not think it was. Despite the panel's finding that Pamela Dickenson recognized the importance of preserving the relationship between the father and their son, was not motivated by a desire to disadvantage the father, and also had an obvious, sincere reason for the move—to accompany her new husband, Mark Salwasser, who wanted to move to California—did not allow her to remove the child to California. The panel, instead, ruled that Pamela's desire to accompany her new husband was not a good reason for the move and was not in the best interests of the child.

Thus Family Court Judge Edward F. Donnelly, Jr.'s denial of Pamela Dickenson's request for permission to remove the parties' minor child to California was affirmed.

Anecdote #3.

Six months after *Dickenson* was decided, the appellate panel deciding *Pizzino v. Miller*\[140]/ concluded the opposite, however, to wit, "that a sincere desire to be with a spouse is, *per se*, a good and sufficient reason that requires a finding that there is a real advantage to the custodial parent in moving. It is not our function as judges to conduct reviews of the wisdom of decisions of competent adults to marry."\[141]/ ". . . the desire of a spouse to be with his or her marital partner is a natural and appropriate response that the law is required to acknowledge. A finding that there is no 'real advantage' to the spouse in such a move is illogical and impermissible."\[142]/

The most significant difference between *Dickenson* and *Pizzino* is that Judge Chouteau Merrill was the first wife of Pamela Dickinson's new husband, Mark Salwasser. Do you suppose that the appellate panel was biased in favor of Chouteau Merrill and prejudiced against Pamela Dickenson?

Do you suppose the common denominator of *Attorney* Chouteau Merrill as Gloria's lawyer and *Judge* Chouteau Merrill being the first wife of Pamela Dickenson's new husband, Mark Salwasser, had anything to do with the diametrically opposed opinions of Judges Gould and Donnelly? Do not forget that both Gould and Donnelly were formerly registers of probate and family courts—Donnelly, not having to read a law case for 16 years, from 1983 to 1998, and Gould, not having to read a law case for 18 years, from 1974 to 1991—before being appointed to the bench.

Chouteau was not involved with the *Pizzino* case. Judge Michael J. Livingstone was. He had denied the former wife's motion to modify her divorce judgment so that she could move from the Commonwealth with the two minor children of her former marriage, but the appellate panel, finding that there was a real advantage to amending the divorce judgment to allow the former spouse to move from the Commonwealth with the former spouses' minor children, vacated Livingstone's judgment in part and remanded the case to the family court.

The possible reason for the appellate court's opinion: Livingstone was under investigation after serious charges were filed against him in November 2005 and July 2006 prior to the *Pizzino* case being heard. His butt no longer was going to be protected. In April 2008, Livingstone agreed to retire officially—on June 12 after using 40 days of accrued leave—from the bench to settle the misconduct charges that he violated judicial rules by, among other things, running a real estate business and collecting attorney's fees while serving as a judge. Upon being appointed in 2002, he gave his cases to an attorney friend, who then appeared before him.\[143]/

I do wonder to this day whether "the Livingstone problem" applies also to Chouteau. Not only had Chouteau practiced for a decade at a huge, prestigious law firm in Boston with a large family-law department but also, very soon after her divorce, married William Levine, a well-known, well-heeled, well-connected family-law lawyer whose surname she did *not* take and who is a partner in a renowned family-law boutique. The danger: most parties in family-court cases would not know whether their opposing counsel knew Chouteau in the past or whether their opposing counsel is a partner of her present husband, Bill, or associated with his lawfirm.

Anecdote #4.

In 2000, in *Meuse v. Paine,* an out-of-wedlock case, Judge Mary McCauley Manzi found that the child's mom unlawfully took the child to Florida, but Manzi then never ordered the mother to return to Massachusetts with the child. Dad had to get the child himself. When found and captured by a SWAT team in Oklahoma, he faced a Parental Kidnapping charge.

In 2006, another out-of-wedlock case, Mary McCauley Manzi allowed the mother's request to relocate the child out of state, and the father appealed.

The differences demonstrate how entrenched Manzi's bias for women is: In *Meuse v. Paine,* Brian had filed to establish paternity and had been awarded custody by a district court judge, but neither Manzi ordered Mother Paine to bring the child back to Massachusetts nor the district-court judge ordered Paine's arrest when she showed up in his courtroom.

In *Wakefield v. Hegarty,* the mother filed a paternity complaint in order to get the court to determine who the father was, and was allowed to remove the child to another State.\144/ The father's request to share legal custody of the child was based allegedly on the evidentiary record as a whole. The Appeals Court affirmed the permission to relocate with the child.

Anecdote #5.

In *Abbott v. Virusso,*\145/ the mother had been awarded primary physical custody of one of the couple's two children—a boy and a girl—and filed a motion to relocate with her child to Arizona to join her fiancé, Dr. Seder. The daughter, blaming Dr. Seder for the divorce of her parents, was living with her father and refused to move to Arizona with her mother.

Judge Edward J. Rockett, J., denied mother's motion to relocate with the son and Mother appealed.

In a 2:1 decision, Appeals Court Judge Fernande R. V. Duffly vacated the denial on the grounds (1) that the mother had established a good, sincere reason to relocate with the child to Arizona; (2) that in determining whether it was in best interest's of child to relocate with mother, the trial court was also required to consider mother's interest in relocating, her relationship with child, and her quality of life; and (3) that upon remand to the family court for further findings, the trial court was required to make an electronic recording of *in camera* interview with the 11-year-old minor child.\146/

The ultimate issue, it appears, in removal cases where the custodial parent seeks to move to be with a significant other, is the best interests of the child.\147/ In *Abbott,* the appellate panel noted that in both "the *Dickenson* and *Pizzino* cases involved the mother of children seeking to relocate to be with her new husband. Whether a different analysis should be applied where the mother seeks to move to join her fiancé, as here, is best left for another day."\148/ Both of the parties, Abbott and Virusso, also wrongly relied\149/ on *Yannas v. Frondistou-Yannas,*\150/ in which the removal involved the one parent who had sole physical custody. They should have relied on *Mason v. Coleman,*\151/ in which the parents had joint physical and legal custody, which the "'best interest' calculus"\152/ is appreciably different.

Anecdote #6.

Baltzer v. Cleri[153] / for which E. Chouteau Merrill was again the trial judge and she allowed the mother, Lorraine Baltzer Cleri, who was awarded sole legal and physical custody of the minor children, to relocate with them to New York from Massachusetts. Chouteau then gave the father both an actual visitation schedule and a "virtual visitation" schedule—virtual visitation being visitation via computer. His virtual visitation with the children was scheduled to be "twice per week, on Tuesdays and Thursdays from 6:00 p.m. to 7:00 p.m., and at such additional times as the parties may agree. To facilitate the virtual visitation each party shall forthwith purchase and install a video camera attachment and the related software for his or her computer."

Chouteau's order was technologically oriented:

- Unless otherwise specified, notice may be by telephone so long as the parties actually speak to one another, or by email so long as the receiving party indicates having received the email.

- The Wife shall provide the children with telephone and electronic mail access so they may communicate with the Husband.

- The Husband and the Wife shall each provide the other with reasonable telephone access to the children while the children are in his or her respective care. Both parties shall encourage said contact and not impede or permit others to impede the same.

- During either party's away from home vacations with the children each shall exchange itineraries, telephone contact numbers and addresses where the children will be staying at least one week prior to the vacation. The non-vacationing parent may telephone the children once per week during the vacation. The children may telephone either parent at any time.

A great deal of publicity arose out of the *Cleri* case owing to the order of "virtual visitation." Chouteau became known as the "virtual visitation" judge. Although the unpublished decision appearing on Westlaw does not, of course, mention it, Paul Cleri, who later phoned me, complained of Lorraine's failure to give the children a computer for the so-called virtual visitation.

Anecdote #7.

In 2006, E. Chouteau Merrill was once again the judge in a removal case. The case was *Cartledge v. Evans,*\[154]/ another 2:1 decision. It was a case between Titans. Representing Jennifer was a new associate in the lawfirm of the aging Monroe Inker, the granddaddy of family law, who has since passed. Representing Mark Evans was Janice Bassil, a hardball-playing piranha.

Having been burned with negative publicity as a result of the *Cleri* decision, Chouteau denied Jennifer Cartledge's motion to relocate with the child and ordered Jennifer to return with the child to the Commonwealth. Chouteau was, as mentioned, overturned.

Chouteau Merrill had made the following findings: (1) "The Wife's claim that she is only able to find employment in Connecticut is not credible"; (2) "The Wife's claim that she has no support system in Massachusetts is not credible"; (3) "The Wife's claim that she cannot afford to stay in Massachusetts is not credible"; and finally (4) "A move of 115 miles from his father is not in [the child's] best interest." Each of these findings is thoroughly documented and analyzed, and is well supported by the record.\[155]/

Ironically, Chouteau could have argued the exact same things about Gloria in 2000, but did not. Why? Because she did not have to argue anything before Gould . . . because there was no hearing. And, of course, she was not only being well paid to argue the opposite if she had to argue something at all, Chouteau had to have known of the beneficial interest given to GAL Beardslee for her then-upcoming trial testimony..

Given the capriciousness of the court decisions, a party needs to rub a bottle with a genii in it to make his or her wishes come true!

Anecdote #8.

Gloria and Luke Stockdale Again! Collateral Action to Reverse Removal.

Gloria was given a temporary order allowing her to remove the children to her father's home in Maine. Her husband, Lucas, was not asked for his consent and was not given an evidentiary hearing as the law requires. Gloria's father, George, was a suspected pedophile and Lucas, a gentle man who adored his sons, was fearful that the children would be molested. After the children had been removed to Maine and came to visit Luke at home, he observed that their behavior had changed. His fear was enhanced by what he saw. All the red flags had been raised. He was certain then that the children had, indeed, been molested.

Unable to get the Massachusetts courts to order the children into his custody in Massachusetts, Luke decided to file a diversity case against Gloria and George in U.S. District Court in Portland, Maine. *See* Chapter 1, page 3. As noted there, a "diversity" case requires all the plaintiffs to be from one State and all the defendants to be from States other than State in which the plaintiffs reside or are domiciled. Here, the plaintiffs were Lucas and the children, who, because they were still under the jurisdiction of Massachusetts and they were in Maine only according to a "temporary" order, Lucas considered them to be Massachusetts residents or domiciliaries. Chief Justice D. Brock Hornsby of the U.S. District Court in Portland took on the case.

Gloria and George immediately filed a Motion to Dismiss for lack of jurisdiction, on the grounds that the children were now domiciled in Maine and not in Massachusetts. Because of the sensitivity of the molestation issue against one of their well-established citizens, Judge Hornsby heard arguments around a conference table in his chambers.

Gloria argued that she was a domiciliary of Maine and because she was, so were the children. We argued not only that the children were in Maine only temporarily and were still under the jurisdiction of the Massachusetts family court but, specifically, that the children were too young either to know or to understand what "domicile" or "domiciliary" means and certainly were too young to choose where they will be domiciled.

Despite the fact we were ready for this attack with a handful of cases from around the country, Hornsby found that the children were domiciled in Maine and advised Luke to bring the suit in a state court in Maine. Having seen the arbitrary and capricious ignoring of procedural and substantive law in Maine, the last thing Luke and I wanted to do was bring a case of this character into Maine courts. It would be like jumping from the Massachusetts pot into a fire in Maine. (Other folks would say that both States are already in the hellfire.)

Appealing against Hornsby in the First Circuit would have been futile.

Chapter 7

Restraining Orders

Gang-banged in court or in jail. It's the law.

> Every married woman shall be free
> from bodily correction or stripes by her
> husband, *unless it be in his own defense*
> *upon her assault.*
>
> — The Body of Liberties (1641)
> Massachusetts Bay colonists
> [emphasis added]\[156]

> VAWA has turned the mere **assertion**
> (false or not) of 'fear' into the trigger
> that instantaneously turns non-violent
> American fathers into homeless and
> childless outcasts from society. And
> it is doing things just as terrible to the
> children of these fathers who are being
> made fatherless. The American family
> unit, and the development of America's
> children, is doomed to regress further
> and further if the VAWA is renewed.
>
> — Marc Snider, Letter to Congress
> (New York Civil Rights Council, 2005)

The Violence Against Women Act (VAWA) was drafted by Senator Joe Biden and passed into law in 1994 during Bill Clinton's first term as President. In FY 95, the Department of Justice began the STOP Violence Against Women Grant Program through VAWA funding.\[157]/ STOP is an acronym for **S**ervices, **T**raining, **O**fficers, and **P**rosecutors.

In 2001, VAWA was extended by George W. Bush for five more years. VAWA and its progeny (for example, Victims of Crime Act and Family Violence Prevention and Services Act) have created a humungous industry worth about $1 billion a year. That money allegedly goes to provide victim services and enhance law enforcement efforts. It doesn't.

"The Violence Against Women Act has also spawned the passage of about 1,500 state-level laws."\[158]/ Those laws include the Domestic Violence Guidelines of each State. Although they are entitled "guidelines," they are considered "laws" and many of the guidelines are incorporated into local police department manuals and handbooks.

"VAWA inspired DV laws clog our courts with false claims of domestic violence, which prevents true victims from getting help."\[159]/ R.A.D.A.R., 9/20/08.\[160]/

Most men and women in our society do not have a clue that there is something known as VAWA. They only learn about it in court . . . a criminal or civil court. If they go to their local criminal court, the women will learn from the so-called Victim Witness Advocates that they can get a Protective Order, which will keep their significant other or their husband away from them . . . and from the children. Victim Witness Advocates then accompany the women to the bench, where the judge sits. If the women are filing for divorce in a family court, their lawyers advise them to apply for a restraining order. If they have no lawyer, then a Victim Witness Advocate or a Family Service Officer or Probation Officer will tell them how to apply for a restraining order.

What the women are told universally—that is, across this nation—is that all they have to say is that they "fear" the men. The law requires that they fear "imminent serious physical harm" by their man, but most judges dispense with that requirement. Judges have heard "I fear him. His eyes—they are blue—looked different than they usually looked." Such a statement causes a restraining order to issue immediately and be given to some law-enforcement officer for service. Sometimes the woman calls the man and merely says, "Do not come home."

A former president of the Massachusetts Bar Association spoke candidly about the problem: "Everyone knows that restraining orders are granted to virtually all who apply... In many cases, allegations of abuse are now used for tactical advantage." Another legal expert agrees with her: "With child abuse and spouse abuse you don't have to prove anything. You just have to accuse."\¹⁶¹/

These tactics have become so widespread that divorce lawyers euphemistically refer to them as "silver bullets," "slam-dunks," or "divorce planning." Legal commentators have expressed alarm over the perversion of justice. "New Jersey attorney David Heleniak sums up the process this way: 'In ten days, the hypothetical husband has gone from having a normal life with a wife, children and home to being a social pariah, homeless, poor, and alone, trapped in a Kafkaesque nightmare.'"\¹⁶²/

And the men, they learn the effect of the DV laws when they get a notice not to go home again and to stay away from their wife or significant other and the children, if any, involved. That notice might say Protective Order or Restraining Order or Abuse Prevention Order at the top right-hand corner. They may not go home for their clothes, their tools, their bank records, or anything else. If they do go home, their wife or significant other will call the police and if the man is still on the premises when the police arrive, the man will be arrested for violating a restraining order, will be kept overnight, will not be allowed to be bailed out, and will have to wait until morning, when he will be brought before a judge. No one but a judge may release a man arrested for a "DV" incident.

The man may eventually go home only in the presence of a police officer, who will give the man about fifteen minutes to collect belongings. Except for obviously personal clothes, the wife has veto power over what hubby is able to remove. This process essentially gives the wife a license to legally steal her husband' assets.

Often when a man is arrested, a man is stunned because he knows he was not violent. What he does not know is that the U.S. Department of Justice defines "domestic violence" as being "any physical, sexual, emotional, economic, or psychological actions or threats of actions that influence another person. This includes any behaviors that intimidate, manipulate, humiliate, isolate, frighten, terrorize, coerce, threaten, blame, hurt, injure, or wound someone."\¹⁶³/

The man is entitled under the law to get a hearing before a judge within 10 days. He might not, however, get that hearing, despite his entitlement to one. His right to due process, that is, notice and a right to be heard before any order issues against him, was violated on the day the *ex parte* order issued against him.

Because the original *ex parte* order is likely to be extended for a year, the most critical time for the defendant is that so-called "10-day hearing" because all too often that one-year restraining order is extended for another year and ultimately becomes a permanent order.

So it is truly imperative at that 10-day hearing to cross-examine the applicant (likely your wife or girlfriend or your ex-wife or ex-girlfriend) meticulously. If she is the manipulative type, go after the manipulation. If she is the mendacious type, go after all her history of lies. If she has a lover or random boyfriends, do not worry about being gentlemanly. You have to "dirty her up." Hopefully, you will have saved the nicest birthday cards, anniversary cards she ever sent you. The more lovey-dovey they are, the better. Get her to admit "that's her signature" on it, admit it into evidence, and then READ it into the record. Read it with enough passion to get the clerk to cry. The woman might be affected emotionally and say that you are as gentle as a dove, the most gentle man she had known.

Buy (in the clerk's office) the tape of the proceeding as soon as you walk out of the courtroom . . . whether you "win" or "lose" . . . because some of the women are like Energizer Bunnies: they will repeatedly apply for restraining orders for years. So you will want a record of each and every hearing just in case you need to impeach her over and over again.

Once the so-called temporary order is in place, it can be a nightmare to remove.

The following is an excerpt from a court transcript in which a respondent's attorney requested District Court Judge Margaret A. Zaleski to vacate (i.e., discontinue) the order:

MR. GREGORY HESSION: "Can you please state your name and your address for the record?" [The Court argues with counsel as to whether Mr. L can testify.]

THE COURT: "I don't believe I need to hear any evidence from your client. I'm going to deny your request to vacate the restraining order."

What began as a civil matter in family court will end as a criminal matter if the man violates the unconstitutional order that issued *ex parte. Ex parte* means that one party to a law case has no knowledge that the other party has secretly communicated with the judge. That is a No, No.

Byron Watson, a man recently caught in the maelstrom of divorce, has asked the question so many before him have asked, Why is there a statute for domestic violence when all the criteria under the statute is covered by the assault or assault and battery statute?\[164]/ The domestic violence statute\[165]/ only serves to cater to special interest groups and to bolster support of politicians who intentionally created a very flawed statute that is easily abused. Restraining orders are only effective against the innocent and risk the creation of an emotionally charged individual who may commit extreme acts."

The answer to that question is quite simple. Each State reports the DV activity to the federal government yearly and can expect to receive an annual bonus the next year.\[166]/\[167]/\[168]/

The federal government has recommended policies:

- Many jurisdictions have instituted "no-drop" prosecution policies. No-drop means that even if the alleged victim recants the allegation and requests that the case be dropped, the prosecutor must still pursue the case. These programs operate under the doubtful assumption that most partner conflict requires heavy-handed legal intervention.\[169]/\[170]/

- A "soft" no-drop policy is one in which the prosecutor may drop charges in some circumstances, including instances when the victim decides to leave the batterer or the alleged victim recants the allegation or requests that the case be dropped.\[171]/

- The Duluth, Minnesota Police Department functioned as a testing site to determine which of three law enforcement options was most effective as a deterrent of violence:

  - arrest of the perpetrator or
  - separation of the parties for a "cooling off" period or
  - restoration of order\[172]/

- As of 2001, forty States had implemented some form of mandatory arrest.\[173]/ Other States have arrest-preferred policies, which are the Department of Justice's recommendations in an annual grant entitled "Grant for the Encouragement of Arrest-preferred Policies and the Enforcement of Protection Order Programs."\[174]/ This grant is administered by the Office of Violence Against Woman (OVW).

After the first few years, studies of VAWA laws were inevitable. One researcher concluded that the effectiveness of restraining depended upon how much the target of the order was intimidated by the court. If the target was an abuser, it was highly probable that he will continue to be abusive and highly *un*likely that the offender will hesitate to violate a restraining order.\[175]/ So what is the sense of using an unconstitutional law and a piece of paper as an *un*likely deterrent.

In 1993, two co-authors concluded that racial and class stereotypes influence arrest decisions. Whether correct or not, they further concluded, "Generally, arrest is made far less frequently in cases involving minorities as police deduce that violence is a normal way of life for these individuals.\[176]/ By 2007, other researchers contradicted the earlier study: "A disproportionate number of arrestees are Black."\[177]/

Another team or alleged researchers claimed that while an officer's race does not affect his or her tendency to make an arrest, both the officer's level of experience and gender is related to arrest outcomes. "Specifically, female officers make fewer arrests than male officers and older more experienced officers are less likely to make arrests in comparison to younger officers.\[178]/

In 2007, R.A.D.A.R. reported that 26 States require the divorce courts to consider domestic violence when determining what is in the "best interest of the child," that 23 jurisdictions have a rebuttable presumption against shared parenting, and 4 States have explicitly prohibited shared parenting when there has been an allegation of domestic violence true of not.\[179]/

Unfortunately the judiciary rarely serves as a buffer against unfounded claims of partner abuse. Why? Because "the Violence Against Women Act funds judicial education programs that have been shown to be ideological and one-sided. Rather than helping judges to balance the legitimate needs of the accuser with the due process rights of the accused, the training sessions do the opposite, instructing judges to grant a restraining order if there is 'any hint whatsoever that there's a problem.'"\180/

"At one New Jersey program, a trainer openly advised judges to ignore due process protections: 'Your job is not to become concerned about all the constitutional rights of the man that you're violating as you grant a restraining order. Throw him out on the street, give him the clothes on his back, and tell him, "See ya' around."'"\181/

Each year civil restraining orders are issued against about 2–3 million persons in the United States and about one million persons are arrested under criminal law for intimate partner violence,\182/ of whom 77% are male.\183/ The Massachusetts Trial Court revealed that half of the orders Massachusetts issued were not based on even an *allegation* of physical violence."\184/

"One report by the Ms. Foundation for Women expressed the concern that overly aggressive law enforcement has led to 'mass incarceration of men, especially young men of color, decimating marginalized communities.'"\185/

> As a result of aggressive law-enforcement and prosecution efforts, our nation's domestic violence system amounts to "state-imposed *de facto* divorce," explains Harvard Law School professor Jeannie Suk.\186/ The government "initiates and dictates the end of the intimate relationship as a solution to DV."\187/

See RADAR's "A Culture of False Allegations: How VAWA Harms Families and Children," pages 9-10, to read the detailed, authoritative list of the effects on children who live apart from their fathers and are at risk for a broad range of social pathologies, including educational, behavioral, and health problems. Given that "[m]ore than one million American children experience divorce each year,"\188/ and that false allegations of DV are made during the course of 55% of the divorce proceedings, of which 59% could not be substantiated as true,"\189/ "each year, many thousands of children experience divorces in which false allegations of partner violence are made, allegations that often serve as the basis to deprive children of contact from one of their parents."\190/

" 'A community that allows a large number of young men to grow up in broken families, dominated by women, never acquiring any stable relationship to male authority, never acquiring any rational expectations about the future—that community asks for and gets chaos.' "\[191]/

Domestic Violence

Bob Parks,\[192]/ the Republican candidate for State Representative in the Second Franklin District of Massachusetts, wrote on his blog:

> . . . *most citizens have no idea how much of their tax money goes to domestic violence programs, how ineffective they are, or how much harm they cause to families.* . . .

> *First, the money: Each year the federal government spends over $1 billon dollars for various programs designed to stop domestic violence.   That money goes to law enforcement departments, prosecutors, and abuse shelters.   Then add the money from state and local government, as well as private contributions, and we're looking at a $4 billion industry.*

> *If that $4 billion was actually stopping domestic violence, I think we'd all agree it was money well spent.*\[193]/   *But the truth is that domestic violence programs have not worked.*

This is what industry insiders are saying:

- *"We have no evidence to date that VAWA has led to a decrease in the overall levels of violence against women," according to Angela Moore Parmley, PhD at the U.S. Department of Justice.*

- *"At worst, the criminal justice system increases violence against women. At best, it has little or no effect," notes Linda Mills, PhD, New York University vice provost and author of Violent Partners.*

A cynic might say, "Another ineffective government program – so what else is new?" The problem with domestic violence programs in Massachusetts is that they are actually harmful. Here's why....

Much of the problem can be traced to the Commonwealth's legal definition of "abuse," which includes "placing another in fear of imminent serious physical harm." Now, almost anything counts as partner "violence"—raising your voice, an honest airing of differences, and even "possessiveness" all invite legal intervention.

As a result, scarce resources end up going to cases that are minor and/or frivolous. As a result, real victims of violence can't get the help they desperately need.

In short, we have created an abuse-reduction system that is ineffective, unaccountable, and even harmful. These problems are documented in a series of reports by RADAR—Respecting Accuracy in Domestic Abuse Reporting.

So how do we go about fixing a costly system that has gone astray? An effective approach to curbing domestic violence needs to incorporate policies that:

- *respect fundamental constitutional guarantees of due process and equal treatment under the law*
- *are based on the best available research and are able to withstand scientific scrutiny*
- *assure that interventions are based on an individualized assessment, respect victims' wishes, acknowledge cultural differences, and do not impose a one-size-fits-all approach*
- *emphasize counseling and treatment for minor/one-time cases, rather than law enforcement and criminal justice intervention*
- *discourage the making of false accusations*
- *do not engage in discrimination*
- *assure accountability at all levels*

Many people have been unjustly incarcerated, while the person who may recant can do so without so much as saying "sorry" while lives are ruined and reputations are destroyed.

Anecdote #1.

Paul's wife had gotten a permanent restraining order against him. He had not seen their children for several years. Paul's mother was dying and told him she wanted to see her grandchildren before she passed. He knew the order forbade him to contact either his now-ex-wife or their sons, but he did want to grant his mother's last wish. So he found a sympathetic telephone operator, begged her to phone his ex's sister and ask the sister to call his ex-wife and tell him Grandma wants to see the children before she dies.

The operator did as she promised: she called the ex's sister, who called the ex, and then the ex then dropped a dime. Paul was arrested. His mother died, never having seen the children before she passed on. From prison, the correction department people brought him to his mother's wake in shackles: handcuffs and ankle bracelets. His family, seeing him that way, thought he had done something terrible and never spoke to him again. Paul was not brought to his mother's funeral. He was held in prison for 9 months. He had no lawyer.

Anecdote #2.

Luke's wife got her first restraining order against him on the same day she filed for divorce. He had stepped on a plastic Halloween candy basket the kids left on the floor and she claimed he was going to kill her and disappear with the children. That order ran out a year later.

In the meantime she had moved to another State and got another, a second, restraining order against him in that State. He had not been in that State after she relocated there.

After the Massachusetts order expired and believing the court would order them to sell the marital property, Luke wanted to complete renovations he had begun before his wife filed for divorce. So he went there with his tools and materiels (precut window and door trim and baseboards) to finish the renovations. Surprise! His wife had put her stepbrother into the condo. The stepbrother and the wife each phoned the police. Luke was arrested at his own home, strip-searched, and held on bail, although he had no prior criminal involvement at any time of his life.

At the arraignment, he was both appointed a defense counsel, Lisa A. Grant, and handed a Complaint with four charges against him. Two of the four charges were for "attempting to violate a restraining order" and for "violating a restraining order," although the restraining order had expired a month earlier. The other two charges were for destruction of property (allegedly the lock on his front door) and for possession of a burglarious tool (his screw driver to install the trim).

Concerned that the appointed counsel, Grant, was doing nothing (but who is currently one of the members of the Board of Bar Overseers), he asked me to accompany him to court on the day of trial. My bit of backchannel communication with the assistant district attorney convinced her to move to dismiss the case. Never having seen Grant get any case dismissed, the judge looked over at me—given my hearing and the bad acoustics in the courtroom, I was sitting alone near the court officer's seat on the side and as close to the bench as possible—and then to Luke and asked him if I were his mother. Luke said, No, my divorce lawyer. The judge grinned broadly, dismissed all four charges and told Luke to take me out to a great dinner.

Wifey then applied for another Massachusetts restraining order (#3). Although she no longer was a resident of the Commonwealth, she was awarded it. I hammered away that he never had a 10-day hearing and eventually before a replacement judge, I got the order vacated.

Because the out-of-state restraining order expired, the wife applied for a second restraining order in her new home state (#4 RO). The out-of-state Court told Luke and me that he would do whatever Massachusetts did, given that the accusation was identical to that in Massachusetts. So on our next court date out-of-state, we had the papers to show that Massachusetts had vacated the order. While we were waiting, Luke's wife's lawyer, Michael P. Asen, walked through the door at the rear of the courtroom leading to the judge's chamber. The judge, we were led to understand, was either an old friend or a former partner of Asen's.

Although we do not know what occurred in the judge's chamber that day, we do know that instead of holding the RO vacated—as promised in open court—the judge immediately ordered us to trial that day. We had not brought documents for trial or had served subpoenas, because we believed the out-of-state court would vacate the order as promised. We tried to access the file and order the tape, but learned that the file had been cleansed . . . totally. There was **no** record of the previous proceedings in the case . . . not even the names of the lawyers on the case. Amazing. And that State does *not* tape its proceedings unless someone orders it at least 24 hours in advance.

Around a year later, Luke was ordered by the Massachusetts family court to make available for appraisal the marital condo on a certain day at a certain time. The wife could attend if she so wanted. Without telling Luke that she would be there, Luke's wife showed up from out-of-state and her local lawyer called the police from his cellphone and reported that a violation of a restraining order was taking place (i.e., RO #4, the out-of-state restraining order; RO #3 had expired). Fortunately, Luke had allowed the appraiser to inspect the property and had left with him before the police arrived. Had he stayed at the premises, he would have been arrested again.

Notwithstanding that the police did not see anything, the wife convinced the police to levy charges and then managed to convince the District Attorney to give the second State's order Full Faith and Credit. As a result, the DA brought against my client two of four charges (all enhanced) for violating a domestic violence restraining order.

I argued for dismissal on the grounds that there was no active restraining order in Massachusetts and that the wife had also not followed the Massachusetts statutory procedure required to seek full faith and credit for the out-of-state order.\[194]/ Judge Sally A. Kelly denied the motion, so I brought an interlocutory appeal, but the Appeals Court rubber-stamped the very wrong decision below.

A year-and-a-half later, Judge Thomas C. Horgan, in Boston Municipal Court, dismissed the criminal prosecution, saying to the assistant district attorney, Do you think I'm going to tell a jury in my courtroom to ignore the Massachusetts order and find that the out-of-state order is the one he should have followed? Not in my courtroom. With that, the trial judge dismissed the case *sua sponte* and challenged the District Attorney's office to appeal the dismissal.\[195]/ The DA did not appeal.

Luke's wife was like an Energizer Bunny. There was no stopping her short of filing two malicious prosecution cases.

Anecdote #3.

A fireman got lucky. His ex-wife was dating a big, brawny policeman. The district court judge found she was not in danger of suffering imminent, serious physical harm. Her new boyfriend would be able to protect her. There was no need for a restraining order.

Anecdote #4.

Harry Stewart had a restraining order that allowed him to drop off his child at the outside door of the apartment building in which his wife and child resided. He was not to get out of his car. Harry would sit in his car and watch through the window until his ex-wife appeared to collect the child. One night, Harry opened the front door of the foyer of the apartment complex because his 5-year-old son couldn't open it and had to go the bathroom. The child had messed his pants two weeks earlier trying to get in. Harry never made contact, or saw Mother that night.

Because Harry had entered the building, his ex-wife, like Paul's, called the police, and he was arrested for violating the restraining order. Six weeks later, he was convicted, given a six-month suspended sentence, and ordered to participate in a batterer's program. Because Stewart refused to sign a statement admitting he was a batterer, a condition of the court-ordered counseling, he was sent to the Dedham jail to serve the six-month sentence.

The case infuriated members of the Fatherhood Coalition, who garnered national publicity and staged weekly protests outside the jail in Harry's support. The Coalition's founder Mark Charalambous sponsored a bill in the Legislature to make these fundamental changes in the restraining order process:

- Evidence of actual and intentional harm would be required before an order could be issued.

- Prosecutors would be required to consider perjury charges against anyone who files a false petition for a restraining order.

- Those who violate restraining orders unintentionally would not be punished.

- A person under a restraining order would be allowed to visit his or her children, provided that no parental abuse allegation had been made.

Anecdote #5.

Because of another insane fact pattern, Steve, too, was sentenced to 30 days in jail for an alleged violation of a restraining order. He came out, he committed suicide in Waltham, Massachusetts. I would have, too, had he been my client. I believe he represented himself in court. Other than hearing his story through the men's gravevine and the local newspaper, I have no personal knowledge. I believe the court had thrown him out of his home and had sold it.

Anecdote #6.

Bob, too, had a restraining order that prohibited him from communicating with his wife and children or being closer than say 500 feet or yards from them. Bob was a runner. One Wednesday, around 5 o'clock in the evening, he was exercising on the school track. His car was parked on the other side of the wire fence not too distant from the track. His ex-wife saw his car, cellphoned the police, and claimed that one of their daughters was playing soccer in a nearby field and saw him. He was arrested and held overnight, he phoned me, we appeared for his arraignment, after which he was released on personal recognizance.

The following Sunday, he went to church. Not to a morning service, but to an early evening service. He had expected his family to have gone to morning services. As he opened the door, his ex-wife turned and saw him. When he noticed her seeing him, he left immediately. She again phoned the police, but Bob was not on the church grounds by the time the police arrived.

When in the local district court for trial, I told the judge that the restraining order was improper. The court made the assistant district attorney get the papers, for the copy I had was almost illegible. Giving a defendant "almost illegible" papers is a trick ADAs often use. Bob and I waited the half-hour or so for the ADA to return to the courtroom. Only then did I say what it was I believed was improper. It was the date. A hearing had been set for the 10th of the month but the notice had been served on the 11th of that month, resulting in Bob being found in default on the 10th, when he did not appear. Not getting notice is a violation of due process.

I had kept my mouth shut prior to that trial date because it would have given the ADA an opportunity either to "correct" the original notice or to replace it with a newly created notice. This is a commonplace occurrence. Troublesome because you and your client do not know in advance with what the client is being charged.

The judge was a visiting judge, i.e., a judge from a distant court and unfamiliar with the ADAs in the court in which we were awaiting trial. That is always helpful. No friends or favorites have yet been formed with the ADAs. The ADAs have not become one of the judge's court family.

The actions against Bob were dismissed on the grounds that the restraining order was improper and could be no violation of an improper order.

The ADA had apoplexy. The judge remained firm and told her to appeal if she had a problem. I stood mute. CAVEAT: Do not shoot yourself in the foot. Shut up when the court is making your legal argument for you!

A Breakthrough of Sorts!

A New Jersey Superior Court found that the Prevention of Domestic Violence Act is violative of the New Jersey and United States Constitutions.\[196]/ The *Crespo* decision by Judge Schultz was a "trial court" decision and is NOT a precedential case.

Judge Schultz ruled that the burden of proof in New Jersey domestic violence cases should be "clear and convincing," not "by a preponderance of the evidence," and that application of the latter standard constitutes a due process violation. Due to this alleged constitutional defect, Judge Schultz reversed Crespo's conviction under the New Jersey Prevention of Violence Act.

The Attorney General has filed an appeal on behalf of the State. It is *Crespo v. Crespo*, A-0202-08T2 (App. Div. filed Sept. 12, 2008),\[197]/ but it has *not* yet been decided.

If New Jersey has a two-tier appellate system, the appellate decision might or might not be appealed to New Jersey's highest court. That appellate decision *might* also be published.

Recommendations to Stop False Allegations of DV

RADAR's recently released White Paper presents 10 needed changes to federal and state domestic violence laws to correct this insidious problem of false allegations.\[198]/

1. The definition of domestic violence should be consistent with statutory definitions of physical assault.

2. Harassment and stalking should be objectively defined in terms of specific acts by the alleged offender, not the perceptions or feelings of the alleged victim.

3. Partner abuse that does not fall within the above-described definition of domestic violence, harassment, or stalking should be addressed by counseling, treatment, and mediation, not by the law enforcement or criminal justice systems.

4. In order to obtain a restraining order, petitioners must provide hard evidence of physical assault, harassment, or stalking.

5. Restraining order petitioners may not make a petition for child custody while a temporary restraining order is in effect.

6. Because restraining orders can affect constitutionally protected parental rights, judges should use the evidentiary standard of "clear and convincing evidence."

7. Restraining orders should be issued during *ex parte* hearings only when objective evidence is presented that the violence, harassment, or stalking represents an immediate credible threat to the petitioner's physical safety.

8. States should enact laws that penalize the filing of false complaints or engaging in perjury. These laws should pertain to the actions of plaintiffs, attorneys, domestic violence shelters, and other organizations that engage in such activities.

9. Prosecutors and judges should be encouraged to vigorously pursue such violations.

10. Government-funded legal services must be made equally available to both the petitioner/plaintiff and respondent/defendant.

Your state and federal lawmakers need to make these reforms. The epidemic of false allegations of domestic violence must end.

Alan Karmin, author of *The Measure of a Man*, which documents his "battle against the odds after a false accusation of domestic violence and [his] quest to fight back against an unfriendly family court system," citing a RADAR report, states that "at least one million restraining orders are issued each year in which violence is not even alleged. There is no other court in the land where the penalty for perjury does not exist—you can lie and not be punished for it, but actually be rewarded for it. There is no other court where you are presumed guilty until proven innocent. And for non-custodial parents . . . especially fathers . . . going through a divorce . . . and the never-ending litany of custody issues and all the rest that goes with it . . . it can feel like eternal damnation.

"Current domestic violence laws define abuse so broadly and provide so many incentives to file a claim that the system has become flooded with minor cases. As a result, true victims have trouble getting the services they need, according to the RADAR report.

"The RADAR analysis notes that a false allegation creates a 'ripple' effect that can persist for many years, harming the alleged person's reputation, legal standing, security clearances, career prospects and financial status. In many cases, it also affects the person's relationship with their children, a relationship that could be harmed permanently.

"False allegations not only damage the individual falsely accused, they also affect other family members who then may be barred from seeing a grandchild, nephew, or niece.

"When you have the system backlogged with so many false allegations, the true victims of domestic violence will not get justice. There are just too many things wrong with VAWA. If someone heard their car go 'clunk' they wouldn't ignore it, they would drive immediately to a mechanic. Well, this clunker (VAWA) needs to get to be put on a lift.

"Despite the best of intentions, our nation's effort to curb domestic violence is not working. Current solutions not only fail to reduce domestic violence, but also create other severe problems. Families are being undermined and children harmed. Innocent Americans are penalized based on false accusations. And victims of violence are re-victimized by a rigid system that ignores their wishes, or excludes them altogether."

Chapter 8

Contempts

A Woman's Heaven and a Man's Hell

> Non-compliance with court ordered
> visitation is three times the problem of
> non-compliance with court ordered child
> support and impacts the children of
> divorce even more.
>
> — J. Annette Vanini and Edward
> Nichols,\[199]

There are three types of contempt: summary, civil, and criminal contempt.

Summary Contempt

Summary contempt is a crime. The crime is contemptuous conduct in a courtroom *if* the presiding judge can see or hear the conduct and *if* the conduct was committed within the actual presence of the judge.\[200] The contemnor, the person who committed the crime, may be punished summarily if the judge determines that immediate punishment is necessary to maintain order in the courtroom.\[201] Anyone in the courtroom may be found in summary contempt, even lawyers.

Anecdote #1.

In a Massachusetts courtroom, as we were approaching the current millennium, in which legal acrimony was at its height, one attorney, Freddie, leaned over and said to opposing counsel, "if you want discovery, you're going to get discovery up the ass."\[202] The motion judge thought he heard the word "ass." It was only after opposing counsel called the judge's attention to the statement that the judge concluded that contumacious conduct occurred.

The appeals court concluded that though the attorney's statement was crude, unprofessional, and vulgar, there was no indication that the statement disrupted the court's business or that the statement was violative of a previous warning. "The only reason the defendant's obnoxious conduct was not summary contempt was that it was not disruptive of the proceedings and not an insult directed at the judge."\203/

Civil and criminal contempts

Civil and criminal contempts require complaints in writing, or Complaints with a capital "C." Civil contempt is what you have committed when you do not comply with a clear and unequivocal order commanding you to do something. If you do not comply, the court will likely put you in jail to coerce you to decide to comply with the court order.\204/. You will not be imprisoned for a definite term. You will hold the key to the cell door. When you pay the money, the cell door will open. If you show that it is impossible for you to comply with the order, you must be released."\205/ When you do not hold the key to the cell door, the contempt is criminal.

Criminal contempt is for exclusively punitive purposes.\206/ Where there is no aggrieved party and no benefit is going to accrue to any entity, incarceration is a punishment for affronting the law. Affronting the law makes the contempt criminal, which calls for a criminal-type punishment.\207/

All courts have the inherent power to hold an entity in contempt for violating their orders. This inherent power is, however, recognized only if the order is valid. The only time a party may ignore a court order and attempt to evade being sanctioned for contempt by litigating the validity of the order itself is when the court "lacked jurisdiction to make the order, or where the order was 'transparently invalid.'"\208/

If the contempt issue is one of money, the court must find that the person has the ability to pay at the time the contempt order or judgment is entered.

A problem might arise if the judge determines that you have the ability to pay when, in fact, you do not and that you have a clear intention to disregard the valid court order. He or she might then find you in criminal contempt.

The determination of whether a contempt is civil or criminal can be problematic when documents are involved or if the underlying order was politically motivated. One such example is a contempt finding that I suffered during my fight to keep my Bar license.

Anecdote #2.

Supreme Court Justice Francis X. Spina, acting in the single-justice session, ordered me to answer written questions posed by the Office of Bar Counsel and/or the Board of Bar Overseers, the Siamese twins that together allegedly regulate the practice of law. Because the dynamic duo already had all the requested information, there would have been no benefit whatsoever to accrue to them. He also wanted me to produce written notices of withdrawal to clients, opposing counsel, and courts.

I did not want to withdraw from my current cases because **(1)** my clients had not complained about me, **(2)** they wanted me to continue representing them, **(3)** it would have been difficult, if not impossible, for them to find replacement counsel, **(4)** they had a right to counsel of their choice, **(5)** ordering their counsel of choice to withdraw from their cases would damage their property, which was their interest in their respective cases, and **(6)** my primary obligation was to my clients and not the court.

I argued, therefore, that I was justified in not writing and given that justification, there was no affront to the law and a finding of contempt, civil or criminal, was inappropriate..

If the judge were to find me in contempt, I argued, the contempt was not civil, it was criminal and I wanted a jury trial.

But Judge Spina, whom I perceive as being the axe man for that court, held that it was a civil contempt and sent me to prison until I answered the questions and provided the documents.

I disagreed. I said it was criminal contempt, which entitled me to a jury trial. Where Judge Spina knew or should have known that it was impossible for me to comply with his order while incarcerated, the contempt was criminal in nature. The contempt should also have been deemed criminal, not civil, and heard by a jury because I was jailed solely for punishment.\²⁰⁹/

In sum, incarcerating me for noncompliance was too harsh, un-constitutional, and certainly a clear error of law, making it mandatory to vacate the finding of contempt. "[C]riminal contempt proceedings are exclusively punitive"\[210]/ and I was being punished for challenging the court. Where no party would be aggrieved and no benefit would accrue to any entity, my incarceration was a punishment for affronting the law, making the contempt criminal.\[211]/

On appeal to the full panel of the Supreme Judicial Court, I ar-gued that where the charge was for criminal, not civil, contempt in the Supreme Judicial Court for Suffolk County, and I was not allowed a trial by jury, the finding of contempt was a clear error of law and must be reversed and the Judgment of Contempt vacated.

Punishment for Contempt Depends on the Court in Which Contempt Arose

In Massachusetts, whether you are entitled to a jury trial and the length of the maximum time for which you can be imprisoned de-pends up which court found you in contempt. Formerly, one had a statutory right to have jury issues framed in the Probate Courts for trial in the Superior Court. However, the statute was repealed.\[212]/ Cur-rently in Probate Court, "there is no provision for a jury trial."\[213]/

Currently in Massachusetts Superior Court, jury trials are available for criminal contempts if incarceration imposed shall be for more than six months. "There is no constitutional right to a jury trial in a criminal contempt proceeding in which the penalty is six months' imprisonment or less."\[214]/

Currently there is, however, no statute or case law addressing the is-sue of incarceration for criminal contempt in the single-justice session of the Massachusetts Supreme Judicial Court.\[215]/ In reality, however, the practice has diverted from strict compliance with the Massachu-setts Rules of Civil Procedure and is presently governed by a hybrid of formal rules and historic customs and practices.\[216]/

In fact, the Commonwealth has "never been squarely presented with the question of the extent to which the Constitution of the Com-monwealth requires jury trials of criminal contempt proceedings."\[217]/ Thus, where the contempt charge brought against me was *de jure* crimi-nal, the County Court had no jurisdiction either to hear or sentence me to any incarceration, definite or indefinite. Even the Massachusetts Rules of Criminal Procedure fail to provide a jury in the Supreme Judicial Court for Suffolk County.\[218]/

Further, where there is no rational basis for the distinction which permits jury trials in some courts but not in others, I was deprived of equal protection of the laws. The only basis was set out\[219]/ by this Court, viz, that there was a rational basis for permitting jury trials for criminal contempt in Superior Court,\[220]/ but not in Probate Court, because there is no such provision for the latter court.\[221]/ That basis is not rational, it is contrived. Thus, the SJC's reasoning was clearly wrong. Essentially the SJC stated, with nothing more than a bald statement such as *Well, Probate Court is different than the other courts,* that there was a rational basis for the disparate treatment. That was reversible error.

The United States Supreme Court had earlier stated, "[W]e will not overturn such a statute unless the varying treatment of different groups or persons is so unrelated to the achievement of any combination of legitimate purposes that we can only conclude that the legislature's actions were irrational."\[222]/ What was the Court saying? It was saying that the Court will only strictly scrutinize whether, say, a man and a woman are being unequally protected by legislation if the legislation is impermissibly interfering with the man's or the woman's exercise of his or her fundamental right or is operating to peculiarly disadvantage the man or the woman.\[223]/ Certainly being charged in one court versus being charged another gives one defendant a peculiar disadvantage.

Assuming *arguendo*—very hesitantly—that there was strict scrutiny of the statute, I, resorting appropriately to the vernacular, asks, *What in the world made this Court find that the same alleged crime can be punished differently because it was brought in two different courts?* The rational action would have been either to make the rules the same for both courts or to disregard the location of the accidental birth of the crime and allow the crime to be tried in one court.

For example, the Massachusetts Supreme Judicial Court ruled that, in essence, birth as a gay person should not deprive the child of the right to marry.\[224]/ Why, then, should the birth of a criminal-contempt charge in one court deprive the defendant of the jury trial to someone who was lucky enough to be charged in another court with the same crime? Thus to deprive someone charged in probate court—or, as in the instant case, in the County Court—rather than in superior court, of the right to a jury trial is a blatant act of disparate treatment and *un*equal protection.

Criminal Procedure Rule 44(a) must then be extended to apply to all courts so that all defendants charged with the same crime are treated equally regardless of the court in which they are charged. Simple and rational. No other rational solution exists.

Now, for those of you in the other 49 States, you must look up the contempt statutes. Be sure to trace them as I did for Massachusetts. If you are charged with contempt, always, always, always demand your right to a jury trial.

Similarly, certain sections of the statute for the Unauthorized Practice of Law\225/ must be uniformly changed. Where there is incarceration, **(1)** the sections must be removed from \226/ a section of statutes applying to civil actions and inserted into the chapters setting out criminal statutes, **(2)** the word "equity" must be stricken, and **(3)** language providing a jury trial must be inserted. Uniform charge, uniform sentencing, and uniform rights to a jury trial would be uniformly correct.

Where I was deprived of equal protection, the finding of contempt was a clear error of law and should have been reversed and the Judgment of Contempt vacated.

I want to remind the reader that this book is not about me, but about everyone. Use the information regarding my experience to understand how warped the law can be implemented and how serious the need for court reform is.

Answer to Complaint for Contempt for NOT Paying Child Support When You Had NO Custody or Visitation

Anecdote #1.

In Drano #77 on my website, I provided a copy of an Answer I filed on behalf of a client who was served with a Complaint for Contempt for NOT paying child support when he had no custody or visitation. My theory of defense was that the order he allegedly violated was a court-approved Settlement Agreement, was still a lawful order, and was neither void nor void *ab initio*—as regards the issue of support.\227/

I contended and still contend that the Settlement Agreement is a contract, which was executed by the parties and soon thereafter breached by the ex-wife, Lynda. As soon as she breached it, the ex-husband, Paul was thereafter, in accordance with well-settled law, under no obligation to perform under it.\228/

Lynda was to fulfill a condition precedent, so that Paul could have visitation with his sons, but she failed to do so. She therefore breached the contract and thereby not only relieved Paul of any financial obligations to her but also failed to perfect any rights she might have had under the Settlement Agreement.\229/

To seek equity, Lynda had to come into court with clean hands, and she had long since the date of the parties' Settlement Agreement violated that order not only on a continual basis but on a continuous basis.\230/ To seek equity, there had to be no direct connection between the couple's problems or the way Lynda handled them and her claim for specific enforcement of the Settlement Agreement,\231/ but Lynda's allegedly inequitable conduct did, indeed, directly affect her claim for specific performance.\232/ To seek equity with unclean hands is a No, No. With unclean hands. Lynda should not have caused harm to Paul,\233/ but she did, indeed, cause him harm by her unclean acts. And, lastly, to seek equity, Lynda should not have wanted to benefit by her own turpitude.\234/

And most significantly, the relevant part of the order that was allegedly violated had to be clear and unequivocal, and in this case, that part of the order was clear and unequivocal. It was clear that Lynda had to take the children to counseling prior to providing visitation to Paul. So she refused to take them and then denied Paul visitation with them and alienated their affection for him. So she was not entitled to a judgment of contempt or to an order for payment of alleged arrearages, given that she had refused to take the children to counseling and refused to allow him to visit with the children.

Of course, that the court approved such a Settlement Agreement was outrageous, particularly where Lynda had been denying the children any time with their dad. This was either negligence or intentional judicial inequity. Were the judges held accountable, they would not be so careless as to approve such an agreement, one agreed to by Paul only because he was threatened or intimidated by a court bending over backwards to help the woman. The court always makes the excuse that their decisions are in the best interests of the children, but clearly such stupid or careless or just plain mean decisions are *not* in the best interests of the children.

Finally, where the child-support "guidelines are based on tradition-al custody and visitation arrangements,"\235/ they simply did not apply to the case where Paul did not get any parenting time with the couple's children.

Therefore, Paul was justified in not paying child support and not in contempt of court.

I have considerably simplified Lynda and Paul's story here, for my sole purpose was to show how a complaint for contempt can be defeated. Lynda had had very dirty, evil hands. In 1994, Paul's mother was dying of cancer and wanted to see her grandchildren before she died. Paul could not simply call Lynda or the children because Lynda had procured a restraining order against him. (I discuss restraining orders in Chapter 7.)

So he thought of another way. Logically, he thought it would be harmless and that he would be abiding by the restraining order, but . . .

Paul convinced a telephone operator to call his sister-in-law, Lynda's sister, and ask her to tell Lynda that Grandma wanted to see the children before she died. The operator, clearly a compassionate soul, called Lynda's sister, who called Lynda, who then dropped a dime on Paul. He was arrested. Grandma did not get to see the children before she died. Paul was brought to her wake in ankle bracelets and handcuffs. He was never brought to her funeral. Seeing him in chains and ankle and handcuffs, his family thought that he had done something horrible and broke off any relationship with him. He remained unlawfully incarcerated for 193 days in 1994-1995 for an alleged violation of the restraining order as a result of the third-party contact with the telephone operator.

The final issue in this case arose when the Department of Revenue brought a Contempt case on Lynda's behalf for failure to pay child support. After I served the DoR with two sets of interrogatories and two sets of requests for the production of documents—one to be answered by DoR and the other, by Lynda—which if answered would have revealed both DoR's share of the money collected (as a result of its contract with the court) and information about Lynda's finances, Lynda declared in open court that she had not wanted the DoR to bring the case on her behalf. The next time we were before the court, the DoR, which had refused to produce the discovery on their own behalf as well as on behalf of Lynda, dismissed the case. The judge, Judge James V. Menno, a decent man who attended Harvard Divinity School prior to getting his law degree, looked shocked, but he had no choice but to allow the dismissal of the $25,000 child-support arrearage/contempt case. It had to become a classic "The One Who Got Away" case.

Usually in these child-support arrearage cases, the men go to jail without passing "Go" or they borrow tens of thousands from friends and relatives to get released from the holding cell in the courthouse. The usually-dimeless men make up the bulk of the nonviolent prison population\[236]/ for which the Commonwealth wastes $60,000 per man for a year's incarceration.\[237]/ Not only has the man been sent unconstitutionally to debtor's prison, his court-ordered child-support obligation continues to accrue while he is there. (The issue of child support is further discussed below in Chapter 4.)

Delilah and Samson and a Judge Who Is Displeased by Cross-Examination

Anecdote #2.

Day 1 of the Delilah-Samson divorce trial. Consolidated with the divorce was a trial on a Complaint for Contempt brought by Delilah against Husband Samson on in December.

A month earlier, when Samson appeared pro se (representing himself), Judge Catherine R. Sabaitis had found him in contempt of not paying alleged out-of-pocket medical costs of $865. When he retained me to represent him at trial, Samson had insisted that no bills by medical practitioners were ever presented to him. Delilah's attorney, GH, simply wrote the amount on the Complaint. That writing is **not** evidence. At no time was Samson allowed to cross-examine his accusers; at no time was Delilah required to produce evidence that she had expended $865 out of pocket for medical expenses. The December Complaint for Contempt was based on the November order.

On the first day of trial, while cross-examining Delilah, the first time in over a year that she had been put on the stand, Judge Sabaitis refused to allow me to ask about what bills and/or expenses comprised the $865. Sabaitis in a nasty voice said the issue had been adjudicated and that it was *res judicata*. I responded that the first order was unlawful, in that no evidence had been taken to reach the determination of contempt and that an unlawful order is void *ab initio*, and therefore Samson had no need to comply with it. I offered to supply her a brief. She did not want one.

My attempts, too, to cross-examine Delilah on one of her Financial Statements were also aborted by Judge Sabaitis. The cross-examination was far from complete, but given the injudicious rulings of Judge Sabaitis, the prognosis of that examination was not good. Clearly tSabaitis's notions of due process did not comport with those of the highest courts in the Commonwealth and our country.

One of the judge's colleagues, Judge Prudence McGregor, had given custody to the father forthwith because the mother lied on her Financial Statements.\[238]/

Delilah had similarly lied on her Financial Statements, and Samson had gathered documentary proof of the prevarications. If a party in a divorce action were not allowed to cross-examine on the items in the Financial Statements, there would be no sense of the court to make filing them mandatory. Inequitable asininity is both costly to both clients and their counsel, and unacceptable for any system purporting to be a justice system.

A while later, on the second day of trial, we sought a mistrial several times when Sabaitis did not want me to use certified copies of Delilah's bank statements—already marked as exhibits—when cross-examining Delilah. That was intolerable. I persisted. Each time I asked about a discrepancy between Delilah's Financial Statement and her bank statements—for instance, on your Financial Statement, you declared your monthly income to be $1000, where then did the $4000 shown as a deposit on your January bank statement come from?—her attorney, GH, objected, the judge sustained, and I moved for a mistrial. Finally the judge relented, called a mistrial, and recused herself.

Fortunately Delilah and GH saw the handwriting on the wall. With a different judge, the outcome might have become unpredictable—that is, the female might not have won—given not only the quantity of documentary evidence we had of the financial discrepancies but also the nature of the circumstantial evidence of from where the money came. The case settled.

Samson has remarried to a Twiggy Delilah, has a new family, and gets what appears to be sufficient parenting time with his children from his first marriage.

Interviewed by a reporter for the Massachusetts Lawyers Weekly, Judge Catherine Sabaitis stated that what displeases her the most is "[r]epetition of arguments already made; interrupting opposing counsel; long-winded arguments and examination of witnesses." She certainly showed Samson and myself that she was displeased to have to listen to the cross-examination of Delilah.

Inescapable Bias and Gender Discrimination

Anecdote #3.

The wife, Gloria, was to maintain a life insurance policy on herself for $100,000. The husband, Lucas, was to be the beneficiary as trustee in trust for the children. The husband was to maintain a life insurance policy on himself for $100,000. The wife was to be the beneficiary as trustee in trust for the children.

Wife brought a contempt action against the husband for not having the $100,000 life insurance policy. When the landscape turned ominous over the contempt issue, Luke brought a contempt against Gloria for not having the policy.

At trial, Luke produced evidence that he had over $100,000 in a Fidelity Trust account for the children and had named the wife as trustee. Gloria admitting to knowing Luke had been maintaining this account.

After the hearing on the contempt action, Judge John M. Smoot found Gloria not guilty of contempt while finding Luke guilty of contempt. That Smoot's finding of Lucas in contempt and Gloria not in contempt for the same alleged wrongdoing is an unconstitutional act of gender discrimination. That the findings are discriminatory in nature is re-inforced by the Smoot having taken evidence that Lucas had in place the financial vehicle with a then-current value of $130,391.96, that Gloria, as trustee, was the primary beneficiary (100 percent) of that vehicle, and if Gloria were not alive, then the twins were to share in it 50-50 . . . and that Gloria had not had any vehicle in place to protect the children in case of her death.

With these circumstances, in which Lucas clearly believed that his financial vehicle protected the children to a greater extent than that which even the divorce judge had ordered, and Gloria had not thought to protect the children at all, Smoot revealed an **invidious gender bias** resident in the Court by his inappropriate findings and orders given the great discrepancies in the parties' positions. If anything, Smoot should have found Gloria in contempt and Lucas not in contempt.

An additional discrepancy in the orders is equally as offensive and discriminatory. To require Lucas, on one hand, who has considerably less financial ability than Gloria, to provide documentation within 30 days and to give Gloria, on the other, 11 months to provide documentation is horrifying: The gender discrimination is so blatant! It appears as if a radical feminist, rather than a fair Court, made the findings and crafted the orders.

Further, given the number of proven falsities that Gloria averred as truths in her Complaint for Contempt against Lucas, it was inappropriate that the Court came down harder on Lucas than on Gloria. Given the totality of the circumstances, the Court made more than a mere harmless error.

Given the inexcusable, inescapable bias, the husband, Lucas, did not appeal, for he had lost all confidence in either tier of appellate courts in the Commonwealth to find judicial bias, or if they did, to publish their decision. Details of this contempt action may be found on my website at Drano #152.\[239]/

Significant is that John Smoot never practiced law prior to Mike Dukakis nominating him for a judgeship. John Smoot had been only a pencil pusher—an Assistant Register for 9½ years and a First Assistant Register for 1½ years—before becoming a judge in 1990. It is unlikely he had read a law case during those 11 years in which he was pushing a pencil and using a rubber stamp in the clerk's office. One can only wonder what assistance Smoot gave to Dukakis during his successive campaigns for public office.

Digression: There are about another dozen or more family-law judges whose primary experience was being a pencil-pusher assistant register with little, if any, experience in the law prior to becoming a judge. Smoot is not alone. Ineptness for the position is widespread.

In that same year, 1990, Dukakis also appointed Catherine Sabaitis, Samson and Delilah's judge.

We can only thank the gods on Olympus that Dukakis looked like a fool in the tank when he was running for the presidency of this country. He did enough damage with his judicial appointments while he was governor of the Commonwealth.

Hypothetical Anecdote.

When the child-support order issues, the courts generally work according to a set of guidelines, which although called "guidelines" have the effect of a quasi- mandatory statute. "Quasi-mandatory" because the judges are given great discretion, which if exercised, is used almost 100 percent of the time to the disadvantage of the obligor, who is almost 100 percent of the time, the male of the family. And if the judge is biased or has some other prejudice against the father, the judge will impute income to the father and thereby cause the father's child-support payment to be larger—often far in excess of what his real income is.

One often sees imputed income added when a man has been, for instance, a middle manager but then loses his job due to the economy or illness or accident. The judge says, I see that you were qualified to make $80,000 a year. Make X number of job applications a week. I find that you are working as a cab driver to avoid a higher child-support obligation. The judge has no evidence to reach that conclusion, but will, nevertheless, reach it and the appellate courts will not correct the prejudicial conclusion. Rubber-stamping and summary dismissals of interlocutory and final appeals are routine. Why? Because in family-law cases, the higher the child-support orders, the higher the annual bonuses from the federal government. The more wage-assignments collected by the DoR, the greater the value of the courts contractual share.

The dad will then use up any assets he might still have, goes broke, and goes to jail for civil contempt. The new wrinkle is to have the prisoners pay for their own unconstitutional incarceration in debtors' prison. And if his family or friends are not monied and/or generous, the dad stays in jail and becomes alienated from his children.

The Massachusetts' formula for guidelines produce if not the highest child-support obligations, then the next highest orders nationwide. They are not based on the needs of the child but on the income of the parents. In no time, the men become not "deadbeat dads" but "deadbroke dads." Excluded from the guidelines are the following items which the fathers also must usually pay.

Alimony	GAL fees	Private school fees
Supervised visitation	Depositions	Summer camp
Psychological test fees	Subpoena costs	Expenses when children are
Psychologist's or psychia-	Service of process fees	with dad
trist's fees	Medical copayments	Dad's living expenses
Wife's attorneys fees	Health insurance	Taxes, federal, state, local,
Dad's attorneys' fees	Life insurance	sales, excise
Children's attorney's fees	Car insurance	Social Security
Special master's fees	College tuition	

Clearly not all men must pay all of the above, but many, many do. Although some of these expenses appear on each party's Financial Statement, but the expenses on the Financial Statements are *not* considered on the Child Support Guidelines Worksheet. The judge might or might never look at the expenses listed on the Financial Statement, making, therefore, the only constructive use of the Financial Statement is when you are cross-examining for truthfulness. If a judge, like Catherine Sabaitis, does not allow one party to cross-examine the other party on the entries made on the Financial Statement, the Statement is a waste of time and totally unnecessary.

All too often, as described above, civil contempt is used as a tool in Family Courts to extort child support from fathers who do not have the money to pay the amount of child support ordered. That of course is the prelude to debtor prison. A debtor's prison, a place where people are sent although they had no choice to violate or obey the order; they simply did not have the money to pay. They had no intent to commit a crime. It is the law that has no moral compass, not the people. To say that civil court reform is needed, especially in the family and probate courts, is an understatement.

Chapter 9

Rape and Date Rape

When is rape not rape?

There has been a technological revolution in the forensics of rape, and it's revealed some ugly truths. Thanks to DNA technology, dozens of men spending years in jail after being convicted of rape in the '70s and '80s have been found innocent of those crimes.

Rape is a terrible, violent crime, and we must, as a society, do all we can to help rape victims get over any trauma they might suffer. It is almost impossible, however, to protect women from getting raped. A violent "stranger" rape is one thing. A consensual bedding is another. Many women get into bed with a man who turns out to be a lousy lover, even for one night, and she changes her mind in the middle of the intimacy because she feels like she is being raped . . . but that is not rape. She might feel as if she were used as a waste basket—which she might as well have been—but her feelings do not make the intercourse physical rape. It was, at most, mental rape.

Then, given that our society puts every woman yelling rape, whether physical or mental rape—on a victim's pedestal, she yells, "Rape!" And the next thing the man knows, his life is on the way to being ruined.

Because we are in an Age of Feminist Hysteria as well as Feminine Rebellion, the charge of rape has become—regardless of its incipience—a crime which has unreliable data because no one is asking the relevant questions of the alleged rape victims. Many women do not want to admit to themselves or to anyone else that they were damn fools for getting in bed with a man they barely knew and that they were sorry or angry afterwards so they cried rape.

The problem is societal. Men raised and residing in countries like Italy, Greece, France, are taught to pride themselves on being "lovers." The psychological course is as important as arithmetic is in grade school. In this country, the U.S.A., boys compare their sexual experiences according to the bases they reached—first, second, or third—and swell, at the very least, with pride if they reached Home Base. They have been taught very little at home, in school, or in their community.

And now that millions are brought up in homes devoid of fathers, they are taught nothing about normal sex. They are often taught by their divorced mothers that men are no good. And often the children hear female-female moaning from the master bedroom. They certainly do not wake up and ask, Mommy, what were you and Daddy doing last night?

And because Sophia Loren and Marcello Mastroianni films are no longer shown in movie theaters, no kids are sneaking in through the side doors reachable through the alley to see them. Instead, the kids are learning at school about homosexual sex and reading books about King-King and Queen-Queen families, books published to teach primary-schoolers to feel good about their "gender" feelings.\[240]/

Rape, both physical and mental, will increase as our young people know less and less about what male-female intimacy is supposed to be or supposed to be like. That is a shame. No wonder some of today's marriages are measured in weeks, months, or a year or two.

But as bad as rape is, or whatever the cause, it is not as bad as an innocent man being sent to jail for 20 years for a crime he did not commit.

Unfortunately, false and mistaken accusations of rape are not uncommon. Four to seven percent of all rape charges are simply lies, lies brought by women either seeking attention for themselves or trying to get even with a man for some real or imagined wrong.

When a woman is raped by a stranger, and subsequently identifies the rapist, 25-30% of the time she identifies the wrong man. (This is actually not a surprising figure: Over 25% of eyewitness identifications in all crimes are wrong.)

Despite these high false-accusation figures, men are often assumed to be guilty on the basis of a simple accusation by a woman. A man who attempts to defend himself is often prevented from doing so by rape shield laws, which prevent him from presenting exculpatory evidence. Even worse, as some well-publicized cases have shown, women who knowingly make false accusations of rape are not prosecuted. Essentially, they are given a free pass for committing a crime.

The result is that the credibility of real rape victims is destroyed. Since the rate of false rape accusations is so high, and since false accusations are not prosecuted, women are essentially encouraged to make false accusations of rape for political purposes, and the public has no way of knowing whether a rape accusation is real or not.

Court reform should include the following two initiatives with regard to rape: Additional protections for men, to allow an adequate defense against false charges of rape. Prosecution of women who, knowingly and maliciously, make false charges of rape.

Anecdote #1:

A gentle gentleman came to me after he was served a notice of a restraining order and had to go to court for the 10-day statutory hearing. That he was nervous and concerned was of no surprise. The affidavit of the so-called victim was that of the elder of his two daughters. "Never. I never put a hand on my daughter."

We sat down and I began asking questions. I wanted to be well-prepared for cross-examining the young woman on the stand.

As Chris (a pseudonym) answered my questions, I typed both summary biographies of his family and friends and of his ex-wife and her family and friends, and a chronological list of events in his life. It took us 12 hours and a great order of Chinese food to get us through the night. They were all Christians—Bible thumpers—the people who often remind you they are Christians. (As an atheist, it drives me crazy!) Okay, church-goers. The elder daughter, the one who made the accusations, was at a "Christian College" in the Midwest and her former boyfriend was at a "Bible School" in a State close to New York.

Chris and his wife, Pamela, had been divorced a few years prior to this calamity taking place. He bought a house a few miles from the family home, to be close by for "visiting" with his daughters. There had been no prior restraining order on him, so the kids could come by his house whenever they wanted to do so. His new home had bedrooms both for the girls and his biofamily. For a while, a brother lived with him. (Another brother, newly married, was a reservist called up for duty in Iraq.) Another time, his parents, between selling their "family" home and buying another in Florida and between returning from Florida and buying another home up here (they missed all their kids). Whenever he had to go to court, they were there. So was his best friend. All as supportive as anyone would hope their family to be. Wonderful people.

Grandma was a charmer. She had a hobby. That hobby was keeping in bound books a diary of all the family events, including all the times Chris saw the children, and all the trips her children and grandchildren took. She kept notes about who was present, what they did, sketches, *and* dozens upon dozens of photos of the happiest kids you ever did see at picnic tables, poolside, and playing. Abuse was nowhere to be seen in that family!

When a date had to be confirmed, go to Grandma. To use for Chris's defense, she sent me copies of the bound folios. They were our confirmation. They were as contemporaneous as could be.

Then his ex-wife remarried. Whom did she marry? A Mafioso, literally, a man who had aided and abetted the murder of a Mafia headman: he drove the van that took the body to its final resting place. Whoa!!! My client's ex-wife had met the conspiracist when he was released on parole from a federal prison.

"Have you, Chris, ever met him?"

"Yes."

"When?"

"I had promised the girls to take them for ice cream. As I drove to the house, I saw Pamela, the girls, and a man walking. I stopped the car and said, 'Okay, girls, ice-cream time.'

"'No,' the man said.

"I got out of my car and walked up to him and said 'I don't know who you are, but I'm telling you, 'Do not interfere with the time I have with my girls.'"

It was only later that he learned that this man was a Mafioso. Let's call him Tony.

For me, that was the beginning of the G-2 work.

"Chris, Tony is likely not accustomed to gentle people telling him off. Dollars to donuts, he's the one behind all this."

Did Tony work? If so, where? What does he use for money? How much do the girls see? How much do they understand? Tony probably did not want Chris to learn too much about him and his habits and the girls would be Chris's sources of information.

I was ready.

We got to court. I insisted that "Jeannie" take the stand to testify, not merely say a few words standing before the bench. The victim witness advocate, improperly acting as lawyer, asked the court to suspend the hearing so that she could talk with Jeannie. After a half hour or so, they returned and asked for a continuation so that Jeannie could get a lawyer. The continuation was granted.

Late on that same night following the court appearance, I got a phone call from Chris. The police had paid him a visit at around 11:30 P.M. He had been indicted on 28 counts of rape and sexual molestation. The indictments accused him of raping his daughter weekly for years. Each indictment covered a defined range of dates.

Holy Cow.

Chris came again when he got off work. His job was one of those for which he was on call several days and then off several days.

We had learned from a few police reports that Jeannie had been getting psychological or psychiatric care at her college. Then she was sent by the college to a State on the Pacific Coast for more treatment for almost two months. That did not make sense. Given that her biofamily and all her relatives were in Massachusetts, why would a Midwestern college send her 2000 miles farther away from her Home State?

Insurance, had Chris received any insurance bills? Yes! Those bills gave us considerable data. One piece of data was very interesting; it was a sum of money for an obstetrics department. She must have been pregnant. A D&C? The price was right. Maybe the "Christian College" sent her out west to hide the fact that one of their students had become pregnant on their campus. We kept that conclusion quiet. Chris could not have been the man doing the impregnation. He had not seen her. After Chris had met Tony, the visits to and fro his daughters drastically decreased, and during the previous year, the alleged victim, Jeannie, was away at college. Chris had seen her only for an hour or two at a family get-together at Christmas time. Allegations against him appeared to be a cover for a girl who was expected to be more moral than other, less-Christian girls, but wasn't. Her stepfather, Tony, likely helped in the cover-up plan. Tony himself might have been Jeannie's impregnator, and that act might have been the reason Jeannie needed the help of so-called mental health professionals.

The police Lieutenant who wrote one of the several police reports was extremely forthright and helpful. He identified for us the sergeant who had taken the intake information from Jeannie. The sergeant's reports explained some of the missing details.

So when Chris arrived at my home-office and was at my side, I phoned the college. Although one of the people I was trying to reach was in Russia proselytizing for the summer, I did manage to reach someone who knew where she had been sent out west. I asked Director X, "Why did they send her out there?"

"Her brother was out there."

She had no brother!

Then we managed to find Jeannie's ex-boyfriend.

Tony must have a son, we speculated. Fortunately Tony's last name was not all that common. Google time. Bingo. We found a Tony, Jr., about 45 minutes to an hour away from where Jeannie was shipped. We gave his bio to Chris's best friend, who was skilled enough to enlarge a picture showing Tony, Jr., in an interesting environment.

After a few inquiries, I found an ace investigator and an attorney who could make an appearance in that State 3500 miles away and serve subpoenas if required. By the time the private-eye got there, Tony, Jr., had moved from his seashore hide-away, one on the incoming drug route.

A few weeks later, we went to court again. Jeannie did not show. The judge granted my oral motion for dismissal of the temporary restraining order, but noted that she would set the matter up for a bindover under Rule 12. I had warned Chris about that, i.e., if we asked for a bindover hearing, the DA might nol pros\[241]/ and change the venue immediately to Superior Court, which is usually where the case goes once the indictment(s) issue. But the assistant DA wanted more time. The case worker interviewed by the investigator more than likely had immediately let the police know she had been found and contacted. The government's case was unraveling.

Two months later, I had been unable to resolve my Bar problem, so Chris had to find another Massachusetts attorney. He did, but Chris complained that the attorney never spoke to him and would not respond to phone calls. Fortunately, as soon as Chris's case was called, the assistant DA moved to dismiss it. Word had gotten back to the police and then, of course, the DA, about all our discovery. They knew they had no case against Chris.

That afternoon he called and said, "Thank you, I know it was your discovery that did it. My new attorney barely spoke to me." This was the reason I moved in the Massachusetts SJC to allow me to finish my representation of this man . . . and ended up being found both in contempt for not voluntarily withdrawing from his case and in jail as punishment for the contempt. I feared Chris would spend the rest of his life behind bars on false accusations. The Mass. SJC justices did not, of course, give a damn. They are the hypocrites of justice.

Later, upon receiving the word that Chris's case was dismissed, the western attorney voluntarily sent Chris's few thousand dollar retainer back to Chris.

He hasn't seen his daughters, but he is, otherwise, fine. Sadly, so is Tony. He managed to force Chris out of the girls' lives and to keep his habits secret.

Jeannie, of course, was not prosecuted for reporting false allegations to the police. And they were serious. Her father could have gone to jail for life for crimes he never committed.

Anecdote #2:

Two children were being taped by their dad to get an answer to a question the guardian *ad litem* had asked him: When did he learn that the children had seen their mother making love to her boyfriend? Dad was surprised. One, he suspected but did not know for sure that Mom had a boyfriend. Two, he never knew that the children knew that she had a boyfriend. Three, he never knew that the children had seen their Mom making love to a boyfriend.

The GAL later did, indeed, at trial and in her report admit to asking Dad the question.

So Dad, Stockdale, told the children he had a question to ask them.

STOCKDALE: I need to ask you guys some questions on the tape recorder. And the first question is: Have you seen mommy make love to BOYFRIEND?

TWIN1: Yes.

TWIN2: Mom was on top making sex.

STOCKDALE: Uhuh, Is that true, TWIN1? Did you see that too?

TWIN1: Ye-e-es [hesitantly].

STOCKDALE: What did you see, TWIN1?

TWIN1: What did I see? I saw -- umm -- BOYFRIEND-Pop's penis going into my mom's 'gina hole. . . . Keep that a secret!

STOCKDALE: Why should we keep that a secret? Who told you that?

TWIN1: My mommy.

STOCKDALE: Ohh, this is not so good. [*Pause.*] How long after I get kicked out of the condo did BOYFRIEND-Pop move in?

TWIN2: I'm bored.

TWIN1: One day. [*Pause.*] Keep that a secret. [*Excitedly.*]

I hired the foremost forensic linguist in this country and internationally, Anne Graffam Walker. She wrote in her report, "The naturalness of the dialogue was also supported by the general flow of the verbal exchanges, intonation of all speakers, and Mr. X's sighs, indrawn breaths, and 'asides' (lines 14 and 103).

"Finally, TWIN2's 'I'm bored,' and 'I wanna go' (pencilled in; not transcribed), and the twin's excited admonition to their father to keep something secret is typical of naturally occurring conversation, and would seem inconsistent with coached responses."

STOCKDALE: Is that true, TWIN2?   Did BOYFRIEND-Pop . . . How long after I got kicked out did

BOYFRIEND-Pop move in?

TWIN1: Whispering to TWIN2 "one day."

TWIN2: . . . One da-a-ay [*very hesitantly*].

The taping stopped for a while and then the discussion on tape turned to something else. We do not know why the children added the word "Pop" to the boyfriend's alleged name. They did always call their maternal grandfather, Pop-Pop. Why "Pop-Pop," who knows?

STOCKDALE: Let me ask you this question. Has anybody ever hurt you?

TWIN1: Yes.

STOCKDALE: Who hurt you?

TWIN1: Ahhh . . . Pop.

STOCKDALE: Is this BOYFRIEND-Pop or Pop-Pop?

TWIN1: Pop-Pop.

STOCKDALE: And now, what did Pop do to you to hurt you?

TWIN1: Um . . . Jumped up and down on me and put his penis in my poo-poo hole.

STOCKDALE: Say that again. [*Surprised.*]

TWIN1: He jumped up and down on me and putted his penis in my poo-poo hole. My mother said to keep it a secret. [*The child's voice had become louder with tears in it, as if he was saying to his Dad, Why aren't you hearing me?*]

STOCKDALE: Are you sure he did that to you?

TWIN1: Yes.

"There is no indication in this dialogue between Mr. Stockdale and his sons that the children have been 'coached'; certainly they have not been coached by Mr. Stockdale to give rehearsed responses to the questions he asked," Graham-Walker concluded.

The first judge and only judge, Angela Ordonez, to hear the tape of the children took away Lucas Stockdale's visitation of parenting rights for a period of time. She killed the messenger.

The second judge, Nancy M. Gould, whom Lucas wanted to listen to the tape, refused to listen to it. Instead, Gould found that Pop-Pop was a "pillar of the community."

The third judge, Lisa A. Roberts, refused to listen to it, refused to allow it into evidence at trial, refused to allow the expert, Graham-Walker, to testify at a *voir dire* (although Walker was sitting in the courtroom waiting to be called to the stand) or at trial, but did allow Stockdale to testify to what he heard. Stockdale found it difficult emotionally to repeat what the children said.

Seven years later: Lucas Stockdale has been seeing the children since the divorce trial and has a panoply of rights regarding the children, including the right to phone and receive phonecalls from them on any day at any time, to attend their events in and out of school (for instance, soccer games, band, parent-teacher meetings), to receive school report cards, to be in communication with all medical professionals, and have them live with him every other weekend as well as every other school vacation, every Father's Day, their birthday each year, every summer between July 4th and the opening of school. In fact, as they have grown older, if one of them does not want to go with mom on vacation, he is dropped of at dad's for the week or 10 days. He and the children are quite close, sufficiently close enough to conclude that the children were, indeed, sexually abused and feel safer at Dad's house and that one experienced significantly more emotional damage than the other. The Courts—Gould, Roberts, and Ordonez—of course, the GAL, and their mother, Gloria, aided and abetted the sexual abuse.

Certainly judicial immunity must be abolished so that the children may be enabled when they reach majority to sue the judges for the pain and suffering the youngsters are still trying to overcome.

* * *

To unravel these false allegation cases, you must keep in mind that nothing is ever quite like it appears. Think of yourself as a novelist and try to write summaries of the personalities of those folks involved. Do not rein your brain in. You want to let it be able to stumble on the truth or, at least, stumble onto the road leading to the truth.

Date Rape

Colleges are creating Kangaroo courts, which they call internal hearings. Not only are the young people not allowed to have lawyers assist in examining their accusers, at some colleges, they cannot even have their lawyers present. The young men must approach the college peacefully but aggressively.

Emotionally, these hearings and the hysteria of society are putting young men in a position where they are afraid to trust young women. This, too, needs lively addressing.

<u>Anecdote #3</u>:

A female student, Kat, told some of her friends that she had been sexually assaulted by a male student, Don, in a parked vehicle after she and Don had attended a rehearsal of a play. It is believed that during the next five days, Kat's friends told a Resident Assistant, who told the Campus Police, who told the Boston Police Department that the accused, Don, sexually assaulted Kat. It is not known who brought the allegation to the attention to the Dean of Students. Don denied any wrongdoing.

A transfer student, Don was already a published author and a playwright whose work had been performed. His prospects for a stunning career were significant and impressive until the incident which was the subject of the complaint filed either orally or in writing with the college and with the Boston Police Department.

Upon Don's transfer to the college, he received a copy of the Student Handbook and Planner, which constituted a contract between the college and Don.\242/ In it, the college represented that as a student, Don retained his constitutional rights, including his right to due process and a fair hearing. It also asserted that a complainant was required to submit: the name of the accused, a clear explanation of the nature of the incident, the names, addresses, and phone numbers of witnesses, and the names, addresses, and phone numbers of those filing the complaint. The sanctions, which are penal rather than remedial in nature, may be "probation, suspension, dismissal." The Handbook also outlines the information which a student is to receive prior to a Board hearing if the student is accused of an infraction of the Student Code of Conduct.

On March 5th, a detective in the Boston Police Department "heard about" a complaint of sexual assault from the defendant college's Campus Police, who received a complaint from a college Resident Assistant, who received a complaint from the several Jane and/or John Does, as-yet unidentified but believed to be one or more of Kat's friends.

On the same day, the BPD detective contacted Kat, who informed him that she had not reported the complained-of incident to the college authorities. He then told her that until after the police finished their investigation of the matter, she should not report the incident to the college, and Kat promised the detective that she would not contact the college until the police investigation was complete.

On the 7th, Don met with the BPD detective and denied any wrongdoing. On that same day, Don heard from the Dean of Students: "A situation has been brought to my attention requiring a need for me to meet with you. . . . I expect to hear from you by March 8th" So it was on the 8th that Don spoke to the Dean, who informed Don that Kat had complained that she had been sexually assaulted by him on February 28th, that the procedures at the hearing would be as outlined in a document, that the College Conduct Board would expect Don to plead "responsible" or "not responsible," that Don's advisor—any person NOT trained in the law or cross-examination—could only "suggest" questions to be asked of the complainant (Kat) and her witnesses, and that the behavior of which Don was accused was "not only considered an extremely serious violation of the college's Student Code of Conduct, but also a criminal infraction of Massachusetts state law."

Neither the Dean of Students nor the President of the college provided Don with a written statement by Kat, so that other than the naked allegation of "sexual assault," Don knew none of the particulars of what he was accused.

Neither the Dean of Students nor the President provided Don with a list of witnesses on Kat's behalf or with a written statement by Kat, her friends (the Jane Does or the John Does), the unidentified Resident Assistant, or the Campus Police, or by anyone else.

According to the Handbook and the Hearing Procedures, Don would be expected to take the stand without the benefit and protection of counsel. Don's taking the stand could conceivably be construed as a waiver of his right to remain silent should a criminal complaint issue.

No provision had been made to memorialize the testimony at the hearing; that is, no provision had been made to tape record or for a stenographer to be present at the hearing.

On March 16th, the Dean informed Don that he had scheduled a hearing on March 28th and that Don could not bring a lawyer to the hearing. Don's concern was that there was an ongoing police investigation and that without the benefit of counsel, an innocent remark by him might be misconstrued, and work to his detriment.

On March 19th, the Dean sent to Don a letter listing nine people from whom the panel of five would be chosen.

On March 25th, Don received from the Dean an email containing notice that his attorney would not be allowed into the hearing room, but by that date, Don had still not received (a) a bill of particulars. (b) a clear explanation of the nature of the incident, (c) the names, addresses, and phone numbers of witnesses, and/or (d) the identification of the person or persons who filed the complaint with the Dean or the college's agents, servants, and/or employees.

Significant, also, is that the college and the Dean of Students refused to continue the hearing until some time after the completion of the police investigation, refused to refrain from holding the hearing at which his lawyer is forbidden to attend, and threatened Don with suspension or expulsion should he not attend the hearing.

Given that false details of the incident were published to many people who had no need to know anything about the post-rehearsal incident, whether there was a sexual assault or not, Don's personal reputation at the college and his professional reputation was harmed.

Furthermore, an allegation of sexual assault in our society is a stain that can never be removed. He worried that he would not be picked as a cast member in college productions and that his viability as a successful, credible, and reputable literary figure—an author, a playwright, and actor—in the future would be threatened, and that the damage would be irreparable.

By the time March 28th arrived, I had given the Dean a proposed complaint, motion, and an order for an injunction to stay the college from holding a hearing that was designed to deny Don a fair hearing, the right to due process, a meaningful opportunity to cross-examine witnesses against him and to present evidence on his behalf, and the right to have an attorney of his choice to represent him at the hearing, particularly where the BPD has not yet completed its investigation into the complained-of incident.

Inherent in conducting a civilian trial penal in nature without legal counsel simultaneously with a police investigation, I argued, presented the danger of immediate and irreparable harm. Should Don be forced to appear and participate in the hearing process without legal counsel, he would be vulnerable to immediate and irreparable harm. If Don were to not cooperate with the College Conduct Board and not participate in the disciplinary hearing process, he would be found in default and would suffer punishment.

Fortunately my arguments and the proposed pleadings prepared to be filed in the trial court worked. I was allowed to argue, no one took a witness stand—Kat never showed—and the complaint against Don at the college was dismissed.

Fight, fight, fight. Do not give in to college programs that deny your children or you your constitutional rights to due process and equal protection.

Ramifications of the false allegations are far-reaching. The statutes must be rewritten to address the horrendous consequences\243/ caused by the existing statutes written during the current Age of Hysteria, arising out of the Age of Feminist Rebellion.

Chapter 10

Child Protection Services

Wars Against Governmental Kidnapping

This is an area of the law in which I have not worked. It is a horrendous area of the law if I am to believe the zillion mothers who have phoned me or who have sent emails to me and the world. Some of the stories can be mistaken as scripts for Saturday Night Live or CI or CSI films.

The mothers of the children taken want to rid the world of social workers, police officers, doctors and nurses, judges, and lawyers. They want to do the impossible. Most of the people they want to sue have some sort of immunity: absolute immunity, judicial immunity, qualified immunity, prosecutorial immunity, statutory immunity, or common-law immunity. To sue the few dozen named defendants would take a lawyer months of writing briefs in opposition to the dozen or more motions to dismiss. Most of the briefs would be for naught, that is, would yield no money to pay the lawyer's own bills, and would be futile.

Anecdote 1.

Dawn had an absolutely beautiful face, . . . but she weighed somewhere over 300 pounds. I was defending her against a charge of vandalism for allegedly writing a very scary message on the wall of a stall in a woman's restroom of a supermarket where she had a part-time job. The incident was being treated as a bomb scare. Whoever wrote it had a lot of anger.

I wanted to get to the bottom of it. I learned that she had been in more than a dozen foster homes and had been allegedly raped by a group of boys when she was 14. She was of normal weight when she was raped. The weight was her protection. "Boys don't like fat girls" was her mantra. She had the anger. Did she write the message on the wall?

Every time I saw her, Dawn crossed her fingers and said, I'll be 18 years old in a few months. I'll be able to go to see my mother, my real mother. Tragedy followed. Her mother would not see her. Mother had been so traumatized and intimidated and harassed by the agency (then "DSS") that she feared she would have to live through that experience again.

Immediately after the criminal case was dismissed, Dawn disappeared, drove from Massachusetts to Ohio, met some 41-year-old man, got pregnant, and married him. Shortly thereafter she called the two people who had secretly helped her to escape the clutches of DSS, and told them she was safe.

As told to me by Dawn, the family's six children, ranging from 2½ years to 10 years old, were taken from their parents. The young woman said her "littlest" brother used to call hot dogs "raw dogs." ("He always managed to get one from the refrigerator," she cried, "I'd take it from him if I noticed him soon enough.")

Someone heard him say he eats raw dogs and reported that the family was in a cult that practiced rituals in their back yard. Those alleged "rituals" were the summertime barbeques ordinary families have when the weather is pleasant.

Where dad was when she turned 18, I do not know. I am unsure whether she learned where he was. He had, indeed, been with the family when DSS took the kids. "We were a happy family. We always had fun," she tearfully recalled. "My parents were good parents. We loved them and they loved us."

The State got $40,000 per child from the federal government when they took the kids. None of the kids was a special-needs kid when taken, but a few of the kids acted out after they were taken and they were given Ritalin. It did not help the kids, but the State's take increased to $90,000 per child on the drug. The people who hid Dawn for two years figured out one day that Dawn's family was worth $1 million dollars to the State.

A possibility of it getting worse.

During March 2009, the U.S. House of Representatives passed the Mothers Act (H.R.20). The Mothers Act was sponsored by Sen. Robert Menéndez (D-NJ) and reintroduced in the U.S. Senate (S. 324 introduced January 26, 2009).

If passed, the Mother's Act will mandate that all new mothers be screened by means of a list of subjective questions that will determine if each mother is mentally fit to take their newborn home from the hospital. Just imagine that after your child is born, you are told that you can't take the child home because you did not answer a multiple-choice questionnaire correctly. Just imagine being told that the only way you can take your child home is if you or your spouse goes into treatment or on anti-depressants, which we know causes psychosis, delusions, and even homicidal thoughts.

Unfortunately, this bill is on a fast track—*no* public debate, *no* public disclosure of the broad impact on our society—and that is why we need you to act now! To send a letter, go to *http://salsa.democracyin-action.org/o/1918/t/7870/campaign.jsp?campaign_KEY=26855*. Also call the Senators on the H.E.L.P. Committee and tell them to let the Mothers Act die in committee.

Lisa Murkowski, R: 202-224-6665, AK	Jeff Bingaman, D: 202-224-5521, NM
John McCain, R: 202-224-2235, AZ	Sherrod Brown, D: 202-224-2315, OH
Christopher Dodd, D: 202-224-2823, CT	Tom Coburn, R: 202-224-5754, OK
Johnny Isakson, R: 202-224-3643, GA	Jeff Merkley, D: 202-224-3753, OR
Tom Harkin, D: 202-224-3254, IA	Bob Casey, D: 202-224-6324, PA
Pat Roberts, R: 202-224-4774, KS	Jack Reed, D: 202-224-4642, RI
Edward Kennedy, D: 202-224-4543, MA	Lamar Alexander, R: 202-224-4944, TN
Barbara Mikulski, D: 202-224-4654, MD	Orrin Hatch, R: 202-224-5251, UT
Richard Burr, R: 202-224-3154, NC	Bernard Sanders, I: 202-224-5141, VT
Kay Hagan, D: 202-224-6342, NC	Patty Murray, D: 202-224-2621, WA
Judd Gregg, R: 202-224-3324, NH	Michael Enzi, R: 202-224-3424, WY

Kathleen's Story.

Kathleen W. wrote,\[244]/ "*We are organizing a class action lawsuit against the Counties, States, Government, hospitals, police, and all parties involved in unlawfully detaining and holding our children against our will and without cause. We have documented the deep, imbedded corruption in the 'social services' agencies nationwide. We have filed three lawsuits so far, and are looking for other families who have also been annihilated by this evil. Email us at fightcpscalifornia@gmail.com to join the fight to save our children."*

Kathleen W.'s personal story: *"Riverside County and CPS adopted out our beautiful, healthy, infant daughter, completely AGAINST OUR WILL, and against the law when she was only EIGHT HOURS OLD. They already had it all set up with their KANGAROO COURTS AND THEIR TURN-KEY ADOPT-A-WHITE-BABY COMMERCE SYSTEM. Neither parent had any history nor usage of any illegal drugs, and our daughter was born with an APGAR score of 9.8, with absolutely NO DRUGS in her or her mother's systems. The Palm Springs Desert Regional Medical Center staged a urine test that was tampered with and was wrong, and they refused to use the mother's blood or re-test her at all. The one urine test was the ONLY basis for their illegal abduction of our newborn infant, and it has been an illegal "legal loophole" battering of our daughter and our Parental rights ever since.*

On August 8, 2007, our newborn daughter was illegally and forcefully taken by William Michael Biles of Banning CPS, with the help of eight others at Desert Regional Medical center, with no court order nor warrant, and no police present. He physically threatened mother and newborn with the statement "Give me that baby NOW, or you and her will be physically hurt!" and we have fought for our daughter since.

CPS contrived multiple hearsay untruths and presented falsifications to the court, without our knowledge. Judge Christopher Sheldon approved the criminal ADOPTION, then granted us a "Contested Jurisdictional Hearing," and then suddenly, the case was transferred to Southwest Adjudication Center, where Commissioner Fernandez declared he lacked the power to render a Judgment on another Judge's decision to have the Contested Jurisdiction Hearing, then Fernandez took it off calendar, where it stands today......we have been denied our daughter in this illegal kidnapping, and we have located proof that the County of Riverside and DRMC routinely set new mothers up this way, very often to take newborn white, healthy, drug-free babies to sell them on their own twisted underground baby market. We have been violated entirely, and we will keep fighting for our daughter."

Some might think Kathleen W.'s story merely the raving mother who is heartbroken because her child was taken from her. Others will say, No, Barb, this is exactly what happened to us! Kathleen W. is correct:

- *CPS manufactures multiple nonexistent/fictitious abuse case scenarios to offset true statistical abuse case information.*

- *CPS concurrently processes these children from foster care to Adoption, in order to obtain perverse monetary incentives in the form of bonuses.*

- *CPS provides a market to neighboring agencies and the courts (Judges, psychologists, visitation monitors, court mandated behavioral class instructors, court appointed legal counsel, etc...), in order for them to financially benefit from the foster care/adoption system they themselves perpetuate.*

- *CPS victimizes innocent financially challenged families, and draws them into a corrupt system to utilize their children as pawns for this corrupt child commerce.*

- *CPS is utilized by family court officials and attorneys as an adverse tool to extricate children from one parent to the other, with reference to "parental alienation syndrome," where in truth, the CPS caseworkers are the ones initiating the alienation of these children from their own birth parents. Caseworkers are never allowed to testify in court under the cloak of "CPS Authority" due to possible misuse or conflict of interest related to right to privacy laws (Very convenient)*

- *CPS utilizes unlawful & coercive measures to persuade vulnerable parents to submit to statements of nonexistent abuse, forcing desperate parents to "plea bargain" to a CPS fabricated crime, for the return of their children from foster care.*

- *CPS fabricates false allegations and most of their "investigations" to purposely mislead or misdirect a case.*

- *CPS intentionally fails to prosecute Parents accused of child abuse, since in the majority of cases, no initial crime has been committed. However, CPS continues to claim a crime has been committed, as THEY abuse/neglect the children.*

- *CPS knowingly abandons children into the foster care system, conscious that some individuals in these homes physically and/or sexually abuse those in their "protective" custody. CPS ignores crimes committed in foster care through failure to investigate.*

- *CPS fails to question these individuals for their abusive conduct, whereby, if it were a birth parent or not a foster care parent, these individuals would be prosecuted to the fullest extent of the law in criminal court.*

- *CPS represents themselves in positive personas by omitting, altering, and falsifying documents, so as to mislead the public and or government of their true actions as listed above. Thereby publicly grandstanding, displaying an inaccurate social martyrdom for the well being of children.*

The Police should determine if children need protection from their own parents, since child abuse is a Criminal offense.

Kathleen W. went on to name 14 people she claimed were "guilty of knowingly lying in this abduction of our child": one doctor, one nurse, six CPS employees, one judge, one court clerk, and four attorneys.

* * *

Another Kathleen, Kathleen D., wrote: *"About me: Single Mother. Activist, Researcher, Lobbist. I investigate CPS abuse cases and work with politicians who are commited to making real change. I have spoken with hundreds of CPS victims, State and Government officials. I have appeared on local TV and national radio. I have done interviews and published several articles on the subject. I am currently working on a book and a TV talk show. In my spare time I do local public access and support other CPS victims.*

"My daughter Jennifer D. was kidnapped by CPS because of Title IV Federal funds. Judge Picquet would not allow the facts to be presented in court and he refused to let my daughter speak on court record. She was kept in foster care for 6 months and intimidated into giving coerced testimony by CPS officials. My daughter was never abused or neglected and CPS lied in court. They presented false evidence and violated HIIPA laws. They hired therapists to write false statements so they could profit off my daughter. Jenny turned to drugs and began cutting herself because of what CPS and therapists in San Luis Obispo did to her. This agency needs to be reformed."

Kathleen D. added a postscript which, I assume, she believed was persuasive.

P.S. DEDICATED TO: "CRAZY OLD BITCH"

> *THIS WOMAN IS WRITING TO MY DAUGHTER'S SPACE PAGE (the nerve). This is in response to her HAM CASSEROLE dish she posted online. She works for an attorney & we all know how much money attorney's are making money the CPS kidjacking!!*
>
> *Current with dad mood: aggravated Mother Corrupt-O-Meter-80%*
> **RECIPE FOR DISASTER (A delicious dish of DECEIT that CPS cooks up)**
>
> *1 Previously happy teenager*
> *3 cup of police*
> *20 Gallons of social workers (substitute with Sociopaths and child molesters)*
> *10 pints school officials*
> *6 foster homes*
> *10 Therapists*
> *5 Doctors*
> *1 Nosy "crazy old bitch"*
> *3 Myspace pages*
> *1 Concerned Mom*
> *1 Set of Nasty Grandparents*
> *1 Vindictive Dad*

[Instructions how to mix ingredients intentionally redacted.]

> *PS. HEY CRAZY OLD BITCH - I DON'T KNOW YOU. I DON'T KNOW YOUR INTENTIONS. LAY OFF FOR NOW. STOP WRITING MY DAUGHTER ON HER MYSPACE PAGE. GO FIND SOME FRIENDS YOUR OWN AGE.*
>
> <u>*COMING SOON*</u>: *AMBER ALERTS, MILK CARTONS, NATIONWIDE LAWSUITS, AND POLITICAL REFORM*

Kathleen D. ends, "*It's amazing how corrupt CPS has become. My heart goes out to all of the other children and families who are victims and who's lives CPS has destroyed. Many former foster children become depressed and turn to drugs and our prision is filled with former foster kids. It is a shame that our Government allows CPS to continue to devestate the future of hundreds of thousands of children each year. They hurt more children than they help and the system is completely broken. I think CPS should be abolished and we should start over.*

"*I just found this site today: http://www.california-adoption.org/nationalnews.html*

CPS also has this site: www.adoptuskids.org. I need someone to help me find all the websites CPS is advertising children at. They are offering Federal Grant money to people for adopting children and it __looks like they have nice little racketeering operation going on__. ASFA just doubled so they will be on a kid finding frenzy soon".

KATHLEEN D.

What DYFS Cannot Do

It has been clearly established that absent probable cause and a warrant or exigent circumstances, neither police nor social workers may enter a person's home without a valid consent, even for the purpose of taking a child into custody, much less to conduct a search. It has also been established that the warrantless seizure and detention of a person without probable cause or exigent circumstances is unreasonable.

Many of the thousands of cases dismissed across this nation by courts holding that the defendants allegedly have absolute or qualified immunity, that there was no violation of the Fourth Amendment, that there was no deprivation of constitutional rights, that the courts had to abstain from hearing the cases on the basis of some abstention doctrine lead one to the suspicion that the government has failed to abide by constitutional constraints. Each time that failure was repeated likely had deleterious long-term consequences for the child and, indeed, for the entire family.

TO DOs

- Require agencies/departments to provide unredacted copies of the families' case files automatically to the families being investigated, so that they have their due process right to receive notice of the accusations and an opportunity to defend themselves by being able to prepare for cross-examining their accusers and testifying.

- Enact statutes to put in place mandatory sanctions against police and social workers who enter a home lacking a signed warrant and unlawfully seize a person and/or property and detain a person without probable cause or exigent circumstances.
- Privatize the foster care system.
- Trace the money the agencies/departments receive from the federal government as an incentive to take children from their biological families and put them out for adoption. That money creates an ethical conflict and an incentive for the agencies/departments to destroy families rather than to fight for ways to keep them together or to reunify them.
- Investigate agencies/departments entirely.
- Revamp agencies/departments entirely to ensure competency and moral, ethical, and legal honesty.

Chapter 11

Fraud, Fraud on the Court, and Complicity by the Court

From Riches to Rags

Fraud by accountants and receivers, who are often attorneys, is frequently encountered. You can sue them in court, but your case will dismissed on the grounds that they were given immunity by the courts who appointed them.

Fraud by plain ol' attorneys is also not infrequent. They have no immunity if they have not been appointed by a judge. So you may sue them or report them to the regulatory agency in their State. Some state regulatory agencies operate fairly to both sides, some do not, and some are as corrupt as the attorney about whom you are complaining.

Fraud on the court . . . you may not sue. The judge must take action, but rarely, rarely, rarely does.

<u>Anecdote #1.</u>

An auto body shop yielded about half a million dollars a month to the owner, who had a wife and three children, and they were all living in a lovely 4-bedroom home in an affluent suburb of Boston. Now that is not strange. It, in fact, is enviable. But that the wife slept nightly with the children on the living floor was strange. The wife would not allow the children to sleep in their beds. Dad did not object to the arrangement. He didn't think it was strange, because his wife told him it was not.

But one day, the wife wanted a divorce. She retained one of the nastier-type attorneys and filed in family court. Casey retained Jon Benson, who left no record of competency and partner of Roberta Benjamin, a matured woman who, I recall, used to swish around Concord Courthouse in a lengthy, sumptuous mink coat. I couldn't see the middle of her, but I envied her slim, slim ankles.

While Casey was in Arizona visiting his sister, Benson, in my opinion, stupidly stipulated to a receiver taking over Casey's highly successful cash auto-body business.

Judge Judith Dilday, a two-fer-one whose husband was the President of the Massachusetts Black Attorneys Association, approved the
receivership in Casey's absence. Outrageous . . . even though Casey's
attorney, Benson, stipulated to same.

Within weeks the business was raked or raped and taken apart.
Casey's wife helped the receiver and was allowed to work at the register
and take cash. The receiver sold off the company's tools, equipment,
and inventory almost immediately, and the sale of the real property
was in the offing. The fees of the receiver, HIS attorneys, two accountants and THEIR attorneys were extraordinary and unwarranted and
allowed by the court.

When I was retained, the business was next to being unsalvageable.
Casey thought maybe he could pull it back together despite the devastation. His rationale: he built it from scratch, he could rebuild it from
almost scrap. His business reputation was excellent.

But Judge Dilday would not vacate the receivership, and did not
appear to understand the implications of what she had done and how
her orders allowed an unconstitutional taking. It was rape by judicial
order.

After Casey complained to the Commission on Judicial Conduct
about Dilday and had to reappear before her in Cambridge, she was
furious, but did recuse herself from the case. (That was my first day
on the case and I did not know he had written to the CJC. Surprise!)
Judge Edward Ginsberg, now retired, was assigned to the case and
heard in Concord my motion to vacate the appointment of the receivership. The thrust was a thorough explanation of the facts and considerable citations supporting Ginsberg's right to *undo* the order of a
judge on the same judicial level as he. Ginsberg refused to follow the
common law giving him the power to *undo* Dilday's order.

Casey believed that an appeal would have been futile, for the business property was on the verge of sale. There would have been nowhere to rebuild Casey's auto-body shop.

Casey's family went from riches to rags in a few short weeks.

Very adaptive, almost passive, and resigned, Casey took a job as
a sales clerk at a local chain of department stores, Lechmere's, and
shared an apartment with some other men and a dog. With his life

free from a nagging wife and children who ignored him because they had been alienated from him, he seemed quite happy. Liberty is a wonderful thing. When Lechmere's in Cambridge closed down, Casey moved to Arizona, near his sister. He would not have been successful suing the receiver, because the receiver would have been protected by absolute immunity and the case would have been dismissed.\[245]/

In his father's absence, Casey's son stopped sleeping with his mother and sisters on the living room floor, went into the drug distribution business near the local high school, attracted the attention of a federal DEA swat team, was arrested and convicted and sent to Federal prison. A common occurrence for children who have been made fatherless by Order of Court.

Anecdote #2.

The doctor was ripe for picking. The lawfirm's bills demonstrate that the lawfirm believed that. After decades as associate and partner at a well-known prestigious firm, the founder of the firm sat on the judicial bench for four years before seemingly voluntarily retiring and setting up his lawfirm for the benefit of his son, who had been within months sworn into the Bar.

Like many, many lawfirms, the lawfirm used the "team" approach and they charged handsomely for that approach. For instance, the client was served a divorce Complaint (usually a form), a lead attorney was assigned to the case, charges the client for looking at the Complaint, a lesser attorney or a paralegal was assigned to write the Answer, the lesser attorney drafted the Answer and brought it to the lead attorney for checking, the lead attorney gave it back to the lesser attorney or the paralegal for correction, and then the Answer was sent to a secretary. The client was charged for 6.10 hours allegedly spent by the two people to write a one-page answer. The lead attorney was responsible for 5.10 hours of the 6.10. It is difficult to imagine what the lesser attorney added to the Answer by her hour's work which the lead attorney had to correct for another 5.10 hours.

Depositions: The firm charged for preparing for one of them, but did not hold the depo.

Discovery: For almost 2 years, there is no record of any discovery being served on the wife's counsel. But the doctor was charged for alleged preparation. Given that the discovery was never sent and the doctor received no benefit from all the "busy" work, that amount had to be credited to his account.

Pleadings: The firm allegedly prepared and charged for them, but did not serve or file them.

Appraisal of marital home: It's difficult to conceive of 20 hours spent on the appraisals. The home was a simple split-level in an area where the homes are not dissimilar.

Internal conferences: Close to a dozen or more internal conferences for which everyone in the firm charged their hourly fee. The records do not contain any notes taken at these conferences. Maybe the scones, donuts, bagels and cream cheese, and Starbucks coffee took up the space on the conference table.

Phonecalls: The firm charged for the lead attorney spending approximately 73 hours on the phone. To whom? It was just a divorce, albeit an acrimonious one with some serious issues, but there was only one wife and one attorney . . . and with one lover of the wife and his attorney.

Bill: The invoices are inconsistent, but they appear to total upwards of $80,000.

The client paid $34,579.35 and thinking, What is getting done?, he balked at paying all of them. Things were just getting worse.

There were two primary issues: the wife alleged that the doctor had raped her three times and the wife wanted gold that he had in his home country and had never brought to this country. The lead attorney spent all her time discussing the gold with the wife's counsel, with whom the lead attorney did not get along!

The doctor, prestigious in his own right, feared criminal charges would be brought against him as a result of his wife's false allegations. When he discussed that with the lead attorney, she confessed that she knew of the epidemic of false allegations, but she had never handled a case with them and did not know how to handle them. He asked her if he found someone experienced with such cases, would she be willing to use that person as a consultant. She replied that she would.

The doctor found me and asked if I would be willing to work as a consultant with the lead attorney, who was well-known in her own right. Although the lead attorney and I had never met or communicated in any way, I told him, Sure, if she agreed to work with me. By the time he told the lead attorney, she had changed her mind, so their attorney-client relationship ended.

She and I appeared in court the same day, she to withdraw, I to file my appearance. And she handed the doctor another bill. She and I spoke long enough to tell me that she had scheduled a half-day deposition of the wife to take place on the last day of the discovery period. Holy Cow! Three allegedly false allegations of rape, the financials, and only half a day scheduled for the wife's deposition on the last day of discovery!

When I arrived, the lead attorney, who we agreed would question on the gold issues, of which I had no knowledge, was almost finished. I had the hour a half remaining to question the wife. She was cooked. We knew there would be no more heard of the rape charges. Her counsel and I spoke before we left the prestigious lawfirm. We got along well and he agreed there was no way rape charges ever could be brought.

He and I took the next 10 days to write and revise and re-revise a settlement agreement. We went assiduously over each word in every sentence. We only had to go into court once and get the approval of the judge.

The prestigious lawfirm still wanted to be paid. I advised the doctor to let them sue him and he could countersue for malpractice if they did. That firm would not want to be sued for malpractice. That would make news. We were able to settle the lawcase. Because the doctor also did not want to see his names in any lawbooks or newspapers, he gave them a few thousand dollars more and they wrote off the approximately $30,000 remaining on the bill.

Moral: Dissect your attorney's bills. Do not automatically pay them. Question everything that appears to be in error or an error. Do not accept the "team" approach. That is when you're screwed the most. It's as bad as going to a teaching hospital, where you are attended to by students called interns and charged by an unseen, amorphous registered doctor and discover you have been misdiagnosed and improperly treated. The only difference between lawyers and doctors is that the doctor will get paid, at the very least, by the government, if not by a private health insurer. The only risk the doctors face is not collecting on the 20 percent co-pay.

Anecdote #3.

Susie's husband died and she became the administrator of his estate. There was nothing in his estate except two business lawsuits that were pending. I handled one of them and the case settled fairly quickly.

On the other case, the lawyer her husband had retained disappeared, literally, so Susie hired another lawyer to locate the file. He did, but after obtaining it, he did little. Displeased with him, she hired a third lawyer: Attorney GJ, who rented office space from another attorney, Steve Gordon, in Worcester. GJ and Gordon argued over money. Gordon then put an attorney's lien on the case GJ was handling for Susie. Gordon did the same on the cases of District Attorney Conte's niece, who also rented office space in Gordon's office.

Susie never met Gordon, had never been to his office, had never spoken to or seen Gordon. GJ's representation of Susie was not successful. The judge, St. Cyr, allowed Gordon to put the attorney's lien on Susie's case, but would not allow GJ to appeal.

I learned what was going when, in October 1993, Gordon served on both me and GJ a Motion for Assessment of Attorney's Lien for $8500.00 and Order of Payment and Affidavit, in which Gordon represented that he was counsel for Susie. Upon receipt of the motion, I contacted GJ regarding it. At that time, I learned that GJ wanted to withdraw from the case\[246]/ and also got the impression from GJ that the posttrial motions were still under advisement and that his retransfer request would have to be refiled when judgment was entered into the docket.\[247]/

Faced with Susie's immediate need to oppose Gordon's motion for fees, and fearing for her well-being at the time, I, a few days later, served and filed my Notice of Appearance and pleadings in opposition to Gordon's motion for fees. It being nigh to impossible for Susie to find yet another attorney to represent her at that juncture in the case, I became successor counsel.

The first thing I did upon entering Wrentham (MA) District Court was to get a certified copy of the docket sheets. The docket sheet did not reflect what St. Cyr gave as his reason. There had to be, I speculated, a connection between the judge and the defendant company. (I learned later that St.Cyr had been town counsel in the small town in which the defendant company was located and did business.)

At oral argument in December 1993, and in his pleadings to the Wrentham District Court judge, Gordon misrepresented that he represented Susie in the action, that GJ had been his employee while GJ was working at Gordon's office, and that Gordon was therefore entitled to attorney's fees.

Following argument, the District Court judge allowed the parties to file memorandum on the application of the retransfer statute.\[248]/

In March 1994, the WDC denied the retransfer to Superior Court and awarded Gordon judgment entitling him to $5000.00 fees for his alleged representation of Susie in the underlying action. On 1 April 1994, WDC again denied Susie's subsequent request for retransfer. During April 1994, Susie filed a Petition for Draft Report,\[249]/ which was also denied.

Keeping with my habit of getting certified copies of the then-handwritten docket sheets, I obtained a second copy of the docket sheet, but it had been amended by inserting an alleged order by St. Cyr . . . to cover his butt for his reason for denying Attorney GJ his appeal. So *in toto*, I had two certified docket sheets, one not showing the relevant order by St. Cyr and one showing the insertion in pen of the relevant order, as well as one unsigned order by St. Cyr and another signed order by St. Cyr. Clearly the so-called judge was crooked and was playing games in his clerk's office with the docket sheets.

Digression. Docket sheets are now computerized. You will not see handwritten insertions or other corrections, but you might stumble on different versions of computerized ones. So still be sure to check them. If you see that the version is different than the set you have, purchase the new set of docket pages. Those pages will be proof that the court might be pulling something untoward. It is *not* uncommon for grievous acts to show up on docket sheets. **End of digression.**

The judge, John F. St. Cyr, who had been the Town Counsel of Millis, where he resided, and Medfield between 1963 and 1976 and knew the defendant company, Millis Used Auto Parts,\[250]/ was a Special Justice of Wrentham District Court between 1972 and 1983; and the Presiding Justice of Wrentham District Court between 1983 and 1996. He then returned to private practice from a lifelong guaranteed appointment with wonderful health benefits and a pension at almost full pay. Why would a judge do that? Why? An accumulation of complaints to the Commission of Judicial Conduct sometimes causes the secret return of a judge to private practice If this was the case, how many complaints had been filed against him? I suspect that was likely the reason he interfered with GJ's efforts to go forward with an appeal, and then with mine. Had St. Cyr been taking pay-offs for favorable decisions to certain parties? If so, how large were the pay-offs? I would love an aggressive investigative reporter to snoop into St. Cyr's background. My visibility and notoriety is too pronounced to do the same.

Aside from satisfying my curiosity, a solution still had to be found for getting Susie's money for her. Given the rule of law that a person cannot swear, say, Yes, to one question in one court and No, to the same question in another court . . . and given that Gordon had sworn in Wrentham District that he was Susie's lawyer, and that the amount she was awarded when GJ was representing her was less than what it should have been, suing Gordon in Superior Court for legal malpractice might be productive.

The theory, the one that holds true for all legal malpractice cases: Had Gordon not committed malpractice when allegedly representing her, she would have gotten a better result from her case in Wrentham District Court.

The story of the legal malpractice case can be seen in Chapter 20.

Anecdote #4.

Beware of the fancy titles the family courts give their appointed sycophantic troglodytes—flunkies! Four of them were in Lucas and Gloria Stockdale's divorce case. Three, all lawyers, are involved in this anecdote. Gerald Nissenbaum, who was appointed as a so-called "Discovery Master," never helped Lucas get one piece of paper from Gloria; he was a fake, undeserving and arguably very corrupt. James J. McCusker, who was appointed as a so-called "Special Master" charged with researching one legal issue, namely, the competency of the children, got, instead—with Nissenbaum's misguidance and unbeknownst to me or my client—involved in the custody issue. And also unbeknownst to Lucas and me, McCusker made a deal with both Martha Rush O'Mara, another attorney frequently participating in the discussions in Massachusetts Lawyers Weekly online MassForum, to do some work for him and Nissenbaum.

When Nissenbaum was appointed a little more than a year before trial, he filed his first report recommending that Lucas get custody of the couple's children. The two judges, Nancy Gould (judge in April when Nissenbaum filed his report) and Lisa Roberts (substituting, as of the following November, for Gould who went off the case after I sued her in federal court), refused to hold any hearing on or even refer to Nissenbaum's report at any time.

During those seven months, Gloria's attorney, E. Chouteau Merrill, was nominated and appointed to a family-court judgeship and Nissenbaum's mindset turned 180 degrees. Why did it change direction? **(1)** Did Nissenbaum get Gould's message—directly or indirectly—that she was displeased with his report? **(2)** Was Nissenbaum intimidated by Merrill's judicial appointment and the prospect that he wanted to be on "her" side should he suddenly have one of his own cases before her in the near future? **(3)** Did Gloria's multimillionaire father persuade Nissenbaum to do everything he could to ensure all matters be disposed of in Gloria's favor? **(4)** All of the above? **(5)** None? Or **(6)** Other?

When Nissenbaum recommended that Judge Lisa Roberts appoint McCusker, I objected on several grounds, but Roberts overruled my objection. Inevitably McCusker took Gloria's side.

Because there was so much political corruption involved in the case, there was a 59-day divorce and political corruption trial, which ran sporadically over 11 months' time.

On the stand at trial, McCusker **(1)** admitted on cross-examination that he acted outside the scope of his authority, **(2)** testified that only Martha Rush O'Mara—and not he and O'Mara, as charged on his bill—had made a trip to the out-of-state home of Gloria's multimillionaire father (whom Lucas was accusing of sexually molesting the couple's children, whom Gloria had brought with her to live in her father's home), and **(3)** revealed that O'Mara paid him 60 percent of the money she was allegedly receiving for her work on the case—which is unheard of in the "legal" community. In my opinion, McCusker had paid Nissenbaum half of the 60 percent referral fee—which, if true, was the type of backroom deal kept secret from everyone. I was not allowed to get the answer to the question as to how much of the 60 percent he paid to Nissenbaum.

Of course, as could be expected, the fees, whether or not split 40-30-30, were to be paid by Lucas Stockdale. Dirty, dirty, dirty!

Ironically, in the final week of trial, we learned at trial that the information brought back from out-of-state by McCusker and/or O'Mara was entirely inaccurate and prejudicially false.

Shame, shame, shame on Lisa Roberts, Nissenbaum, McCusker, and O'Mara.

Worse is that Roberts was protected from suit and liability by judge-made absolute immunity, and Nissenbaum and McCusker had quasi-absolute immunity because they were court-appointed. Whether O'Mara, who had not been appointed, had quasi-immunity was never tested. It is imperative that such immunity be abolished. Without accountability, the courts will lose face as dangerously as our dollar is losing value today and will continue to do tomorrow.

While calamity is anticipated for our economy, the calamity for the courts is unanticipated by the populace who has not yet been pulled into the courts.

What is "fraud on the court"?

A judge is an officer of the court, as well as are all attorneys. Federal and state judges are paid to act impartially and lawfully. A judge is not the court.\[251]/

When an officer of the court commits fraud during a court proceeding, the officer is engaged in *fraud upon the court.* "Fraud upon the court is fraud which is directed to the judicial machinery itself and is not fraud between the parties or fraudulent documents, false statements or perjury. . . . It is where the court or a member is corrupted or influenced or influence is attempted or where the judge has not performed his judicial function—thus where the impartial functions of the court have been directly corrupted."\[252]/

Fraud upon the court has been defined to "embrace that species of fraud which does, or attempts to, defile the court itself, or is a fraud perpetrated by officers of the court so that the judicial machinery can not perform in the usual manner its impartial task of adjudging cases that are presented for adjudication."\[253]/ "[A] decision produced by fraud upon the court is not in essence a decision at all, and never becomes final."\[254]/ Fraud upon the court makes void the orders and judgments of that court. It is also clear and well-settled Illinois law that any attempt to commit fraud upon the court vitiates the entire proceeding. "The maxim that fraud vitiates every transaction into which it enters applies to judgments as well as to contracts and other transactions."\[255]/\[256]/ "It is axiomatic that fraud vitiates everything."\[257]/ Under Illinois and Federal law, when any officer of the court has committed fraud upon the court, the orders and judgment of that court are void, of no legal force or effect.

When Seeking Review of the Fraud: Seek Extrinsic Fraud

". . . where the ground for a bill of review is fraud, review will not be granted unless the fraud was extrinsic. . . . The distinction between extrinsic and intrinsic fraud is not technical but substantial."\[258]/ The classical example of intrinsic evidence is a witness's perjury.

While perjury is a fraud upon the court, the credibility of witnesses is an issue the judge or jury must determine in order to reach a final judgment. An allegation that a witness perjured himself is an insufficient basis on which to seek review "because the materiality of the testimony, and opportunity to attack it, was open at the trial."\[259]/

Only extrinsic fraud may be the basis of a bill of review. Review will not be granted to permit relitigation of matters which were in issue in the case that was concluded by a judgment or decree.\[260]/ (*See* Chapter 15.)

"Where the authenticity of a document relied on as part of a litigant's case is material to adjudication, . . . , and there was opportunity to investigate this matter, fraud in the preparation of the document is not extrinsic but intrinsic and will not support review."\[261]/

To justify a bill of review, the new evidence of fraud (1) must have been undiscoverable (meaning that you used reasonable diligence to find it but could not) before the time it would have been used at trial, (2) could not have been obtained before judgment was entered, and (3) must have been unknown prior to judgment.\[262]/ Only then would the new evidence be deemed "extrinsic" and sufficient to justify the bill for review of the judgment.

Chapter 12

Immigration Fraud\[263]/

*The new internal terrorism: marital immigration and
artificial insemination for anchor babies and ultimately child support*

Marriage to an American is the most common way for foreign nationals to become a U.S. citizen.\[264]/ Because so many persons wanted to obtain work authorization (known as a Green Card) and American citizenship, sham marriages became widespread. As a result, Congress passed the Immigration Marriage Fraud Amendments (IMFA) in 1986. Under IMFA, a citizen may petition to have either his wife or his fiancée be given conditional two-year legal residency. They have 90 days to get married if they haven't already done so. Within 90 days of the expiration of the foreign spouse's two-year conditional residency, both must certify in writing to United States Citizenship and Immigration Services ["CIS"], formerly the United States Immigration and Naturalization Service ["INS"], that the marriage is intact and sound. Failure to do that automatically revokes the foreign spouse's right of residency and he/she must leave the country. Also, if the couple gets a divorce within two years of the marriage, the foreign-born spouse must depart the country.

But the Violence Against Women Act, VAWA (pronounced Vah-Wah), first passed into law in 1994, provides an end-run on IMFA. *Now, any alien who claims to be "battered" moves to the front of the immigration line and is entitled to a broad range of services and welfare benefits, rather than being required to leave the country.* According to a recent report, VAWA-supported immigration fraud now costs American taxpayers $170 million a year,\[265]/ reports RADAR, Respecting Accuracy in Domestic Abuse Reporting, a much respected organization using reliable statistics.

Now, Almost Anything Counts as "Extreme Cruelty"

Originally, VAWA allowed immigrants who could demonstrate "extreme cruelty" to bypass the two-year marriage requirement and file a "self-petition." Self-petitioning means the battered immigrant spouse can apply for a Green Card without her spouse's knowledge or support.

There are an abundance of women's groups catering to foreign women. The first thing they tell their clients is to file for a restraining order.

Anecdote #1.

One man whose Polish wife filed a restraining order against him waited until the day after his wife's two years legal residency had expired, and then filed unilaterally and demanded her deportation. He repudiated any claim that their marriage was intact and any claim she might make later on of abuse. He noted he'd been found not guilty of such accusations at jury trial and also provided transcripts of polygraph examinations.

He was told that she had not met her obligation to file for an upgrade to permanent residency within the required time. So in this case, she ought not subsequently have been allowed to avail herself of any claim of abuse.

He does not know what happened, but does know that somehow, subsequently, she was granted permanent residency, even over his objections.

* * *

When VAWA was re-authorized in 2000 and 2005, definitions were expanded. *Now, any form of abuse, even if there has been no physical violence, can be counted as "extreme cruelty."* For example, VAWA-funded Legal Momentum openly claims any of the following should be taken as proof of extreme cruelty:

- Emotional abuse
- Possessiveness
- Minimizing, denying, and blaming

Second, evidentiary requirements were relaxed. *Now, hard evidence of "extreme hardship" is no longer required.* Susie Kinoshita of the VAWA-funded ASISTA project openly advocates for what she calls the "subjective test," which she defines as "the self-petitioner's own declaration."

Seven Other Ways VAWA Promotes Immigration Fraud

VAWA encourages immigration fraud in seven other ways:

1. Providing free legal support to the self-petitioner, sometimes assisting her to file additional fraudulent claims of abuse.
2. Barring any investigation of immigration document fraud.
3. Prohibiting any evidence of an incriminating nature to be placed in the self-petitioner's file.
4. Centralizing self-petitions to an office in Vermont staffed by VAWA-trained personnel.
5. Allowing illegal aliens with a criminal background to self-petition.
6. Allowing deportees to qualify for self-petitioning.
7. Absolving the self-petitioner from any responsibility for bringing false claims of abuse.

The bottom line: VAWA provides legal immunity to any person who claims abuse regardless of prior criminal activities or current legal status.

Holding Perjurers Accountable

The following changes need to be incorporated in the 2010 reauthorization of the Violence Against Women Act. This will re-establish the integrity of our immigration system and hold accountable those persons who make false claims of abuse.

1. All battered spouse self-petitions should be investigated for previous marriage fraud. Material evidence of prior fraud must be included in the self-petitioner's file. Self-petitions should be denied if prior marriage fraud is documented.
2. Overseas consular officers should be asked to assist when conducting investigations on suspect cases. In-country officers often have local knowledge that can expose marriage scams.

3.   A determination of false statements should be cause for depor-
     tation. Deportation laws should be enforced.
4.   VAWA-funded attorneys who engage in suborning perjury
     should be subjected to fines and other disciplinary action.
5.   If marriage fraud is suspected, the American spouse should be
     notified and that person's testimony obtained.

Harming True Victims of Abuse

VAWA sends a perverse message to the underground world of illegal immigrants. It also hurts the real victims of abuse because widespread false allegations of abuse inevitably cast doubt on the validity of
real victims' claims.

The VAWA immigration provisions urgently need to be reformed
so American citizens are no longer subjected to scurrilous allegations
of abuse that are so easily made for personal gain.

Father X Speaks.

Anecdote #2.

According to Father X, artificial insemination was used against
him to create a baby to circumvent immigration laws and to commit,
in effect, Immigration & Paternity Fraud and to remove the child's
rights to a father.

The background: Father X had married a Senegal woman while he
was a post-graduate student and she was a visiting professor. After he
married her and sponsored her visa, he became suspicious about the
circumstances behind her leaving her position with the college.

She had a lot of problems with consummating the marriage. The
one successful attempt to have sex ended with an ectopic pregnancy.

"For me," Father X iterated, "the combination of my wife not being able to copulate during marriage and her failure to reveal to me
her visa sponsor with details about her separation from her last visa was
grounds for termination the marriage."

He continued, "She requested that I undergo an examination to
help her identify why she had an ectopic pregnancy. She claimed that
it must have been something wrong with me and that it was all my fault.
So as she requested, I agreed to have a Sperm Count procedure.

"When I went to Mount Sinai, I went not to a fertility clinic but to a regular physician's office, where I met the nurse, who handed me paperwork to fill out. I did as she asked but I clearly wrote on the documentation that my semen was to be used for testing purposes only and not to be used for anything else. The nurse assured me of that! Then I signed the paperwork.

"My insistence was because I believe my right to say how, when, and where to have a baby should have been protected at all cost. No Doctor has the right to take this away.

"Later on, I assumed my ex-wife and the Doctor—Dr. Tanmoy Mukherjee—conspired to perform an IVF—an in-vitro fertilization test—using my semen. They did this without me ever meeting the doctor, talking with the doctor, or signing any consent to the IVF procedure. This was all confirmed during a NYS Department of Health Investigation.

"During the NYS Department of Health Investigation (another cover-up), my ex-wife and the Doctor claimed that they used another man's semen but lost all medical records/consent forms for that so-called other donor. Then, saying that I was not the victim because another man's semen was used, the Department of Health immediately closed the case."

The "malicious plotters" to strip Baby X of his rights to have a father were, Father X claims, Mother X, Dr. Tanmoy Mukherjee, of the Mount Sinai Hospital/Reproductive Medical Center of New York, and Judge Edward Torack in Bergen County (New Jersey) Family Court.

BUT according to the N.Y. Department of Health, "In 2000, there was no express statutory or regulatory requirement for a semen bank to obtain the written informed consent from a man providing semen for use in the artificial insemination of his wife or intimate partner. Therefore, our office will not be filing any citations regarding lack of informed consent."

Baby X was created by unauthorized artificial insemination by Dr. Mukherjee for Father X's wife, who was facing deportation to Senegal for defrauding a university. In order to avoid deportation, Dr. Mukherjee and the mother of Baby X conspired to use the semen of a U.S. citizen and create an "anchor baby." It was his semen, Father X asserts, that they conspired to use without his consent to create the "anchor baby." With the baby, Father X's wife could get him burdened with the responsibility of child support. Because Mother X already had a green card, she had no fear of deportation to Senegal.

During hearings at Bergen County Family Court, Father X presented a copy of Mother X's immigration records (showing, according to Father X, a history of immigration fraud) and got Mother X to admit under oath at trial that she had the child via an Unauthorized Medical Experiment/IVF with Father X's semen.

Immediately after clear evidence was presented in court that Baby X was created by an Unauthorized Medical Experiment for the purposes of Immigration Fraud, the father was completely banned——by Judge Edward Torack of Bergen County Family Court—from all courts and all judges .

The end result: Father X was stripped of all rights to the child except to shut up and pay. Thus the State of New Jersey also stripped Baby X's right to have a Father!

Today, Father X writes not only that *the State of NJ Family Court uses children as weapons but also that:*

There is no such thing as appealing.
There is no such thing as court protecting my rights.
There is no such thing as a medical treatment for what was done to me.
There is no such thing as the police protecting my rights.
There is no such thing as a prosecutor protecting my rights.
There is no such thing as a civil rights organization protecting my rights.
There is no such thing as family for me.
There is no such thing as having children for me.
There is no such thing as a government that represents me.
There is no such thing as finding a wife.
There is no such thing as requesting help from traditional churches for me.
There is no such thing as health organizations to protect my rights.
There is no such thing as elected officials to protect my rights.
There is no such thing as real ACLU or any other illusion.

But what I do have is the ability to let people know that they must keep on complaining, writing, petitioning, speaking to those who will listen, and letting people know that our government is out to destroy us!

Anecdote #3.

Another Judge Torack case.

Maria Jose Carrascosa says that "Carrascosa and Innes married in 1999 in Spain, and resided in New Jersey. They had one child, a daughter, Victoria. The marriage broke in 2004 after several years of domestic abuse, and Innes abandoned the family home. Thereafter, Maria Jose filed in Spain a petition to annul the marriage and was granted full custody of her daughter. Mother and child then moved back to Spain in January of 2005.

At that point, Innes filed for divorce in New Jersey and accused Maria Jose of illegally taking their daughter abroad, even though there was no such requirement or court order that she remain in the USA."\[266]/ Innes pressed his case in Spain simultaneously. Valencia (Spain) high court of appeals sided with the lower courts in granting full custody to Maria Jose.

Despite the State Court of Valencia ruling on the custody issue and ordering the confiscation of the child's passports in order to prevent her leaving Spain, New Jersey Judge Torack proceeded along in a parallel process and granted custody of Victoria to Innes.

When Maria Jose went to the US in order to demonstrate to the court she had been granted custody and that custody had been upheld on appeal, her passport was confiscated, and she was given 10 days to turn Victoria over to Innes.

In November 2006, a team of 17 police agents arrested and shackled Maria Jose in leg irons and hauled her before Judge Torack, who threatened her with incarceration of 40 years if she did not turn over her daughter. She has been held prisoner in the Bergen County Jail since then, the judge refusing all pleas to free her.

Father X asserts that Judge Torack lied about conducting motion hearings that never happened in Father X's case, too, and that no one commenting on this case is allowed access to the court records without Judge Torack's permission! He points his readers to two websites"

http://web.archive.org/web/20070129074109/www.jap4all.us/Spotlight.htm and
http://web.archive.org/web/20050313030925/www.jap4all.us/ACJC.htm

both of which were created by still another "Torack victim" and refer to Judge Torack's background in and out of court. Torack has obviously created an abundance of anger against him in New Jersey. Father X questions: Is Judge Torack a criminal?

Anecdote #4.

Recently Roy Den Hollander, a New York attorney with impressive credentials, filed a class-action law suit against four government officials. He himself was one of the four plaintiffs. A target of the suit, in part, is the "Female Fraud Act," which is what he calls VAWA.\\[267]/

The suit arose out of his belief that "As the law created by feminist lobbying now stands, alien females prone to criminal pursuits can become permanent residents and eventually U.S. citizens by simply saying their American husbands abused them, and it will not matter that these females are lying, committed crimes of moral turpitude, violated drug laws, worked as prostitutes and procurers, or used fraud and perjury to gain entry into the U.S. and to stay here."\\[268]/

In his Complaint, Hollander wrote:

11.   The alien wives of class members have and continue to manufacture public records of alleged abuse by their U.S. husbands so that those records will be relied upon by the defendants to find husbands responsible for abuse. Such records include an alien wife:

  a.   Making false allegations of abuse to obtain an ex parte temporary order of protection—no permanent order required by the defendants;

  b.   Falsely claiming or intentionally causing the violation of a temporary or permanent protection order in order to have the U.S. husband arrested—no final adjudication required by the defendants;

  c.   Making false accusations of domestic violence to the police that often require the police to arrest the husband—no conviction required by the defendants;

  d.   Faking minor injuries—no judicial decision on who caused the injuries required by the defendants;

  e.   Filing various complaints with the police that falsely accuse the U.S. husband of any number of crimes—no conviction required by the defendants;

f. Making false statements to government social service agencies—no investigation or hearing required by the defendants; and

g. Responding to leading questions from social workers for Federally funded feminist advocacy groups in order to make out a fraudulent prima facie case for permanent residency.

12. These records harm a husband's reputation, honor and integrity with false statements and with respect to non-false matters reveal intimate private conduct that injures a husband's privacy interest.

13. When an alien wife, her lawyer, and feminist advocacy group invoke the permanent residency process, the mere allegation of abuse, causes the defendants, under IIRIRA, codified as 8 U.S.C. § 1367(a)(2), to drop a curtain of secrecy over all immigration proceedings by prohibiting the disclosure of any information to the U.S. citizen husband concerning allegations of and the defendants' findings of fact that the husband committed "battery," "extreme cruelty," or engaged in an "overall pattern of violence" against his alien wife.

14. These proceedings, considered law enforcement by the Justice Department, are kept secret from the very person against whom findings of facts of abuse are made—the U.S. husband.

15. Behind the Star Chamber curtain, the alien wife, feminist advocates, and profit-driven immigration attorneys are free to submit fabricated, irrelevant, untrustworthy, hearsay, and character trait information of criminal, no convictions required, and non-criminal conduct by the U.S. husband because there is no one to refute their statements nor attack their credibility.

16. Virtually any lie, prevarication or dissemblance is used for showing "battery," "extreme cruelty," or "overall pattern of violence" under the Orwellian newspeak terminology "credible evidence" as set forth in 8 U.S.C. § 1154(a)(1)(J), 8 C.F.R. § 204.2(c)(1)(iv), 61 Fed. Reg. 13,066, and Virtue INS Memorandum, 76 Interpreter Releases 162, 168-169 (1999).

17. In the end, "credible evidence" means whatever the defendants decide it to mean. Id.

The feminist establishment was responsible for getting VAWA enacted into law. The feminists' purpose was to intimidate American men into looking for wives at home—not overseas. It does that by creating the risk of the Government punishing a citizen man by violating his rights, invading his privacy, and ruining his reputation without any of the usual Constitutional recourses that protect against secret, arbitrary decisions by the Government.\269/

In sum, by his suit, Hollander sets out clearly how the VAWA provisions challenged in this federal case violate an American man's constitutional rights, namely,

- freedom of speech by preventing him from standing up and speaking on his own behalf and in his own defense;

- freedom of choice in marital affairs by telling him to either support his alien wife's application for permanent residency or be found guilty of "battery," "extreme cruelty," or an "overall pattern of violence" *in absentia*;

- procedural due process by failing to provide notice, an opportunity to be heard, and non-biased decision makers;

- equal protection as to national origin by discriminating against Americans on the face of the statutes and sex as the statutes are applied by biased Government officials and as intended by the feminist establishment.\270/

Chapter 13

Employment Discrimination
Dirty!

Employment discrimination cases are fact-intensive. No matter the similarity, each case is unique. The personalities involved are unique. The employers are each unique. The state policies toward business are unique. The unique facts also make employment discrimination cases law-intensive. Just determining which laws are applicable or in which court you will have a greater likelihood of success or, in fact, which court has jurisdiction or whether the Federal law preempts the state law can be challenging.

The defense bar—those attorneys who represent companies—play hardball. They fight giving access to people in the company for depositions. They fight giving access to—that is, seeing or producing copies of—documents to plaintiff attorneys. The defense bar never represents plaintiffs, and the plaintiffs' bar never represents defendants. The premier organization for the plaintiffs bar is the National Employment Lawyers Association (NELA), which has chapters in each State across the nation.

Prior to the Internet, the plaintiffs bar—of which I was a member—did not have easy communication with other plaintiffs' attorneys. Today the opportunities for communicating and sharing ideas or problems with fellow attorneys is incredibly enhanced. In Massachusetts, for instance, the NELA-affiliated chapter has a listserv which provides immediacy. One member asks a question, five answer it.

Whether this ability to ask one's professional colleagues has numbed an attorney's need to do his or her own research or has made an attorney lazy is unanswerable. But for one who used to have to haul the law books down from the shelves, copy the cases, highlight the relevant portions, take notes, and have to restack the dozen or so books, to read some of the questions asked on the Net is both startling and saddening. How can the young attorneys learn the many alternative arguments on a given issue? The answers they are spoon-fed on the listserv are equal to Westlaw's headnotes. While being quite helpful, Westlaw headnotes are not always correct and do not include the opposing points of views. They also overlook some stunning and extremely useful statements and declarations by the courts. Ditto the answers on the listservs . . . although the member plaintiffs' lawyers on the MELA listserv are some of the most brilliant lawyers in the profession. I have inordinate respect for them. Most of them would, however, soon go to a mental institution if they had to deal with family-law judges. The lack of due process and equal protection would, literally, drive them wild. Family-law judges and ordinary family-law lawyers are from one species and employment-discrimination lawyers are from another.

Although electronic legal research, too, can provide immediacy, many attorneys simply do not do the requisite research on their own. Instead they rely all too much on the answers they get from one listserv or another.

Ultimately, however, once the case is off and running, the success or failure of employment discrimination cases depends upon the judge.\271/ Will he compel the defense attorney to comply with the discovery rules, that is, to produce the documents requested and to answer all the interrogatories propounded by the plaintiff? If the plaintiff's attorney's attempt to get those answers or the documents requested is allegedly too zealous, will the judge sanction the attorney or will the judge compel, instead, the plaintiff to pay the defendant's attorney's fees?

Judicial rulings midtrial can be dangerous if they are about unforeseeable subjects.

One case in particular comes to mind. A few words about the case might help put it into context. The primary defendant was an environmental-consulting company. The company alleged that six women had formed a group with the intention of taking down the company. After the allegation was made, one of the women (Lily) voluntarily left on her own. A second was fired. A third left (Maxine) on her own. A fourth was fired. A fifth left on her own. The sixth (Inez), who was the plaintiff in this case and who had been at the company the longest, was fired.

My client, Inez,\272/ was a toxicologist, a working mother with three sons, two of whom were twins. Her husband, John, at one point left his job with another environmental-consulting company and became a stay-at-home dad. He was a wonderful dad, but was not as careful in preparing the couple's tax returns.

At Inez's deposition, Defense Counsel Mark C. O'Connor, was extremely aggressive and threatened that he would turn in her husband to the IRS for tax evasion and/or tax fraud.\[273]/ This was O'Connor's *modus operandi*, his "MO." At an earlier deposition in another case in which he was also defense counsel, O'Connor admitted that being offensive and cruel was part of his intentional style. His goal, to intimidate the deponent.

The threat at Inez's deposition arose because Inez had not produced copies of her and John's joint State and Federal tax returns. The defense counsel's offensive behavior continued until the end of the day.

As my client and I walked out of the conference room, we decided to stop in the ladies' room, given that traffic out of Boston at the 5 o'clock rush hour could make the trip north unpleasantly long. In the ladies' room, Inez fainted. I immediately sought the assistance of the receptionist to call for an ambulance. After facing considerable unexpected resistance to calling for an ambulance, I insisted that the receptionist summon the Managing Partner of this old, large prestigious firm. Only then was the ambulance called. When it arrived, Inez was still unconscious on the floor of the ladies' room.

The ambulance took her to New England Medical Center. I followed in my own car and stayed present until the results of all the tests were complete. The results confirmed that my client had had an anxiety attack. Because she was late in returning home, Inez had to tell her husband about her trip to the hospital, but she decided to keep the cause of her anxiety from him. John was an excitable, passionate type and was against her bringing the wrongful termination lawsuit in the first place.

I had earlier reported defense counsel to the Massachusetts Board of Bar Overseers.

My client and Lily, a geologist who was the first of the six women to leave her employment with the company, had maintained a close friendship. That weekend Lily called Inez. When Inez got off the phone in the kitchen—pre-cellphone days—John asked, What was that all about? During the week, she relented and told him. By Thursday, when he was fishing with his cousin, he was all upset about the events that had taken place at Inez's deposition. By Monday afternoon, John had a heart attack. The EMTs arrived, the defibrillator was broken, John, husband and father, was dead upon arrival at Lahey Clinic. He was 40 years old. His father, too, had died around that age. Because of the family history and the broken defibrillator, making a case that his death was caused even indirectly by the opposing defense counsel would have been difficult if not impossible. And the case law was solidly against being able to sue opposing counsel for wrongdoing. In the back of our minds, however, we, having already concluded that O'Connor was an evil man, considered him a murderer.

Ironically, about a week or so prior to John's death, I received written notice of the dismissal by the BBO of my complaint against Defense Counsel O'Connor.

Ultimately, the time for trial approached. When the defense counsel arrived for trial, he had with him a document not previously produced. It was allegedly a document showing the finances of the company. All financial documents had previously not been produced and were not compelled to be produced by the judge, Judge Judith Fabricant.\[274]/

From its face, it was clear that the document was fabricated solely for trial. I objected. The judge sustained my objection and disallowed the introduction of the document. Whoopee!!

At the very end of trial, while the defense was putting on its last witness, Theodore "Ted" Barton, the president and CEO of the company, defense counsel was about to put a "chalk"—like a poster—on an easel in front of the jury. A chalk may not be displayed to a jury before ALL the facts on it have been introduced into evidence.

When I saw the chalk, I was amazed. It was a 3-foot blowup of the exact document that had been disallowed or deemed inadmissible earlier. So again I objected, not only on the basis upon which I had previously objected but also on the basis that none of the facts had been introduced into evidence. The judge overruled my objection.

Fabricant then astoundingly not only allowed the defense to use the chalk but allowed President and CEO Theodore "Ted" Barton to testify standing up in front of the jury for an hour.

Had Judge Fabricant been reached? What made her flip her previous ruling 180 degrees and disregard all the law regarding chalks as well as the admissibility of evidence? I'll let the readers decide. My best guess would be Tyco CEO Dennis Kozlowski, who had bought the defendant company . . . and who currently is ensconced in federal prison, caused the flip of Fabricant.\\[275]/

Up until that time, it was clear that Inez, the toxicologist, had won her case. Witness after witness had testified in her favor.

The jury trial was never appealed. My client did not have $12,000 for the trial transcript . . . and after having lost her husband and having the children attending weekly sessions for grief therapy, she had had enough with the legal system. It was time for Inez to go forward.

In a companion case, that is, one against the same employer—but different individual defendants—the defense counsel was the same. The case had been brought by Lily, the geologist who was both Inez's close friend and the alleged whistleblower and ringleader of the so-called women's group. Lily had quit her job after being hospitalized. She believed she had taken ill because she had to work continuously on contaminated lands without the proper protective clothing . . . and the company refused to provide that clothing. She had discussed that refusal with Maxine, another of the six women in the alleged group.

Not only was Maxine responsible for preparing papers in compliance with EEOC regulations—EEOC being the Equal Employment Opportunity Commission—Maxine's husband, Bill, was a civilian employed by the U.S. Air Force at Hanscom Airbase to oversee compliance with contracts between companies and the federal government.

Lily also met with Maxine's husband, Bill, and described the company's use and reliance on fraudulent timeslips on projects being performed for the federal government. For instance, the company was supposed to charge a maximum of 8 hours per day and 40 hours per week per person and the timeslips of those assigned to the projects were to be filled out in pen and signed by the worker, generally a professional employee. The people were working 10 hours per day and 50 hours per week—depending on the job, of course—and were ordered to fill out the timeslips in pencil. A "special" assistant—who ironically left the company and became a police officer in Virginia—charged the extra 2 hours per day and the extra 10 hours per week either to the following week or to another job for which there was sufficient money in that project's budget to pay the overage. Over a short time, the professional had enough time in the fraudulent timeslips to cover a vacation to Europe or some other venturesome destination. These vacations were not deducted from the yearly vacations dictated by company policy.

One day, after having some pillow talk with Maxine the previous evening, Bill put his compliance hat on, and an 8-month audit by a group of investigators from the federal Department of Labor (DoL) was off and running. Lily was long gone from the company, but the DoL found that the remaining women, including Inez, were earning less than the men, were not promoted when they should have been, and were, in effect, suffering gender discrimination. It was during the DoL investigation that Lily learned why "things" had been made so uncomfortable for her. The DoL investigator had phoned her, sought information from her, and brought her up to date.

It was the same DoL investigator whom I later subpoenaed to Inez's trial. The federal government moved to quash his subpoena as well as the subpoenas of other DoL staff on the grounds that it was against federal policy to allow federal employees to testify. Judge Judith Fabricant therefore quashed the perfectly legitimate subpoenas and then would not allow the certified DoL reports into evidence. So months of expenditure of taxpayer money by the federal government was a total waste. The report was eventually watered down and the company's wrist was only slapped.

After hearing from the DoL investigator, Lily phoned me. By this time, Lily had moved to California and had doubled her pay with a national company that did not discriminate when paying women. The time for bringing a case for discrimination had run out, but Lily, being a neo-feminist, wanted to sue.

So on her behalf, I brought the whistleblower case in Massachusetts Superior Court, which then remanded the case to Concord District Court. Judge Paul McGill was in charge of the district court. He is a very dark black man, born of a white mother and a black father who had worked, it is rumored, for a railway. They divorced and mother moved to Dorchester, Massachusetts, and her then-significant-other paid for Paul to attend the Mt. Herman School, a private school for the children of the affluent. Paul then went to Harvard University and eventually Northeastern University School of Law. For a few years, he was a public criminal defense attorney in Roxbury\[276]/ District Court, in which criminal charges brought primarily against black men were heard. He was known as "Motions McGill." Shortly before Lily's case was remanded to District Court, McGill was appointed as First Justice of that court in Concord, a lily white, affluent community.

The first thing the defense counsel did was bring his clients' Motion for Summary Judgment for the second time. It had been denied in superior court prior to the case being remanded to Concord. It was denied again by McGill.

The discovery phase began. I sought documents. Amongst the documents Lily and I were seeking were copies of more timeslips. Defense counsel said the company had been bought and the old documents were in 26 boxes. He would not reveal who bought the company. The company was still infused with rage against Lily.

McGill also allowed some of our requests to compel discovery, but the company refused to comply. I sought McGill's help again, but, strangely, he began reversing himself. I finally said, at least let me go through the documents in the 26 boxes. McGill gave us a date to go to the facility.

I then received a FAX from defense counsel. The letter contained a list of instructions. I would even be accompanied into the ladies' room. They also would not allow anyone to accompany me to help me go through 26 boxes in 2 hours. I smelled trouble.

I phoned Concord Police Department and requested a paid two-man detail—no need for them to be armed—both to escort me to the facility and to be percipient witnesses. The chief's right-hand person, a female officer, said she would get back to me. Several calls back and forth. Ultimately, I was told they would not provide the two-man escort because I was not a taxpayer in Concord. Unbelievable, someone who goes to Concord cannot expect police protection because they do not pay taxes in Concord, Massachusetts. Outrageous.

I then arranged for Burns agency to provide a two-man team to escort me. Defense counsel wrote that he would allow no one to escort me into the facility. Naturally, I could not dare to go in alone: I would have no witness to confirm that I acted professionally.

I managed to get a court date for March 1st (1995). Defense counsel and I waited. At some point, he disappeared. As soon as the courtroom clerk, Ed Sulesky, was available, I asked, When are we going to be called? His response was, The case is continued to March 3d. Mr. O'Connor could not wait. He had to be at another court.

On March 3d, we were back in court. As we approached our respective podiums, O'Connor handed me a few motions. Follow the rules of procedure? No way. Fortunately the clerk, Sulesky, wrote at the top of the motions, **FILED IN COURT MARCH 3.** Judge McGill did not care that I had had no time to prepare and file written oppositions to the motions, despite having seen Sulesky's immediate and unforgettable notice of the violation of the rules of procedure.\[277]/ That day, McGill ruled on a half-dozen motions.

A few days later, on March 7th, Sulesky wrote a list of the motions heard on the 3d and the dispositions of each and served it on counsel. That list made it into the docket sheet, thereby memorializing what happened in court. The last motion, Paper #157, McGill took "under advisement." The tape clearly recorded McGill's voice saying he would take it under advisement and the transcript correctly noted what he said.

On March 22d, we were back in court. McGill found me and Lily in contempt for not paying money he allegedly ordered us to pay when he allowed "Motion #157." I was shocked. He had never decided Motion #157. No order ever issued. We were found in contempt of a *non-existent* order!

During the next nine months, the case became a circus, one filled with complex, convoluted legal procedures, some accomplished by the lies of defense counsel and the anxiety of the judges to get rid of the case!\[278]/

By December 1995, Judge McGill reversed himself at least four times, imposed against me *in terrorem* fines (fines for each day the fines were not paid), lowered the amount Lily was from several thousand dollars to a little over $200 dollars, declared it was too confusing to keep the contempts against me and against Lily separate, and stated that he was splitting the case into two—one, a case for contempt against Lily, and the other, a case for contempt against me.

An attorney, Elaine Whitfield-Sharp, who later achieved her 15 minutes of fame by being one of the defense team in the "Nanny case," in which English nanny Louise Woodward was charged with the murder of an infant by shaking him,\[279]/ was in Concord court that day. She introduced herself to me and ended up lunching with me and a friend who had accompanied me to court that day. Whitfield-Sharp offered her legal services free of charge. She empathized. She, too, had suffered at the hands of a questionable judge . . . in Michigan.

The case against Lily bore the original title and docket number of the case. The case against me became Mark C. O'Connor v. Barbara C. Johnson and was given a new 1996 docket number. My defense to the contempt of nonpayment was the inability to pay. O'Connor replied expressing disbelief; he wanted my personal financials. (These are what Attorney Richard Fine in California refused to produce to court and he, too, was jailed and targeted for disbarment. As of this writing, Attorney Fine has been in jail several months.) O'Connor said he did not understand how I, if I had no money to pay, could afford to reside in affluent neighborhoods. After objecting strenuously, Whitfield-Sharp produced copies of my personal financials to McGill in his chambers. McGill wrote nothing either in a memorandum, a decision, or an order about my financials or my ability to pay or not to pay, but found me in contempt of not paying fines associated with frivolous motions. Again, there was no existing order issued on March 3d, no ruling holding that any motion was frivolous, and no clear and unequivocal orders.

On my behalf, Whitfield-Sharp appealed. One of the several issues was whether I was charged with criminal or civil contempt. The Massachusetts Appeals Court affirmed the lower court's decision in the summer of 1998.

The original defendant company, a "Baby Bear" environmental-consulting firm that had been absorbed into a "Mama Bear" firm, had been sold again, this time to a "Papa Bear" international company, Tyco Internatiional, Ltd., whose CEO was at the time Dennis Kozlowski. Kozlowski's attorney, O'Connor, once again sought my personal financials. Each time he came into court he requested the judge to tell me to bring my tooth brush next time.

Believing both the decision and O'Connor to be outrageous, I had contacted a newspaper investigative reporter, Laura Brown of the Boston Herald. Laura had said, "Barb, unless you're put in jail, there is no story."

In December 1998, McGill had wanted me to produce my 1998 financials. I had not gathered them. This was a harmful error, given that the time for measuring one's ability to pay an order is when it issued. In this case, the alleged order allegedly issued in March 1995, almost four years earlier. When I had produced my financials in January 1996, McGill had never acknowledged that I had produced them, that they supported my claim of inability to pay, and that it was appropriate to dismiss the contempt complaint. I did not want to spend days to do what would again be a futile task.

On the day of the scheduled hearing, December 17th, Whitfield-Sharp's husband, Dan Sharp, also an attorney and coincidentally also in Concord District Court that day, handed me a ream-sized box containing the papers I had produced to the court in 1996. They had been returned to Elaine at some point in time. McGill, seeing the box on the table beside which I was standing, told me to give the box to O'Connor. I began to say, in words for all intents and purposes, No, Your Honor, these are not the 1998 papers, they are the 1995 papers which you have already seen. I got as far as the "No," when McGill said "Lock her up."

I was escorted by the court officer to a holding room. Because the officer had known me for years, he broke the rule and let me use his phone to make a phone call. I phoned one of my sons and told him to call Laura, the reporter, immediately and tell her I was going to jail.

That was the day after Bill Clinton launched a three-day bombing attack—Operation Desert Fox—against Iraq as punishment for Sadaam Hussein's refusal to allow a United Nations team to inspect for weapons. On the 17th, Clinton gave a briefing and the news media was full of military reports. The media suggested he launched the attack on the eve of impeachment to divert attention from his escapades with Monica Lewinsky. It didn't. What it did was take up space in the Herald that Laura's story of my plight might have gotten had it been a slow-news-day.

My son spent the next day in Concord court trying to find out what had to be done to get me out of Framingham Correctional Facility. It took the court clerk's office an entire day to figure out what the ransom amount was. There had never been an order telling me whom to pay, how much to pay, or by when to pay. So much for a clear and unequivocal order, which an order must be before someone may be found in contempt of it! Sometime around 9 in the evening of Friday, 18 December 1998, I was released from the woman's prison.

A day later, on Saturday, 19 December 1998, after almost 14 hours of debate, the 105th Congress approved two articles of impeachment—one for lying under oath to a federal grand jury and the other for obstructing justice—against President Bill Clinton.

Yes, a U.S. President could be impeached, but I could not sue McGill. Judges have given themselves absolute or judicial immunity, which means they are protected from suit, even if they act maliciously or corruptly. That Article V of the Massachusetts Declaration of Rights mandates that all persons from the three branches of government be accountable to all the people all the time no longer matters. The courts ignore the article\[280]/ and judges such as McGill cannot be sued.

Eight years after I had been jailed for a day, former CEO L. Dennis Kozlowski was found guilty of 22 out of 23 indictments charging him with conspiracy, grand larceny of hundreds of millions of dollars from Tyco, falsifying business records, and violating general business law. On 21 June 2005, Kozlowski was sentenced to serve between 15 and 30 years in prison.

During his tenure as Tyco's top executive, Kozlowski's lavish spending included a $2 million birthday party he threw for his wife on the Italian island of Sardinia and a $6,000 shower curtain allegedly purchased with company funds.

By the time I was jailed in 1998, during Kozlowski's tenure as Tyco CEO, the former "Motions McGill" who worked for $30 an hour, the kid from Dorchester, the new Judge McGill was living in a home next door to Digital Equipment Corporation CEO and President Ken Olsen in Maynard, Massachusetts. Contrarians say, Ken Olsen lived very frugally and had lived in the same home for years. Might be that he did, I reply, but it was not an area where you'd find Section 8 housing.

When the Kozlowski story broke, I wondered whether lavish birthday parties and $6000 shower curtains were the only outlandish thing Kozlowski bought. I again let the readers decide.

Chapter 14

Estates and Trusts

Judges make paper hay

Beware of executors of estates. Beware of the heirs of the estates. Beware of the lawyers representing estates. Beware of the judges hearing these cases. Remember there is sometimes big money available to spread around.

Anecdote #1.

Gizella was suing an estate for the money she claimed David, the decedent, promised to pay her during his lifetime but never got around to doing it before he died.

Gizella and David were lovers. They met on Cape Cod while vacationing. She was a petite, well-proportioned blonde from Germany near the border of Italian-speaking Switzerland. She knew her sewing, her cooking, the restaurant and construction businesses, and her men.

David was a Jewish widower, portly—the body type loved by German females—and made wealthy by several car dealerships and land holdings.

They did not marry. It was too soon after WWII for a German-Jewish couple to formalize their relationship. The Holocaust was too fresh in societal memories. So they became Trans-Atlantic lovers. He traveled frequently to meet her in the scenic locales in Germany, Switzerland, Italy, and France. She even introduced him to her family on the family farm, which had been, fortunately, distant from the war-fronts and spared the grief of serious wartime tragedies. When she could leave her business, she made it across the pond to Cape Cod, where he bought a duplex condo in which they could enjoy their romantic interludes.

There came a time when because of her businesses, a local Italian lover, and her dying mother needed her attention, Gizella did not come to this country. David continued, however, to pursue her by letters.

Another decade passed and David wrote that she must come to him. She responded, telling him that her construction business had failed due to the economy and that she intended to go into the restaurant business in Texas. A friend of hers had become quite successful there and told her not to pass up the opportunity.

David wrote her still another letter. In it, he attempted to dissuade her from going to Texas. At the very least, he said, she must stop off in Florida on her way to Texas. He must see her.

Her mother having passed on and her local Italian lover not in the picture, she relented and flew to Florida to meet David. She was shocked by how sickly he looked.

He begged her to stay and care for him. She became conflicted. She told him, she, too, was older now and needed to plan financially for her old age. He said he would see to it that she had enough money for her old age. Recalling their allegedly torrid affair, she felt she had to stay.

For five years, she gave him nursing care and provided housekeeper, cooking, personal attendant, shopping, tailoring, and chauffeur services. Because they traveled between his year-round home, his Cape Cod vacation home, and his condo in Florida, she also prepared their residences for his arrival. For instance, she drove his car to and fro Florida while he took a plane there and back. He was suffering from a myriad of illnesses—diabetes, cancer, heart problems, circulation problems— and frequently had inpatient hospital care, but he never wanted to stay long in the hospitals. He would carry on and tell the doctors he had Gizella and she could give him whatever care he required. She gave him his shots and she took of the bandages on his infected legs, applied medication, and rebandaged them. When he lost an extraordinary amount of weight, she took in and professionally tailored his dozens of suits and shirts so that he appeared at all times as grandly attired as he did when he was well.

From time to time, when she asked for her money, he told her he had taken care of it, inferring that he had established the trust for her as promised. His deceased wife's best friend, Stella, had become best of friends with Gizella also. When visiting Gizella and David, the friend was witness to one of these arguments over money. Privately Stella told David that Gizella was golden and that he must take care of her and David responded that he had and would continue to do so. Eventually he asked Gizella which property she wanted. She told him the Cape Cod condo. And one day coming out of the bank, she began crying, and he said, Why are you crying? I just gave you $250,000. That was later revealed to be untrue.

After an emergency which put him once again into a hospital, David died. There was no trust and no money set aside for her.

His younger son, Solly, who lived with them in the year-round home and whose "elevator did not go to the top floor" and who had "a few loose screws," signed the death certificate stating that his father died in Massachusetts. Shortly thereafter, Solly, who related to Gizella as if she were his mother, showed her a second death certificate for his father, David. The new one declared that David had died in Florida. Solly told Gizella that the executor of David's estate, Joe Garb, had requested he amend the original one . . . for tax purposes.

Not being knowledgeable about probate procedures, Gizella waited to be told what to do by the executor. Soon after that, she was referred to me for legal services. I learned that the estate was being probated in Florida, not Massachusetts, and that the time within which creditors must file their claims had expired. I wrote a Complaint and filed it in a superior court in Massachusetts and wrote the pleadings appropriate for the Florida probate proceedings and filed them, too, along with a motion to have them treated as if filed by a Florida attorney.

Fast forward here past a few tears. We won in the Florida court. The estate appealed and lost. We were then able to continue with the Massachusetts case.

Eventually we were in the middle of a trial. Judge Alan van Gestel (now retired) presided. The first thing he told counsel was that he had been on the Civil Procedure Rules committee for four terms. One of the first things I did was move for dismissal of the estate's counterclaims. The executor wanted money from Gizella for the Cape Cod condo. I sought dismissal of the estate's counterclaim to get from Gisella or at least to get credited for the value of the Cape Cod condo. The condo was never part of the estate.

The facts being entirely in our favor, the estate's lawyer, Franklin Levy, agreed to the dismissal of the counterclaim. The reasons for his acquiescence were clear. Instead of putting the condo in Gizella's name, David had put the condo in his and Solly's names as joint owners. And the registered deed showed the condo was never in the estate. By operation of law, when David died, the title to the condo passed solely to Solly. In other words, the condo became solely Solly's, and therefore never was an asset of the estate. And because Gizella had been like a mother to Solly and Solly knew that his dad had told Gizella that the condo was hers and since Solly did not like the trip to the Cape, he had deeded it over to Gizella.

When the executor, whom I intensely distrusted, took the stand to testify, Levy sought his testimony regarding the estimated fair market value of the condo, I objected. It was irrelevant. It had nothing to do with the estate. But van Gestel allowed the executor to answer Levy's questions, including about the value of the condo. The executor was not familiar with the condo and only guessed the value . . . a very high guess. His testimony on the issue of value absolutely should not have been allowed by van Gestel. This was judicial insolence, not only clear harmful error. This from a judge who bragged about his knowledge of the Rules and evidence. Discretion had nothing to do it. Under these circumstances, the judge was not allowed discretion. Because the condo was not given to Gizella by the estate, but by Solly, the estate had no right to be credited with the value of the condo.

An owner who is familiar with his own property may, indeed, testify to the value,\[281]/ but the executor was not the owner and not familiar with the property, so he was, according to the law, not entitled to give his opinion of the estimated fair market value. The estate needed an expert real estate appraiser for such testimony. The judge, van Gestel, wrongly overruled my objection.

I also filed Gizella's Motion for Directed Verdict on the counterclaim seeking the return of a $100,000 bequest (which the heirs had given Gizella in a "compromise of the will"). A "compromise of the will" is an agreement signed by all the heirs to give something to someone who was not in the will. In this case, the heirs and the executor claimed that Gizella agreed that $100,000 was what she was owed to her by the decedent. We had been able to prove that Gizella was not present when the heirs signed the "compromise" and that she knew nothing about the compromise, and had never entered into any agreement with the heirs.

During the critical days, when the executor was testifying, the father of Levy's partner appeared in court. Why is this significant? The father was a recently retired judge, Judge Herbert Abrams, who used to sit in the same trial court. Clearly he knew the judge on the bench, van Gestel. Why was Abrams there? He was not there to see his son, Attorney Abrams, perform. His son was not defending the case, his son's partner, Levy, was. And from Judge Abrams' face, he knew I was curious as to why he was there.

When the jury came back with a question about the condo and the bequest Gizella had received by agreement of the heirs, van Gestel told the jurors they could set off—subtract—the award with the $100,000, which was the bequested gift, and the alleged value of the condominium. Allowing the setoffs was reversible error. An estate may not use property not in the estate as payment for the estate's debts.

Why the 180 degree turn from allowing Gizella's Motion for Directed Verdict to allowing the jury to set off what he had already denied? I have no proof, but I did wonder, Did Abrams make a sidetrip into van Gestel's chamber? Did he have a cash pay off with him when he walked into van Gestel's chamber? I'll never prove it, but I shall never stop believing it.

We appealed. One of our issues was the denial of Gizella's motion for an additur, i.e, for an amount of money to be added to the amount awarded by the jury. Another: Whether the appropriate measure of the amount Gizella needed to support herself for the rest of her life was by computing her annual need until her death by using a life-expectancy table or by a percentage of the net estate, a value set by the promisor. The Appeals Court affirmed the judgment below.

During the time the case was on appeal, the estate's lawyer moved to put the jury award into a non-interest bearing account held by the court. Over my opposition, the court allowed the estate's motion without holding a hearing. My understanding was that the money was delivered to the court and put into an account. When the appellate rescript issued, I sought the money for Gizella.

The court claimed it had no record of it. The money had disappeared!

When Gizella did not believe me that it disappeared, I was disgusted with her nastiness and told her to hire another lawyer to find it, which I believe she did. Whether the other lawyer found the money, I do not know. I do know that I never received a dime for my work over a decade. Gizella had, however, paid the costs, overnight trips to

Florida, depositions, filing fees, etc., a requirement under our contingency contract.

Gizella's case is a good example of the Appeal Court's rubberstamping of the lower court judges and then deciding not to publish the case. The Appeals Court held (1) that the jury's determination that the value of Gizella's services was $210,000 was adequate, (2) that the award of $210,000 was properly offset by $100,000 and (3) that the value of the condominium which Gizella had received was the result of an earlier will compromise. The bequest had been a "gift" and the condo had never been a part of the estate and never part of a compromise. Either stupidity or malice prevailed in the Appeals Court. Your choice at to which it was. The members of the appellate panel were not identified.

The appellate panel wrote further: "The condominium was not actually part of the estate; it passed by survivorship to the decedent's son, [Solly], but nevertheless was included as part of the overall will settlement." The panel then referred the public to see another case regarding a will compromise agreement that included both estate property and non-estate property. The problem here was, of course, that Gizella was not present when a will compromise was discussed or signed; she did not know, in fact, that it had ever taken place until she received a check for $100,000 (before I ever met her).

Gizella's case is an excellent example that the courts can and do, indeed, knowingly misstate the facts and the law to reach a predetermined decision. *See* endnotes 307-308 (for Chapter 16), which describes a federal court judge (Edward Harrington) do the same thing and worse. This is why the abolishment of judicial immunity is mandatory. Only then will the judges have to defend their misconduct in a court of law. Given that Gizella's award should have, had the jury instructions been proper, been around $750,000, the multimillion-dollar estate, too, had plenty of money for spreading around a few gifts.

One good thing did happen, however, Gizella made a "fortune" in the stock market success during the '90s. She had said to me at one point, "I don't care. I don't need the money anymore."

* * *

In passing from Gizella's case to another, I must add: You may not sue on a promise to leave you something in a will.\282/ The cases amply illustrate, a plaintiff may recover the fair value of services furnished on the basis of an oral promise to make a will.\[283]/ A promise to give you money must be a promise to give you money while the decedent was still alive.

* * *

Anecdote #2.

Bébè sued the estate of her former business partner and lover, Alfred, for back pay and her interest in the commercial property they were renovating and the community of residential condominiums they were developing. Each of them took a minimal salary and invested the rest into the partnership's projects. Alfred died before they were ready to take their money out of the business.

His heirs, his sons from his first marriage, contending that money was not due her, vigorously contested Bébè's claims. Their probate lawyers, although well-known in their community for their talent and skills in probate law, were not litigators, i.e., not the lawyers who do trials with witnesses. So to represent the estate in the trial court, they retained a litigator, who had a gentle, professional demeanor but who played hardball . . . softly.

Bébè had considerable documentary evidence to support her claims. The sons asserted that she had forged their father's signature on some of them, so they retained a handwriting expert. I quickly schooled myself in handwriting analysis by reading many books on the subject, including the FBI manual. It was worth it. The cross-examination of the so-called expert could not have gone better.

At trial, the litigator over-defended by calling excessive witnesses. He might have known the facts of the case, but he did not know or understand the personalities of the sons or the dynamics of their relationships. He knew less about the decedent. He did not know that the decedent, Alfred, was actively bisexual. He did not know Alfred's boyfriend, whose notes to a bank Alfred had co-signed without any consideration, that is, for no ostensible reason or benefit. He also did not realize that Alfred had another girlfriend. That meant the litigator did not know the very things he had to know before going to trial. He was, in a nutshell, unprepared for trial. (He had also lied on his application to get favorably rated by Martindale-Hubbell. I assume he knew that Martindale-Hubbell does NOT check the applications for truth. See my website—*http://www.falseallegations.com/hubbell.htm*—for a letter from Martindale confirming that sin.)

The litigator even put the probate lawyer on the stand. Lawyers are known to make bad witnesses. And this one was offensively pompous. The jury laughed throughout his testimony. The probate lawyer thought the jury was laughing with him. They were laughing at him.

When his last witness, one of the sons, described his father's relationship with the woman with whom he was when Bébè was absent on personal family business (she, too, had grown sons). Upon hearing that son's testimony, the jurors let out, literally, a syncopated groan. It took them around two hours to render a verdict in favor of Bébè.

Did the estate pay Bébè? Of course not. The probate lawyer at whom the jurors laughed had been moving around the money held in a limited liability partnership and in a trust or two. They changed the trustees. They changed the ownership of the properties. The tricks they pulled are those tricks which make every lawyer say that collecting the award is often more difficult than winning the trial.

I sought and argued for help from Superior Court Daniel A. Ford at a hearing at which there were seven lawyers opposing me. Ford, an obese man who did more grunting than speaking, was of no help. It took a few years to collect that money, but collect it we did, plus 12 percent annual statutory interest for every year since the date she filed the Complaint. Had Bébè been paid after she won the verdict, she would not have been able to invest the money at such a favorable interest rate. That was her motive for waiting patiently until we collected it. She was, indeed, a professional business woman. She knew that invested at 12 percent annual interest, money will double in six years and that she would become a rich lady.

Daniel Ford was playing cute when he refused to help collect the money. In the end the sons and Alfred's first wife lost a lot of money. Of course, the judge lost nothing. Whether he gained something, we do not know.

Ford was the judge on Bernard Baran's case in the mid-'80s. Baran's case is the earliest conviction in the epidemic of day-care sex abuse cases of the mid-1980's, in which people were accused of "ritual abuse" and grotesque sex offenses against children and adolescents. Like the others, Baran was convicted by juries carried away by emotion and a media feeding frenzy, regardless of the flawed interviews and contradictory, fantastic testimony of children. It was a triumph of junk science in the courtroom.

Baran was a 17-year-old homosexual accused of sexually molesting children at a nursery school. A few years ago, Baran was released when more evidence of his innocence came to light. Given the outrageous amount of unlawful evidence admitted in Baran's case by Ford, a man like Daniel Ford should not be on the bench.

Chapter 15

Criminal Cases, Including Parental Kidnapping, Paternity Fraud

Does the number of imprisoned guilty convicts exceed the number of imprisoned innocent convicts or vice versa?

The most troublesome problem in the criminal area of law is plea-bargaining. Both the guilty and the innocent accept offers by prosecutors to plead guilty in exchange for reductions of sentences for the crimes they are charged with committing.

The consequences of plea-bargaining are both very good and very bad. Good: Court-congestion dwindles. Prison population rotates quickly. The cost of paying appointed private defense counsel lessens. Bad: Prisons are populated by many innocent people, people who should never have been warehoused in them. When released, a prison record hinders their efforts to the workplace. Opportunities of all kinds diminish: to work, to have a profession, to establish families.

All plea bargains are inherently evil. To diminish the volume of criminal cases is an insufficient reason to push pleas. Plea bargains encroach not only on a defendant's right to a fair trial but also might some day encroach on yours. If the defendant is guilty, Justice is not short-changed, but if the defendant is innocent, plea bargains amount to coercion. Justice is supposed to be a search for the Truth. In plea bargains, the truth of a situation is irrelevant, since it is process that is sought, not Truth or Justice, what we have hoped or defined as the American Way. But, today, is it?

If the crime charged is of a sexual nature, the prisoner—whether innocent or not—is likely to suffer being gang-banged. Gang-banging is frequent, but less so, if the crime charged is not sexual in nature. If the innocent prisoner is put on a sex-offender list, his future outside prison is as bleak as that of a guilty prisoner. These are the hidden, undisclosed consequences.

Reassessment of the sex-registry laws is appropriate. They are regressive in that they might cause more of the very kind of crime they are intended to prevent. They can turn both the rightly- and wrongly-convicted sex offenders into outlaws and outcasts . . . for how can anyone called an offender possibly function in a society that compels him to keep on moving, that allows him no secure place to live and no secure job? If truly a sex offender, there is nothing to prevent him from doing again what got him into that position in the first place. If not truly a sex offender, he is apt to be forced into some kind of outlawry.

Another of the most egregious practices is that of the prosecutorial enhancement of the charges brought against defendants. Change enhancement is a perjurious scam universal to all state or county prosecutors. Where district attorneys are elected, they want high conviction rates to brag about during the election season. Therefore their assistants are taught, literally, how to enhance the crimes they bring against a defendant. For instance, if a young boy-man is rowdy outside a saloon, the police are called, they arrive at the scene, and try to arrest the young boy-man, who says, "Don't touch me. What did I do? I haven't done anything." The police arrest him.

He is arraigned in the morning. The prosecutor brings against him not only the charge of Disturbance of the Peace but also Resisting Arrest and Assault and Battery Against an Officer. At this point the young boy-man, who feared being convicted of all three charges, bargains for a lesser sentence, whereupon the prosecutor drops a charge or two. A rowdy kid ends up in prison and learns there what he might not have learned on the street.

Later, out of prison and needing a job he cannot get, he uses some the "stuff" he learned in prison. The unnecessary criminalization of a kid, a boy-man.

In October 1997, an English nanny, Louise Woodward, was put on trial for causing the death of an 8-month-old infant, Matthew "Matty" Eappen, by shaking him. She was sentenced to life for second degree murder, with a minimum of 15 years behind bars.

She had been charged with First Degree and Second Degree Murder and Manslaughter. When it came to objecting to the instructions to be given the jury, Woodward's legal team, made up of a group of four prestigious lawyers, objected to the giving of instructions for all the crimes. The lawyers "apparently believed that the jury would choose to acquit her entirely rather than find her to be a murderer."\[284]/

Relying on her lawyers' advice, Woodward opted for an "all-or-nothing" verdict, meaning the only available choices for the jury would be conviction or acquittal. The rationale: there was insufficient evidence to prove that the child was murdered and that the manslaughter charges would give the jury an easy way out of choosing properly. They wanted Woodward out of jail completely and not in, even for a short time.

The judge then gave the jury instructions for murder in the first and second-degrees but not the jury instructions on the lesser charge of manslaughter. After the conviction for Second Degree Murder, three shocking events occurred: One, the jury was heard to report that they did not want to find her guilty of murder, and that they would have found her guilty of involuntary murder had they had the choice. Two, the defense pled for the murder charge to be reduced to manslaughter, which was not part of the original all-or-nothing strategy. Three, a week later, Judge Hiller Zobel reduced the Au Pair's sentence to involuntary manslaughter and cut the sentence to 279 days, exactly the period of time she already had spent in prison, which meant she was free to go . . . but she was ordered to remain in Massachusetts until the prosecution appealed.

So heightened was the interest, that when the court's email system failed, Zobel's entire Memorandum and Order was published on the Internet.\[285]/

Upon her return to England, Louise Woodward attended law school and joined North Ainley Halliwell in January of 2004.

Watching the trial on CourtTV, I was horrified to see a well-known Whore of the Courts in Massachusetts and beyond, Eli Newberger, a medical doctor in Massachusetts who is M*ephistopheles*, a "liar" and "destroyer of the good,"\[286]/ allegedly imitating Woodward shaking the baby. I was also offended by Prosecutor Gerald Leone's quasi-dramatic performance, particularly in his closing, where he purposely fell to the floor to allegedly imitate the baby.

One trial observer objected to the theory of the "shaken baby syndrome," and in particular to this case. "What is the *clinical* basis for determining whether a baby has been 'shaken to death'?," he pondered, given that there is *no real forensic* evidence that can prove whether a baby has been shaken or not. "The *only* way to build a profile of shaken babies is to perform medical experiments on live babies worthy of Dr. Mengele. You take a pool of babies, shake half of them to death, and kill the other, the unshaken half, and do autopsies and determine the differences. *That* information could then be used to prove in subsequent cases whether a given baby has ever been shaken. But it is unthinkable to do such experiments. So therefore, given this unthinkability, there is *no such thing* as an expert who can testify whether a baby has been shaken to death." The observer continued, "The scientist in me *knows* that anecdotal experience is NO substitute for clinical trials. And NO doctor has anything BUT anecdotal experience in this field." He later added, almost as an afterthought, "Could the baby not have simply died of natural causes?"

Of course, even assuming that the Eappen baby was shaken to death, there was no provable evidence as to who might have done it.

In my opinion Matty's mother, Deborah Eappen, M.D., caused the child's death by badly injuring the child's brain several weeks earlier. It was that injury that Woodward allegedly caused to re-bleed. Also in my opinion, the child's disposition during those three weeks was a giveaway that death was imminent. I do not actually recall the details of why I "convicted" Deborah Eappen, I simply remember having a very firm conclusion. That which was very compelling to my opinion of Matty's parents was the fact that each of the Eappen children had to wear two sets of clothing because the heat in the house was kept at an extremely low temperature. Given that both parents were well-paid medical doctors, they had no excuse whatsoever for improperly heating the home. It was cold that year. I knew that. I lived only a few blocks away on West Newton Hill . . . and home-heating oil was still cheap.

Given the tragic societal belief that medical doctors are gods, Woodward was a young, vulnerable scapegoat. The prosecution's enhanced charge of murder would not be questioned.

Parental Kidnapping

Anecdote:

The family court had not given custody to either parent. The Court, Judge Mary McCauley Manzi, had found that the mother had unlawfully removed the child from Massachusetts to Florida, but had not ordered the mother to return the child to Massachusetts. Sitting in Haverhill District Court, Judge Allen G. Swann reviewed the family court records and confirmed that there had been no child custody order in place when Brian Meuse took the child a year later from Florida by plane to Massachusetts.

At trial, the prosecutor was unable, in fact, to prove where the so-called kidnapping had occurred or when it occurred, and whether what happened was, indeed, a kidnapping.

We proved that Florida had no active custody order, that Florida had dismissed the case the mother had brought in Florida upon her arrival there, that without a Florida custody order, no kidnapping had occurred in Florida, and therefore Florida wanted nothing to do with the criminal case in Massachusetts. We also proved that Meuse was not in Massachusetts on the date he was alleged to have kidnapped the child.

At trial, I put a copy of the statute on an easel in front of the jury and focused on the meaning of each and every word in the statute, for each word in each statute must be given meaning. If the word had no meaning in the context of the proposed statute, the legislature would not have included the word in the statute.

Clearly the Commonwealth could not prove that it had the jurisdiction to try Meuse for parental kidnapping and could not prove the elements of the charge.

The trial took 4½ days and less than 1 hour to find Meuse not guilty. Several months later, the paths of Meuse and one of the jurors crossed. The juror asked Meuse, "Why did the trial go 5 days? We had our minds made up on the second day." Why, because the judge, minutes literally, before the trial was to begin, decided not to allow me to use the "necessity defense." That was critical. So I had to prove circuitously that Meuse had a necessity to take the child from her mother . . . and we did.

Clearly the DA knew that Massachusetts had no jurisdiction and that they could not prove the elements of the charge. Without hearing the facts, Swann could not know that. My theory was quite simple: If there was no custody order in Massachusetts (and the judge had agreed in a decision 10 months *prior* to trial) and the child was not taken from the mother in Massachusetts, then there was no kidnapping and no crime committed in the Commonwealth, which meant that Massachusetts did not have jurisdiction.

Although the trial judge had precluded Dad's photos of the child, by the end of the trial, he changed his mind and allowed me to give them to the jury. I don't think he would have allowed that to happen had he not been convinced that Dad had had, indeed, a necessity to take the child in order to save her from the mother's egregious neglect—which is beyond the scope of this book.

Conclusion: the DAs' conduct across this nation must be scrutinized and restrained by the courts and the DA's judge-made immunity from suit and liability must be abolished. The pain and anxiety caused Meuse and his family and friends during the 5-day trial was caused, of course, not only by the DA's office but also the judge.

False Reporting to the Police

False reporting to the police is a crime in Massachusetts,\[287]/ but the statute is never enforced. This selective enforcement of the law must be changed. Strict adherence and restitution must be effected. Not only do men suffer legal abuse by the non-enforcement of the false-reporting statute, so do women who are truly abused. Unfortunately, the false reports are so numerous that the courts cannot discern which of the voluminous reports are true and needing special attention.

The caselaw clearly states that cross-examination is to be used to expose false testimony, which, in my opinion, is fine, but the problem is that the person who has falsely reported or falsely testified is never put on trial for that behavior and therefore never sanctioned or punished for it. Trials for perjury, a criminal act, are rare.

Paternity Fraud

Paternity fraud must be wiped out by statute. If a woman lies as to who the father of the child is, she should be charged criminally. That criminal statute must be drafted and passed. The consequences of that crime are cruel. A man who believes the child is his, he loves and bonds with the child. When he learns the child is not his, he is not only devastated, he does not want to tell the child of this out of fear that the child will suffer emotionally. Will the child worry that his or her dad will not love him or her anymore, or that dad will move away? If the child is old enough to understand what divorce is and the "parents" begin divorcing, will the child worry that he is the cause of the divorce? Because the man was married to the woman when she conceived or bore the child sired by another man, he will be responsible for child support. Because he loves the child, he will not want to harm the child by fighting a potential child-support order. And the family-court judges make no effort whatsoever to compel the mother to reveal the identity of the putative father or to order the biological father to pay child support to the mother.

So the deceived father suffers, the child *or* children suffer, but never does the deceptive woman or her secret lover suffer. And the courts could not care less. They will throw the deceived dad into jail should he fall behind in his child-support payments. The court has taken the position that if the man has acted as if he were the father, then he must continue to support the child even after divorce or separation . . . so that the child is not hurt emotionally.

Who is kidding whom? The child might need to know his or her biological parent for medical reasons. So the question becomes, when should the child be told the truth of his paternity? Should the time line be fixed or decided on a case-by-case basis?

Does that mean that the child will know some adversity. Yes, it does. But adversity comes with life. No one promises each child a rose garden to live in for life. A little adversity early in life often builds character, and should not necessarily be looked upon as a "bad" thing. In fact, the earlier the child learns the truth, the hurt might be easier to accept. The child will overcome the bad news. And in the long run, knowing the truth will be best.

Justice and fundamental fairness and truth must be the overriding factor here.

To put some fairness into the system, the mother must be compelled to reveal who the biological father is or be punished, and the biofather must be ordered to pay child-support. If there is any dispute regarding who the natural father is, DNA testing must be ordered and the DNA results must be determinative of a man's child-support obligations.

Until now, an independent action to set aside judgment based on fraud has been governed by the extrinsic-intrinsic fraud distinction (discussed in Chapter 11), and only extrinsic fraud has supported setting a judgment aside.

A few courts have ruled that the wife's concealment of the husband's nonpaternity constituted extrinsic fraud.\[288]/ "Courts in Alabama, Arkansas, Oklahoma, South Carolina, Texas, and Vermont have held that a wife's misrepresentation regarding paternity in a dissolution of marriage proceeding constitutes intrinsic fraud, not extrinsic fraud.\[289]/ The distinction is important because of the limitations in the various States for filing a motion for relief from judgment.

An allegation that a witness perjured himself is insufficient to get review of the judgment "because the materiality of the testimony, and opportunity to attack it, was open at the trial."\[290]/ "Where the authenticity of a document relied on as part of a litigant's case is material to adjudication, . . . , and there was opportunity to investigate this matter, fraud in the preparation of the document is not extrinsic but intrinsic and will not support review."\[291]/ The preparation of a particular article in *Hazel-Atlas* was extrinsic because the article was spurious, and, subject to other relevant rules, would support a bill of review.\[292]/

Some courts, however, have declared that "misrepresentation of the child's paternity to the divorce court constituted a fraud upon the court."\[293]/ A party may not sue the other for fraud upon the court. The court must act on that fraud. In Indiana, if a party establishes that an unconscionable plan or scheme was used to improperly influence the court's decision, and that such acts prevented the losing party from fully and fairly presenting his case or defense, then "fraud on the court" exists.\[294]/ The doctrine of fraud on the court, through which judgment may be set aside, is limited to the most egregious of circumstances involving courts.\[295]/ "An action for fraud on the court is not subject to the doctrine of laches and may be raised at any time."\[296]/

In Indiana, the court of appeals held, "medical evidence refuting paternity and mother's admission that she misled court originally as to paternity required that finding of paternity be set aside as matter of justice, and based on extrinsic fraud and fraud on court."\[297]/

In my opinion, the distinction between the three types of fraud denies relief to the party wronged. Fraud can be so elusive that it is all too common and easy for the wronged party not to discover the deception until after the trial. Considerable harm can be caused between the time of trial and the time the fraud (by silence, by perjury, or by documentation) is discovered.

And as I wrote above, both the enhancement of charges and plea-bargaining must be stopped. To use the threat of longer prison sentences if a person does not say he or she is guilty of a crime he or she has not committed is a crime, a violation of one's civil right. There is no rational reason why prosecutors should be allowed to escape the liability that all of us must bear should we violate someone's civil right. For instance, the Massachusetts Civil Rights Act imposes liability on someone who threatens, intimidates, or compels another to do something that would deprive that person of his or her civil rights. Why should prosecutors be allowed to violate that law and be protected by immunity? There is no justifiable excuse for forgiving anyone, regardless of position, of punishment for wrongful acts.

And the judges intentionally and voluntarily go along with, if not encourage, these damnable practices. May those judges be damned and not be protected by immunity.

Chapter 16

Relief from Wrongdoing in Other Actions, Malicious Prosecution
Pro se-ers Suing the World
Opportunity or No Opportunity to Succeed?

Your ex-wife learned that you had a new girlfriend or that you were getting re-married or that you had gotten re-married. Out of jealousy or spite or revenge, your wife falsely reported to the police that you violated a temporary restraining order (TRO). You were arrested. A criminal charge was brought against you. At the arraignment, bail was required. You were strip-searched during the intake at the jail, where you stayed until a friend paid your bail. You were fired when your boss learned you were charged also for assault and battery. The case was dismissed or the jury found you Not Guilty. You had to pay your lawyer $5,000 for defending you.

You began to fall behind on your child support when you lost your job. Your wife filed a Complaint for Contempt for violation of child-support order. You hired a lawyer to represent you in the contempt action in family court. Ignoring your lawyer's common sense argument, i.e., that your expenses had ballooned and you no longer had a job, the court threatened you: *Pay Up or Prison!* You have to get a friend to give you a loan so you can pay your family-law attorney and the arrearages, which were growing weekly.

In the meantime, the TRO was still open. Your wife had told the judge that not only she was in fear of you, so were the children. You had to stay away from all of them and absolutely do not contact them directly or indirectly. Indirectly? That meant, you could not even send your children birthday cards through one of their aunts. You then had to pay the family-law attorney to help you modify or vacate the TRO. This was important. You wanted to restore the relationship you had with the children before you were made into a leper by your wife with the unworthy help of a judge . . . and Joe Biden through VAWA.

To ask the court to remove the children from the TRO required more pleadings (a motion, a memorandum, a reply to your wife's opposition) and another court hearing, and more waiting . . . for a decision.

When will it end? Your expenses for a lawyer and child support will not end. The restraining order, open or vacated, will stay on your record and cast a shadow of a criminal even though you are not one. Potential employers might or might not understand.

How can you get reimbursed?

Federal Civil Rights Act: Section 1983 of Title 42 of the United States Code (42 U.S.C. § 1983)

Suing under section 1983 requires you to prove that the defendant acted under the color of state law in such a way that he, she, or they deprived you of a well-established fundamental constitutional right. When you claim you were deprived of a well-established fundamental constitutional right, you are raising a "federal question."

So . . . depending on the facts of the case, you may sue your wife and the police officers in their individual and professional capacities under the Federal Civil Rights Act for maliciously prosecuting you for a crime you did not commit and for which the police had no probable cause to complain.\[298]/ You may also sue the police department.\[299]/\[300]/

You will not be successful suing the judge who issued the TRO or the assistant district attorney who prosecuted you. They have judge-made immunity. Any case against them will be dismissed after the attorney-general files a motion to dismiss. In Massachusetts, SJC Francis X. Spina dismissed a case against a judge as soon as he saw it; he did not even wait for a motion to dismiss to be filed. (More about immunity will be explained below and in Chapters 18 and 19.)

Go to my website, *http://www.falseallegations.com*, and see samples of section1983 actions. You will have to show that your wife was a "state actor." The cases you may use to make that showing are in the samples.

In Massachusetts, there is a crime for false reporting to the police, but there is no such case in the law books. That does not mean that no one has ever been prosecuted for that crime; it simply means that no one ever appealed being prosecuted for that crime.

If you want a Criminal Complaint to issue against your wife, you will have to fill out an application for the criminal charge to issue and sign it as the "Complainant," which will leave you vulnerable to be sued by your wife. The court clerk will send your wife notice of a scheduled "show cause" hearing. Your wife and her attorney will appear. It is likely the clerk/magistrate will find that you have no probable cause and will not issue the Criminal Complaint against your wife.

If the wife freaks out upon being served with the criminal complaint, she sometimes retaliates by alleging yet another false accusation, so that when the husband appears in court for the scheduled hearing, there is a new warrant for your arrest waiting for you. Instead of getting your hearing, you get arrested. Of course, the hearing never happens. "It happened to me," said a victimized husband.

Because the crime of false reporting falls under a state statute, the federal court will not get involved. If, however, you decide to sue in federal district court, your wife might countersue for abuse of process when you, identified as the Complainant of the Application for Criminal Complaint, sought a criminal charge issue against her. So trying to get a criminal charge against her for false reporting to the police is likely not worth it.

Your boss is not at fault for firing you. That was his prerogative. You can try to sue your wife for causing the firing, but the facts of your case will have to be extraordinary and compelling.

If you prevail on your malicious prosecution case in federal court and you remember to plead in your Complaint that your damages include the $5,000 you paid for your criminal-defense attorney, you will be reimbursed the $5,000.

The contempt for not complying with a child-support order is state business. You can appeal the finding of contempt, but it will be a waste of time, effort, and money. The federal court will not interfere with state business on comity grounds\[301]/ and will neither vacate nor amend a State order regarding marital status or child custody or child support.\[302]/ You will not be reimbursed for your counsel's fees for representing you for the contempt action in family court or for any interest you might have had to pay to your friend for the loan. Nor will you be reimbursed for fees to oppose your wife's motion for you to pay her attorney's fees.

The only possibility for reimbursement of your losses is by winning from the federal jury an award for the false arrest, the strip search, the few days of imprisonment, and the negligent or intentional infliction of emotional distress they caused you.

Of course, the main problem is that the family-court judge repeatedly made rulings that were not gender-neutral and that although you may sue the judge, the judge has immunity from suit, so any suit against him or her will be dismissed.

Immunity is judge-made law. I have been fighting judicial immunity for, at the very least, a decade. You cannot break the glass ceiling of judicial immunity even if the judge acts maliciously or corruptly on the bench. That is actually what the cases read: A judge must retain his independence even if he is malicious or corrupt. The cases are saying, Let judges be malicious and corrupt, just so long as they retain their independence. Let them stay on the bench and be malicious and corrupt again. Insanity, America, insanity. None of us should countenance this judge-made law.

I was, in 2006, disbarred for criticizing judges. The criticism is, according to Professional Conduct Rule 8.4, "prejudicial to the administration of justice." The rule's purported purpose is nothing but a cover for judicial asses.

Anecdote #1.

Other ways in which the courts create their own injustice. For instance, in a malicious criminal prosecution case, Federal Magistrate-Judge Robert B. Collings could have done a number of things (too many and complicated to detail here):

- After the arresting officer *admitted* on the witness stand

    o   that the signature on the Criminal Complaint was not his but a forgery,

    o   that the Application for Complaint he filled out was not the one used to obtain the Criminal Complaint against my client,

    o   that the Application for Complaint used to obtain the Criminal Complaint against my client was a totally fraudulent document filed in the BMC by City of Boston Attorney Eve Piemonte Stacey on behalf of the City of Boston and its police department;\[303]/ (details are in the endnote),

- Collings did not sanction Attorney Eve Piemonte Stacey who knew that she produced fraudulent documents in response to my discovery requests for the documents filed in the BMC, assuming, of course, that she, the City attorney, was producing a legitimate Application for Complaint and a legitimate Criminal Complaint. There were other issues, too, but too many to describe here;

- Collings did not compel the police department to produce the other subpoenaed officers, whose home addresses they kept secret and who could have produced oral and/ or documentary evidence proving who replaced one Application for Criminal Complaint for the original, written by the arresting order, who changed the criminal charges brought against my client, and who forged the arresting officer's signature on the Criminal Complaint;

- Collings improperly bifurcated the case-in-chief, thereby keeping from the jury that part of the case which would have supplied the motive for both the officers to lie and their City attorney to produce fraudulent evidence;

- although federal caselaw allows judges to put a time limit on testimony in advance of trial, Collings abused his discretion by not extending that time limit for examining the two defendant-officers once the documents were admitted by one officer to be fraudulent and once it was shown they were lying on the stand about the other physical evidence;

- Collings denied my client's motion for a directed verdict. In so doing, he approved of prosecuting a man for crimes brought forward on an Application for Complaint that was not the one filled out by the arresting officer and, according to the testimony of the arresting officer, a forged Criminal Complaint.

Anecdote #2.

Another malicious prosecution case presents similarly bizarre facts. U.S. District Court Justice Edward Harrington refused to take jurisdiction over the state pendent claims and sent those claims to the state superior court to resolve the action, including potentially a trial. (State "pendent" claims are those claims brought under state law, not under federal law, and have not been disposed of by the time you bring a federal case.)

As soon as FOX Television Stations, Inc., and National Center for Missing and Exploited Children found themselves in state court, they again filed to dismiss the case on the grounds that the "fair report privilege" applied to the case. They had lost their motions in federal court on that ground and lost their motions again in state court. They then filed an interlocutory appeal of the denial of their dismissal motion. They lost again. FOX and NCMEC next petitioned the SJC for relief from the Appeal Court's denial of relief from the Superior Court's denial of their motions to dismiss the three claims pending in the lower court: defamation, conspiracy, and emotional distress.

I never got around to uploading Meuse's winning appellate briefs to my website because of my ongoing war about my license.

Then I was disbarred and ordered off the case in Essex Superior Court to which Judge Harrington sent the state causes of action against FOX, AMW, NCMEC, opposing counsel. Meuse had to get a new attorney but did not find one. Both Meuse and I got screwed. I could have retired with some cash—finally—and Meuse did not get a remedy for that which he had suffered.

Judge Harrington had also wrongly applied the Westfall Act, which allows the U.S. Attorney-General, without any knowledge, to write a certification that the FBI agents were working within the scope of their employment. That document gets the FBI off the hook.

Are we surprised? People betrayed by the U.S. Congress.

Harrington was again in the news recently for helping rogue FBI agents: "Federal judge praises Connolly role."\[304]/ Called as the first defense witness for Connolly at the murder trial, Harrington credited Connolly with playing a star role in the dismantling of the New England Mafia in the 1980s. You decide:

The background: "Connolly, who retired from the FBI in 1990 after 22 years, was convicted of racketeering for protecting James 'Whitey' Bulger and Stephen 'The Rifleman' Flemmi I from prosecution and warning them to flee before their 1995 indictment on racketeering charges."\[305]/ Connolly, who is currently serving a 10-year prison term and accused of plotting with longtime informants Bulger and Flemmi, is now standing trial in Florida for the 1982 gangland killing of a Boston businessman. "Bulger, still wanted for 19 murders, is one of the FBI's 10 Most Wanted."\[306]/

"After testifying as a defense witness in Connolly's federal case in Boston, Harrington wrote a letter to the sentencing judge on federal court stationery, urging leniency. He later withdrew the letter, acknowledged it was a violation of the code of conduct for judges, and apologized."\[307]/

As a result of my little knowledge. I formed a conviction that Harrington should have recused himself from the Meuse case, given that two FBI agents from the same Boston FBI office were defendants in the case. I have a similar firm conviction that his bias for FBI agents, of course, was the very reason the case was assigned to him. Another case in which the assignment to Harrington made the news also fed into my conclusion. See the endnote for details.\[308]/

Ah, politics. What would our lives be worth without politics being played in the courtroom? Clearly, justice is not to be found in our constitution but in whom we know!

A bit of the background of the case: Meuse took his child from the mother in Florida. There had been no order of custody prior to his taking the child. In his absence, a state criminal complaint issued with the charge of Parental Kidnapping on it. Critical here is that Meuse was not a fugitive from justice under federal law. A dubious State *misdemeanor* arrest warrant had issued from a state district court, but a warrant under 18 U.S.C. §1073 for the Unlawful Flight to Avoid Prosecution ["UFAP"] requires a State *felony* warrant before a UFAP warrant may legally issue. Further, the alleged UFAP warrant was UNsigned by the magistrate-judge whose name had been typed on the warrant form as being the "Issuing Officer," or by any other judicial officer. The alleged federal warrant included the false statement that

Meuse had been charged with "Unlawful Flight to Avoid Prosecution" in violation of 18 U.S.C. §1073, but there was **no** State felony warrant, which was required before a UFAP warrant could legally issue. So the alleged federal warrant was invalid and void.

Thus, where the warrant was controvertible and Meuse was not a fugitive under federal law, when FBI agent Charles S. Prouty was interviewed on a FOX TV show and several WANTED posters were published nationwide, Prouty not only did not take the requisite extreme care to avoid statements branding Meuse as guilty of a crime of which he had not been convicted,\[309]/ the oral statements on television and the several WANTED posters were breaches of the specific limitations imposed by federal law.\[310]/\[311]/

I argued the Westfall Act was not applicable. Substitution of the United States for the FBI defendants was inappropriate. And the district court did have jurisdiction over the case at least until the scope of the FBI agents' employment was determined.

Where Meuse asserted that Agents Prouty and Kelly acted outside the scope of their employment despite the U.S. Attorney's certification to the contrary, the burden of proof was on Meuse.\[312]/ But Meuse had to be given the opportunity to meet his burden. And he was not.

Judge Harrington acted immediately on Assistant United States Attorney Michael Sullivan's certification, substituted the United States for the FBI agents, and dismissed Meuse's case against the agents. Doing so denied Meuse an opportunity to get relief from the consequences of the FBI agents' tortious and unlawful acts. "[W]hen a federal official commits an unconstitutional act, he is necessarily acting outside his official capacity."\[313]/

Harrington also cheated Meuse out of relief by declaring that Meuse's claims against the FBI agents were *Bivens* claims.\[314]/ *Bivens claims are claims under federal, not state, law, and used that finding as a reason to dismiss Meuse's §1983 claims against the agents. It was then, after I challenged the characterization of those claims as being Bivens* claims, that AUSA Sullivan wrote his dishonest certification based on provable fabricated facts.

In sum, without a felony warrant from Massachusetts, the FBI had no authority to seek a federal UFAP warrant, so they faked it. Rogue Special Agent Charles P. Kelly signed an affidavit that there was a state felony warrant. There never was one—so testified the Haverhill police detective at Meuse's Parental Kidnapping trial. In addition to Kelly's false affidavit, which was produced by one of the several counsel for the defendant Rupert Murdoch's companies, were two more documents: one purported to be the Criminal Complaint entitled *USA v. Meuse* and the other purported to be the federal warrant to arrest Meuse . . . but the federal warrant was UNsigned and the Criminal Complaint appears to have many discrepancies. (*See* Drano Series #116 on my website. The link to it is in note 13 in the margin of Drano #116.)

STF/AMW and FOX TV, on behalf of themselves, tried to prove a federal case was filed against Meuse in U.S. District Court at Boston during October 2000, but it was not; they tried to prove the FBI had filed in support of that complaint an affidavit in November 2000, but the FBI had not filed an affidavit in support of the complaint against Meuse in November 2000; they tried to prove a federal warrant to arrest Meuse had issued in November 2000, but it had not issued.

Left in U.S. District Court were the mother of the child Meuse sired and the police Detective Lieutenant, the Captain, and the city police department. Relying on the misapplication of law and outright lies, the FBI agents got off the hook. All the other defendants, including the mother's lawyer, became defendants in the state court.

When I was disbarred in Massachusetts and the SJC sent notice to the federal court, Judge Harrington stayed the remainder of the case. It remained stayed until the First Circuit Court of Appeals issued a decision on my appeal.

The First Circuit did not find in my favor. Judges Juan R. Torruella, (of Puerto Rice), Kermit Lipez (of Maine), and Jeffrey R. Howard showed themselves to be political whores of the judiciary, like many others of their brotherhood, ignoring that there were no witnesses against me, no opportunity to cross-examine alleged adversaries, or to present a defense, and nothing resembling a trial.

Because the likelihood of being granted cert by SCOTUS is minimal, I have not bothered to exercise my right to petition SCOTUS. Instead I have decided not to waste more of my valuable lifetime. I have now fully tested justice in both the state and federal courts. Clearly, justice has lost and corrupt politics has won.

Anecdote #3.

The problems burdening people who represent themselves are of a different nature. Generally their cases do not stay open long enough to amass incremental injustices. They are very often dismissed immediately for some procedural error. I saw such a Complaint recently. The plaintiff had not served the Complaint properly on some of the defendants. The court extended the time for him to perfect the service. The guy seemed not to understand what it was that he had done wrong. If he had read the federal rules on service, he should have been able to figure it out. That is one of the few sets of rules that is spelled out in some detail. Then the plaintiff had to amend the Complaint two times.

After he received a few motions to dismiss, he failed both to oppose them in a timely fashion and to ask for an extension of time to oppose them. His failures likely were the result of his not knowing how to oppose them. Then, of course, the court dismissed his case. The judge likely had no choice. But you can be sure that the man was remarking to his friends how corrupt the judge was . . . even though the man had nothing to support his negative opinion of the judge!

Other Problems *Pro se*-ers Have

Another problem *pro se* filers have: They sue the world. Unfortunately, the plaintiffs do not think ahead. Why? More than likely because they do not know what is supposed to happen after they file their Complaint. Well, the defendants must file a "responsive" pleading. As I explained in the Introduction, both a Motion to Dismiss and an Answer are responsive pleadings. Motions to Dismiss are generally filed first. So when the plaintiff sues five people and/or unnatural entities, that plaintiff will likely receive five motions to dismiss. That means the plaintiff must oppose up to five motions to dismiss. It might take a *pro se* plaintiff two weeks to draft an opposition to a Motion to Dismiss. If the plaintiff is lucky, a few of the defendants might double up on one Motion to Dismiss.

Unfortunately I've received Complaints that have two dozen defendants. The plaintiffs of those Complaints—should they survive the round of motions to dismiss—will have to plan on sitting before their computers for many, many months without a breather.

Some *pro se* plaintiffs are bright, have the skills to write a sentence, know punctuation, and learn quickly how to research the law. After surviving the round of dismissal motions, they must learn what is involved in the discovery process.

The discovery stage is where those incremental inequities by judges begin. At this point, the primary goal of many judges is to get rid of as many of their assigned cases as quickly as possible. Incompetent judges are simply incompetent. The primary goal of unfair judges is to deny you access to the documents and people you need to complete your discovery.

At the summary judgment stage, the War of the Facts begins. Very few *pro se* plaintiffs get this far.

The Attorney-General's Office Will Not Help You

The Massachusetts Attorney-General's office needs to be split into two distinct offices. There is an inherent conflict of interest in his powers. Compare this description with that in your State. My suggestions might have significance for you, too.

On one hand, the AG is the attorney for the PEOPLE.

On the other, he must sue on behalf of the Commonwealth and defend it against you.

In consumer protection, for example, he acts for the folks from time to time, but he and his predecessors have done almost nothing in the area of civil rights.

For instance, when John Doe sues the Commonwealth for violations of civil rights by the State and its agencies, departments, etc., the AG defends the state entities against John Doe.

Given the publicity, the AG knows or should know that many married or unmarried men should not be paying child support under the guidelines because the guidelines contemplate (1) that the couple have a traditional custody and visitation arrangement and (2) that the parents are to be sharing equally in the support of the child(ren).

Where has the AG been on this issue?

Nowhere . . . because he is more interested in defending the Commonwealth: it is, after all the political and powerful side of the conflict. He has chosen to let the people be damned.

I want to see two offices with two different AGs at the helm. It is a must!!! People need help.

Chapter 17

Federal Abstention Doctrines and the Domestic Relations "Exception" to the *Rooker-Feldman* Doctrine

A heavily legal chapter only for the highly motivated reader

> "The Privilege of the Writ of Habeas Corpus shall not be suspended, unless when in Cases of Rebellion or Invasion the public Safety may require it." Art. I, § 9, cl. 2. The word "privilege" was used, perhaps, to avoid mentioning some rights to the exclusion of others. . . . [T]]he only mention of the term "right" in the Constitution, as ratified, is in its clause giving Congress the power to protect the rights of authors and inventors. See Art. I, § 8, cl. 8.)
>
> — *Boumediene v. Bush*, 128 S.Ct. 2229 (2008).

After three acrimonious years in family court, Harry and Hilda were finally divorced. All things important to him—child custody, if not shared custody, and property—went to Hilda.

Moustaffa, a Nigerian, owned a nightclub on property down South that his neighbor, a white church, wanted for expansion. His neighbor made false allegations about him and Moustaffa was jailed—eventually for taxes— and the neighbor got the property.

Tim had had a tax problem and ran into FBI agents in the middle of it. Under the Westfall Act, the FBI got out of the case.\315/ The FBI should not have gotten immunity from suit and liability.

And all of them——Harry, Moustaffa, and Tim——were as mad as hell.

To top it off, Harry's attorney charged him $125,000 and the court ordered Harry not only to pay his ex-wife's attorney's fees but also to pay extraordinarily high weekly child support. The guardian *ad litem* wanted $19,000 for her services. Because the GAL was court-appointed, if he did not pay her, he would be found in contempt and be immediately emprisoned. This is not speculation. While incarcerated, his child-support arrearages would continue to accrue. This is not speculation. And he would lose his start-up company: he was its only employee. This is not speculation.

Harry heard about "section 1983," the Federal Civil Rights Act, and decided to sue in federal court, but he could not only afford another attorney, he could also not find one who took federal civil rights cases. So he decided to represent himself. He would file a Complaint on his own, *pro se*. He thought he had learned about how the law works during those three horrible, anxiety-producing years in family court.

Moustaffa would still be incarcerated when the statute of limitations would run, i.e., when the time within which he would have to bring his suit would have passed. There are a few cases which hold that incarceration will stay the statute for the time a plaintiff is in jail.

Tim had enough problems with the IRS, he was afraid and broke. The last thing he needed was another lawsuit.

Harry's law case was dismissed. He could not overcome the many technical obstacles, obstacles he never heard of in family court. He concluded there was no justice.

Comity

Comity arises out of both this country being a union of separate state governments and the belief that the national government will fare best if the States and their institutions are left free to perform their separate functions in their separate ways. Perhaps for the lack of a better and clearer way to describe it, this is referred to as 'Our Federalism.'. . ." \[316]/\[317]/\[318]/

Comity is a self-imposed rule of judicial restraint whereby the federal courts act to avoid collisions of authority. It is not a rule of law but "one of practice, convenience, and expediency"\[319]/ which persuades but does not command.

Recent decisions emphasize comity as the primary reason for restraint in federal court actions tending to interfere with state courts,[320] for example, the U.S. Supreme Court has cited comity as a reason to restrict access to federal habeas corpus[321] and to limit interference with State tax systems.[322]

Abstention

If and when States have so-called "important"' interests in pending civil proceedings between private parties[323] and the litigants can assert their federal rights in the state court, comity requires "abstention," meaning that the federal district court must abstain from taking jurisdiction of the case. By so doing, the federal courts are allegedly showing "proper respect for the ability of state courts to resolve federal questions presented in state court litigation."[324]

Other strands of the doctrine are that a federal court should refrain from exercising jurisdiction in order to avoid needless conflict with the administration by a State of its own affairs. [325] Also, while pendency of an action in state court will not ordinarily cause a federal court to abstain, there are "exceptional" circumstances in which it should.[326]

For example, the federal court has jurisdiction both where the relevant state law is settled[327] and where it is clear that the challenged state statute or action is unconstitutional no matter how the state court construes the state law.[328]

In fact, federal jurisdiction is not ousted by abstention; rather it is postponed.[329]

Tensions between the federal and state courts would be ameliorated if the federal courts believed that state courts would adequately protect the constitutional liberties and that the federal courts would not be thwarted by state programs. Were the tensions ameliorated, federal courts would benefit because time and effort would not be expended in deciding difficult constitutional issues which might not require decision.[330]

During the 1960s, the abstention doctrine was in disfavor with the Supreme Court, suffering rejection in numerous cases, most of them civil rights and civil liberties cases.[331] Time-consuming delays[332] and piecemeal resolution of important questions[333] were cited as a too-costly consequence of the doctrine. Both consequences may be alleviated substantially if the States adopted procedures that would make it easier for federal courts to ask the State's highest court to decide unsettled state law which would dispose of the federal court action. The Supreme Court has actively encouraged resort to certification where it exists."\[334]/

Actions brought under the civil rights statutes seem not to have been wholly subject to the doctrine,\[335]/ and for awhile, cases involving First Amendment expression guarantees seemed to be sheltered as well, but this is no longer the rule.\[336]/ Abstention developed robustly with *Younger v. Harris*,\[337]/ and its progeny. "There is room to argue whether the *Younger* line of cases represents the abstention doctrine at all, but the Court continues to refer to it in those terms."\[338]/

The most common abstentions doctrines are *Younger, Rooker-Feldman, Burford, Pullman*,\[339]/ and not quite an abstention doctrine, but a mutant doctrine, to wit, the "second prong" of the Eleventh Amendment.

Caveat

> *This is a difficult chapter because the subject matter—the various exclusion doctrines—defy simple, common-sense explanations of what they are and what they do and why they do it. Skip a section if you feel overwhelmed or become disinterested. Some of the sections you will likely find interesting, so be sure to skim, at te very least, the chapter so you will not miss the "good" parts.*

Exhaustion of State Remedies

A complainant will ordinarily be required, as a matter of comity, to exhaust all his state legislative and administrative remedies before seeking relief in federal court where such remedies are, of course, available.\[340]/ To do so may make unnecessary federal-court adjudication. The complainant will ordinarily not be required, however, to exhaust his state judicial remedies—to appeal to your State's highest court—inasmuch as it is a litigant's choice to proceed in either state or federal courts when the alternatives exist and a question for judicial adjudication is present.\[341]/ *But when a litigant is suing for protec-*

tion of federally-guaranteed civil rights, he need not exhaust any kind of state remedy.\342/

That guarantee bloomed when the Fourteenth Amendment, one of the post-Civil War Reconstruction Amendments, was ratified in 1868. It is the source of the Supreme Court's power to decide whether a defendant in a state proceeding received a fair trial, that is, whether he was deprived of life, liberty, or property without due process of law.\343/

Unfortunately, the Fourteenth Amendment has been treated as an orphan of the law. To help the orphan, the Federal Civil Rights Act\344/ came into being.

A question of whether a constitutional violation occurred is a pure question of federal law. Yet, in a bar discipline case,\345/ the U.S. Supreme Court said that a disciplinary action is quasi-criminal in nature, but declined to hear such a case from Massachusetts Supreme Judicial Court. In fact, the Massachusetts high court proclaims bar discipline cases to be administrative in nature—despite the fact that in Massachusetts, bar cases are not even administrative in nature, they are what is called *sui generis*, which means, "We shall do whatever we want to do." The essential differences between a case judicial in nature and one administrative in nature is that due process and the rules of evidence are followed in the former and not in the latter.

The Supreme Court so proclaims, that the resolution of whether a constitutional violation occurred is a pure question of federal law and should be applied uniformly throughout the Nation, but the Court has left some wiggle room to back out of that statement. It wrote that availability or nonavailability of remedies is a mixed question of state and federal law.\346/

In practice, they take the political view and do not hear bar disciplinary cases that are political in nature. For example, in the case against me, there were neither witnesses against me nor any proceeding resembling a trial, all my trial witness subpoenas were quashed, and the audience to what was to be a public trial was commanded out of the hearing room in the middle of my Opening Statement.

Principles of federalism protect the prerogative of States to extend greater rights under their own laws than are available under federal law. But do the federalist principles allow the States to shrink under their own law the people's rights under the federal law?

We know, clearly, that the States do shrink our constitutional rights under the States' laws, but do the federalist principles allow the States to do it?

The Court posed the question, Is the availability of protection under the Federal Constitution—specifically, under the Confrontation Clause of the Sixth Amendment? Yes, it inferred. Since it "is no intrusion on the prerogatives of the States to recognize that it is for this Court to decide such a question of federal law, and that our decision is binding on the States under the Supremacy Clause."\³⁴⁷/

The *Younger* Doctrine

The test of the applicability of the *Younger* doctrine in criminal contexts has changed ever so slightly from case to case over the quarter-century since the *Younger* opinion was published.\³⁴⁸/

There are three factors in the "test" to determine when the Younger doctrine applies:\³⁴⁹/

(1) the state criminal proceedings are judicial in nature;
(2) the proceedings implicate important state interests;
(3) they provide an adequate opportunity to raise federal constitutional challenges.\³⁵⁰/

You will have to discuss each of these items when opposing a defendant's motion seeking the application of the Younger doctrine.

CAVEAT: Very Dirty (Dishonest) Trick by Opposing Assistant Attorney-General: It Could Happen to You

In my case against the Board of Bar Overseers and a few other defendants, the defense counsel, Assistant Attorney-General John Hitt, altered the statement allegedly being quoted from the *Middlesex* case.\³⁵¹/ The true statement allegedly quoted is "*It is clear beyond doubt that the New Jersey Supreme Court considers its bar disciplinary proceedings as 'judicial in nature.'*"\³⁵²/   Assistant AG Hitts' falsified quotation is "*It is clear beyond doubt that [Massachusetts Supreme Judicial] Court considers its bar disciplinary proceedings as 'judicial in nature.'*"\³⁵³/

I wrestled with AAG Hitt's false assertion—with which the District Court and the First Circuit panel concurred—that *Middlesex*\[354]/ was relevant to my case. Hitt and the courts concluded that *Middlesex* expanded the reach of the *Younger* doctrine to attorney-disciplinary hearings. To reach that conclusion, all three entities fraudulently insisted that such hearings were judicial in the Massachusetts.

I conceded that recent cases rely on *Middlesex* to expand the reach of the *Younger* doctrine, but contended that Massachusetts has held fast to the notion that its bar disciplinary proceedings are administrative in nature, not judicial. Why? The reason is starkly clear: Because were the proceedings "judicial in nature," the Massachusetts SJC would have to change how the BBO is doing business. The SJC **(1)** could not allow the BBO to continue to operate as a quasi-administrative body under the Administrative Practice Act and **(2)** would have to acknowledge that there are well-settled rules of evidence and procedure, rules that the BBO and the Massachusetts SJC now blithely ignore in attorney-discipline cases.\[355]/

Those rules are the safeguards of which the Court\[356]/ spoke when deciding to extend judicial immunity to hearing officers performing adjudicatory functions in federal administrative agencies: "[F]ederal administrative law requires that agency adjudication contain many of the same safeguards as are available in the judicial process."\[357]/ Not one of those safeguards exists in the Massachusetts disciplinary proceedings.

Therefore, AAG Hitt's false quotation had a significant purpose: he had to lie in order to give support to the weak and false, but politically correct, finding that Judge Young was expected to make as a member of the Black Robe Club. The lie was but to create a smokescreen. And Judge Young got the political message.

Examples of Some Problems You Can Encounter: Avoid Them!

- Bettencourt was a physician seeking reinstatement of his medical license. His petition for review by the Massachusetts SJC was pending and provided him with an adequate opportunity to raise federal constitutional claims, so *Younger* applied.

Problem.   "[Bettencourt] waited until **after** the Board had rendered its decision, and after his review petition to the SJC had been filed, before he brought this federal action. The district court [was] not being asked to defer to future or contemporaneous unconstitutional conduct. [Bettencourt's] case [was] for the alleged past denial of due process and equal protection, a claim which the SJC, having jurisdiction, is equally competent to entertain."\[358]/

In sum, Bettencourt waited too long. The state court had already had taken the matter under consideration·

- Gibson appears to have been an optometrist. Beyond his name being in the caption, his name does not appear elsewhere in the case. The case was essentially between groups of optometrists. Judicial bias was recognized as a basis for derailing the *Younger* abstention.\[359]/

   Problem.   Gibson "sue[d] **before** the Board's hearings occurred. The district court then would have evaluated plaintiff's allegations of bias on the part of the board members."\[360]/

- In *Middlesex*, the executive director of the National Conference of Black Lawyers,\[361]/ Hinds, constitutionally challenged the proceedings.\[362]/

   Problem.   Hinds was defeated by the *Younger* abstention doctrine in federal District Court.

"the Third Circuit reversed on the ground that the state bar disciplinary proceedings did not provide a meaningful opportunity to adjudicate constitutional claims."\[363]/ The reason: disciplinary proceedings are "administrative, 'non-adjudicative' proceedings"\[364]/; they are "analogous to the preindictment stage of a criminal proceeding."\[365]/ The proceedings in *Middlesex* were "unlike the state judicial proceedings to which the federal courts usually defer."\[366]/

While the petition for rehearing brought by Hinds' opponent was pending at the Third Circuit Court of Appeals, the court learned that the New Jersey Supreme Court would directly consider Hinds' constitutional challenges and consider whether they would change the (N.J.) Supreme Court rules. Notwithstanding the new rule providing for interlocutory review, "the Third Circuit declined to alter its original decision."\367/

The United States Supreme Court, however, disagreed with the Third Circuit. Applying *Younger*, USSC (more commonly known as SCOTUS) reversed on the grounds that Hinds now had available an avenue in state court for an interlocutory appeal in which he could raise his constitutional challenge to the proceedings.

- Brooks was the lover of his attorney, who bore his child. When the attorney sought to dismiss Brooks' paternity suit, he complained to the Professional Conduct Committee. He filed in both state and federal courts. The First Circuit said he did not have enough proof of judicial bias to satisfy the third factor of the test to overcome *Younger*.

(a) Like Gibson, I sued before the Board's hearings occurred; **(b)** unlike Hinds, I tried five or six different ways to exercise my constitutional rights at the BBO and in the Massachusetts SJC, **(c)** unlike Hinds, I have not been fortunate to have a new avenue of interlocutory appeal made available to me, **(d)** unlike Brooks, my allegations of judicial impartiality are anchored to specific facts, and **(e)** like Gibson, I am facing not only a "Board that might have 'preconceived opinions' with regard to [my case] before them," but also a judiciary that has a possible pecuniary interest should judicial immunity be abolished.

In exceptional circumstances, *Younger* does not apply. For example, the *Younger* doctrine does not apply "in cases of proven harassment or prosecutions undertaken by state officials in bad faith without hope of obtaining a valid conviction and perhaps in other extraordinary circumstances where irreparable injury can be shown."\368/

In unusual circumstances, a plaintiff may secure relief in the federal courts—even though doing so would interfere with ongoing state-initiated proceedings—by demonstrating "bad faith, harassment, or any other unusual circumstance that would call for equitable relief."\[369]/ . . . The Supreme found one of these "unusual circumstances,"\[370]/ permitting federal-court interference, to have occurred when a state administrative board was so constituted as to be fundamentally biased.\[371]/

Bettencourt had not contended that any unusual circumstance was present, so the court found, "Having failed to raise the issue,\[372]/ [Bettencourt] has waived it."\[373]/ Unlike Bettencourt, I raised all my issues. And unlike Bettencourt, in my Complaint\[374]/ I was not "asking the district court to interfere with proceedings in progress before a state judicial tribunal as to which claims of irregularity by the Board do not apply."\[375]/ *Bettencourt* was thus inapposite to my federal case.

The defendants failed to refer to *Gibson*, where Gibson (unlike Bettencourt) pled and the District Court found the administrative process to be "so defective and inadequate as to deprive the plaintiffs of due process of law" that neither the *Younger* nor the exhaustion doctrine forbade a federal injunction.\[376]/ There, in *Gibson*, the Court noted,

"Such a possibility of bias was found to arise in the present case from a number of factors. First, was the fact that the Board, which acts as both prosecutor and judge in delicensing proceedings, had previously brought suit against the plaintiffs on virtually identical charges in the state courts. This the District Court took to indicate that members of the Board might have 'preconceived opinions' with regard to the cases pending before them."\[377]/

It was in this context that the Court found that "neither statute nor case law precluded [the District Court]" from adjudicating the issues before it and from issuing the injunction if its decision on the merits was correct.\[378]/

The First Circuit Court opinion in *Brooks v. New Hampshire Supreme Court*\[379]/ was as original as anticipated when Justice Selya is the author. He reiterated an element seen in several other cases and one element not seen or required elsewhere: **(1)** the need to seek recusal of "allegedly biased judges"\[380]/ and **(2)** the need to make startling allegations of general institutional bias, for instance, to plead evidence of "a potential conflict of interest . . . or a pecuniary stake in the outcome of the litigation."\[381]/\[382]/

Nevertheless, my evidence came close if not sufficient to jump the almost insurmountable hurdles placed on the track by the court in *Brooks*:

One.

Unlike Brooks, I did "employ available procedures for recusal of allegedly biased judges"\[383]/:

a. First I moved for a jury trial,\[384]/
b. I moved to preclude Defendant Chair Carpenter from sitting on any committee or deciding any motion in the actions,\[385]/
c. I moved to recuse Defendant Special Hearing Officer ["SHO"] Phillips,\[386]/
d. I moved to remove the Assistant Bar Counsel as prosecutor.\[387]/ I requested that the Full Board (not the Chair alone) issue subpoenas requiring attendance and testimony at trial,\[388]/ and
e. I moved for a conference with the 12-member Board.\[389]/

Brooks' failure to employ such procedures as seeking recusal was fatal, according to Judge Selya: "For this reason alone, his claim must fail," Justice Selya said about Brooks,\[390]/ citing for that proposition *Middlesex*,\[391]/\[392]/\[393]/\[394]/\[395]/

Two.

"To implicate due process, claims of general institutional bias must be harnessed to a further showing."\[396]/ My further showing was my crusade for court reform and the abolition of judicial and quasi-judicial immunity.\[397]/ In fact, approximately a third of the OBC's trial exhibits consisted of pleadings uploaded to my website, *falseallega-tions.com*, where I not only exercise my First Amendment rights to free speech and political expression but also fulfill my obligation to make public the unscrupulousness of certain courts.\398/

Three.

And unlike Brooks, I included, in the Complaint addendum, doc-umentary evidence of almost each and every allegation of deficient procedures and bias and the predisposition and follow-through of the BBO and the Chair not to uphold their own policies and rules.\399/

In sharp contrast with the demands the court made on Brooks, the court made light of Brooks' Complaint that the New Hampshire Supreme Court "agree[d] to entertain his petition, but only *in cam-era*"\400/ and "that the NHSC [was going to] only hear oral argument on his petition behind closed doors."\401/ Brooks' Complaint, accord-ing to the Appeals Court, was but a "frenzied brandishing of a card-board sword"\402/ and the "Justices' interest (if any) in maintaining the privacy of attorney disciplinary proceedings appears to be purely Platonic."\403/\404/

.In contrast, although—being somewhat of a crusader for full dis-closure, exposure, and accountability—I found Brooks' plight some-what sympathetic, I pled specific, concrete facts—of which there is documentary evidence—as to why a closed trial would be spooky:

- At a prehearing conference on 17 November 2003, Phillips told the stenographer repeatedly that the proceeding was "off the record" when I spoke;\405/

- on 2 December 2003, two of my witnesses appeared and Phillips asked whether they were there because of my subpoenas, and when they said, Yes, Phillips excused them and told them the subpoenas were invalid and they could leave;\406/

- during my Opening Statement, the Assistant Bar Counsel falsely claimed that a pre-existing protective order of 10 September 2003 precluded me from mentioning names of witnesses, including a complainant;\[407]/ there was no such order;

- Phillips then ordered the public audience from the hearing room on the first day of the scheduled trial.\[408]/

This behavior was not perceived by me as being "Platonic," as the court in *Brooks* claimed the Justices' behavior was.\[409]/ Without a complete and accurate stenographic record, without witnesses, without the public in attendance, I was vulnerable to being scathed by whatever falsity the defendants chose to fabricate . . . as had been done in the Bar Counsel's Petition for Discipline.

Bad Faith

Defendants also sought dismissal on the grounds that I failed to plead bad faith sufficiently. They cited *Bettencourt*\[410]/ for that proposition, and *Judge*,\[411]/ for the proposition that I had to plead my claims of bad faith or illegal motive with more specific and nonconclusory facts from which such a motive may reasonably be inferred, not merely by generalized asseveration alone."\[412]/

I disagreed. In my Complaint\[413]/ were not only the paragraphs that show bad faith and illegal motive on the part of the defendants. I pled as follows:

- I referred to my political motivation ("a motion to enjoin my political and free speech");\[414]/

- I impliedly referred to the defendants' bad faith in petitioning against me.\[415]/ In those subparagraphs, I wrote that the defendants "failed to state the authority giving the Bar the right to censor my website and stifle my political speech and free expression, failed to state the scope of the website censorship sought, failed to state how the censorship was to be implemented, failed to state the authority giving the Bar permission to override my First Amendment rights";

- I referred again to the defendants' desire to stifle "my views on the need for judicial accountability and the need for court reform [which] are well-known to the courts";\[416]/

- I commented that I "believe[d] the award was to smite my crusade to abolish judicial immunity";\[417]/

- I pleaded, "The motive of Carpenter and likely persons unidentified was to preclude me from showing that the lower-court orders were not only 'bad,' they were based on fabricated facts and findings and on, literally, a materially altered document";\[418]/

- I wrote, "The merits of the underlying case of Count I constituted my defense that public scrutiny is necessary to guard against unscrupulous judicial proceedings and that it was because of unscrupulous judicial proceedings …"; \[419]/

- I wrote, "The BBO and the Bar Counsel disagree with me that I have a right to pierce immunities not made into law by our legislatures.\[420]/ The BBO and the Bar Counsel disagreed with me that article V of the Mass. Declaration of Rights makes all magistrates and officers of all three branches of government accountable to all the people, including me, at all times."

In determining whether the state disciplinary action was commenced in bad faith or was intended to harass me, the court must look at three factors:

> (1) whether it was frivolous or undertaken with no reasonably objective hope of success; (2) whether it was motivated by defendant's suspect class or in retaliation for the defendant's exercise of constitutional rights; and (3) whether it was conducted in such a way as to constitute harassment and an abuse of prosecutorial discretion, typically through the unjustified and oppressive use of multiple prosecutions.\[421]/

Element 1.

Certainly the OBC's case was going to be successful. Given the taint of the administrative process employed by the OBC and the BBO, "flagrantly and patently violative of express constitutional prohibitions,"\[422]/ the OBC was guaranteed success. The OBC and BBO are figuratively Siamese twins. They share the same executive officers (the SJC). The SJC appoints, approves, and/or hires the directors, staff members, counsel (both Bar Counsel and the General Counsel and the assortment of assistants to both the Bar and General Counsel). The OBC and BBO share office space, internal staircase, receptionist, telephone, and restroom keys. They give each other instructions, and as prosecutor and adjudicators, they indulge in *ex parte* communication at will.

Element 2.

During my gubernatorial campaign, I ran on a platform advocating court reform, particularly of the family-law courts, and judicial accountability, to be accomplished by abolishing judicial immunity and the derivative quasi-judicial immunity. The OBC/BBO and the judiciary are unhappy with my activism.

Element 3.

The entire OBC process went on for years against me. There is no other way to describe it except as being intense and harassing and threatening.

In so doing, I have been caused irreparable injury.\[423]/ I shall be defending myself to both the public and the "legal" community for years henceforth.

Lastly, the "exhaustion of remedies question." That question requires that the claims are the same in both the state and federal courts. Here, they were not.\[424]/ Because **(1)** the claims in my federal case alleged deprivation of federal constitutional rights and state procedures that were contrary to federal law and thus invalid under the supremacy clause and **(2)** there was no pending state case involving the claims presented in the federal case, neither the exhaustion of state judicial remedies nor the *Younger* doctrine in that context applied.\[425]/

Therefore, because the federal claims raised in the instant action could not be either raised at the BBO or resolved in the ordinary route of appeal in the Commonwealth of the BBO disciplinary proceeding, *Younger* was not implicated in the case.

As Justice Douglas wrote, dissenting, in *Younger*:

> The eternal temptation, of course, has been to arrest the speaker rather than to correct the conditions about which he complains. I see no reason why these [speakers] should be made to walk the treacherous ground of these statutes. They, like other citizens, need the umbrella of the First Amendment as they study, analyze, discuss, and debate the troubles of these days. When criminal prosecutions can be leveled against them because they express unpopular views, the society of the dialogue is in danger.\[426]/

I found myself walking the treacherous ground under the penumbra of the OBC/BBO's power to prosecute and judge me in my capacity as an attorney who believes she, like ordinary citizens, is protected by the First Amendment and entitled to express views unpopular with the judiciary or those in power in the judicial system. Calling for both court reform—— in particular, but not only, the family-law courts—— and the abolition of judicial and quasi-judicial immunity, not only as a citizen and but also an attorney, I found myself falsely accused of unethical conduct.

Rather than "study, analyze, discuss, and debate" the problems identified by me, and acknowledge that I had a professional obligation to alert those in positions of power, the OBC/BBO has instead asserted that my website files offend the professional rules of conduct.

Where, with the approval of the BBO, the OBC subsequently leveled a disciplinary prosecution against me because I expressed views unpopular with both the state and federal judiciary, the society of the dialogue is in danger.

Rooker-Feldman

Under the *Rooker-Feldman* doctrine, lower federal courts are precluded from exercising appellate jurisdiction over final state-court judgments.\[427]/

The *Rooker-Feldman* doctrine, the court explained, includes three requirements: **(1)** "the party against whom the doctrine is invoked must have actually been a party to the prior state-court judgment or have been in privity with such a party"; **(2)** "the claim raised in the federal suit must have been actually raised or inextricably intertwined with the state-court judgment"; and (3) "the federal claim must not be parallel to the state-court claim."\428/

"The *Rooker-Feldman* doctrine takes its name from the only two cases in which we have applied this rule to find that a federal district court lacked jurisdiction. In *Rooker*, a party who had lost in the Indiana Supreme Court and failed to obtain review in [the U.S. Supreme Court] filed an action in federal district court challenging the constitutionality of the state-court judgment. We viewed the action as tantamount to an appeal of the Indiana Supreme Court decision, over which only this Court had jurisdiction, and said that the 'aggrieved litigant cannot be permitted to do indirectly what he no longer can do directly,'"\429/ meaning that he cannot take the indirect route of seeking relief in the federal district from the denial of his appeal in the state court.

"*Feldman*, decided 60 years later, concerned slightly different circumstances, with similar results. The plaintiffs there had been refused admission to the District of Columbia bar by the District of Columbia Court of Appeals, and sought review of these decisions in federal district court. Our decision held that to the extent plaintiffs challenged the Court of Appeals decisions themselves—as opposed to the bar admission rules promulgated nonjudicially by the Court of Appeals—their sole avenue of review was with this Court."\430/

Over time, the *Rooker-Feldman* doctrine has been narrowed both by Congress and be common law. Having been so complicated, it is beyond the scope of this book. For those interested, see Endnote\431/, where I have placed excerpts that you should read if you are in the middle of a court fight involving the *Rooker-Feldman* doctrine.

Anecdote #1.

Lucas Stockdale brought a federal district court against four judges for acting outside the scope of their authority and for intentionally violating his constitutional rights,\432/ Specifically, Stockdale complained-of **(a)** the unconstitutionality of the guardian *ad litem* statute,\433/ **(b)** the appointment of a guardian *ad litem* ["GAL"], **(c)** Trial Court

Memo #14, authored by Defendant Retired Judge John J. Irwin, Jr., instructing sitting justices to violate the GAL statute by shifting the burden of paying the GAL's fees from the Commonwealth to the parties, (d) the continuing violation of the GAL statute by Judge Nancy M. Gould, who, before ordering the parties to share the cost of the GAL's fees, neither assessed the parties' ability to pay the GAL's fees—as instructed to do by Trial Court's Memo #14—nor complied with the statute, (e) the violation of the child-removal statute,\[434]/ by allowing the removal of the Stockdale children to another State without Stockdale's consent or a showing of just cause, (f) the violation of the Massachusetts Child Custody Jurisdiction Act ["MCCJA"],\[435]/ by allowing the removal of the Stockdale children to another State prior to depriving Stockdale of his constitutional and statutory rights to an opportunity to cross-examine the GAL, Barbara O'Brien Beardslee, who recommended the removal *ultra vires* (that recommendation was not part on the reference of appointment, namely, the court order on which the tasks being authorized are listed) and to rebut any materials adverse to him which Beardslee might have had, and (g) the failures of Judge Sean M. Dunphy to train Judge Gould, to enhance her performance as a sitting justice, to protect and prevent injury to the Plaintiff, and to take corrective action.

Stockdale had told GAL Beardslee that he feared his wife taking the children out of state because if it were true what her family had let him to believe, that his father-in-law was a pedophile, his children's wellness would be jeopardized. At 5 years of age, they were vulnerable. His fears, he learned later, were valid. Later, rather than at the time, because Gould refused to correct the dangerous situation. In fact, Gould had repeatedly declined to hear my client's motions regarding the children. (Stockdale had fired his first lawyer and then came to me to try to reverse the injustices that had occurred in family court.)

After I had taken all avenues possible in family court——filing a motion to recuse Gould from the case and interlocutory appeals——I decided to bring the Federal Civil Rights case. The case was dismissed on immunity grounds but around five days after the federal Complaint was served on her, I learned that Gould was off the case. Whether she recused herself or was administratively removed from the *Stockdale* case is still unknown. Judge Lisa A. Roberts, mentioned elsewhere in this book, became a substitute for Gould on the divorce case.

During August 2008, at 66 years of age, Gould quietly retired from the bench. Constitutionally judges were appointed for life, but because of dementia and Alzheimer's, the constitution was amended to make 70 the age at which all Massachusetts judges must retire. Whether her retirement was voluntary or involuntary has also not been made public.

In the federal suit, the opponents filed a motion to dismiss the Complaint. Lucas Stockdale argued that the *Rooker-Feldman* doctrine did not apply because Stockdale was not seeking reversal of decisions rendered by Judge Nancy Mary Gould or the voiding of her holdings in the Stockdales' divorce action.\436/ But he was both facially challenging a state statute and seeking money damages from Judge Gould. Because the federal district court did not need to decide any issue either actually litigated in the Massachusetts court or "inextricably intertwined" with issues so litigated in the state probate court, there was no jurisdictional bar.\437/

Stockdale also filed under the Federal Civil Rights Act (section 1983) for an injunction that governs the judges' future conduct and for money damages against the individual officers who had acted outside their jurisdiction and unconstitutionally. Where he was not challenging the merits and not seeking the review of the merits of the underlying divorce action, the *Rooker-Feldman* doctrine did not apply.\438/

The defendants conceded that Stockdale brought the action challenging the constitutionality and the defendants' administration of a Massachusetts statute governing the appointment of guardians *ad litem* in probate court actions, "particularly as that statute has been applied in a divorce action currently pending in Massachusetts Probate & Family Court."

Judge Gould unlawfully and knowingly acted contrary to the requirements of mandatory statutes.\439/ Absent authorization to do what she did, she acted without jurisdiction. When someone, including judges, does not stick to their job definition, that someone is acting *ultra vires.* . . . a reason for denying Gould protection from immunity and entitling Stockdale to sue for relief. In such cases, relief can be granted without impleading the Commonwealth when the judge lacks delegated power\440/ . . . another reason that must keep a judge from being protected by the judge-made judicial immunity.

Because Judge Gould violated the law and that conduct is forbidden, she was not shielded by immunity\441/ and her claim to judicial immunity for engaging in unauthorized and forbidden conduct should have been denied.\[442]/\[443]/\[444]/ Judge John Irwin, another of the defendants, also violated a mandatory statute. He, too, should have been stripped of any claim to judicial immunity.

That the divorce action was still pending is of no relevance. The marital status of the Stockdales was not material to the claims in the suit. The custody of the children was not material to the claims of the suit. The damage to the children had already been caused by Judge Gould's intentional violation of the existing laws. The eventual distribution of personal and real property was not material to the claims of the suit. And the claim for a declaration as to the constitutionality of the first two sentences of the GAL statute was not subject to the *Rooker-Feldman* doctrine.

If Stockdale complained of the eventual decision on child custody or child or spousal support or property distribution after the divorce trial, he would have filed an appropriate and timely appeal in the Appeals Court of Massachusetts. Those issues were not included in the federal case.

The primary issue at bar was the facial challenge to the constitutionally of the GAL statute. The secondary issues were part of "a species of tort liability" created by section 1983 "in favor of persons who are deprived of rights secured by Federal law."\[445]/

Defendants baldly asserted that Stockdale sought to have the federal district court review and reverse Judge Gould's decisions, but, significantly, the defendants failed to identify which decision Stockdale asked to be reversed. They failed to do so because there was none.

Defendants also complained that the causes of action against Judge Gould were for violations of state law. As stated, this action is a species of tort liability under sec. 1983 for the deprivation of Stockdale's rights secured by federal law. Monetary damages for a tort would not be available in the divorce action in the Massachusetts Probate & Family Court, a court of limited jurisdiction which does not include jurisdiction over tort cases.

The First Circuit Court of Appeals panel of three, without a hearing and without an opinion, wrote, "The judgment of the district court is affirmed essentially for the reasons stated in its Order." And the U.S. Supreme Court denied *certiorari*.

Anecdote #2.

In the appeal of my case against the Board of Bar Overseers of Massachusetts, M. Ellen Carpenter, Esq. (Chair of the Board of Bar Overseers), Herbert P. Phillips, Esq. (Special Hearing Officer), Office of Bar Counsel, Daniel Crane, Esq. (Bar Counsel), and the Commonwealth of Massachusetts. I challenged the validity – i.e., the constitutionality – of the BBO Rules and proved that my reliance on *Feldman*\[446]/ was not misplaced, contrary to lower-court Judge William Young's assertion.

To prove that his reasoning was specious required discussion of **(a)** the inconsistency of the Judge Young's conclusions that the nature of a bar-disciplinary hearing in the Commonwealth was judicial, which it absolutely is not and there are many Massachusetts cases that support my opinion, **(b)** the relief I sought, and **(c)** the Judge Young's misinterpretation of two cases\[447]/ as to when *Rooker-Feldman* is applicable and when it is not.

The First Circuit Court of Appeals did not discuss this issue in its judgment containing four paragraphs of a few lines each. The judgment, while not boilerplate, was an abortion.

Given that disciplinary charges were brought against me two months after the November 2002 election, in which I ran for governor on a platform of court reform, the need for judicial accountability and the abolishment of judicial and quasi-judicial immunity, the decisions in each of the courts were politically motivated.

The Tricks That the Court Played

To **_not_** apply *Feldman,* the district court had to find that a Massachusetts disciplinary proceeding is administrative in nature. To apply the legal proposition in *Feldman,* which **would** inure to my benefit, the federal district-court judge had to find that a Massachusetts disciplinary proceeding is judicial in nature. So he did! Be damned the truth.

Judge Young's change of the nature of Massachusetts disciplinary proceedings from "judicial" in nature to "administrative" in nature precluded the application of *Feldman* and gave him cover for his result-oriented specious conclusion.

I had argued that the *Feldman* case permitted me to attack the validity of the BBO rules in the district court because my challenge was **not** to a decision or judgment out of the Bar disciplinary proceeding, for there had been at that time no decision or judgment, and was therefore **not** barred by *Rooker-Feldman.*[448]/

The judge in a memorandum wrote,

> "The Court carefully distinguished between 'general challenges to state bar rules, promulgated by state courts in nonjudicial proceedings'—for which there is jurisdiction in the lower federal courts—and 'challenges to state-court decisions in particular cases arising out of judicial proceedings,'—for which there is not." *Schneider*, 917 F.2d at 628 (quoting *Feldman*, 460 U.S. at 486).

Then the court stated, "Were Johnson not engaged in *state administrative proceedings* involving the same rules as those cited in her complaint, *Feldman might well permit* her to challenge the constitutionality of those rules in federal court." Therein lies not only District Court Judge Young's error, but also proof of his maliciousness and corruption.

Domestic Relations "Exception" to the *Rooker-Feldman* Doctrine

Anecdote #3.

Plaintiff BT was divorced from his wife in Maine, and she was not a defendant in this case. Through this lawsuit, he sought neither a divorce, custody, nor a change in child support. He sought only remedies, including but not limited to money damages, for his claims sounding in civil rights and torts. Plaintiff LJ has never been married, but has one son born out of wedlock. The mother of his son was not a defendant in this case. Through this lawsuit, he sought neither a divorce, custody, nor a change in child support. He, too, sought only remedies, including but not limited to money damages, for his claims sounding in civil rights and torts.

The jurisdiction of the district courts extends to "all civil actions" between diverse parties involving the requisite amount in controversy.\[449]/ Neither the *Younger* nor the *Burford* abstention from exercising diversity jurisdiction was appropriate.\[450]/

The *Younger* abstention was inappropriate on the facts before the court in *Ankenbrandt* because there was neither any pending state proceeding\451/ nor any assertion of important state interests.\452/ The *Burford* abstention was inappropriate where the status of the domestic relationship had been determined as a matter of state law, and the status of the relationship had no bearing on the underlying torts alleged.\453/

"[T]o the best of my knowledge, a court is not at liberty to craft exceptions to statutes that are not at issue in a case."\454/

> Whether or not the domestic relations "exception" is properly grounded in principles of abstention or principles of jurisdiction, I do not believe this case falls within the exception. This case only peripherally involves the subject of "domestic relations." "Domestic relations" actions are loosely classifiable into four categories. The first, or "core," category involves declarations of status, e.g., marriage, annulment, divorce, custody, and paternity. The second, or "semicore," category involves declarations of rights or obligations arising from status (or former status), e.g., alimony, child support, and division of property. The third category consists of secondary suits to enforce declarations of status, rights, or obligations. The final, catchall category covers the suits not directly involving status or obligations arising from status but that nonetheless generally relate to domestic relations matters, e.g., tort suits between family or former family members for sexual abuse, battering, or intentional infliction of emotional distress. None of this Court's prior cases that consider the domestic relations "exception" involves the type of periphery domestic relations claim at issue here.\455/

> "In general, lawsuits affecting domestic relations, however substantially, are not within the exception unless the claim at issue is one to obtain, alter or end a divorce, alimony or child custody decree,"\456/ where the counts for breach of fiduciary duty and for negligence and waste were not foreclosed by the domestic relations exception.\457/ "This narrow construction led the

Court in *Ankenbrandt* to hold that the exception did not apply to tort claims there at issue despite their intimate connection to family affairs."\[458]/ Both counts were central to the defendant's "alleged misfeasance or wrongful nonfeasance in allowing Dunn's private insurance policy to lapse."\[459]/

Where "petitioner's claims [ ] involve a federal question or statute—the presence of which would strongly counsel against abstention—petitioner's state-law tort claims for money damages are easily cognizable in a federal court. All these considerations favor the exercise of federal jurisdiction over petitioner's claims."\[460]/ Justices Stevens and Thomas concurred in the judgment.\[461]/

Federal district court also has subject-matter jurisdiction over claims seeking relief from family-court orders which emanated under procedures that allegedly violated due process, equal protection, and other federal statutes such as the sec. 1983 civil rights statute.\[462]/ Where the *Agg* case had been brought under sec. 1983 and alleged deprivation of federal constitutional rights and state procedures that were contrary to federal law and thus invalid under the supremacy clause, the domestic relations exception doctrine, which concerned federal jurisdiction based on diversity, did not apply.\[463]/

In *Rubin v. Smith,*\[464]/ too, the motion court held that the domestic relations exception did not apply to a sec. 1983 civil rights suit. There a mother and daughter had alleged that the police had violated their constitutional rights by seizing the daughter pursuant to a Connecticut child custody decree without notice and hearing. Even though the claims arose out of a custody dispute, the suit was not a diversity case: it had raised constitutional questions and sought damages for deprivation of their constitutional interests without due process of law. Adjudication of the child's custody was not sought.

Many other cases involving the "domestic relations exception" may be found at endnote 465.\[465]/

Burford

The *Burford* abstention\[466]/ is appropriate where the status of the domestic relationship has not been determined as a matter of state law, and the status of the relationship has a bearing on the underlying torts alleged.\[467]/ The *Burford* abstention is also appropriate where the plaintiff has not asked the District Court to issue a divorce, alimony, or child custody decree.\[468]/

Conflicts of Jurisdiction: Federal Court Interference with State Courts—Habeas Corpus: Scope of the Writ

The Eleventh Amendment bars only suits against a State by citizens of other States, but in 1890, the Court\[469]/ barred suits against a State by citizens of its State. This judge-made law became known as Eleventh Amendment immunity, and having had the same effect as an abstention doctrine, it has done humungous harm to countless people across this nation by dismissing their petitions for relief from the federal courts, and must vanish from our body of law. Because no United States Congress ever enacted the law, the law cannot be repealed. Why? There is no Act to repeal.

In 1908, a seminal case\[470]/ in American constitutional law created a "fiction" by which the validity of state statutes and other actions could be challenged by suits against state officers as individuals.\[471]/ (A "fiction" is a fact that is not real but is made real by a court calling it a "fiction." In this case, the fact was already real but the court did not want to admit it.)

The 1890 prong—the second prong of the Eleventh Amendment—is a "fiction," like Casper the Ghost; it was never and still is not part of the Eleventh Amendment. The Court and all the other courts are simply pretending the Eleventh Amendment does not allow you to sue your own State. The Eleventh Amendment does not say that at all. The courts are lying to you because they know you are willing to take whatever they say as true. Sorry, a few hundred thousand of you, maybe even many millions of you, have been snookered!

The various rules of restraint flowing from "comity" considerably reduce federal interference, but there still remains inevitable conflict between federal and state courts when the federal courts are open to persons complaining about unconstitutional or unlawful state action, particularly when your suit could be brought in a state court as well as in a federal district court . . . and perhaps so brought by other persons. It is in three areas that institutional conflict is most pronounced.

Federal Restraint of State Courts by Injunctions

To enjoin proceedings in state court, the party must overcome several barriers, among them the abstention doctrine\[472]/ and an equity doctrine requiring that an injunction be withheld "in any case where plain, adequate and complete remedy may be had at law."\[473]/ The latter principle explains the reluctance of federal courts to interfere with a State's good faith enforcement of its criminal law.

To overcome the reluctance, the High Court has required a litigant seeking to stop a threatened state prosecution not only to show irreparable injury which is both great and immediate but an inability to defend his constitutional right in the state proceeding. The cost, anxiety, and inconvenience of having to defend against a single criminal prosecution, are generally insufficient to be considered irreparable ... even if the state criminal statute is unconstitutional ... *provided* that the person charged under it may seek a remedy by raising his constitutional defense in the state trial.\[474]/ If circumstances make it impossible for a defendant to protect his federal constitutional rights during the state criminal proceedings, a federal court injunction may properly issue.\[475]/

After 1965, the law changed frequently\[476]/ from fewer to more cases in which the Court held the allegations and offers of proof may have been sufficient to establish that the "irreparable injury'" justified federal injunctive relief.\[477]/ Until 1971, the allowance of requests for injunctive and declaratory relief increased. Gradually, the expansion spread out from First Amendment areas to other constitutionally-protected activities.\[478]/

In 1971, however, these developments were highly controversial and after three arguments on the issue, the Court in a series of cases receded from its position and circumscribed the discretion of the lower federal courts to a considerable and ever-broadening degree.\[479]/ The important difference between the old and new series of cases was that in the latter for particular reasons there were no prosecutions pending whereas in the former there were. Nevertheless, the care with which Justice Black for the majority undertook to distinguish and limit the old series signified a limitation of its doctrine, which proved partially true in later cases.

Moreover, in a companion case, the Court held that when prosecutions are pending in state court, ordinarily the propriety of injunctive and declaratory relief should be judged by the same standards.\[480]/

A declaratory judgment is as likely to interfere with state proceedings as an injunction, regardless of whether the federal decision is treated as *res judicata* or whether it is viewed as a strong precedent guiding the state court. Additionally, "the Declaratory Judgment Act provides that after a declaratory judgment is issued, the district court may enforce it by granting 'further necessary or proper relief' and therefore a declaratory judgment issued while state proceedings are pending might serve as the basis for a subsequent injunction against those proceedings to 'protect or effectuate' the declaratory judgment,\[481]/ , and thus result in a clearly improper interference with the state proceedings."\[482]/

And, in fact, when no state prosecution is pending, a federal plaintiff need not demonstrate the existence of the *Younger* factors to justify the issuance of a preliminary or permanent injunction against prosecution under a disputed state statute.\[483]/

Of much greater significance is the extension of *Younger* to civil proceedings in state courts\[484]/ and to state administrative proceedings of a judicial nature.

Chapter 18

Immunity and the Pseudo Eleventh Amendment
Formulas for the Courts' A-bombs

All power residing originally in the people, and being derived from them, the several magistrates and officers of government, vested with authority, whether legislative, executive, or judicial, are their substitutes and agents, and are at all times accountable to them.

— Constitution of the Commonwealth of Massachusetts, Part the First, art. V, ratified on 16 June 1780

"'The history of liberty is the history of due process.'"\[485]/ Due process is at the core of our American system of justice. It requires basic fairness in any procedure that can lead to punishment.\[486]/

Instead our system of justice is reminiscent in many, many ways of the Star Chamber, the most reviled court in English history.

The Star Chamber was established after an act in 1341.\[487]/\[488]/ The Chamber was the "ancient meeting place of the king of England's councilors in the palace of Westminster in London, so called because of stars painted on the ceiling."\[489]/ Over time, the composition and jurisdiction of the court became uncertain, but "[i]n practice its jurisdiction was almost unlimited."\[490]/ Certainly its jurisdiction had superseded that of the ordinary courts of law in cases where the ordinary courts were too weak to act.\[491]/

After the act of 1487, "the Star Chamber became the great engine of the royal tyranny"\[492]/ and within 25 years, under the leadership of

Wolsey and Cranmer,\[493]\ /\[494]\ / it not only performed the very necessary and valuable work in punishing powerful offenders who could not be reached by the ordinary courts of law,\[495]\ / it also became a political weapon for bringing actions against opponents to suppress opposition to the royal policies of Henry VIII.

Originally open to the public, the Court of Star Chamber sessions came both to be held in secret and to represent the misuse and abuse of power by the king and his circle. "Its procedure was not according to the common law."\[496]\ / There were no witnesses (it could proceed on rumor alone), no juries, no right of appeal, and punishment was swift, flexible, and severe to any enemy of the crown. "It could apply torture; it could inflict any penalty but death."\[497]\ /

Between 1628 and 1640, the Court of Star Chamber became a substitute for Parliament and in the 1630s banned all "news books." Charles I made extensive use of the Court of Star Chamber to persecute dissenters, including Puritans who fled to New England. Star Chamber proceedings were used to gain not only arbitrary convictions, but also arbitrary acquittals for guilty parties whom the crown wished to protect. The abuses of the Star Chamber by Charles I were one of the rallying cries for those who eventually executed him in 1649.

In sum, because it "characteristically departed from common-law traditions . . . and . . . specialized in trying 'political' offenses, the Star Chamber has for centuries symbolized the disregard of basic individual rights."\[498]\ /

A little more than a century after the Star Chamber was abolished in 1641 and more than fourteen years before the first 10 amendments to the U.S. Constitution were ratified by Massachusetts, the founders of Massachusetts accepted at the Constitutional Convention the Declaration of Rights as written by John Adams. Article V of the Massachusetts Declaration of Rights tells us that the three branches of government must at all times be *accountable* to the people.

Never has Massachusetts' Article V been repealed. Never has the impact of the Eleventh Amendment of the United States Constitution on Article V been considered and determined by a Massachusetts court. Never has the word "accountable" as used in Article V been interpreted by a Massachusetts court. Not even in an impressive account of the history of sovereign immunity set out by the Massachusetts Supreme Judicial Court\[499]\ / was Article V cited.

The article suggests that if an entity is held accountable for some wrongdoing, that entity must make restitution or compensate the victim or provide some equitable relief for the wrong—the fundamental right to a remedy being clearly established in Article XI, Mass. Declaration of Rights.

In 1793, a man from outside Georgia sued the State of Georgia\[500]/ and won. The decision "created such a shock of surprise that the Eleventh Amendment was at once proposed and adopted."\[501]/ Reading, "*The Judicial power of the United States shall not be construed to extend to any suit in law or equity, commenced or prosecuted against one of the United States by Citizens of another State, or by Citizens or Subjects of any Foreign State,*" the Eleventh Amendment was ratified in 1798 by the legislatures of three-fourths of the States. And simply, it means that a citizen of one State may not sue another State.

In 1871, judicial immunity was added to the mix by the justices of the U.S. Supreme Court,\[502]/ which relied upon a case from England.\[503]/\[504]/ In one fell swoop, even though we had thrown off the yoke of tyranny more than 100 years earlier, the U.S. justices wrote "*that judges of courts of record of superior or general jurisdiction are not liable to civil actions for their judicial acts, even when such acts are in excess of their jurisdiction, and are alleged to have been done maliciously or corruptly. . . .*"\[505]/ The Court then gave its excuse: "*This provision of the law is not for the protection or benefit of a malicious or corrupt judge, but for the benefit of the public, whose interest it is that the judges should be at liberty to exercise their functions with independence, and without fear of consequences.*"\[506]/ This means that in order for judges to maintain their independence, they must remain immune from suit by the people even when the judges have acted maliciously and corruptly. The reasoning of the Supreme Court was and remains unconscionable. It was allowing malicious and corrupt judges to remain seated on the bench to protect their independence. What? To allow them the independence to be malicious and corrupt again? Insanity!

The practical effect of giving immunity—judicial, quasi-judicial, and qualified immunity—has been to wipe out accountability. With no allegedly legal requirement of accountability, gross negligence, incompetence, bad faith, ulterior motives, and the like, have been allowed to blossom and proliferate in abundance. The public has thereby suffered the loss of their constitutional right to seek a remedy, to seek recourse to the laws, for wrongs committed against them.

During the century-plus since 1871, the guarantee of accountability in Article V of the Massachusetts Declaration of Rights has become only a ghost in the shadow of the multitude of state and federal cases holding that accountability is to be frowned upon. Enronization of the judicial system thus stands on an infirm foundation.\[507]/\[508]/ It stands only on the judges saying absolute judicial immunity is the law. But it is not! Article 6 of the United States Constitution—containing what is known as the "supremacy clause," meaning federal law about a certain issue trumps the state law on that issue\[509]/—cannot defeat Article V of the Declaration of Rights of the Constitution of the Commonwealth of Massachusetts.

But what about the other States, which do not have the equivalent of Article V in their constitutions? Well, Article 6 of the U.S. Constitution does not apply to them either. Why? Because the U.S. Congress had nothing to do with the creation of judicial immunity, and Article 6 may not be invoked unless Congress intended to create the law. And when the Supreme Court created judicial immunity in 1871, Congress was not at the party at the bench. It had not even been invited.

Where judicially-created law does not fall within the penumbra of Article 6 of the U.S. Constitution, the judicially-derived judicial immunity may not reign supreme over the command of accountability in Article V of the Declaration of Rights.\[510]/

In April 2004, I filed in the U.S. Supreme Court a Petition for Writ of Certiorari to test the High Court's waters involving the issue of the longevity of judicial appointments in both the federal and Massachusetts constitutions. The petition can be seen on my website at *http://www.falseallegations.com/drano120-supreme-court-judicial-immunity-gould-42304.htm*. The questions presented to the Court in that petition are presented here for your convenience. They arose out of a case in which I had sued four state judges in federal district court in Boston.

1. Whether the judicially-created doctrine that declares judges absolutely immune from suit may bar claims against judges by a person exercising his First Amendment right to petition the Government for a redress of grievances.

2. Whether a judge's intentional and knowing contravention of existing mandatory, nondiscretionary, statutes violates the "good behavior" clause of the United States constitution and thereby makes the protection of judicial immunity unavailable.

3. Whether a judge's intentional and knowing contravention of existing mandatory, nondiscretionary, statutes constitutes "bad behavior," making the award of judicial immunity unavailable.

4. Whether a judicially-created amendment, the unratified, second prong of the Eleventh Amendment to the federal constitution, may bar money-damage claims against the Petitioner's State's judges under 42 U.S.C. §1983, the state and federal constitutions, and common law.

The Pseudo Eleventh Amendment

In 1890, the U.S. Supreme Court created what I call the "second prong" of the Eleventh Amendment.\511/ You'll never find that expression in the law books. Why? The judiciary does not want you to know that the law they always call the Eleventh Amendment when they dismiss your case is *not* the Eleventh Amendment ratified by Congress but judge-made law. The words "Eleventh Amendment" are only a smokescreen created by the judiciary to hide what the United States Supreme Court did. They do not want the public to know that the Court did not honor the constitutional mandate that the three branches of government shall remain separate to guarantee that we have a system with checks and balances, a system requiring "the separation of powers."

That second prong said not only shall citizens of one State not be allowed to sue another State, citizens shall not be allowed to sue their own State unless their own State says, Okay. The original and still current Eleventh Amendment reads, as I wrote above: "*The Judicial power of the United States shall not be construed to extend to any suit in law or equity, commenced or prosecuted against one of the United States by Citizens of another State, or by Citizens or Subjects of any Foreign State.*"

Over the years, courts have expanded the meaning and power of the real Eleventh Amendment. Now, although the United States Congress never amended or repealed the Eleventh Amendment, courts across the nation have ruled (1) that the Eleventh Amendment bars suits against nonconsenting States by their own citizens, but it doesn't(!), (2) that each State has immunity from being compelled to appear in the courts of another sovereign against their will, but it doesn't(!), and (3) that the Eleventh Amendment bars suit by private parties seeking to impose liability which must be paid from public funds in state treasury, but it doesn't!

And the courts have ruled (4) that the Eleventh Amendment restricts judicial power under Article 3 of Constitution,\512/ but it doesn't(!), (5) that Article 1 cannot be used to circumvent constitutional limits placed upon federal jurisdiction by Eleventh Amendment,\513/ but it doesn't(!), (6) that it made each State into a sovereign entity in the federal system, and (7) that each "sovereign" State may not be amenable to the suit of an individual without the State's consent.

In a nutshell, the judges have gone on and on and on making law barring the people's rights to get a remedy or relief from the wrongs done them by a State or any part of them.\514/ Simply put, the Supreme Court's sovereign-immunity decisions put protecting state governments ahead of safeguarding people's rights. . . . Sovereign immunity undermines the basic principle, "The very essence of civil liberty certainly consists in the right of every individual to claim the protection of the laws, whenever he receives an injury."\515/

Only a few voices have been heard complaining about the unconstitutionality of the courts taking over the legislature's lawful tasks, but those few voices have not been powerful enough to change the course of the centuries' old courts' unlawful and/or unconstitutional actions. Thomas Jefferson (1743–1826) repeatedly warned the union. Some heeded him, but no one acted to remedy the problem.

> *"The Constitution . . . is a mere thing of wax in the hands of the judiciary which they may twist and shape into any form they please."*

— Jefferson letter to Judge Spencer Roane,
September 6, 1819

> *"The judiciary of the United States is the subtle corps of sappers and miners constantly working under ground to undermine the foundations of our confederated fabric. They are construing our constitution from a co-ordination of a general and special government to a general and supreme one alone."*

— Jefferson letter to Thomas Ritchie,
December 25, 1820

"The germ of dissolution of our federal government is in the constitution of the federal judiciary; an irresponsible body, (for impeachment is scarcely a scare-crow) working like gravity by night and by day, gaining a little today and a little tomorrow, and advancing its noiseless step like a thief, over the field of jurisdiction, until all shall be usurped from the States, and the government of all be consolidated into one."

— Jefferson letter to Charles Hammond,
August 18, 1821

"On every question of construction [of the Constitution], carry ourselves back to the time when the Constitution was adopted, recollect the spirit manifested in the debates, and instead of trying what meaning may be squeezed out of the text, or invented against it, conform to the probable one in which it was passed."

— Jefferson letter to Justice William Johnson,
June 12, 1823

"At the establishment of our constitutions, the judiciary bodies were supposed to be the most helpless and harmless members of the government. Experience, however, soon showed in what way they were to become the most dangerous; that the insufficiency of the means provided for their removal gave them a freehold and irresponsibility in office; that their decisions, seeming to concern individual suitors only, pass silent and unheeded by the public at large; that these decisions, nevertheless, become law by precedent, sapping, by little and little, the foundations of the constitution, and working its change by construction, before any one has perceived that that invisible and helpless worm has been busily employed in consuming its substance. In truth, man is not made to be trusted for life, if secured against all liability to account."

— Jefferson letter to Monsieur A. Coray,
October 31, 1823

"One single object . . . [will merit] the endless gratitude of the society: that of restraining the judges from usurping legislation."

— Jefferson letter to Edward Livingston,
March 25, 1825

In 1984, a century after the naissance of the obscene judge-made prong of the Eleventh Amendment, U.S. Supreme Court Justice Stevens, in a dissent, wrote, "'From the fifteenth-century English common law . . . , courts have never held that prohibited conduct can be shielded by sovereign immunity. That rule makes good sense—since a principal cannot authorize unlawful conduct, such conduct is of necessity *ultra vires.* There is no reason to abandon such a well-settled and sensible rule.'\\[516]/

And, but a year later, Justice Antonin Scalia, delivering the *Supreme Court Historical Society's 1985 Annual Lecture,*\\[517]/ said, "At the time of *Marbury v. Madison*\\[518]/ there was no doctrine of domestic sovereign immunity, as there never had been in English law. As Marshall notes in passing in the portion of his opinion establishing the proposition that there is no right without a remedy: 'In Great Britain, the king himself issued in the respectful form of a petition, and he never fails to comply with the judgment of the court.'"

Where the primary reason for any State to retain immunity is solely to protect the State's coffers, any taxpayer can reasonably suggest that where he contributes to the State's coffers, he is entitled to compensation for the wrongs committed by the State and its subdivisions against him.\\[519]/\\[520]/

That reason lends credence to the notion that a plaintiff in a lawcase has a right to seek equitable relief under section 1983 and under state law.

What can the public now do to regain their constitutional right to petition against the States and the federal government where wrongs were committed against them? In each State, different actions must be taken. One example may be seen in the Commonwealth of Massachusetts.

For instance, where the Commonwealth consented to suit by waiving its sovereign immunity completely in its Constitution in the 18th century and some of its alleged immunity by statute (the Massachusetts Tort Claims Act)\\[521]/ in the 20th, Eleventh Amendment sovereign immunity is unavailable as a defense to any of the claims brought in an action. Specifically, any John Smith may contend that there are four explicit sources showing waiver or sources containing indicia of the intent not to have sovereign immunity or, at a later point in time, to do away with sovereign immunity in the Commonwealth:\\[522]/ **(1)** Article V of the Massachusetts' Declaration of Rights, **(2)** Article XI of the Massachusetts' Declaration of Rights, **(3)** the Massachusetts Tort Claims Act,\\[523]/ and **(4)** the judiciary as well as the legislature.\\[524]/

As of 1977, "Massachusetts [was] one of only five remaining States which retain[ed] the common law immunity at both the state and local levels. . . . All except thirteen States ha[d] abolished or limited the defense in suits against the State."\\[525]/ "'[Any] limits to governmental liability and exceptions to the rule of liability [should be] based upon considerations of justice and public policy.'"\\[526]/

The judge-made immunities—sovereign immunity, judicial immunity, quasi-judicial immunity—must go. *Accountability* must be restored. Folks have to be able to find legal remedies for the wrongs committed against them. Folks have to be able to sue folks who have done them serious wrong.

One or two cases where immunity is denied would change the entire legal landscape! All the so-called mental-health and child-protection workers would have to clean up their acts immediately. It would not take long at all. One or two winning cases would put these fraudulently protected workers on notice to take care because they shall be accountable for their conduct as are the rest of us.

That is not to say that there are no bright social workers or psychologists or evaluators or family service officers or guardians *ad litem* or judges. Of course, there are bright and responsible and caring ones . . . *but* without accountability, no need to take responsibility for their work, no need to care about the quality of their work, and no fear of being sued because they have been protected by very, very foolish zealots, lots and lots of bad apples have spoiled the bunch . . . and literally millions of families across this nation have been despoiled and ravaged and driven into desperation because of the foolish zealots and the very rotten apples. All of these issues must be addressed, not swept under the proverbial rugs.

Privacy and Public Scrutiny are rivals in this area. I suggest that the complaints against judges be made public BUT with Numbers substituted for the judges' names. If, after true investigation of the alleged misconduct, there are public outcries, and they are based on reasonable outrage, then the alleged wrongdoer's name should be revealed. This is a precaution given that many, many complaints are frivolous, but certainly, once it has been determined by scrutinizing the facts that it is not a frivolous complaint, the public has a right to know.

Anecdote #1.

Suffering from osteoporosis, GiGi, a 90-year-old widow, crushed her cervix and broke a rib on a fall from a bench on which she was sitting talking to friends. In need of monitoring of necessary painkillers, she entered a hospital and from there went to a nursing facility. There she got inadequate care, e.g., she fell three times because she was unassisted, the last time resulting in a broken arm and a broken hip, which required an emergency operation. Like a little broken bird, and overmedicated, her mind began going. She began to recover at another rehabilitation facility.

When her 100 days of state care ran out, she left that facility and went to live in a private residence with a friend. There she received excellent private care for a number of months, and using a walker and receiving therapy three times a week from a visiting therapist, she began to be mobile again, but hallucinations became a daily occurrence. Ultimately a serious threat of suicide voiced to an elder-service caregiver caused her to be sent to the hospital and observed in the psychiatric ward. That day, she thought it was the year 1001.

Although there appeared to be no official diagnosis, she was housed in the ward for those with symptoms of dementia and Alzheimer's. From the hospital, she entered a facility for long-term around-the-clock medical and nursing care, for which the costs were not paid because the Division of Medical Assistance (DMA) denied her application for MassHealth.

She was denied MassHealth because she had more than $2000 in her bank account. Her counsel went to a hearing and brought with her originals and copies of those documents showing that GiGi's money had been earmarked to pay other outstanding bills. The hearing officer, Matthew Levin, said he did not need the documents or copies.

Following that hearing, MassHealth coverage was denied her. GiGi then filed for an internal appeal with the DMA.

When she lost the internal appeal to the administrative agency, she appealed by suing in the trial court. The defendants were the DMA, the Executive Office of Health and Human Services, Hearing Officer Matthew Levin in his individual and professional capacities, Commissioner of the DMA Wendy Warring, the Commonwealth of Massachusetts, and John and Jane Doe.

After GiGi's filed suit in the trial court, the skilled-nursing facility filed suit against her for $38,824, allegedly payment due as a private patient because the defendants in the instant case denied her Medicaid/MassHealth coverage. Without coverage by MassHealth, GiGi was denied her right to that essential medical and nursing care,\[527]/ for she did not have the financial ability to pay approximately $6500 (the then-going rate) per month as a private patient.\[528]/\[529]/

The defendants relied on immunity defenses: sovereign, judicial, and quasi-judicial immunities. In particular, Levin defended by claiming that GiGi had not provided certain documents to him. That was untrue. GiGi had offered to supply those documents at the original hearing *well before* she brought suit, but Levin had said that he did not need them.

Judge Richard Welch. III stayed glued to the myth that the Commonwealth had sovereign immunity and that, pursuant to the Massachusetts Tort Claims Act, he could substitute the Commonwealth for the individual state employees. This, Welch said, has the effect of precluding suit against the state employees in their personal capacities and entitling Hearing Officer Levin to quasi-judicial immunity.

"In any event," the judge added, "Levin is also protected by the doctrine of judicial immunity. The plaintiff correctly argues that such immunity (be it absolute, or quasi-, or qualified immunty) is the product of judge made common law and is not contained in any constitutional or statutory provision. Still, little reason has been given to overturn this well established precedent."

Although the DMA and its hearing officer, in their defense, claimed that they had insufficient evidence to deny GiGi long-term nursing coverage by MassHealth, Levin acted in bad faith by itemizing as allegedly requisite to a finding in favor of GiGi those very documents which GiGi had offered and he had not accepted on the grounds that they were unnecessary.

Judge Welch's decision was, in my opinion, double-talk and the defendants got away with not paying GiGi's attorney's fees.

Postscript.

Fighting also behind the scenes, GiGi managed to get MassHealth coverage.

Discussion.

Where Article V of the Massachusetts Declaration of Rights requires all public employees of the three branches of the government of the Commonwealth of Massachusetts to be accountable to the people at all times, the court was precluded from applying to GiGi's case the Massachusetts Tort Claims Act, upon which Defendants Levin and Jane and John Doe relied to give them absolute or quasi-judicial immunity from suit.\530/

According to a case around 10 years ago, the Supreme Court clearly wrote that under common law, too, the Commonwealth is subject to suit by its citizens: *"Several colonial charters, including those of Massachusetts, . . . expressly specified that the corporation body established thereunder could sue and be sued.... If a colonial lawyer had looked into Blackstone for the theory of sovereign immunity, as indeed many did, he would have found nothing clearly suggesting that Colonies as such enjoyed any immunity from suit.* "\531/

". . . There is also the postulate that States of the Union, . . . , shall be immune from suits, without their consent, save where there has been 'a surrender of this immunity in the plan of the convention.' "\532/ And that surrender and consent to suit by its citizens was the plan of the Massachusetts convention adopted in 1779–1780.\533/ That instrument "is still in force today as the organic law of the Commonwealth of Massachusetts."\534/

Ignoring Article V would make it impossible for Article XI (also ratified in 1780) of the Massachusetts Declaration of Rights to perform its magic. For example, Article XI states that every Massachusetts subject "ought to find a certain remedy, by having recourse to the laws."\535/ With absolute judicial immunity and quasi-judicial immunity, the guarantee of Article XI would have been a misrepresentation.

Therefore the "generation of the Framers thought the principle so crucial that several States put it into their constitutions."\[536]/

If immunity for the people populating all three branches of state government does not exist because Article V of the Massachusetts Declaration of Rights is deemed to be operative, making waiver unnecessary and consent to suit in state and federal courts explicit, then judicial, quasi-judicial , and qualified immunity also do not exist, and thus could not preclude any of GiGi's claims against Levin and Jane and John Doe.

Given also that "officials seeking absolute immunity [other than legislators or judges] must show that such immunity is justified for the governmental function at issue" and that Levin or Jane Doe or John Doe made no such showing, they were not entitled to quasi-judicial immunity.\[537]/

Levin's and Jane and John Doe's acts or failures to act violated GiGi's civil rights under the federal or state constitutions. Therefore, notwithstanding the Article V issue, those defendants should not have relied in GiGi's case on the Massachusetts Tort Claims Act.\[538]/

Further, where "governmental privileges or benefits necessary to basic sustenance have often been viewed as being of greater constitutional significance than less essential forms of governmental entitlements,"\[539]/ by denying GiGi's application for MassHealth, the defendants, in effect, denied her the necessities of life; to wit, her long-term medical and nursing care, inasmuch as she could not afford between $6200–$6500 per month, the charge for private-patient care.

Given the evidence of Levin's and the Does' incompetence, to which the administrative decision to deny GiGi's application gave testament, even were they to have had immunity, it would not protect them. "Qualified immunity protects 'all but the plainly incompetent OR those who knowingly violate the law.'"\[540]/

Faced with insufficient evidence to deny GiGi long-term nursing coverage by MassHealth, Levin acted in bad faith by itemizing as allegedly requisite to a finding in favor of GiGi documents which had never been requested by Jane and/or John Doe. Levin had to know he was acting outside of the scope of his authority when he fabricated for his written decision a new list. This was a fraud on GiGi, an act violating her right to due process and equal protection of the laws, and consequently an act done in bad faith. That there was no written request for these documents noted on the boilerplate letter, one used as a matter of policy and practice, is evidence that Levin's conduct was malicious and in bad faith.

Therefore the Mass. Tort Claims Act, which affords immunity to public employees under certain circumstances, cannot apply. Reasonable good faith is necessary in order to be protected by either qualified or absolute immunity.\[541]/ "Good faith" is, in fact, a synonym for "qualified immunity."\[542]/\[543]/ Therefore, if we assume *arguendo* that Levin is to be protected by qualified immunity, he would have to prove that he did not know or could not have known that expanding the list of documents allegedly required of GiGi—only for the purpose of enhancing the decision against her—would violate GiGi's constitutional rights. Clearly, Levin's mere possession of GiGi's entire file is evidence of Levin's bad faith and/or malicious intention to deprive GiGi of her constitutional rights or other injury.

GiGi speculated, but did not affirmatively plead, that the Division had received an order to contain approvals in order to reduce the projected MassHealth costs, which had been rising steadily in a time of statewide fiscal crisis.

Anecdote #2. \[544]/

A fifteen-year-old girl's mother went to a state court judge in his chamber and asked him to sign an order approving a tubal ligation for her daughter. The judge had in his possession a petition entitled "Petition to Have Tubal Ligation Performed on a Minor and Indemnity Agreement," which had been presented by an attorney to Judge Stump of Indiana's DeKalb County Circuit Court. The petition was never filed in court.

The mother repeated what was contained in the affidavit-like petition, to wit, that the girl was "somewhat retarded" (although she attended public school and was promoted each year with her class), that she was staying out overnight with older men, and that sterilizing the girl would "present unfortunate circumstances."\[545]/

Granting the mother's request, the judge did issue an order for the sterilization to take place, but the order, like the petition, was never filed in the court.

The girl did not know she was actually being surgically sterilized. She thought her appendix was being taken out. It was not until she was married and unable to conceive a child, that she learned the true nature of the operation, to wit, that she had been surgically sterilized four years earlier.

She, Linda Spitler Sparkman, then sued the judge and others for violation of her constitutional rights and conspiracy under the Federal Civil Rights Act (42 U.S.C. §§ 1983 and 1985(3)), assault and battery, and medical malpractice. Her husband, Leo Sparkman, asserted a pendent claim for loss of potential fatherhood.

The U.S. District Court "clothed" Judge Stump with absolute judicial immunity and dismissed the pendent state claims for lack of subject matter jurisdiction, but subsequently the Seventh Circuit Court of Appeals\546/ held "that the judge acted extrajudicially and that the doctrine of judicial immunity [was] inapplicable to this case."

Discussion.

A compelling case was made that Judge Stump acted without jurisdiction, for when the girl's mother, Ora E. Spitler McFarlin, made her request in the judge's chambers, there was no authority for the judge to hear such a request or to issue such an order. No case had been filed with the court, no docket number had been assigned, there had been no pleadings filed. The matter was handled entirely *ex parte*; neither the girl, Linda Spitler, nor any representative for her was present or allowed to respond.

The Seventh Circuit Court of Appeals had written, "[The judge" may not arbitrarily order or approve anything presented to him in the form of an affidavit or a petition. A claim must be characterized as a case in law or equity in order to come within the statute. In short, it must have a statutory or common law basis." The court continued, even if Stump had acted within the statutory scheme, his action would "be an illegitimate exercise of his common law power because of his failure to comply with elementary principles of procedural due process."\547/

When the case made it all the way to the U.S. Supreme Court, however, the Court declared that because Judge Stump sat in a court of general jurisdiction, he was acting in excess of his jurisdiction, not in the absence of it, the judge was protected by absolute immunity from the suit for money damages.\548/ "Immunity," the Court emphasized, "does not exist if judges act in the 'clear absence of all jurisdiction.'"\⁵⁴⁹/ "A judge is [also] absolutely immune from liability for his judicial acts even if his exercise of authority is flawed by the commission of grave procedural errors."\⁵⁵⁰/ Thus the U.S. Supreme Court reversed the decision of the Seventh Circuit Court of Appeals.

The decision is considered a troublesome one: the narrow construction—"clear absence of all jurisdiction"—of the limitation on absolute immunity allowed Judge Stump to get away with inflicting great harm, without the barest rudiments of procedural due process.\⁵⁵¹/

This, in fact, is tyranny, say most oppositionists.

Oppositionists to Immunity Have Said

Iimmunity ensures some citizens injured by government will have no remedy. Immunity renders illusory the claims that the judiciary upholds the Constitution. Immunity undermines the very essence of civil liberty. Scores of scholars have written about immunity, about the tragic results it causes, about the ineffective efforts to abolish it and correct the justice system. None have given us a cure.

"We fought a revolution because the King did wrong, and did a lot of it. We did not throw off the yoke of the King and secure our independence, our liberty, and our sovereignty, to then be under the yoke—and tyranny—of judges. Absolute immunity is repugnant to the Constitution. Judges giving judges immunity flies in the face of separation of powers," wrote Attorney Gary Zerman.\⁵⁵²/

In the Cato Journal, Robert Craig Waters wrote:\⁵⁵³/

> In the American judicial system, few more serious threats to individual liberty can be imagined than a corrupt judge. Clothed with the power of state and authorized to pass judgment on the most basic aspects of everyday life, a judge can deprive citizens of liberty and property in complete disregard of the Constitution. The injuries inflicted may be severed and enduring.\⁵⁵⁴/ . . .
> Those who are harmed, no matter how extensive and irreparable the injury, they are deprived of any method of obtaining compensation\⁵⁵⁵/ . . . [such that] a victim can be forced to bear the full burden of a serious, irreparable injury

> inflicted by a state-court judge in blatant violation of the Constitution.\[556]/
>
> . . . Those subject to a corrupt judge's power may find little comfort in the Supreme Court's pronouncements that judicial immunity in effect is a necessary evil, the price to be paid for a 'fearless' judiciary. With power to abridge liberty and seize property, state-court judges are the masters of everyday life in America.\[557]/
>
> . . . By resort to the current immunity doctrine, an unscrupulous judge could escape liability even for acts of revenge, gross favoritism, improper seizure of property, unjust incarceration, or serious injury inflicted 'in a judicial capacity.'\[558]/

I heartily agree with Waters' statements above, but I even more heartily *dis*agree with his willingness to accept immunity as an acceptable doctrine.\[559]/ In fact, his "cure," in my opinion, is horrendous and entirely unacceptable. For anyone interested in his so-called cure, see it in endnote 560.\[560]/ My comment after studying it closely is, Never, never, never should there be an irrebuttable presumption of immunity allowed in our justice system. Never, never, never should there be immunity, p-e-r-i-o-d. Waters' plan is totally unacceptable. It is too open to too many abuses and misuses.

The Judicial Accountability Initiative: South Dakota 2006 Amendment E

A group calling itself Jail4Judges sponsored Amendment E in South Dakota in 2006. Amendment E was an attempt to amend the South Dakota Constitution to create a "Special Grand Jury" to hear cases of alleged judicial misconduct, to strip judges of their immunity, and to expose them to possible fines and jail terms. If Amendment E had paased, South Dakota would have been the first State in which citizens could sue judges for official acts in order to rein in judges who deliberately disregard law and violate people's rights.

In those States where judges are elected and review procedures are available, judges tend to be more accountable. In those States where judges are appointed—as in Massachusetts, by a governor until the age of 70— and there are no review procedures, there is absolutely *no* accountability . . . ever.

Abolishment of Absolute Immunity

Abolishing absolute immunity would open the door to litigation, but officials can be protected "from meritless suits by employing strict pleading requirements or aggressive use of summary judgment"\[561]/ rather than by according them absolute immunity, which is an evil, not a necessary one. There should be no fear where a judge acts fairly, considers all the facts, and properly applies the law. There is no need for irrebutable presumptions to preserve the integrity of the judicial process.

Without immunity, a judge would be allowed the fundamentally fair due process that is guaranteed in the constitution for everyone: notice of what they are being sued for civilly or charged with criminally, an opportunity to be heard—that is, the right to cross-examine witnesses and present a defense—and a fair trial, not one with only the appearance of a fair trial. Once you get into "appearances," the door opens and double talk stalks in.

So that there is no doubt that immunity of all kinds os abolished, the federal and state congresses should enact legislation to guard against its renaissance in any other form.

Chapter 19

Quasi-judicial, Prosecutorial, and Qualified Immunities

Protecting Judges' Parasites, the Other Enemies of the People

Anecdote #1.

Brown and Linnehan are parents who were illegally denied to be parents of their children and were suing in federal district court for themselves individually and on behalf of other parents whose children also suffered parentectomies.\[562]/

The defendants were:

- Eli Newberger, a doctor who was the director of Children's Hospital Family Development Program and thought to be evil by many parents;

- Children's Hospital, who with gross negligence did not properly oversee what Newberger was doing and perceived the program headed by Newberger as a cash cow;

- Amy C. Tishelman, a doctor who assisted Newberger by signing false sexual evaluations in order to deprive children of their parents;

- Barbara A. Cohen, an alleged therapist who was incompetent and left the Brown children in harm's way by not telling Brown that his wife and their children were living with an admitted sex offender who was receiving alleged sex-offender therapy at the Whitman Counseling Center, where Cohen worked;

- Whitman Counseling Center, which failed to inform DSS that Dell Smith was living with the Brown children, one toddler and one six-year old, and failed to inform Brown that Dell was an admitted sex-offender;

- Trial Court of Massachusetts, which maliciously and corruptly deprived plaintiffs of due process and equal protection, left the Linnehan and Brown children in harm's way, and aided and abetted that harm by so doing;

- Department of Social Services, which deprived plaintiffs of their constitutionl rights, left the Linnehan and Brown children in harm's way, and aided and abetted that harm by so doing;

- Eileen Kern, a social worker who, despite not having any reasonable suspicion or any proof of sexual abuse, filed a report with the alleged child-protection department for abuse and recommended to the court that Linnehan's son be evaluated by the Collis Center for sexual abuse

- Sandra Fyfe, a Collis Center social worker who, although having no reasonable suspicion that the child had been sexually abused by anyone and despite four therapists recommending that Linnehan be allowed visitation with his son, acted on her own and wrote a report recommending that Linnehan not be allowed visitation—with or without supervision—with his son;

- Christopher Salt, a court-appointed investigator wrote two reports replete with misstatements and without any proof of sexual abuse, recommended that Linnehan be denied visitation; of the more than 73 appointments he was given by the court, all were by Judge Ronald Harper, leading to the suspicion that Salt was Harper's toy boy;

- Jack McCarthy, allegedly a psychologist, in 1994, 1995, and 1998 relied on Newberger's report as the basis for again recommending that Linnehan not be allowed visitation with his son, and in 1999, McCarthy relied on that report to recommend that Linnehan's parents, enneagenarians, not be given court permission to see their grandson.

Some of the entities filed reports in court. Some of the defendants' reports were filed by the wife's attorney. Some of the entities did nothing. Some of the entities did things they should not have done. Some were appointed by the court. Others were not appointed by the court. Some were clearly "state actors," which one must be to be sued under the Federal Civil Rights Act. Some were less clearly state actors. All should have been liable for their wrongdoing to Brown and Linnehan. None were . . . according to Judge Robert Keeton of the U.S. District Court in Boston.

After reading Salt's report, Dick was so traumatized by the false accusation of sexual abuse that he spontaneously lost his voice. Over the years, many diagnoses have been rendered: hyperfunctional voice disorder, maladaptive vocal and respiratory habits, vocal chord nodules. . . .

Of the 70-odd appointments of Salt to conduct investigations, all but three of the appointments were made by Harper.\[563]/ How many investigators had Harper appointed during the time frame in which he appointed Salt? What was the connection between Harper and Salt? What did Salt give or provide Harper in return for the favored appointments? Given the amenability of the British culture to put their sons into unisex boarding schools and overlook sexual adventures between the boys, was Salt the judge's toy boy?

After Salt filed his report, replete with falsities, Ronald Harper *allegedly* ordered the Collis Center to perform the sexual assessment. Sandra Fyfe, employed by the Center, met with Jamie and Robyn but never interviewed Dick or observed him and Jamie together.

After her boss, Collis Center Executive Director Thomas Tanguay, met with Dick, Tanguay recommended supervised visitation. Yet, despite Tanguay's recommendation that Dick be allowed visitation with the child, Fyfe wrote a report recommending that Dick not be allowed visitation—with or without supervision—with his son.

There is a major dispute as to whether Fyfe's report was ever filed with the Juvenile Court, for the docket was impounded.\[564]/ If not appointed, Fyfe would neither have immunity nor be a state actor, and any Federal civil rights action against her would be dismissed on the grounds that she was not a state actor. If Fyfe was deemed appointed through the Center's appointment, the court would give her immunity from suit and she would be a "state actor," and any Federal civil rights action against her or the Center would be dismissed on the grounds of immunity. Immunity, a judge-made doctrine, saved Fyfe's butt. Immunity must be abolished. There is no logically defensible reason Fyfe should not be responsible for her conduct while you should be responsible for yours!

Although Fyfe's information could only have come from Robyn (the mother of the child sired by Linnehan) and/or Kern, Fyfe never challenged Robyn or Kern or questioned their honesty and/or competence,\[565]/ and then shared what Robyn and/or Kern and her own beliefs with Christopher Salt and with DSS. Deborah Wolf, the attorney who was appointed to represent Jamie, might have filed Fyfe's report with the court, but we do not know that. (In my opinion, Wolf should not be practicing law. She is dishonest . . . also in my opinion.)

Because Dick was never told what occurred when Fyfe interviewed Robyn and the child—if, in fact, she did—Dick does not know whether Fyfe had a reasonable cause for suspicion that someone else abused the child in some manner. Dick was never allowed to call Fyfe for examination.

In retrospect, Dick believes that Sandra Fyfe participated with some of the others in two or more predicate acts against him. They communicated by telephone and letter their biased presumptions, their flawed and specious conclusions and opinions to each other and to third parties that Dick had sexually abused his child. They suggestively and improperly questioned the child until the child allegedly accused him, and rubber-stamped each other's decisions that Dick had sexually abused his child.

The pattern was to receive income from future services which had been made mandatory when sexual abuse—true or not—was found. To Fyfe, a finding of sexual abuse meant more court appointments for her company and referrals by other so-called mental health workers, who would recommend the continuation of counseling by their respective agencies for the children, counseling for the parents, batterer or anger-management programs, sex-offender programs, testing, multiple evaluations, repeated testing, and so on—out of which has grown a multibillion-dollar sex-abuse industry.

When Brown and Linnehan sued the above natural and unnatural entities, the federal judge wrote a lengthy memorandum of decision when he dismissed the case. I explain below not only where and why I disagreed with the court, but also alert you to possible problems if and when you write your own civil rights Complaint. The judge identifies various "tests" the courts use to decide wither defendants are proper defendants in civil rights cases. Those tests are judge-made and have nothing to do with the Federal Civil Rights Act. They are simply some of the tricks the courts use to dismiss your case. You will also be able to watch the issues "in action" that require court reform. My appeal of Judge Keeton's decision is on my website.

The primary cure, as I have continuously advocated, is, of course, to outlaw immunity for judges and the people they appoint. We need accountability from everyone. If we need to be accountable, so must they!

The Intentional Errors the Judge Made

(1) The judge claimed he had to abstain from interfering with state probate and family court proceedings.\566/ Wrong! Plaintiffs were not seeking the federal court to vacate or amend a Probate and Family Court decision, there was no pending litigation, and there was no requirement to abstain. Abstention is not mandatory, it is discretionary.

(2) The judge concluded that the Trial Court and DSS's motion to dismiss should be allowed because the Eleventh Amendment bars plaintiffs' claims against the state agencies. Wrong! The Eleventh Amendment that the judge called the Eleventh Amendment is *not* the Eleventh Amendment. The judge was invoking the FAKE Eleventh Amendment. It has no effect in Massachusetts. Suit against state agencies are *not* barred by the Massachusetts or federal constitutions.

(3) The judge wrote that both the Trial Court and DSS are essentially "state agencies" and agencies are not 'persons' subject to suit under 42 U.S.C. § 1983.\567/ Wrong! The Trial Court is part of the judicial branch of government. This issue of whether a State or a state agency is not a "person" has been controversial for decades.\568/ The controversy arose out of Federal Civil Rights Act itself, which reads, in part: "*Every **person** . . . [acting under state law] shall be liable to the party injured in an action at law, suit in equity, or other proper*

proceeding for redress." Then everyone including the courts asked, Is a State a person? Is a state agency a person?

(4) Brown and Linnehan alleged that the Trial Court and DSS interfered with their parental rights in violation of the due process protections of the Fourteenth Amendment. The court wrote, "To the extent that plaintiffs seek monetary damages from the state coffers on the basis of this claim, the Eleventh Amendment indisputably bars actions for money damages against an arm of the Commonwealth in the absence of a waiver." Wrong! This is untrue. The Eleventh Amendment does not bar § 1983 claims for money damages brought against government officials in their personal, rather than official, capacities.\[569]/

(5) "The Supreme Court 'has consistently held that an unconsenting State is immune from suits brought in federal courts by her own citizens as well as by citizens of another State.'"\[570]/ Yes the Court has done that but in doing so, it has violated the explicit wording of the Constitution.

(6) "The Fourteenth Amendment does not by its own force override the States' Eleventh Amendment Immunity."\[571]/ Wrong! The Eleventh Amendment referred to by the judge is the fake, the unlawful Eleventh Amendment.

(7) "Although the Eleventh Amendment would not bar plaintiffs from seeking prospective injunctive relief against a state official,\[572]/ plaintiffs here have made the fatal pleading error of suing state agencies and not the state officials." Wrong! Plaintiffs did not sue multiple state agencies. Although they sued the Department of Social Services, they also sued Jane and John Does because the plaintiffs did not know the names of the individuals at DSS. Had plaintiffs been allowed to conduct discovery, they wuld have learned the true names of the workers and would have substituted them for the "John and Jane Does."

(8) "Furthermore, plaintiffs have not alleged any continuing violation of plaintiffs' constitutional rights by either the Trial Court or DSS."\[573]/ Irrelevant comment. After the Trial Court and DSS acted, the damage had been done and the cases were disposed of.\[574]/

(9) "Plaintiffs' final claim allegedly arising under federal law is for violations of 'Civil RICO.' Plaintiffs' complaint does not specify whether they intended to sue the defendants under the Federal RICO statute or under state common-law. To the extent that plaintiffs' intended to state a claim under the Federal RICO statute, this claim is barred by the

Eleventh Amendment. The RICO statute does not contain equivocal statutory language sufficient to abrogate the Eleventh Amendment."\575/ RICO is a general statute that does not mention, much less waive, sovereign immunity." Wrong! There is no legitimate sovereign immunity to waive. The Commonwealth is not a sovereign, the people are the sovereigns of the Commonwealth, which is a voluntary association of the people. M.G.L. c. 4, sec. 7. And again, the Eleventh Amendment of which Judge Robert Keeton wrote is the FAKE Eleventh Amendment, a judge-made, *un*ratified alleged prong of the Eleventh Amendment.

(10) "All of plaintiffs' remaining claims arise under state law. This court is without jurisdiction to consider claims that the conduct of a state violated that state's own laws.\576/ The Commonwealth of Massachusetts has waived its immunity with respect to certain tort claims in certain circumstances.\577/ The Commonwealth of Massachusetts did not, however, in enacting [the Massachusetts Tort Claims Act],\578/ consent to suit by its citizens in federal as well as state court.\579/ This court is without jurisdiction to hear these claims, and is without jurisdiction to consider whether, as the Trial Court and DSS argue, plaintiffs' claims would be barred under [the Massachusetts Tort Claims ct]\580/ in any event." Wrong! This is all untrue. Abstention is *not* mandatory. It is discretionary. Given Article V of the Mass. Declaration of rights, there is no lawful immunity in the Commonwealth. The Massachusetts Tort Claims Act is unconstitutional in that article V has never been amended or repealed.

(11) **Plaintiffs' Conspiracy Claims.** "Plaintiffs allege four possible bases for a claim under federal law. The first is for "Interference with Parental Rights," and is claimed under the Fourteenth Amendment to the Constitution of the United States (Count 2). A direct claim under the Fourteenth Amendment is not available, and I conclude that this count is merely an extension of plaintiffs' second federal cause of action, which alleges violations of 42 U.S.C. § 1983 (Counts 3 and 4)." Wrong! "The Supreme Court, Mr. Justice Brennan, held that the complaint containing allegations that a state statute effected an apportionment that deprived plaintiffs of equal protection of the laws in violation of the Fourteenth Amendment presented a justiciable constitutional cause of action, and the right asserted was within reach of judicial protection under the Fourteenth Amendment, and did not present a nonjusticiable political question."\581/

The Motions to Dismiss Claims Brought Under Section 1983

The judge went on to explain that both plaintiffs brought claims under the Federal Civil Rights. All the defendants except Kern based their motions to dismiss, at least in part, on the argument that, as court-appointed evaluators, they were entitled to absolute, quasi-judicial immunity for their actions.

(12) **Salt's Motion to Dismiss.** Salt filed a motion to dismiss under Fed. R. Civ. P. 12(b)(6) and based his motion entirely on absolute, quasi-judicial immunity.

Linnehan identified Salt as being "a Massachusetts court-appointed evaluator," and not entitled to any immunity "because Salt was improperly appointed."\582/   The judge found Linnehan's argument unpersuasive.

"An alleged flaw in the appointment does not change the fact," the judge wrote, "that, from a functional perspective, Salt was acting in close association with the judicial process.\583/   Salt's status as a quasi-judicial actor did not depend on the phrasing of the state statute."

(13) **Fyfe's Motion for Judgment on the Pleadings.** Fyfe filed a motion under Fed. R. Civ. P. 12(c) for judgment on the pleadings and argued that Linnehan waited too long to sue her and the statutes of limitation barred him from suing her.

". . . Pursuant to a court order issued by Judge Harper in the New Bedford Family Court, Ms. Fyfe, on behalf of the Collis Center, was ordered to [and did] perform a court-ordered sexual abuse assessment of [the boy] and his mother Robyn Sylvia," Linnehan's argument that Fyfe was also improperly appointed, the judge concluded, was again unpersuasive, for any procedures in the state statute for court appointment are not determinative. "Rather, this court is guided by a functional approach in making a decision regarding immunity."

Wrong! If a reference of an appointment does not have to be written correctly, why bother require a reference of appointment? This is as bad as the cases—in particular, federal cases— saying arrest warrants need not be signed by a judge or magistrate.

The judge disagreed: "The Court of Appeals for the First Circuit has explained that judges are entitled to 'absolute immunity from civil liability for any normal and routine judicial act. . . . This immunity applies no matter how erroneous the act may have been, how injurious its consequences, how informal the proceeding, or how malicious the motive.'\⁵⁸⁴/ This immunity is based on a long standing principle of the common law: 'Few doctrines were more solidly established at common law than the immunity of judges from liability for damages for acts committed within their judicial jurisdiction.'\⁵⁸⁵/ This doctrine has been expanded to include other actors who are functioning in the judicial process to carry out a judicial order."

What the judge wrote is that the judge-made doctrine of immunity has been upheld by countless judges for a long time. They can do whatever they want, whether it is corrupt of malicuous, and they cannot be sued for those corrupt or malicious acts. And if they give absolute immunity to favored people. Those people, too, cannot be sued for corrupt or malicious acts.

Immunity arose in England in the Star Chamber, the King's court. Because the judges were appointed by the king and were, therefore, to be punished by the king, the judges were given immunity in the court and their punishment, if any, would be decided by the king. No trial was to be public because the king did not want any scandal to "entrench" to him. In the Star Chamber, even jurors were jailed for not performing as the king wanted. Nevertheless, the English kings, too, had to follow the law.

In order to defend giving immunity to their favored people, the judges said, Let's look at their function. It is similar to a judge's function, they are entitled to immunity. But we shall not let them be questioned by the party who is suing them, for the party might learn that those people did *not* function as judges are allegedly supposed to function.

So Judge Keeton wrote, "The functional approach 'requires an analysis of the nature of the duties performed and whether they are "closely associated with the judicial process."'\⁵⁸⁶/ Then he noted that the Massachusetts SJC and the First Circuit Court of Appeals had in the past agreed that those people have absolute immunity,\⁵⁸⁷/ not even qualified immunity.

But notice, that Judge Keeton did not let either Brown or Linnehan examine any of the defendants. Instead, Keeton went along with the other judges in the pack and ignored the Constitution's intent to provide a remedy and relief to anyone deprived of their constitutional rights. The same may be said of Congress. The legislative history and the statutory details and provisions of the Federal Civi Rights Act make it clear that no one, including judges, who knowingly deprived another of his or her well-established constitutional rights was to be protected by immunity.

(14) McCarthy's Motion to Dismiss under Fed.R. Civ. P. 12(b)(6). "McCarthy argues that the complaint should be dismissed against him because 'the complaint fails to allege the deprivation of a constitutional right [and] McCarthy is entitled to qualified and/or absolute immunity.'

Linnehan argued:

> ". . . although McCarthy can produce a stipulation of the parties to choose a therapist, he cannot produce a reference by the court to that position. He was simply a private party. Given that he was to produce reports to the Probation Department, his conduct is, nevertheless, attributable to the state. As a private party, the applicable standard is in *Camilo-Robles v. Hoyos*\[588]/ (nonemployee contract psychiatrists were not entitled to absolute or qualified immunity). 'A private party's conduct is attributable to the state if the state "has so far insinuated itself into a position of interdependence with [the private party] that it must be recognized as a joint participant in the challenged activity."\[589]/

And the court wrote that if McCarthy were court-appointed, the court would find him entitled to absolute, quasi-judicial immunity. If McCarthy were a private actor, he could not be held liable under 42 U.S.C. $ 1983.\[590]/ Plaintiff's allegations that McCarthy was incompetent would not change such a finding; "the immunity would apply however erroneous the act may have been.\[591]/

Ultimately, however, the court wrote, "In view of the inconsistencies in the record, . . . , and the parties' disputes as to McCarthy's status, I do not decide the matter on this ground. Instead, even after drawing all reasonable inferences in plaintiff's favor, I conclude that the complaint alleges no set of facts under which plaintiff can successfully pursue his claims against McCarthy in federal court.

"Plaintiffs try to escape this requirement by arguing for a middle ground. Quoting the opinion of the Court of Appeals for the First Circuit in *Camilo-Robles v. Hoyos*,\[592]/ plaintiffs allege that because McCarthy 'was to produce reports to the Probation Department, his conduct is, nevertheless, attributable to the state.' . . . Although the issue concerning whether a defendant is acting 'under color of state law' is necessarily a fact-based inquiry, it can properly be the subject of a motion to dismiss,\[593]/ when pleadings are insufficient to state even a colorable basis for attributing the actions of the defendant to the state."

This is where I part ways again with Keeton. Plaintiffs should have been able to conduct discovery of McCarthy, such as depose him. Deprived of that ability, they were deprived of the constitutional right to equal protection.

This is also where Keeton relied on a series of three judge-made tests under which a private actor's conduct can be attributed to the State for the purpose of that actor's liability under § 1983 or under which a private actor's conduct can exclude him from liability:.

- whether there was an elaborate financial or regulatory nexus between [defendant] and the [Commonwealth of Massachusetts] which compelled [defendant] to act as [he] did,\[594]/\[595]/

- whether there was an assumption bv [defendant] of a traditionally public function,\[596]/\[597]/ or

- whether there was a symbiotic relationship involving the sharing of profits.\[598]/\[599]/\[600]/ A 'key factor in determining whether a symbiotic relationship exists is certainly whether the state shared in any profits made,' and other factors to be considered include . . . \[601]/

Keeton concluded: "Plaintiff seeks to draw a parallel between McCarthy and the psychiatrists in *Camilo-Robles v. Hoyos*,\[602]/ who were found to be state actors under the symbiotic relationship test. The psychiatrists in *Camilo-Robles* were paid by the police department (and thus by the public treasury), and were 'under contract with the police department to assist in a necessary departmental function: the evaluation of officers.'\[603]/ McCarthy was not paid from state funds, and was not, in performing therapy either with Plaintiff Linnehan's son or the son's mother, performing a governmental function. I cannot infer from the allegations in the complaint that McCarthy was in a symbiotic relationship with the state and therefore liable as a state actor for his actions under 42 U.S.C. § 1983.

"Plaintiff's complaint, therefore, leads [Linnehan] to an inescapable barrier to [his] charges against McCarthy. If McCarthy is not a state actor, he cannot be held liable under § 1983. And the only way McCarthy can be understood to be a state actor under the governing precedents is if McCarthy is understood to be acting in a judicial function. McCarthy's motion to dismiss is allowed.

Wrong! It is imperative that the reader understand the three tests Judge Keeton used to determine whether McCarthy was a state actor or not. You can see how many facets could have gone in many different directions in such analyses. I am still of the opinion that the interpretation in *Camilo-Robles v. Hoyos* and the Supreme Court before it\[604]/ as to how to determine whether a State "has so far insinuated itself into a position of interdependence with [the private party] that it must be recognized as a joint participant in the challenged activity."

(15) <u>Eli Newberger's and Children's Hospital's Motions to Dismiss.</u> Both Eli Newberger, M.D. and Children's Hospital filed motions to dismiss the compaint. Newberger and Children's argued that they were entitled to absolute quasi-judicial immunity and that plaintiffs' claims were barred by the applicable statutes of limitation.

Interestingly, one usually argues immunity when one can be deemed a state actor. So it appears that Newberger and Children's agreed that they were state actors despite the lack of a court-appointment.

"As explained above," the court wrote, "a court's decision on an issue of absolute, quasi-judicial immunity 'requires an analysis of the nature of the duties performed and whether they are "closely associated with the judicial process."'\[605]/ The allegations in the complaint as to how Newberger and Children's Hospital became involved in either plaintiffs case are extremely murky. I infer from the complaint that with respect to Plaintiff Brown, the request for Newberger to perform an evaluation was made by the mother of Brown's children. . . . I also infer from plaintiffs' complaint that Newberger's report was sent to at least two courts. . . . With respect to Plaintiff Linnehan, I infer that Newberger's involvement was initiated at the request of Linnehan's son's attorney. . . . I infer that Newberger's report was again supplied to the court system . . . and that Newberger's report was relied on by other defendants. . . ."

"Based on the allegations in the complaint, I need not reach the issue of Newberger or Children's eligibility for absolute, quasi-judicial immunity. I conclude that plaintiff has not alleged sufficient facts for this court to infer that Newberger or Children's Hospital was a state actor, and therefore subject to liability under 42 U.S.C. § 1983. The only alleged involvement with the state is the submission of reports to family courts in the Commonwealth. Plaintiffs explicitly deny that Newberger or Children's were asked by the courts to perform any function. . . . Plaintiffs make much of the admission by Newberger 'that he knew that the team's reports would be used in court.' . . . But this knowledge, and implicit acceptance of the fact that his reports would used does not show 'an elaborate financial or regulatory nexus between [Newberger] and the [Commonwealth of Massachusetts] which compelled [Newberger] to act as [he] did' or 'an assumption by [Newberger] of a traditionally public function' or 'a symbiotic relationship involving the sharing of profits.'\[606]/

"The mere submission of a report to a court agency, at the request of private counsel, cannot serve as proof of state action even if the party submitting the report is aware that the court may depend on it. No reasonable basis exists for this court to infer from plaintiffs' complaint that either Newberger or Children's was acting under color of state law for the purposes of 42 U.S.C. § 1983.

"As plaintiffs have failed to state a claim against Newberger or Children's under 42 U.S.C. § 1983, and, . . . plaintiffs have failed to state a claim under either the federal RICO statute or 42 IJ.S.C. § 1985(3), I conclude that plaintiffs' federal-law claims against Newberger and Children's must be dismissed with prejudice. In the order below, plaintiffs' remaining claims against Newberger and Children's are dismissed without prejudice for the reasons stated . . . above."

All the words in the previous paragraph well describe not only Newberger and Children's Hospital but also McCarthy. For instance, neither Newberger, nor his team (including Tishelman), nor McCarthy were court-appointed. The counsel opposing Brown and Linnehan filed the Newberger and McCarthy reports in court. Newberger, his team, and McCarthy knew their reports were going to be filed in court. That was the purpose of preparing the reports. The courts accepted the reports for filing and *relied upon* those reports for depriving Brown and Linnehan access to their children.

The judge treated McCarthy as a state actor and gave him immunity. The judge did the opposite with Newberger and Tishelman: he did not treat them as state actors and therefore said they could not be sued under the Federal Civil Right Act. The result was, however, the same: Newberger, Tishelman, and McCarthy got off scot-free . . . even though the court relied on their reports to deprive Linnehan and Brown access to their children.

The hypocrisy of the court is that it looks at the identical situation three times and finds that two are one thing and the third is another. Like someone who operates solely to accomplish its agenda, good or bad, right or wrong, just or unjust. This hypocrisy is what must be exposed and reformed. (The oppositions to all the defendants' motions to dismiss Brown and Linnehan's Complaint are also in the Drano Series on my webste.)

(16) <u>Tishelman's Motion to Dismiss</u>. Brown was the sole plaintiff bringing claims against Amy C. Tishelman. She was a member of Newberger's team at Children's Hospital and was the member who interviewed the younger Brown children.\[607]/ As Brown's allegations with respect to Tishelman were entirely derivative of his allegations with respect to Newberger, the court reached the same conclusion that Brown has failed to state a claim against Tishelman under federal law (statutory, constitutional, or decisional). Plaintiff's federal-law claims against Tishelman were dismissed *with prejudice*, meaning that Brown could not bring the claim again.

All other claims—state-law claims—against Tishelman were dismissed *without prejudice*, meaning that Brown could bring the claim again . . . in state court.

(17) <u>Eileen Kern's Motion for Judgment on the Pleadings</u>. Kern filed a motion for judgment on the pleadings. She argued for dismissal of the case against her on the grounds that the complaint was time-barred, as the applicable period of limitation had run on every one of the plaintiff's causes of action. Linnehan raised a number of questions as to the merits of Kern's motion. In order to decide on the merits of Linnehan's contentions, however, the court would have had to decide unsettled questions of state law.

Continuing on the same tack, the judge wrote, "In these circumstances, I have considered *sua sponte* whether Kern is a state actor for section 1983 purposes and have concluded that she cannot be considered a state actor for the reasons explained below. Thus the federal claims against Kern cannot be sustained, and state-law claims are appropriately dismissed without prejudice.

Linnehan's complaint alleged possible federal claims for violations of 42 U.S.C. § 1983, violations of the federal RICO statute, and violations of 42 U.S.C. § 1985 (3), but the court found that he failed to state a claim against any defendant under either the federal RICO statute or 42 U.S.C. §1985 (3). The only remaining federal claim against Kern, the judge concluded, was Linnehan's claim arising under 42 U.S.C. § 1983. In the complaint, Linnehan stated the facts relevant to Kern as follows:

12. Defendant Eileen Kern is a natural person residing at . . . Massachusetts, United States of America, and who was employed at New Bedford Child & Family in New Bedford, Massachusetts. . . .

116. . . . [T]he initial assessment of Brenden and his mother, Robyn, was conducted by Defendant Eileen Kern in March 1988 at New Bedford Child Family Services.

117. The first court-ordered sexual-abuse assessment was at the Collis Center, which Eileen Kern recommended to Judge Harper.

128. Also despite not having any reasonable suspicion or any proof of' sexual abuse, Defendant Eileen Kern filed a 51A report, DSS social worker Robert Mendez interviewed Brenden, Robyn, and Linnehan. . . .

"Plaintiff does not specify in the complaint Kern's position at New Bedford Child and Family, and does not allege whether Kern was required to file a report under § 51A.\[608]/ . . .

"Filing a § 51A report initiates an investigation by the Department of Social Services. In that sense, it is the occasion for state action. But the mere initiation in this sense is not sufficient to constitute state action under § 1983; if it were, any person who filed a police report leading to an arrest in violation of rights protected in proceedings under § 1983 would be liable as a state actor. This interpretation of the statute exceeds the bounds of reason, and has been rejected by the Court of Appeals for the First Circuit.\[609]/ Plaintiffs have cited no precedent that would lead this court to a different conclusion.

"1 do consider, however, whether the language of § 51A merits a different conclusion. . . . It is conceivable that plaintiff [Linnehan] could claim that Kern was liable as a state actor under the 'nexus' theory of state action. In order for plaintiffs to state a claim under § 1983 under the 'nexus analysis,' plaintiffs must make sufficient allegations for this court to infer that 'the government exercised coercive power or provided such significant encouragement that [Kern's actions] must be deemed to be that of the government.'\[610]/ In short, plaintiffs must allege that 'the State is responsible for the specific conduct of which the plaintiff complains.'\[611]/

"In enacting § 51A, the Commonwealth of Massachusetts mandated that certain actors report suspected incidents of child abuse. The Commonwealth also mandated, however, that these reports not be frivolous. To the extent that plaintiffs allege that Kern's conduct was done without reasonable suspicion of child abuse, or that Kern's report was frivolous, this type of conduct is clearly outside of the conduct mandated by § 51A. In any event, I conclude that the incentives provided by § 51A are incentives only for the filing of legitimate reports based on reasonable suspicion, and that § 51A does not mandate the filing of reports based on less than reasonable suspicion. In other words, I conclude that the state did not exercise coercive power over Kern's decision to the extent necessary for Kern's filing of a § 51A report to be considered state action under § 1983.

"The Court of Appeals for the First Circuit considered a similar claim in *Rockwell v. Cane Cod Hospital*.\[612]/ In *Rockwell*, the [court] considered an allegation that two doctors and a private hospital who, acting pursuant to a Massachusetts statute, authorized the hospitalization of a person believed to be mentally ill, were state actors for the purposes of § 1983. The Court of Appeals . . . concluded that the hospital and the doctors were not state actors. The statute at issue in *Rockwell* was permissive, not mandatory, but the case is nevertheless relevant as precedent here. Although the § 51A mandates the reporting of child abuse, it also declares that making frivolous reports is punishable by a fine. The system therefore leaves discretion in the hands of the persons required to consider § 51A, and mandates an exercise of discretion by those persons in determining when an allegation of abuse is reasonable, and when an allegation is frivolous.

"Under the statutory scheme, the reporting 'decisions ultimately turn on medical judgments made by private parties according to professional standards that are not established by the State.'\[613]/ Persons considering § 51A reports are compelled equally by the incentive to make all reasonable reports (a one thousand dollar fine for failure to do so) and by the incentive against filing frivolous reports (a one thousand dollar fine for so filing). In these circumstances I cannot conclude that 'the government coerced or encouraged the specific [action] that gives rise to [plaintiffs'] complaint.'\[614]/

"Finally, I note that although the Court of Appeals for the First Circuit has not reached the specific question about whether compliance with a state child abuse reporting statute is sufficient to constitute state action under § 1983, the decision explained above is consistent with decisions in other jurisdictions.\[615]/ . . . Defendant Kern's Motion for Judgment on the Pleadings is allowed in the order below with respect to all federal law claims."

The judge repeated what he done before. ". . . all plaintiffs' claims arising under federal law are dismissed with prejudice in the order below. All plaintiffs' claims arising under state law are dismissed without prejudice . . . because it would be inappropriate for this court to make any order interfering with ongoing proceedings in the Family and Probate courts of Massachusetts. . . ." Wrong! There were no ongoing proceedings in Probate & Family courts of Massachusetts.

Analysis

Judge Keeton's goal was to get rid of the case. Every one of the defendants played a role in depriving Brown and Linnhan of access to their children. When each of them acted, the State agreed by finding one more alleged unprovable reason to deprive Brown and Linnehan. The State "so far insinuated itself into a position of interdependence with [the private party] that it must be recognized as a joint participant in the challenged activity."

Each one of the defendants should have been made accountable for their grotesque, malicious acts, all of which were done without justification and without any proof whatsoever. Keeton's decision let monsters get away scot-free from liability for their unconscionable acts.

Prosecutorial and Qualified Immunities

Prosecutors, 99.5 percent (my unscientific estimate) of the time, have absolute immunity, but they do not have absolute immunity when the actions occur during the investigative stage of the prosecution, when the actions are administrative or ministerial.\[616]/ See the endnote for details. Under those circumstances, prosecutors will likely be protected by *qualified* immunity.

Police officers, too, generally are protected only by qualified immunity.

When qualified immunity is given, the plaintiff may conduct discovery. After the discovery phase, the defending prosecutor or police officer may move for dismissal. The plaintiff may then oppose. Caveat: Some judges might not let the plaintiff conduct discovery. Be prepared to fight that ruling.

Chapter 20

Legal Malpractice

Foxes Guarding the Chicken Coops

My lawyer is ripping me off! He is not doing anything for me. He doesn't take phonecalls from me. He doesn't return my phonecalls. . . . I couldn't afford another attorney, 'cuz I had been tapped out, I had to be my own lawyer at trial. . . . My lawyer is a scumbag. I paid him but then he wanted to be paid in advance of my trial. When I didn't give him the advance, he withdrew. . . . My lawyer did not put my witnesses on the stand. He didn't subpoena witnesses to my trial. He didn't object to anything at trial. He did not put copies of my exhibits into evidence. He was like a wimp. He said practically nothing to the judge. He didn't say anything when my wife's lawyer told the court one lie after another. The judge would not let me take the stand and my lawyer did nothing about it!

Anecdote #1.

Susie's Case Against Steve Gordon of Worcester.

As explained earlier, a person can but may not swear Yes to one question in one court and No to the same question in another court. Relying on Steven Gordon of Worcester, having sworn in a district court that he was Susie's lawyer—although he never had been her lawyer—I sued Gordon on Susie's behalf in a superior court on the grounds of legal malpractice. My theory was he could not assert that he was not Susie's lawyer in Superior Court.

He had absolutely no evidence whatsoever that he had ever done one legal task on Susie's behalf. If he had used the skills of an ordinary lawyer, Gordon would have gotten a better result for her in Wrentham District Court. If the case were assigned to a decent, honest judge, the case would have been a shoo-in. It should have settled quickly. Susie would have gotten her money and taken her dream trip.

Susie sent Gordon a demand letter, in accordance with the Consumer Protection Act\⁶¹⁷/ by certified mail and received a reply from Gordon both denying liability and refusing settlement. At least 30 days thereafter, I filed the Complaint in superior court.

To this day, Gordon is still an attorney of record on the *Millis* case docket sheets, but they do not show when he entered his appearance . . . or a withdrawal from the action.

Gordon's Acts and/or Omissions.

Gordon proffered only conflicting testimonial evidence on what legal services he performed. While he claimed, on one hand, that he was entitled to be paid for "Employee GJ's" services and on the other, that he, too, performed services, the only corroborative evidence is the list of alleged activities he attached to his supplemental memorandum for fees in WDC.

Inspection of that document reveals, for example, that the first task Gordon alleged he himself performed on Susie's behalf was "*Review of the file with GJ and discussion regarding the drafting of a complaint*" and that his second task was the "*Review of drafted complaint and rewrite.*" Lies, lies, lies. Boy, that feels wonderful typing those words. Judges chastise lawyers for saying the word "lie" in court. It is equivalent to using the f- word. Even when it is true!

I had rock-solid proof Gordon had lied. The *Millis* case was filed by Susie's husband—while he was still alive—in Norfolk Superior Court four years before Gordon even knew GJ or even heard of the Susie, who became involved in the case as an administrator of the estate only after her husband's death.

Gordon was doing nothing but committing fraud . . . and perjury. In his Answer to the Complaint, Gordon admitted that the Complaint had been filed in 1984 in Norfolk Superior Court during the lifetime of the decedent, whom Gordon admits not knowing. But he could not keep his story straight. In his Response to Request 1 for Admission, Gordon claimed knowing when the underlying case was filed but repeatedly wrote the date of his fictitious activities as "00/00/00."

Significantly, Gordon's "so-called bill" does not controvert Susie's contention that Gordon never advised and/or counseled her. At most, Gordon may have familiarized himself to some unknown extent with the case when GJ had the file in his office that he rented in Gordon's suite of offices, but never did anything proactively with any knowledge he may have gleaned or with any strategies he may have devised.

In sum, Gordon failed to act at all! For example, Gordon failed to know, meet, and communicate with his alleged client, failed to learn what her interests were, failed to properly exercise the responsibilities of the supervisory lawyer he alleges to have been, failed to recommend that Susie seek other counsel to properly represent her interests when he himself was remiss in his duties, failed to zealously represent her, failed to act with reasonable diligence, failed to explain any matter to the extent reasonably necessary to permit her to make informed decisions, failed to file even one pleading on Susie's behalf, failed to conduct any discovery (e.g., depositions), failed to plead properly evidentiary matters during the trial of the underlying case, failed to expedite litigation, failed to protect her right to a trial by a judge, failed to comply properly with Rule 53 of the District/Municipal Court Rules of Civil Procedure, failed to file properly requests for reports of evidence and for rulings of law in accordance with Rule 64 of the District/Municipal Court Rules of Civil Procedure, failed to seek appellate review, generally, failed to petition for a draft report to the Appellate Division so as to effect a review by that Division, failed to file a timely request for retransfer of the remanded action to Superior Court,\[618]/ and failed to resolve all questions in favor of his client.

In sum, there never was any written attorney-client fee agreement of any kind between Gordon and Susie or between Gordon and me, as an individual or fiduciary of Susie. Gordon could not and did not produce any concrete evidence of even one iota of work he allegedly performed for Susie during the period of his so-called representation. In fact, in Susie's district court case, the only documents Gordon filed was his attorney's lien for fees. He never sent a bill to Susie or to me, whom he alleged was Susie's agent.

Further, during his so-called representation of Susie, Gordon never filed any pleadings in Wrentham District Court, never argued a motion in that court, never conducted discovery, never conducted negotiations for Susie in the *Millis* case, and never tried the case in that court or before a Master.

Summary of State of Evidence of Gordon's Representation.

Subsequently, in the Superior Court case for legal malpractice, Gordon filed a third-party complaint against me seeking contribution and indemnification. Judge James McHugh, III, found against Gordon on those claims. Only my damages had to be assessed. Wonderful! McHugh saw through Gordon and said all that was needed then was a trial date.

During discovery, Susie requested that Gordon produce phonebills as proof of the alleged phonecalls he made to me and Susie. Gordon, of course, could not produce any (at that time long-distance phonecalls appeared on one's phone bills), so he moved to compel Susie to produce her and my telephone numbers so that he could allegedly find them on his phonebills. The Court (McHugh, J.) denied his motion and wrote in the decision that Gordon should look up my and Susie's telephone numbers, respectively, in the Lawyers' Diary and the phonebook. Gordon never produced any phonebills; nor did he ever provide a written response to the Court's Order.

McHugh and Judge Wendie Gershengorn shared Courtroom 9A in Middlesex (MA) County Superior Court—six months one, six months the other. When McHugh left Courtroom 9 and Wendie came in, the extraordinary happened . . . or was it so extraordinary?

Some background, during this case Gordon was defended by an insurance defense firm, Burns & Levinson, huge, many decades old, and quite powerful. Well, Wendie's husband was a doctor who had appeared, ao I have been led to understand, as a medical expert for Burns & Levinson. If that were true, Wendie had, therefore, a serious conflict of interest by accepting the assignment of the case. Burns & Levinson then brought a motion for summary judgment and Gershengorn, shockingly, allowed it. Susie was out of luck. A corrupt judge!! There is no question in my mind.

The late Barry Reed, who authored *The Verdict*, in the movie version of which Paul Newman starred, authored several later books. One of them was about a medical malpractice case that arose after a patient fell off the balcony into an atrium several stories below the balcony. Doctors, doctors, and more doctors, and insurance lawyers. The fictional judge, whose husband was also a medical expert for the insurance defense lawfirm, was modeled after Gershengorn. The question posed in the legal genre novel: Would she allow the hospital's motion or would she allow the deceased plaintiff to prevail as she should?

In that book, he also wrote a take-off on McHugh. His book had the case take place in Courtroom 9A in Suffolk County courthouse. But there was no Courtroom 9A in Suffolk, only in Middlesex. When I finished the book, I gleefully phoned Barry to congratulate him for describing McHugh's special smile perfectly, in fact, exquisitely. Barry laughed. "Everyone says I better not ever go back into 9A."

Given that all judges, with a few exceptions (so I've been told), have been bestowed with judge-made immunity, the only way to get back at the judge-made-unaccountable scoundrels is to make fun of them in fiction. Judicial immunity must, must, must be abolished. At least we can send dirty politicians to jail. With judges, we do not even have the opportunity to sue them.

Anecdote #2.

Lucas Stockdale hired the prestigious White, Inker, Aronson lawfirm to represent him in his divorce. Monroe Inker was the granddaddy of divorce law. Recently deceased, Monroe was kind, pleasant, friendly, and expensive. All the monied men went to him for whatever their problem in family court.

Thinking women, those who did not want to be opposed by Monroe, would call him for consultation before they filed for divorce. Learning his rates, they would turn away to another attorney and WIA would lose the "sale." BUT(!) when the husband approached WIA for representation after he was served with the divorce Complaint (formerly "libel"), WIA would check the firm's conflict file and learn that someone in the firm had heard the story from the wife first, and therefore WIA had to refuse to accept the husband's business.

As the incidence of divorce substantially increased, potential-conflict cases did not create a hardship for the firm. There was always some other monied husband to take the other one's place.

In the early '90s, as radical feminism grew and "took over" the courts via federal laws put into place, men began not to stand a chance in court, even when represented by the most competent lawyers. The clients of choice became the wives of the monied men, because the courts would make the men pay for the attorneys of the wives. The American Rule re fees, which required everyone to bear the cost of their own legal fees, became an endangered species of the law.

"Matrimonial law is not what it used to be even 15 years ago," remarked Inker, who noted that the practice now touches upon a wealth of other areas—from fraud to contract. The proof of this, he said, is that over the years he had become involved increasingly in complex litigation that had even brought him to the federal courts. "Many of these cases involve litigation which the average family lawyer never sees," commented Inker, who found himself turning cases away. "I couldn't do them with the resources we have at White, Inker, and we have more than anybody."\[619]/

Granddaddy Inker further attested to guardians *ad litem* being "routinely qualified as expert witnesses"\[620]/ in family cases and then problems arose from the courts by so doing. The problem of guardians *ad litem* is an old one, but now made more common by the ever-growing number of many-fronted wars over the rights of noncustodial parents (usually fathers) in the societally ill Age of Feminist Rebellion.\[621]/

So when his firm took a $45,000 retainer from Luke Stockdale, Monroe knew that it could do nothing for Stockdale with that "small" sum of money to get custody of the children. Monroe also knew that some of the young associates in his firm not only had but a few years experience, they also lacked competence and fire in their bellies. One of them was assigned to Stockdale's case.

From the first hearing in the divorce action until he filed his withdrawal, Attorney Kevin Connelly not only did very little, he did very little, if anything, competently. So Stockdale decided to sue the lawfirm and Connelly for legal malpractice.

In December 1999, Mrs. Stockdale's counsel, E. Chouteau Merrill ["Merrill"], moved that $43,500 in Stockdale's possession be put into an escrow account held by her. Connelly neither opposed Merrill's motion nor objected to the order that issued by Judge Nancy M. Gould ["Gould"] that day. The order commanded Stockdale to turn the money over to Merrill and that no funds be removed "without further order of court."

When Merrill moved for the appointment of a GAL and asserted that there was an agreement that the cost of the GAL's fees would be shared by the parties, Connelly, acting without my informed consent, agreed to the appointment of Barbara O'Brien Beardslee as GAL and stated, "We have no objection" to using the escrow account money to pay Beardslee. Stockdale said he had consented to neither the appointment of a GAL nor the use of his money then in the escrow account to pay the GAL nor the sharing of the cost of the GAL's fees.

The reference of appointment by the judge authorized Beardslee to investigate "custody and visitation" issues in the divorce action. The reference of appointment ordered the parties to share the payment of the GAL's fees, but did not give permission for the fees to be paid out of the money in the escrow account.

The order contravened the GAL statute,\[622]/ which reads in part, "*The compensation shall be fixed by the court and shall be paid by the commonwealth, together with any expense approved by the court, upon certificate by the judge to the state treasurer.*"

On successive dates, without leave of court, Merrill made seven payments out of the escrow account: $3500.00 to Payee Children & the Law Program, $3000.00 to her lawfirm (Brown Rudnick Freed & Gesmer ("BRFG") for psychological testing of Stockdale and his wife, $1815.62 to BRFG for the alleged fees for the GAL, and $2570.75 to Barbara Beardslee herself for her GAL fees. On or around 2 August, the GAL filed her report, and by operation of law, GAL Beardslee's appointment came to an end. Thus, it was only for that period between the day Beardslee was appointed as GAL and the date on her report that the parties were, by court order, to share the cost of the fees.

During November, Beardslee was re-appointed as GAL. Neither Connelly nor WIA objected to the November re-appointment or to the continued payment of the GAL's fees with money from the escrow account containing Lucas Stockdale's money. In the following March, Barbara Beardslee filed an updated report and with that filing, her second appointment came to an end by operation of law. Beardslee had no active appointment after she filed the March report. Four months later, Merrill made a payment of $2967.72 to Law & Psychiatry Service, MGH (for the alleged fees for the GAL out of the escrow account in which Luke's money was held.

Stockdale argued that the money in the escrow account was not his wife's money; it was his. Therefore, when the money removed from the escrow account was used to pay the GAL's fees, his wife was not sharing in the payment of those fees.

Connelly never sought accountings from BRFG of the fiduciary account. Neither Connelly nor any attorney at WIA informed Stockdale of the statute that controls the payment of the fees of a GAL. Neither the consent of nor a stipulation by Stockdale to pay the GAL was sought or obtained by **(a)** his wife, **(b)** the court, **(c)** Connelly, or **(d)** WIA.

Connelly and WIA **(a)** failed to explain to Stockdale what a GAL's function was, **(b)** failed to explain the inherent dangers in engaging a GAL, **(c)** failed to explain that the GAL statute explicitly mandates that the Commonwealth is to pay the fees for the GAL's alleged services, **(d)** failed to object to Merrill's intentional encouragement of the court to violate the existing mandatory statute, and thus participated in an act that violated that existing statute, **(e)** failed to take action, e.g., by filing a Complaint for Contempt.

There was no court order commanding the parties to pay for any so-called services rendered by the GAL in accordance with the second reference of appointment. Each and every fee payment made from the escrow fund was made contrary to the court order in which the court expressly wrote that no funds were to be removed from that account without court approval. Neither Connelly nor WIA took legal action about the unlawful conversion of monies from the escrow account to pay the GAL's fees or to pay any entity for any purpose. Connelly did not notify Stockdale that the fees for the second round of the so-called services rendered by the GAL were being paid from Stockdale's cash in the escrow account.

Given that it was Stockdale's money in the escrow account, when that money was used to pay the GAL's fees, some of it suddenly did not convert into being his wife's money. Therefore, because it was his money that was used to pay the GAL's fees, and none of hers was used, she did not share in the paying of the fees.

Given that the court ordered that the money was not to be removed from that account without further order of the court, and that Merrill did not seek or obtain permission of the court, Stockdale was robbed. Connelly did nothing to stop Merrill or call her contemptuous conduct to the court by bringing a Complaint for Contempt. Neither did WIA.

Had Connelly or WIA informed the court by motion and/or sought an evidentiary hearing, the court might not have sent the Stockdale boys to live in the home of their maternal grandfather, who was suspected of having committed sexual abuse of at least one child, and maybe more.

"I told Connelly about my wife's dysfunctional biological family," Stockdale insisted, "He did nothing as far as I know with that information. After my children were removed to Maine, I told Connelly about the unusual behaviors I was seeing for the first time by my boys. I suspected the worst. Neither Connelly nor WIA did anything to alert the court or the GAL or my wife's attorney. Months later, one of my boys complained to me about his being sexually abused by my wife's father. At the end of trial, when I finally saw my children's school records—the court would not let us get them earlier—there was evidence of possible sexual abuse of the other twin during the first few months of the children being removed to Maine to live in their grandfather's home.

"I had felt helpless when they were first removed and felt even more helpless when I saw my boys' unusual behaviors, heard my child's complaint about sexual abuse, and then saw evidence of my other child's possible sexual abuse. The children regressed in almost every way after their move to Maine. I blame Connelly and WIA. They could and should have properly represented me and my concerns about my sons' safety. Connelly and WIA did not."

When the first restraining order expired, Stockdale wanted to get back into the marital home from which he had been ordered out on the day his wife filed for divorce. His purpose of getting back in was to finish the renovations he had begun prior to his wife deciding she wanted a divorce. He anticipated the court ordering the sale of the home and thought it a good idea to increase the value of the house before he had to put it on the market.

So he told Connelly his representation was terminated and informed Merrill that he, Stockdale, was now representing himself. Stockdale also told both counsel that he wanted the return of his house keys. By Connelly not getting the keys from Merrill, Connelly left Stockdale unable to get them.

Stockdale explained, "Merrill would not respond to my letters because I was still represented by Connelly technically—he had not filed a notice of withdrawal with the court. I had an appointment to meet with Connelly at the WIA office, but Connelly was not there. There were only empty beer cans on his desk. He was nowhere to be found.

"So I hired a locksmith to access the condo in early January. I then returned to my home in central Mass. for my tools and the wood I had precut to finish the renovations in the back bedroom, which

I had begun prior to the divorce. When I returned to the condo two days later, both my wife and her stepbrother phoned the Boston police (she was at her home in Maine and her stepbrother was at our Boston condo). When the police arrived, I was arrested. I was handcuffed, strip-searched, jailed, arraigned, and had to appear in court for a criminal case against me. Fortunately, the case was dismissed at the end of April, but it was an anxious, worrisome time for me. A horrendous time would be more accurate. I incurred expense for my defense. The court-appointed lawyer did nothing and I had to retain my own private counsel to effect the dismissal. Of course, that leaves a criminal charge on a record. I never had a criminal charge against me until that time.

"I blame Connelly and WIA. They could and should have properly represented me and gotten my keys to the condo whether voluntarily from Merrill or by court order. My first request to Connelly was on or around December 5th, so he had sufficient time to move and get a court hearing on the issue. As of December 12th, there was no restraining order, or any other order, precluding me from being at my home. Connelly and WIA did nothing to help me or my boys."

Anecdote #3.

Ethan Emory v. SAF.

When Ethan's attorney's bill reached approximately $78,000 and the divorce was continuing to run into snag after snag, he said, Oops!" and contacted me. I told him to gather all his bills. I then scanned them in and sorted the entries both according to tasks and according to attorneys. Because the lawfirm used, allegedly, the "team" approach, the bills iterated the hours six attorneys had spent on his case, and because some of the entries included more than one task, some of the totals for each entry were approximate.

The scanning in of 80-odd pages and sorting the files were the most time-consuming tasks but also the most important. They made possible both a thorough review of what the SAF attorneys and staff did and did not do on Ethan Emory's case and a reliable conclusion as to whether Ethan Emory owed SAF any money or whether SAF owed Ethan the return of any money he had paid the firm and whether SAF owed him the money Ethan had paid me when I took his case over from SAF. I had settled his divorce case in 10 days and got rid of all the serious collateral problems threatening Ethan's future.

I summarized the work each attorney performed. You should do the same. A few examples:

As to billing $60 for GTP's time. He simply took a phone call made to get SAF to send a transcript to another attorney. All that was exchanged was who would pick up or drop off the transcript(s) and where that would occur. To charge $200 dollars an hour for such a phonecall falls into the unreasonable if not the absurd category. A credit for the $60 would be appropriate.

As to MAC's work: It appears she had 8 conferences with lead attorney, AEE, reviewed some correspondence about something un-named, drafted a motion to continue, and made a few calls to the wife's counsel and to court. What she did with the information she reviewed is not revealed. A motion to continue is generally just boil-erplate. There is nothing in the bill which alerts me to any unusual reason for the continuation. The charge of $798 for that ministerial work is excessive. A credit for the $798 would be appropriate.

Given that on 4/28/98, when SAM was first assigned to the case and reviewed the file, there was not much in it except a few letters and AEE's memo, I attributed almost all the 1.20 hours for the multi-task entry to SAM drafting the Answer and Counterclaim for a cost of $90.00. Then, at a cost of $80.00, AEE revised the document. Next, SAM further revised her copy (.30 hour) and that cost another $22.50, which brought the total cost of SAM's efforts to $112.50. One suspects that AEE could have done it all for the same amount. Not having had the entire file transmitted to me, I cannot make further comment, but generally answers and counterclaims in a divorce case are almost boilerplate.

A month later, SAM reviewed a file for 6 minutes, a file that had vir-tually nothing in it. Three or four days later, SAM reviewed the virtually empty file again. She then allegedly wrote to the client and forwarded documents. Sounds like SAF finally mailed the Answer and Counter-claims to Emory a month after they were written, but that cannot be so because yet a week later, SAM revised the Answer and Counterclaims AGAIN (0.70 hour), bringing the total cost of SAM's efforts to $165. Something seemed terribly wrong with the picture. One week short of two months after the Answer and Counterclaims were written, they were finished: 4/20-6/14/98. Work done on the Answer between AEE and SAM: 6.10 hours. Total time on Answer and Counterclaim: $945. The amount of money charged in 1998 was enormous for one answer to an action for the dissolution of a marriage.

Work in general:

SAM clearly was unable to work without considerable guidance. Although $75 per hour is less than AEE would have received for the same work, more than half of the time SAM spent on the case was taking instruction from AEE. It appears to have been less cost-efficient for SAM to do the work than for AEE to do the work and get it finished. The steps were: (1) SAM would seek instruction from AEE, (2) SAMS sometimes would do some task, (3) AEE would review SAM's work and correct it, (4) SAMS would rework whatever it was she was doing, and (5) AEE would review it again. Such a process not only cost Emory more in both the short and long run, it did not even save AEE that much time, time which she could apply to other cases.

Other examples: it took 2.80 hours to determine what should go into a Keeper of the Records subpoena to one of Emory's part-time employers. Such a task usually takes only a small fraction of an hour. At most, a release would have been necessary. The information would have had to be included in Emory's Financial Statement. Subsequently, SAM researched the issue of objections to Keeper of the Records subpoenas. Why? Emory's wife would have had no conceivable objection to Emory's pay records. She, too, would have wanted them. More credits had to be given.

PAW's lead attorney created issues where there were really no issues. For instance, AEE fought opposing counsel's access to Emory's departmental file. Given that in the file were only awards for clinical and scientific work and no complaints of any type by physician colleagues, medical staff, or anyone else had ever been filed, there was no issue worth 3 hours of time.

In 1½ years, approximately 11.20 hours were devoted to discovery, none of which was served on the wife's counsel or on the wife. Not until almost two years after the discovery process began with SKR, was any further work done to accomplish discovery for Emory . . . and then it was only for SAM to review the discovery documents in the file. And then two days later, a fourth person, CLC, reviewed discovery motions. Next, three weeks later, more conferences took place with AEE regarding the discovery . . . and AGAIN four weeks later, MORE reviewing. Then again, remarkably, more on the next four days. Ultimately, according to the bills themselves, the discovery was never served on the wife!!!!! SAF charged $1,643 for this work which had no benefit to Emory. It had never been sent. Emory was due a credit for all this useless "busy" work.

It is difficult to believe that approximately 20 hours were spent on the appraisal of the marital home, a simple split-level in an area where the homes are not dissimilar.

Conferences and reviews: What did they achieve? The predominant characteristic of this file is the number of "conferences" and "telephone conferences" had by SAM. SAM spent approximately 19.30 hours essentially on conferences with AEE regarding the Financial Statement, Child Support Guidelines, and some tax items. Those 19.30 hours do NOT include the conferences listed as secondary items in other entries. And 11.50 hours worth of more conferences with AEE can be seen in the listing for "telephone conferences," for a total of 30.80 hours at $4,037.00. To fill out a Financial Statement and a child-support worksheet, those numbers are extraordinary. A credit of $4,037 was sought. Please note that the money here is 1998 money.

During the first 7 months of the case, AEE worked the case unassisted by anyone and that she charged almost $1500 for three office meetings with Emory (2.6 hours), phone calls and 11 letters—to Emory, his wife, and her attorney. The subjects of the conferences and the correspondence are not revealed in the bills. Given that the letters were charged out at 6, 12, 18, or 24 minutes, I am assuming they were relatively short, and did not address substantive matters. Clearly I am guessing.

Because there is mention of "Revisions to Agreement," which took 30 minutes—and no mention of drafting one, I am assuming also that opposing counsel drafted a settlement agreement, which apparently was unacceptable ultimately to one or both of the parties to the divorce.

The lead attorney's (AEE's) telephone usage accounted for "roughly" 72.80 hours, or 34 percent, of the 221.20 hours she spent on the case. Of $59,770 charges for AEE's work, 34 percent[623]/ is $20,321.80. How much of this twenty-thousand-plus dollars can be justified? We know that lawyer's fees are not dependent upon success, but the work for which the fees are charged must have some reasonable basis. I cannot imagine spending 72.80 hours on the phone without some definable purpose and definable accomplishment. I am not saying there was no definable purpose and no definable accomplishment, but if there was such a purpose and accomplishment, I do not see them in the bills.

Some reasonable explanation is required.

Legal Services.

AEE did very little, if any, legal research herself, did very little strategizing, very little writing of briefs, and very little learning how to defend against the preposterous and dangerous allegations which had taken center stage in this case. She did not depose any of the DSS people (very critical, and this left the client with an open action at DSS). Neither did she appear to know the significance of letting in the DSS report (even redacted) without cross-examining the author of the report. And incredibly, AEE made no attempt to schedule the divorce trial after the date for the DSS Fair Hearing to give Emory the opportunity to respond to the DSS charges. There is a charge somewhere in the bill that there was some preparation for a deposition of a DSS worker, but apparently, that deposition never materialized. Credit for that preparation is appropriate.

Of critical importance was that AEE left the deposition of the wife until the very last day of discovery, leaving no time to depose the wife about the allegations of physical abuse of the children. But for the deposition by successor counsel of the wife on the issue of the three alleged rapes, the client would likely have suffered a civil suit for rape.

Furthermore, AEE initially agreed to Emory's request to engage a legal expert on false accusations as a consultant to the case, having admitted that this is not her area of legal expertise, but later refused and threatened to terminate legal representation should Emory insist. Then when he did insist on an expert consultant, AEE executed her ultimatum and removed herself from the case shortly before the impending divorce trial, 2½ years into the case, clearly one of the most vulnerable time-points for her client.

It can be argued that she violated Mass.R.Prof.C 1.16 by unilaterally withdrawing from the case when Emory requested that she continue to be lead counsel for all legal issues specific to the divorce, but to work in conjunction with another attorney to be retained for strategy and decisions pertaining to the many and complex false allegations.

Clearly, AEE never had the vision and, one assumes, the experience to recognize or acknowledge that the Emory case was not simply a run-of-the-mill divorce case, but one that involved issues which could and would precipitate actions in other jurisdictions, to wit, in an administrative agency (DSS for the child abuse issue) and in superior court (for the falsely alleged multiple rape accusations and potentially for the appeal of any potential negative decision by DSS after a Fair Hearing). This resulted in significant material adverse effects on Emory's interests . . . and at a tremendously high price—financially, professionally, and emotionally—to him as well as to his children.

In sum, AEE acted more as a case manager, as an administrator, rather than as a provider of legal services. She spent extraordinary time on the phone (2½ pages worth out of 7½ pages of tasks), instructing SAM, and writing letters to new opposing counsel.

The bills are silent as to the purpose of those letters to the new opposing counsel and to the purpose of the letters. We know that very little benefit was obtained from all that communication with new opposing counsel. If the letters were but transmittal letters, then they should have been left to her secretary to do. If they were substantive letters, then what were the issues?

Before I drew a bottom line as to the credit in dollars I thought Emory should get, I wrote to SAF. "Let's see if we can sort out some of the problem areas I identified. I think it's important that you be given an opportunity to fill in some of the information missing from the bills. Then we can reach some agreement to a number that feels fair to Emory and to SAF."\[624]/

I advised Emory not to pay the money SAF claimed he owed. "Let them sue you. Maybe they will. Maybe they won't. If they do, you can countersue for legal malpractice." That is what happened. Emory countersued and won by settlement after a mediation for which the judge—one I knew to be fair, honest, and bright—played mediator.

What to Do to Create Fairness

Complaints Against Attorneys

Privacy and public scrutiny are rivals in this area. While judges continue to be paid during an investigation of them, an attorney's livelihood can be negatively affected during that time. Grievous violations might result in the disclosure of an attorney's name in some States, such as Massachusetts. Pending disciplinary proceedings are revealed on the regulatory board's website. Final decisions are published weekly on the board's website, in the Lawyers Weekly, and in books filled with legal decisions.

With that said, I suggest that all complaints be made public BUT with Numbers substituted for the attorneys' names. This is a precaution given that many, many complaints are frivolous, but, certainly, once it has been determined by scrutinizing the facts that it is not a frivolous complaint, the public has a right to know.

If, after investigation of the alleged misconduct, the Board of Bar Overseers determines that there is wrongdoing or if there are public outcries and the outcries are based on reasonable outrage, then the alleged wrongdoer's name should be revealed.

Chapter 21

Court Reporters

Beware of Transcription Companies

Justice is to be freely given, so say our constitutions. Not if you have to pay $350 to file a lawsuit. Not if you have to pay thousands of dollars you do not have for a transcript of a hearing or trial from which you want to appeal. The right to appeal becomes meaningless. It is not only horrific that the appeals courts have tricks to despoil your right to appeal, the right disappears when you cannot afford to buy a trial transcript, which you need for your appeal.

Why do you need them for an appeal? To prove **(a)** who said what at trial, **(b)** what and when objections were made and who made them, **(c)** what the court's ruling was on each of those objections, **(d)** what exhibits were admitted or not admitted into evidence, **(e)** what the evidentiary purpose was for offering each of the exhibits, **(f)** what legal issues were raised at trial, **(g)** the verbal demeanor of all the witnesses . . . and the judge (if necessary), and **(h)** the effectiveness of your counsel (if this is one of your issues).

People who make a record of a court hearing—whether by typing or talking while holding a mask around their mouths—are generically known as "court reporters." Some are employed by the court and are assigned to the cases being heard. They squabble a lot amongst themselves. Who gets appointed to one judge because she is young and attractive? Who gets appointed to the high-money or high-profile case, which will attract lots of media reporters who will order copies of the daily trial transcripts? Who gets appointed to a case between parties who might or might not buy a copy of a transcript? None of these court reporters is certified. They are (1) simply employed by the judicial branch of the Commonwealth of Massachusetts, (2) they charge the parties whatever they want to charge per page, and (3) they might have their own employees whom they pay to prepare the transcripts from the paper or audio tape. They generally earn a healthy six-figure annual income.

Some "court reporters" are private. They, too, are not certified. They either have private employers or have their own wee or more than wee or substantial company.

Some States do not provide either tapes or reporters unless you tell the court ahead of time . . . and even then, you might or might not get one, so hire your own private one. Maine is a "relaxed" State. The judge's old partner or old buddy can walk into the judge's chamber just prior to trial for a friendly chat. Also significant for people in Maine: A file in the clerk's can be cleaned out and no evidence of a trial having been had can be found in it. Prepare a letter to give to the clerk. Ask the clerk to list the documents in the file and have her certify that those documents were the only ones in the file when she gave you copies of it.

The price of $2.50 per page has slowly given away to $3.50 per page and occasionally $4.75 per page if the copy for the court is added on to your bill. Recently e-transcripts have made their appearance. The charge: $1.10 per page, but you cannot copy parts of it. The e-transcribers do not provide a paper copy, and therefore save the cost of paper and shipping and handling. Other e-transcript transcribers are less honest and still charge the "old" higher prices. So buyer beware.

An index of words is available for each transcript, whether paper or electronically formatted. Some reporters will charge extra for the Index, which used to be a freebie. The e-index for the e-transcript is included in the price of the entire e-transcript . . . as is the miniscript, for the e-transcript software asks how you want to print the e-transcript.

Now the controversy! What is a "page"? How wide are the margins on the left, right, top, and bottom? Another way of asking that question is, How wide is a line? 4"? 5"? 6"? 6½"? How many lines to a page? 54 lines (what the State allows) or 57 lines (what the federal courts demand)? What are the indentions? Huh? What are indentions?

Indentions are the number of spaces from the left at which the transcriber puts the **Q** to identify the question asked the witness, the **A** to identify the answer the witness gave, the word **COURT** to identify the judge's comments or instructions, the name of one counsel, such as

Mr. X, to identify his speech to respond, for instance, to the judge, and **Ms. Y**, to identify the speech of the other counsel.

In plain English: the transcribers generally indent the **Q** and **A**s one tab. The lines below them might go to within one or two spaces of the left-hand edge. Occasionally the **Q** and **A**s are placed a few spaces from the left-hand edge, but then the lines that follow are indented one tab. The reporters' object is to type as little as possible on one page, making the transcript many pages longer than it should be and their bill for the transcript quite steep.

The word **COURT** is generally indented three tabs and every line beneath it three tabs, **Mr. X** ditto, and **Ms. Y** ditto. The result makes the text look like a stripe down the back of a skunk. The width of the line is whittled down to around 3 inches. I have actually received a transcript with only one character on it: the period. That's when I blew my stack. I was not going to advise my client to pay $3.25 for one period! And if you have to pay for a copy for the judge, then it's $6.50 for one period.

When the left- and right-hand margins are a few spaces in from the box for the text, and the indentions are excessive, the width of the lines are anywhere from 3" to 4½" wide. Given that the standard page is 8½" x 11", and a margin is to be 1" all the way around, the line width should be 6½" wide and 57 lines long. The result of enlarging all the margins, the reporters have doubled their income from one transcript.

By the way, the cover page, the attorney page, the certification page are all boilerplate pages. For a multi-day trial, the only item that must be changed is the date, but you will be charged for the three pages for each day of trial. For instance, for a 10-day trial, you will pay 10 times for the attorney page for yourself and 10 times for the judge's copy. So for typing two attorneys' names once, the reporter will charge you 20 times $3.50 (assuming that is the per page price) or $70.

There is a national court reporters' organization, NCRA, which has issued guidelines for the reporters to follow, but the organization is a voluntary one, and does not have any authority to make the reporters play fair when preparing the transcripts.

The courts ignore the excessive costs for transcripts because the high cost lessens the number of cases being appealed. So, in effect, the courts aid and abet by inaction the fraud being committed against the people.

Anecdate #1.

I paid $6700 for services rendered and to be rendered by BG, an independent contractor supplied by a major transcription company. BG used 14-point **bold sans-serif** type for the transcript, kept the right-hand margin set at 5½" rather than 6", and charged a full-page rate for a boilerplate certification page. By using the typeface and type-size she chose, a sample volume of those which BG produced was 129 percent longer than it would have been had she chosen a 12-point type, which is the usual type size, and a `fixed-width` font (typeface).

Then despite an existing contract that specified the rate, BG's employer charged my client for more copies than he ordered and at a higher rate per page than agreed upon . . . and improperly for miscellaneous and diverse things. The employer sued for payment. We countersued for Breach of Contract, Negligence (for breaching their duty to act in accordance with the federal and state fair billing practices acts), Unjust Enrichment (failing to post the payment of $6700.00 to my account, and then, suing without acknowledging the $6700 payment), Violation of Consumer Protection Act, and a few other counts.

Point of interest: The case being tried was a divorce with political implications. Even though we had a private court reporter—BG— Judge Lisa Roberts ordered a secret set of tapes from Janice Eldridge, a court reporter hired secretly by the court. The judge's Assistant Register of Suffolk Probate & Family Court, Maria Rizzo LaFace, had hand-written the order and sent it to Eldridge. Using the excuse that BG had failed to bring her own tape recorder, Roberts gave BG the judge's set of tapes to use to "correct" BG's transcription. I smelled a rat.

Believing that the judge had altered the trial tapes and wanted a set of transcripts to match the altered tapes, I concluded that the judge gave BG a copy of all the tapes so that BG's transcripts would match the tapes and transcripts as altered by the judge. So I initiated a little G-2 investigation. As a result, I managed to get a copy of the handwritten order.\[625]/ All hell broke loose.

As requested by the judge, I wrote a brief explaining why I wanted several clerks as well as LaFace served with trial witness subpoenas. In the morning, the judge quashed all my subpoenas served on anyone in the court clerk's office. Roberts did not, however. quash the one served on Eldridge, whose address I managed to ferret out, but El-dridge did not show. Her attorney did. So I managed to get his admissions on behalf of Eldridge on tape and in a transcript provided by, of course, a replacement transcription company.

In the meantime, the original reporting company was bought out and then the buyer was bought out by a larger company. The new corporation had changed focus. It did not want to take on a case that asked (a) whether there are standards for stenographic services rendered in courts, (b) if so, what are they?, (c) whether there is price-fixing in the industry of stenographic services rendered in the legal arena, and (d) about the political aspects of the case!!

Ultimately, the suit vanished. My client saved over 20 grand. Me? I got the satisfaction of catching the court obstructing justice. This judge was far from the first. In fact, the predecessor judge had altered the tapes of a hearing on the same case the year before. She made them into Humpty Dumpties. Unable to put them together again, the judge could only give delivery of them to us in pieces days apart.

Anecdote #2. \⁶²⁶/

Eight months prior to ECRI bringing suit against my client, I had set out to Armos Eyal, the owner of ECRI both the standards of NCRA, of which ECRI claimed it was a member, and the deficient performance of ECRI. Eyal's issues were **(1)** Why did I not call him right after the receipt of the first transcript? **(2)** Because NCRA standards are only guidelines, he did not need to follow them. He asserted that he follows local custom; therefore I should have verified and confirmed with other court reporters what those customs are. **(3)** He had a right to charge $4.25 a page rather than the $2.35 on the contract my client had signed.

My responses were: **(1)** I had been sent email copies, not 8½" x 11" copies, of the transcripts. Many 8½" x 11" copies did not arrive until long after the proposed findings of fact were due, so I had no need to look at them until much later. **(2)** ECRI held itself out as an NCRA member. I had no need to verify the local custom with other court reporters in the Boston area and compare what they did. My client's contract was with ECRI, not with others. **(3)** My client signed a contract for $2.35 per page, not $4.25.

Usually the attorney—not the client—bargains with the reporting company. Here, the unusual had occurred. I bargained with Armos Eyal before ECRI was asked to perform. We reached an agreed per page price of $2.35. When I saw on the contract that Eyal had added a $100 daily attendance fee (just for the reporter to come to work), I refused to sign it as written. When the reporter showed up in court, the reporter, Julie Bates, gave a contract to my client—unbeknownst to me—to sign. Taken by surprise, my client signed it before asking my advice. The contract also included a change of two terms that were not included in the agreement between Eyal and me. The first was adding a daily $25 ASCII-disk fee and the deletion of ECRI's obligation to provide Mini-Scripts.

On 2/17/04 and 8/29/04, I wrote Eyal regarding the services ECRI provided and the NCRA standards, which ECRI did not follow.

Two months later, on 27 October 2004, Eyal brought suit in district court, but under a different company name, ERSI. Although I alerted ERSI's counsel, Elliott Loew, to ERSI not being the proper plaintiff, Loew failed to amend and change the name of the plaintiff to ECRI, the entity with which Gouin did do business. That failure left my client in the position that had he prevailed on his potential counterclaims, he would not be able to collect . . . even if I had gotten the admission during trial that the plaintiff was wrongly named. Problems could have arisen with the documents coming out of the clerk's office.

My client then brought the case against ECRI in Superior Court, so the proper parties would be involved. (At that time, we did not know that ECRI was not a corporation.)

Because it seemed foolish to fight it out on two fronts, I l suggested to Loew that we negotiate a settlement.

Loew and I began trying to negotiate a settlement. We next found ourselves in a status conference with Clerk-Magistrate Henry Shultz and informed him of our on-going attempt. To give Loew and me time to continue the negotiation strategy, Shultz set a date for a second status conference. That second conference was to occur on April 19th.

Outside the court and after speaking for the better part of an hour, Loew and I came to an agreement as to the steps that had to be taken to reach settlement. My client and I waited for Armos Eyal to perform as promised. Eyal performed something but not that which his counsel, Loew, had promised. (Eyal himself was present at the court that day and waited while Loew and I negotiated.)

Loew responded with a proposed settlement. Because Eyal had reformatted only a few pages and extrapolated the total number of pages from them and because I had reformatted an entire volume and found that the reformatted volume was approximately half as long as ECRI's, I insisted that Eyal do a complete reformatting as agreed upon on 20 January 2005.

While continuing attempts at negotiation with Elliott Loew, I put before Loew more standards, those proposed by a committee appointed by the Supreme Judicial Court, and asked Loew "How is the re-formatting coming along?"

Loew wrote, *"I will talk to you soon about the revised transcript and trying to resolve the case,"* acknowledging the issue raised by me. That was *one* of the reasons for the request to continue the second status conference to 19 April 2005. (The details were *not* communicated to Shultz.)

In the meantime, while waiting for Eyal to perform, I was intensely busy all year with several federal court cases, all of which had rigid time schedules. I had been writing briefs all year under strict deadlines, resulting in my working through the night literally dozens of times.

On April 19th, the day we were due at 2:30 P.M. for the second Status Conference with Clerk-Magistrate Shultz, I shared with Loew and Shultz the problem created because of a confluence of my cases.

I phoned and wrote both Loew and Shultz. Extreme deadlines throughout the year culminated that day in my having no choice but to request being able to attend the status conference telephonically or permission to be an hour late to the conference.

Because I had been under considerable pressure from an enormous amount of work on several cases with deadlines and had worked through the night on one of those cases, I phoned Attorney Loew around 8 or 8:15 in the morning before I went to bed and left him a message about my problem—I was fearful of driving from my home to the court without having had at least a few hours sleep—and asked him to give me a wake-up call around noon.

Loew, instead, responded by email, telling me to call him when I woke. Fortunately my alarm clock worked on time for me to phone him. Loew and I then had a lengthy conversation and reviewed how far apart we still were. There were still a few items that needed cleaning up.

Because time was being eaten up on the phone, I remarked to Loew that perhaps the 2:30 status meeting could still go forward with me on the speaker phone. In that way, I would not be late, which had become inevitable, and would cause less inconvenience for Loew and Shultz. (In federal court, attendance by phone is frequent when travel is inconvenient for assorted reasons, e.g., out-of-state defendants and counsel do not have to make a trip for a few minutes worth of meeting in person.)

Loew and I knew that it was Clerk-Magistrate Shultz who had to make the decision whether a partly telephonic conference would be adequate.

I said I would phone Shultz, which I did. Shultz's secretary—at least, a woman who I believed to be his secretary—took the message, told me to hold, which I did, and then returned to the phone.

Shultz wanted me to put my request in writing and FAX it to him.

I immediately wrote my request in a letter, FAXed it to Shultz, and emailed a confirmation copy to Loew's office. Shortly after I sent the FAX to Shultz, I received a phonecall from the woman saying, in words for all intents and purposes, "He defaulted you."

Where Shultz defaulted my client so inappropriately, I believed that an explanation of the surprising, even shocking, circumstances in a motion to vacate the judgment would be sufficient to restore the case.

There appeared to be no reasonable cause for Shultz to have defaulted my client. His defaulting my client was too harsh an action in these circumstances. There was no evidence before the court that my client or I had been negligent in attempting to defend ERSI's action. The only "evidence" of cause for Shultz's defaulting my client is circumstantial, if not merely speculative: Shultz knew Loew very well, given that Loew's client, Eyal, had **75** small claims cases in Newton District Court between 1/1/97 and 11/9/01 and likely a similar amount during the last four years in both the small- and non-small claims courts.

According to the docket, my client was defaulted at the call of the list. Neither my client nor I had notice that the parties were to appear before the court on that date. It is, therefore, curious that my client was defaulted allegedly at the call of the list.

What exacerbated the wounds inflicted on accommodation, fairness, and justice by Shultz was that the case had not been scheduled to be before the court on April 19th.

While waiting to be helped on the 17th, I thumbed through the Small Claims book for 1/1/97–11/9/01 and found that Armos Eyal had brought **75** small claims cases within that time frame. That number does not include the small claims cases he brought since then, nor the cases he brought—I assumed—in the civil session for *non*-small-claims cases. Note that 67 were brought by Eyal Court Reporting, Inc. Eight others were brought in diverse names, but none in the name of Eyal Reporting Service, Inc.\[627]/

The judge, Dyanne Klein, backed up Shultz and allowed a default. Who knows? Maybe Klein and Shultz are an item. Klein's action was extraordinary. And the Appeals Court and the Supreme Judicial Court of Massachusetts were of no assistance. Of course not. They wanted my butt. You will not find one case in Massachusetts holding any party in default for being late by one hour. Being no rational reason for Klein to do what she did, she must be impeached . . . without a pension. Pensions must not be given to people who act incompetently or corruptly.

My Proposed New Standards Transmitted to the Court

While a court-mandated standard format will relieve practitioners of the need "to say" something to transcription companies after receiving transcripts that look like a stripe down a skunk's back or that were typed using a 14-point bold typeface, there are other needs as acute:

- There is no need to require only transcribers on a "list of approved transcribers." The latter requirement interferes with the law of supply and demand. All court reporting schools have closed in the Commonwealth. The supply of transcribers is small, making a choice of transcribers almost impossible. Given that there is no licensing for court reporters in the Commonwealth, that there is no mandatory testing, and that there is no accrediting agency, there is no reason—other than a reason for payoffs to someone in government—to use a "list of approved transcribers."

- Costs of transcripts are exorbitant. The ordinary party to litigation cannot afford deposition or trial transcripts. The court must consider that economics impacts the litigant's rights to due process and equal protection. Competition must be encouraged. That means allowing people off an unpublicized list to be part of "the supply." Discriminating against those transcribers not on a list that is not readily available to the public is inappropriate. Grandfathering so-called previously approved transcribers is inappropriate.

- Practices that stretch the number of pages produced are rampant amongst any and all court reporters, whether on an approved list or not.

- Billing practices of many transcription firms are, euphemistically, highly questionable.

- The SJC's proposed rules do not adequately take into account the significant technological strides in document creation, management, and storage. Why should we be locked in to double-spaced single columns on one page when MiniScripts are available, less onerous to store, and less expensive to include in an Appendix?

- The SJC's proposed rules do not adequately take into account how transcripts are used during litigation. Appeals are not the only use of transcripts.

Preprinted box.

Each page should have a preprinted box be wide enough to allow a full 6½" line to be typed. To do that, the width of the box should be 6½" plus an extra space on the left and the right . . . to take into consideration the fact that the ordinary word-processing software leaves a space between the margin and the last letter allowed to be typed.

Line width.

The allowable width of a line must be 6½" wide. Transcription companies today typically type lines 5, 5¼, or 5½ inches wide—and that is if the lawyer is lucky. Recently I've received transcripts with lines only 4 or 4½ inches wide. One had a 3½" skunk-type stripe down the middle of the page, and when the court or the attorneys spoke, a 2¾" skunk-type stripe down the middle of the page. And this from one of the so-called "top" firms in Boston and assuredly on the so-called "approved" list.

The narrower the line width, the more costly the product for the litigant, or deponent, or witness. So, the box should be wider, to allow a full 6½" line to be typed.

Line Numbers.

There is one transcription company that is putting the line numbers *inside* a 6" box. There must be an instruction that the line numbers must be *outside* the box. The box must be two spaces wider than 6½"—one space on the left and one on the right of the 6½" line.

Number of Lines per Page.

"Generally, a page is defined as 54 lines of data."\\[628]/ Fifty-four single lines of data yields 27 double-spaced lines of data. Twenty-seven lines would be fairer to the parties who have to pay the cost of the transcripts. Not enough consideration is given to the litigation costs incurred by parties. It would cost the court itself nothing to make this concession. Currently transcription companies waste those lines for the name of their company, a piece of information unnecessary on each page of a transcript.

Content.

Atop each page the numbers of the volume and page and the date must appear. If the document is a deposition transcript, the name of the deponent and the date of the deposition must appear.

Copies.

Transcribers were charging up to $2500 per day for two copies of a transcript. Some transcribers are charging for a minimum of three copies, one copy for each of two parties and one for the court copy. Additionally, they are charging shipping and handling fees that are far beyond the cost of same.   Emailed copies suffice in many instances, which should reduce the cost of a transcript.

Article XI of the Massachusetts Declaration of Rights reads, "He ought to obtain right and justice freely, and without being obliged to purchase it. . . ." A cost of $1250 per day per party for one copy of a transcript is, more often than not, prohibitive for litigants, and thereby violative of a litigant's right under Article XI not to be obliged to purchase it.

Transcribers are, of course, entitled to compensation for their efforts, but $6250 per week is a healthy sum to receive for one's efforts. It certainly should be sufficient to pay for copies for both parties. For 50 weeks, that is $312,500. And that sum is obtainable by charging for only one transcript. The parties can copy the transcript for 10 cents a page, add it to the initial one-copy price, and then split the total cost.

"Once a party or its counsel provides compensation to the court reporter, the party or the lawyer becomes the owner of the transcript."\\[629]/ Since a transcription is by definition a verbatim recording of another person's statements, there can be no originality in the reporter's product Therefore, a "court reporter does not have a copyright as to the contents of the transcript."\\[630]/

To allow transcribers to charge each party for an entire copy— which can be created by merely pushing a print button—allows transcribers to gain an estimated $625,000 per year. That is obscene. It calls out for "usury laws" to apply to transcription companies and transcribers.

Because it would be inappropriate for the Court to interfere with commerce, the High Court should simply say that it is not mandatory for parties to pay twice for one transcript, for the transcribers do **not** own the copyright to the words spoken,\\[631]/ but that the parties and the transcribers may draft and execute contracts to their mutual satisfaction. That would allow supply and demand to impact (1) the contract for which the party and the company have bargained and (2) the final charges.

A copy of the transcript on a CD should be given to the court. There must be no protection or programming codes placed on the CD-ROM that would prevent copying or transferring data. The price of the CD may, at most, be for the few minutes it takes to create the copy on a CD.

The cost of the copy given to the court must be borne by the court receiving the copy. Currently courts have their private transcribers, and often order copies from them even when the parties have their own private transcribers. The purpose is suspect. I scanned and uploaded to my website (*http://www.falseallegations.com*) such an order for transcripts (the ones I mentioned at the top of this chapter) by one Assistant Register, Marie Rizzo LaFace, on behalf of Probate & Family Court Judge Roberts. The purpose of spending thousands of dollars when the court was being supplied copies of the transcripts by the parties was a waste of money appropriated to the judicial branch of government. It is difficult to be sympathetic to those complaining of budget cuts when literally millions of dollars of this type of waste is occurring statewide with regularity.

Indiscernible or Inaudible Speech on Electronic Sound Recording

To avoid the problem of incomplete records of proceedings, transcribers shall use all reasonable means to discern the words that are spoken by each individual. Transcribers shall certify that they have used all reasonable means to discern all of the words that were spoken by each individual, and for each portion of a transcript designated as "inaudible" that the transcriber has replayed separately that section of the tape at least three times from each of the potentially relevant tracks.

Sadly, some of this problem is attributable to the limited vocabulary of some of the transcribers. A word that is more than three syllables or not on a "common word" list is unknown to many of the transcriptionists. (Yes, modern education is that bad and it is more than evident in the transcripts I see. Vocabularies are severely limited, so playing on different tracks might cure some so-called "inaudibles," but not all.)

Furthermore, when a party orders a tape from a court, the tape received is generally not in a 4-track mode but in a mode that plays in an ordinary everyday tape recorder. The availability of a 4-track recorder is scarce and rental is expensive, if found.

Lastly, there are some judges who put their hands over their microphone when speaking. The transcript for one judge in particular, the recently early-retired Nancy Mary Gould, frequently reads, "THE COURT: [Inaudible.]" By so doing, Gould was assured there was no written proof of the outrageous statements she made to either party. Judges must be cautioned that this practice is unacceptable and shall not be countenanced by this Court.

Authentication

The transcriber shall authenticate the original transcript and each copy with a certification on the last page. No additional fee shall be charged for the authentication and the certification. The certification shall appear on the last page of each volume of transcript.

This is an important provision. In a multivolume job with three copies—one for each of two parties and a court—the cost for the certification page runs into hundreds of dollars for one boilerplate page. The same result is obtained—i.e., a charge of hundreds of dollars—when transcribers put two attorneys names and addresses on a separate page.

Transcript Assessment

The transcriber shall include, if the court requires one, a Transcript Assessment Form with each volume of transcript that is prepared, as well as the end user's assessment of the transcript noting any alleged inaccurate or incomplete portions.

BREAKING NEWS

From: "Sandra M. Singer, Esq." [*NOTE: By the way, Singer is an extremely competent, honest attorney. I have read a few opinions of her cases and have watched her responses to other attorneys on a lawyers listserv. One of the best. I have never personally met her.*]

Subject: Re: Superior Court eliminates "per diem" court reporters, switches to digital recording

My recollection is that the court had some time ago either ceased or lessened the use of court reporters.

We need to distinguish between the court cutting making financial cuts which impact justice (which should never occur) and the court making financial cuts so as to cut out financial waste and abuse (which should always occur).

If the use of digital recorders provides an accurate and reliable record of the proceedings then it would be a waste of taxpayer money to pay court reporters and the elimination of court reporters just as the court previously eliminated the elevator man when the elevators changed to push button would be financially a wise and necessary business decision. I am not making a statement regarding whether or not digital recorders are sufficient to accurately and reliably record the proceedings only that the tax payers can not and should not keep paying those functions which have become archaic.

On Thu, Jan 15, 2009 at 7:00 PM, Deborah Sirotkin-Butler [*NOTE: Another excellent attorney*] wrote:

> The impact of the state's budget crunch is being felt already.
> Starting Jan. 19, the Superior Court will discontinue the use of per
> diem court reporters during civil trials, several sources have
> confirmed to Lawyers Weekly. The court reporters will be replaced by
> a tape-recording system.
>
> -Noah Schaffer & David E. Frank
>

> UPDATE: Trial Court spokeswoman Joan Kenney has re-
leased the
> following statement:
>
> As of January 20, 2009, digital recorders will be
used in Superior
> Court civil sessions. Per diem court reporters will
not be used as
> court reporters in these sessions, but they will
continue to produce
> transcripts, as needed. This will help the ongoing
effort in getting
> trial transcripts produced faster for cases on ap-
peal. It is also a
> cost saving measure. The costs associated with per
diem court
> reporters have escalated dramatically in the past
several years.
> Clerks are being trained to use the digital
recording systems.
>
> The other six Trial Court departments use
digital recording systems.

Digital recording is phenomenal. It appears to not let judges alter the tapes prior to transcription. There is no indication, however, that there are standards to which court reporters must adhere: page size, margins, top, bottom, left, right, typesize, font. The issue addressed by the court is the speed in which the "tape" will be produced to counsel.

Chapter 22

Appellate Cases

Fellow Brethren, My Golfmates, "Please save my face. Thanks!"

I paid a filing fee and then they dismissed my case just like that . . . by snapping their fingers.

They dismissed my case against the judge. He has absolute immunity. So did the social worker and the prosecutor.

I filed my notice of appeal, but the clerk never put the papers together for the Appeals Court. I asked the judge to make the clerk "assemble the record." I think that is what they called it. Anyway, the judge did nothing, so I filed another Notice of Appeal. I did that three times. Nothing happened in three and a half years. I finally sued them in the appeals court and that court said that my appeal was not "timely filed." I'm now suing them in federal court for violating my civil rights.

The federal district court said that the defendant was not a "state actor," Of course, she was. She could not have done what she did if she did not have the help of the cops. I appealed the decision to the circuit's court of appeals. They rubber-stamped what the district court judge wrote. So I looked on the Internet to learn how I could appeal to the United States Supreme Court. I found some good boilerplate. All the Supreme Court did was write DENIED. You know, we do not have an appeal system. Since I was a kid, I was told we did. That was a lie. We do not have one, not one that is real, not one that works.

Appeals courts generally hold fast to the time lines noted in the Rules of Appellate Procedure. With state legislation being ambiguously written, with state legislation being badly written by legislators ignorant of the state and federal constitutions, with federal legislation giving annual incentive bonuses to States whose courts find in favor of women, with federal legislation giving annual incentive bonuses to States prosecuting increasing numbers of protection (or restraining) orders, with incompetent judges making egregious decision, with continuing complaints of insufficient money being in court budgets, with dissatisfaction with court decisions and orders being on the rise, and so on, the appeals courts are under considerable pressure to reduce the number of appeals on their dockets. Holding fast to time lines is one way to reduce the number of appeals on their dockets. Being harshly creative while thinking of reasons for dismissal is another.

Interlocutory appeals are more difficult. They are appeals taken while a case is pending in a lower court. The federal courts make it almost impossible to get an interlocutory appeal. All appeals courts avoid discovery disputes. A clerk does not assemble the record for interlocutory appeals. Notices of appeal are necessary if you are appealing from a "final" judgment, that is, for appeals of cases for which "entry of final judgment has been entered onto the docket," not for interlocutory appeals. The rules of your State might be different from other States. Double-check your State rules. I do not know the rules of the fifty States.

Anecdote #1.

Fred's counsel was ill on the day a motion was to be argued. The defendant company moved to default him and the judge, Christopher J. Muse, allowed the defendant's motion. Fred moved to vacate the default, Judge Muse denied it. Fred filed a Notice of Appeal. The defendant moved to strike Fred's Notice of Appeal. He filed a second Notice of Appeal, this time from the order striking his other notice. He filed for the third time. The same thing happened. Judge Muse interfered with justice by depriving Fred of his civil rights. Had Fred been allowed to appeal, it is likely the Appeals Court would have—as they had previously done—held that the lower court erred in striking the Notices of Appeal from the court's judgments.\[632]/ The court reasoned, while the lower court may strike a notice of appeal for procedural reasons, the questions going to the merits of the appeal are for the appellate court, not the lower court, to decide.\[633]/

Anecdote #2.

Lou filed a notice of appeal of a divorce judgment. His wife's motion to dismiss his appeal was granted. Lou filed a second notice of appeal from the order allowing the dismissal. Mabel's second motion to dismiss the appeal was granted. Lou filed a third notice of appeal from a judgment of contempt. Mabel's third motion to dismiss his third notice of appeal was granted.

Clearly believing he could not go to the Appeals Court because his three Notices of Appeal were dismissed—in effect, "stricken"—Lou next filed a petition in the Supreme Judicial Court to invoke the superintendency powers of the high court.\[634]/ And he was shot down by the SJC because *even though his Notices of Appeal were dismissed he retained the right to go to the Appeals Court.*\[635]/\[636]/

That means that Lou could have brought his appeal directly to the Appeals Court even though his Notices of Appeal were dismissed.

> It is clear from the papers reproduced in the appendix and the supplemental appendices, and from the transcript of the lengthy hearing conducted before the single justice, **that the appellant had open to him the right to seek relief in the Appeals Court from the action of the judge dismissing his various appeals.** . . . That court (where the various appeals would have been docketed) could have considered and, if appropriate, rectified (by reinstating the appeals) all of the errors claimed by the appellant in the trial judge's action.\[637]/

Thus, although the striking of his Notice of Appeal appears to be prejudicial to Lou, it, according to the High Court, is not. Of course, the Court was discounting the aggravation and anxiety *and* cost *and* time loss Lou suffered. But . . . it is a bit ameliorative that folks like Lou retain the right to seek review in the Appeals Court of the order of dismissal when a judge has the insolence to strike a party's right to appeal.\[638]/ Over the years, the SJC's decision in Lou's case has become a progenitor of an abundance of cases.\[639]/

As the Appeals Court panel wrote in one of those cases,\[640]/ "Consequently, if the plaintiffs had filed a timely appeal with us, we could have considered and, if appropriate, rectified the errors claimed by the plaintiffs in the motion judge's rulings."\[641]/ As the defendants' list on page 2 of their latest Motion to Strike, Lou timely filed his Notices of Appeal.

But these cases also make clear that Lou was required to file a Notice of Appeal of this court's order of sanctions against Lou. To award sanctions to defendants was reversible error.

* * *

When I began practicing law, I did a lot of court-watching and often heard judges say, "Go'on, take me up. I don't care." Their voices and demeanor belied what they said. Eventually that cry became faint. The appellate courts became more protective of their brethren who were on the lower tiers. Why? As time went on, the new judges met the "old" judges at conferences, sat together on the panels of the same legal seminars, joined their peers who were golfers, seriously imbibed together at the annual judicial conferences at country clubs or luxury vacation hotels. They learned the art of looking out for themselves and each other. They became Brethren under those Black Robes. They learned not to name each other when a case was controversial and the opinion was sure to be panned by the legal community. Nowadays, when appellate briefs are published on Westlaw, even lawyers do not call out the name of the judge being appealed. Instead, they write "the motion judge" or "the trial judge" did this or that. They play along as far as they can to get along. Subtle compulsion.

Judges now simply strike the percipient appellant's Notice of Appeal . . . often several times. Why? Because the judges, increasingly incompetent or egomaniacal as a result of what has become known as the "Black Robe Syndrome," do get embarrassed, despite their contentions to the contrary, by being appealed often, if not in fear of being reversed.

To lessen the publicity of certain appeals, the judiciary—nationwide—releases its opinions as "unpublished" opinions under some State rule. In Massachusetts, "unpublished" cases are called "Rule 1:28 cases." The Commonwealth judiciary does not frown upon "unpublished" cases being cited in legal briefs, but makes it clear that "unpublished" cases have no precedential value. Why? Because, so the high court claims, those appellate cases have not been reviewed by the court to assure that the law cited in them is accurate or applicable to the case. In other words, you folks or your friends or family, the appellants, might have been screwed by an appeals court single-justice or panel.

As to the word "unpublished," it means that the caption and docket number will appear only in a table of other "unpublished" cases in the official and unofficial reporters. You will not be able to learn what the facts and law of the care are. Online is a different story. In Westlaw, you can read the facts and the discussion of law of the unpublished cases If you cite them in a brief, you must put the word "unpublished" inside parentheses after the citation of the case. For example, Doe v. Smith, No. 12345 (date) (unpublished). Unpublished cases are not precedential; that is, the law in the opinions does not need to be followed.

To save the face of some judges, some appellate decisions are signed by a clerk and both the judge whose decision is being appealed and the appellate panel are not identified.

Per curiam is Latin for "by the court as a whole" or "by the entire court." You'll often see "*Per curiam*" at the very top and the very bottom of a case. In our language, it means, *No judge wants responsibility for this one.* So no particular judge will be identified as the author.

A *per curiam* opinion allegedly deals with one or more relatively non-controversial issues, issues that have already been decided in earlier cases, and may be cited as support for a legal argument in a brief. Because the facts of the *per curiam* case are necessarily different from those at issue in the earlier signed opinions, the precedential value of a *per curiam* opinion arises in part from the guidance as to how the settled principles of law were applied. That is, *per curiam*s provide to the lower courts examples of the proper application of the law relied upon to reach the decisions in the *per curiam* cases.

Per curiam opinions also tend to be brief in length. The brevity might be due to the heavy caseload of a court that needs to conserve scarce judicial resources, which prevents a written opinion in every case.

A "*per curiam* affirmed" decision lacks a record for its basis, which precludes further review. PCA opinions are often criticized for this reason.

In contrast, always criticized are the lower-court opinions that are rubber-stamped by the appeals courts. Most of these end up as "unpublished" opinions.

Another characteristic of rubber-stamped decisions arises out of the reason for the appeal. That reason is the appellant complained that the judge abused his or her discretion. Abuse of discretion is extraordinarily difficult to prove. How much discretion did the judge have? What are the outer boundaries of that discretion? Because an abuse of discretion is so difficult to prove on appeal, the judges become quite bold in abusing their discretion and use it against the party whom they want to find against for whatever reason—prejudice, personality difference, politics, to do a favor for a former partner or buddy who is the opposing counsel (the latter is a biggie in Maine).

Some lower-court judges simply write "Denied." By not including any facts or law in their decisions, there is no way to know on what they *did* base their decision. The appeals court will undoubtedly rubber-stamp that sly old fox's outrageously unsupported decision.

There are many caveats that apply to Maine: The lower-court judges rotate between being a lower-court judge in one session and an appeal court judge in another. Let's use John Doe for an example. John has two cases. His judge in Case #1 in the lower court is Judge X. He has appealed the decision in Case #2. Voila, Judge X is the appellate judge in Case #2. ☞ Use your imagination ☞ Court reporters have to be ordered in advance in the clerk's office, although there is no guarantee that the court reporter will assigned to appear in the courtroom. The proceedings, hearings, and trials are not automatically taped or recorded. The court files are emptied. Not even the attorneys' names will remain in the manila envelope. Preserving one's rights in a Maine court is difficult in not impossible. Maine is a dangerous State, where I encountered two judges who gave me concern when I appeared on a *pro hac vice* basis. One was in Portland District Court and the other in York County Superior Court. The latter was G. Arthur Brennan. I never caught the name of the former, and the clerk's office had so emptied the file, the record did not show that there was a trial. Both judges had neither honor nor ethics.

Appeals at the federal circuit level are your last chance to get justice. Believing that you will have a shot of appealing to the United States Supreme Court ("SCOTUS," *Supreme Court of the United States*) if you fail in a federal circuit court of appeals, you will be disappointed. With thousands of "petitions for writs of *certiorari*"—for example, "8,241 filings in the 2007 Term"\[642]/—and only nine judges to decide cases, it is physically impossible to hear them all. In fact, "during that term, 75 cases were argued and 72 were disposed of in 67 signed opinions.\⁶⁴³/ The bottom line: A smidge less than 1 in 100 petitions filed were granted certiorari. Specifically only 0.9 percent. Caveat: Keep your expectations of being granted *cert* low and do not expect to be informed why *certiorari* was denied. Those reasons are kept secret. There is no transparency.

* * *

As you can see, the injustices are incremental but so voluminous that appeals are monumental in scope and tedium with very little chance of success. With such alacrity and laxity, the courts cause the slow disintegration of the constitutional rights that promise you justice and a remedy for the wrongs done you. Then they laugh at you for thinking you will get justice at the appellate level. And you do not get a chance to laugh back, for more frequently than not, the decision of the lower court, whether State or federal, will be rubber-stamped . . . generally without a hearing.

These are predetermined decisions, where the facts that would dictate a different decision are left out of opinion. Keep this in mind when you are doing any research. Look primarily for the legal proposition of the case, not just the facts that led to it. The facts might not be all the facts of the case. They might be only the facts that allowed the legal proposition of the case to be reached. The facts that should have changed the court's mind might have been omitted from the opinion.

Given that a timely remedy is so very seldom available through the appellate route, there is one other route, a preventive one, and one other that can be taken at any time: an interlocutory appeal and a report to the Commission for Judicial Conduct. The former is unpredictable. The latter is predictable; it will get you nowhere.

The rubber-stamping is everywhere. We no longer have legitimate appellate courts. The erosion of the appellate system begins in the offices of the court clerks, where the assembly of records is often sabotaged. Given that there is usually one ordinary, low-paid clerk that handles the assembling of the records of the cases, the order for the delay has to come down from on high. There are simply cases that the court does not want appealed . . . generally not only because they are controversial but because they would tend to open a can of worms. The public would not like the worms.

Chapter 23

Intimidation and Insolence of Judges

Voodoo Club of Judges and Zombies

<u>Anecdote #1.</u>

My first tort—and Warsaw Convention—case was heard before a friend of Teddy Kennedy's, a brand new judge, David Harrison. My brother, "Peter," now deceased, was the plaintiff. (I was too brand new in the business to know that lawyers should not represent friends or relatives.) The primary defendant was Northwest Orient Airlines, which was represented by Meehan Boyle, & Cohen, an extraordinarily successful boutique lawfirm. James Meehan, who was, at that time, considered one of the top lawyers in Boston, was Northwest's trial counsel.

My brother, wheelchair-dependent as a result of multiple sclerosis, and his wife planned a vacation trip to the English countryside. During the air trip, the wheelchair, which was gratuitously transported in accordance with Northwest's Tariff, was damaged to the extent that it was like Humpty Dumpty. It could not again become functionally operable. As a result, Peter's functional mobility was impaired, the couple's vacation trip was ruined, and, as confirmed by the medical expert at trial, Peter's multiple sclerosis was exacerbated by the stress proximately caused by Northwest's continuing misconduct.

Thus, this case also involves the right of a handicapped passenger to have damage to his wheelchair treated as injury to the passenger's body.

When it came time for Northwest to put on its case, Jim Meehan waived his client's right to go forward at that time. He was due in Georgia. A golf game?

The trial stopped and the judge took the case under advisement. Many months later, the 20-page decision came down. Peter and his wife had won. The only thing necessary to do was have a hearing on the damages that would be awarded on their winning action under the

Consumer Rights Act, that is, whether the amount they were awarded would be doubled or trebled.

Meehan then kicked up his heels. How could the judgment, he insisted, be valid where the defendant did not put on its case?

So we found ourselves in an appeal in Superior Court.\644/ Until we arrived back in superior court before Judge James McHugh III, Meehan's firm had brought a Motion for Summary Judgment five times. Three judges had denied their motion. Two judges did not hear it. When we arrived in Judge McHugh's courtroom, the first thing Meehan did was move once again for summary judgment . . . and McHugh allowed it, before I could say, literally, one word.

Because of an agreement reached in district court—and transcribed—between Meehan and myself, I moved for Judge McHugh to reconsider what he did. He allowed my motion and *sua sponte* referred the case to the Appeals Court. His question was, in words for all intents and purposes, Did I do the right thing on April 17th? That meant I had to write an appellate brief.

By the time the Appeals Court made their decision two years later, my brother, Peter, had died. He never learned that we had also won the appeal, meaning that the summary judgment was reversed . . . and the case was still alive and well.\645/

When the case returned to district court, Northwest's counsel stated that he would file a motion to recuse Judge Harrison, but before doing so, Harrison, being intimidated by Meehan, vacated his previous decision in favor of my clients so that Northwest could put on its alleged defense.

I, then, without waiving my objection that Northwest had waived its right to present its defense, moved for a trial date so that Northwest could put on its case before Judge David Harrison. I never got a trial date. The judge declared he did not want to travel from Gloucester on Route 128 to Newton. The traffic, he said, was too great.

Northwest then went into bankruptcy in a distant bankruptcy court.

Then I was disbarred.

After some delay, the bankruptcy judge said my brother's case should be resolved in the state trial lower court, where I could no longer practice. (I do not believe the bankruptcy judge knew that.) The case remains unresolved. Another lawyer is needed. A good one!

Anecdote #2.

Keith got the highest score on the police exam, but was not given a job of his town's police force. We brought the case to the Civil Service Commission. The trial went beautifully. Everyone who had to be impeached was impeached clearly and convincingly. The Chairman of the Commission, Alexander MacMillan, listened well and at one point, to an ego-bloated town detective, "You're not Mark Fuhrman," the cocky, star prosecution witness at the O.J. Simpson criminal trial. Then we waited and waited for the decision. Eventually it came. The case had been dismissed, but not by the chairman who had heard the case at trial.

Shocked, I made inquiry. The new governor had appointed a new chairman. At the transition, there were 2000 cases backlogged. Because of budgetary problems, the new chairman denied all the petitions by budding police officers or firefighters . . . or even employed ones.\[646]/

I wanted more information. So I had a chat by phone with former Chairman MacMillan. The rationale, he told me, was that "they" figured half the plaintiffs would be either unable to afford to appeal or too discouraged or disheartened to appeal. A successful appeal was less likely than not. A plaintiff who appealed *pro se* was likely to make procedural errors that would cause the appeal to be dismissed. Some of the cases appealed would not be meritorious. Some would be dismissed on some boilerplate basis. Dismissing all of them with no basis was a win-win for the Commonwealth and the Civil Service Commission.

Although he fought at a budgetary hearing to retain enough money to staff his commission adequately, MacMillan never assumed any responsibility to speak out to those who were plaintiffs. He let those parties be secretly deprived of their constitutional rights to petition for relief and a remedy. Why would he do something so offensive? Because MacMillan was a political insider. To not go with the flow of the political agenda would have cost him the ability to be appointed or to be chosen to be legal counsel to one commission or another over the many years.

Instead of hiring my client, the police department hired a young man who was about to marry the Captain's daughter. That young man's high school records revealed a misfit. He had an extraordinary number of absences and had not even passed phys ed. The first year as an officer, while he was sitting in his patrol car at a police trap, he was cleaning his gun and accidentally shot himself in this hand. His marriage to the Captain's daughter also did not start off well. Rumor was that they were divorcing. A few years later, on his way to a bikers' summer blast, he had a fatal highway accident.

My client, Keith, who had prepared well for his intended career as a police officer by taking a Criminal Justice course at a local college, by interning at the town's police department, and by coming in first on the Civil Service Exam, was, at first, devastated, but he maintained his control and eventually got hired by another force.

What he learned, however, was that performance on the Civil Service Exam had no value, hiring was based on political or personal connections, and the commission wrote dishonest decisions. Politics was in, merit was out.

Has anything changed in the years since his case was heard? Not really. Nothing really changes in the Commonwealth. Corruption is the sovereign of Massachusetts.

Only while writing this chapter, Speaker Sal DiMasi of the House of Massachusetts was voluntarily stepping down from his position and retiring before he is indicted for numerous offenses. By delaying his retirement until a few weeks after the New Year, he will be receiving a lifetime pension of over $59,000 rather than over $57,000 a year. Talk radio was abuzz all day. Would Sal DiMasi be disbarred from the practice of law if he is convicted?

His predecessor, Speaker Thomas Finneran, left his Speaker's position for a $400,000 job in the biotech industry in Massachusetts. Subsequently he was charged with three counts of perjury and the obstruction of justice (by changing the lines of certain districts, i.e., gerrymandering). Finneran made a deal: he pled guilty to the federal crime of obstructing justice in exchange for avoiding federal prison. The Massachusetts Board of Bar Overseers has only temporarily suspended him, despite the federal conviction. In the meantime, an Entercom radio station, WRKO at 680 am on the dial, has employed him as a morning drive-time talk-show host.

Howie Carr, a columnist for the Boston Herald and afternoon talk-show host on the same station, calls him Finneran the Felon and said recently—while naming the three recent Speakers of the Massachusetts House,[647]/ all of whom left their Speaker position involuntarily because of alleged criminal activity—that Finneran probably had an IQ of only 100. "Buffoons, buffoons, they're all buffoons," Carr chanted.

And as talk radio goes, the subject turned to another, to wit, term limits. Was Carr in favor of term limits? No. There are only a few competent legislators, Carr continued. We do not want to lose the few good ones. Why bother with term limits, when the buffoons can be voted out? The term-limit discussion ended in frustration: But the voters don't throw them out!

<u>Anecdote #3.</u>

In the late '80s, I built an indoor, heated swimming pool. It was a terribly sloppy job, both cosmetically and mechanically. The house was U-shaped; on the left was the original house; on the right were five rooms I had built for my folks, who were getting up there in age; the two "wings" were connected by the pool room.

The first time the pool was filled with water, the water flooded the basement to my folks "wing." The fireman very competently came to the rescue. (They were terrific. Group 2-2.) The swimming pool company had literally forgotten to put in a particular pipe that would have led the water from the pool to someplace *other* than my folks' basement. They had also forgotten to put a light in the light "pocket" at the deep-end of the pool. And they had put the access to all the controls at the very bottom of the wall, where it met the floor. It was an idiotic spot to place them. Anyone had almost to lie down on the floor and peer in to see them. It did not stop there. My brother was handicapped, so I had ramps leading to the deck, 8-foot-wide sliding doors to accommodate his wheelchair, and a hot tub with special hardware to ease his access in and out of the tub. And the company managed to screw that up, too.

So I sued. I hired a lawyer friend. Not usually doing this type of legal work, he wrote the complaint—so that I would not be filing too late—with the proviso that I find a lawyer to replace him. I did.

Around that time, I moved my law office into a suite accommodating 10 solo practitioners. The second lawyer was a very nice young woman who had her practice there. Soon thereafter, she told me that she was tired of the law business. She wanted to open a restaurant. (Which, in fact, she ultimately succeeded in doing.)

Disappointed, I retained the young man who moved into her old office. A nice guy, but he was having marital problems, had his original office still operating, but it was distant, and the time he spent out of the home because of his traveling between the offices was resented by his wife. His primary area of law was workmen's comp and he was being buried alive by what he believed to be arbitrary and capricious decisions. "Barb, I've got to get out of this business. I'm going crazy. My marriage is on the rocks. My dad says I should have followed him into medicine. I have no choice but to withdraw from your case. I cannot concentrate. I'm going to close this office and maybe move elsewhere. But where? I don't know where. I don't know what I'm going to do. I'm sorry, really sorry, I cannot focus. I have to withdraw." Gadzooks! Not again.

Not wanting to get involved with still another attorney on the case, I decided to go *pro se* and finish it up fast. Fast forward to a pretrial conference in the judge's chambers.

Opposing Counsel Neil Rossman, Judge Maria I. Lopez (you might know her as TV Judge Maria Lopez), and I were in her chambers (*read*, office). Lopez had been a Superior Court judge only a few months. The first Latina on that bench. Born in Cuba in 1953, she was in her late 30s and recently divorced with two young sons still in elementary school. Rumor was that she had been having an affair with Attorney-General Francis X. Bellotti, for whom she was working in the civil rights division prior to being named as a district court judge in 1987.\[648]/

Rossman appeared to be in his mid-40s and still attractive. The first words out of his mouth after "Good Morning, Your Honor," were words, for all intents and purposes, "She has had three lawyers. She cannot get along with anyone."

"Mr. Rossman, how dare you say that? That is not true," I said indignantly. I could not believe that he had said that. "If I had known you were going to say something as nasty as that, I would have asked or subpoenaed all three of them to be here. They would have gladly come. We are still friendly."

"I believe him," Lopez quickly retorted. Arrow Number 2. Lopez and I had never met, never seen each other before that day. Her words cut short that meeting. Something was going on. By the twinkling in her eyes and her demeanor, I thought, "Damn, she's trying to make him!"

Fast forward again . . . this time to the trial. We selected jurors, Lopez said the ordinary words that judges say to newly seated jurors, we made our Opening Statements, and then, because I brought the complaint, I was the first to testify.

While I testified, I used the pool company's 4-color brochure. I also had sets of photos taken by my building contractor—he was working on the folks' wing at the time—when the company was building the pool. "I thought I'd photograph what they did so that I could build one at my own place," he told me. "Look at them closely, the rebar is not where it should be."

I looked. His pictures clearly showed what he meant. Rebar (steel bars) is used to reinforce the concrete of the pool. The rebar must be in the center of the thickness of the concrete if it is to be effective. The pool contractor prepares the "hole" to mimic the intended shape of the pool. He puts a "grate" around the bottom and the sides and a lining of cardboard-like material between the grate and the dirt of the sides of the hole. That "lining" will be removed when the concrete is set. He then must put wooden blocks equivalent to half the thickness of the planned pool walls and floor. Then he sprays the concrete.

The images that Don, my contractor, captured on his film showed that the pool contractor had placed only a few of the blocks needed, so that the rebar sat flat on the dirt, meaning that it would not be in the center of the concrete to reinforce it.

The pool company's brochure, a size as large as the old Life magazine, showed this process step-by-step. I wanted to show the brochure to the jury, but I wanted them to see the pictures enlarged. I should have gone to the expense of enlarging those pictures. Pre-Internet and scanning days, it would have cost many hundreds of dollars, if not over $1000 or more. So I asked Lopez for permission to allow me both to "publish" the brochure to the jury and to give them my magnifying glass. In an abusive tone of voice, Lopez denied my motion to give the jury my magnifying glass.

After the jurors looked at the brochure and passed it along to their neighbors, Lopez wanted to see the brochure. Grateful that she wanted to see it and hoping that she would begin to understand the problem, I handed it to her clerk. Then Lopez startled me by saying, "I can't see these well enough. May I have the magnifying glass?"

The morning session ended and we went to lunch. I took mine in the courthouse restaurant, which I knew to be a good one, reasonably priced, and I usually bumped into a few friends there. Finished with lunch, I made for the elevator. Still in decent physical shape in those days, I slipped in even though it was crowded. Suddenly Rossman and his female co-counsel entered. I suddenly heard, "Oh, oh, the enemy camp is here." I turned and saw two of our jurors against the rear wall.

I was seated at my table in the courtroom when the judge was announced as entering. The judge informed us that she had heard that some jurors had already made up their minds about the case. That was wrong, she said. They are not to discuss the case or come to any conclusions until they have heard all the evidence, and are sent to the jury room for deliberation. She then called the jurors in and questioned them as to whether they had made up their minds. They denied they had made up their minds.

The trial resumed. I had a bit more testifying to do. So I continued. Sitting to testify as a witness, and standing when I was doing lawyerly things, such as handing proposed exhibits to opposing counsel, carrying the exhibits from opposing counsel to the clerk, waiting for the judge to make a ruling, and then carrying each exhibit to the jury. Because I was testifying in narrative form, I was also able to address the jury from a standing position, for instance, when I was testifying to the exhibit I was giving them.

At one point, while being cross-examined, the judge interrupted and told me to stop Kaffee Klatching with the jury. "Your Honor, I am not Kaffee Klatching with the jury, I am simply smiling from time to time as I speak."

"Be professional, counselor."

"I am being professional, Your Honor. Being professional does not require me to be funereal." Lopez appeared to be connecting my friendly style of lawyering with the reason why the jurors called Rossman and his assistant "The Enemy Camp." Rossman was extremely formal and when he objected to something, his assistant would also stand and parrot him literally, word for word. Stiff, very stiff. And his assistant . . . she sounded like the head of the Bund. It probably would not have surprised anyone were she to stand up wearing black gloves and boots and holding a whip.

The differences in our styles were remarkable.

At one point, without the jurors present in the courtroom, we had a hearing on a legal issue. Rossman said something, his assistant parroted him, and then Lopez parroted him. Having already asked for a mistrial, I asked again. Lopez refused. We continued with our legal arguments. The same sequence was repeated several times. "Your Honor, when Mr. Rossman speaks, you treat what he is saying as if it is coming from God's mouth and going to your ear. I must move again for a mistrial," I said in so many words. I was disgusted. It appeared to me that Lopez would use her judicial power as much as necessary to make this man. For a beautiful young woman with a job, health benefits, and pension guaranteed for life, she seemed all too desperate. Something funny was going on here. Was she only on the make?

A little while later, Lopez finally declared a mistrial.

Postscript #1.

In 1995, Lopez finally remarried, not to Rossman but to a Boston publisher. Incredibly her former employer and lover, Attorney-General Francis X. Bellotti performed the services as Justice of the Peace. Where Rossman and Bellotti were tall and full-chested men with biceps hidden by well-cut suitcoats, Lopez's groom was short, pock-marked, and pony-tailed as he was in the hippie era . . . and no noticeable or remarkable chest or biceps, but he was as monied, if not more, than either Rossman or Bellotti. But he can be sweeter. (At some point, prior to my becoming a lawyer and pre-Maria, I had worked for him briefly at his newspaper, and bumped into him frequently over the years at a particular local shop.) All of this is, of course, my observations and opinion.

In fact, a few years ago, her groom was going to publish my "Bar" story because of the inequities and unmistakable wrongdoing of the Massachusetts Supreme Judicial Court in the disciplinary case against me. But Maria put the kaybosh on it . . . because of the swimming pool case. She had reported me to the Bar and I had reported her to the Commission on Judicial Conduct. It was a wash. There were, so I have read, many complaints by lawyers against her. Ebony Horton's case, immediately below, was simply the last straw.

Postscript #2.

Charles "Ebony" Horton was tried for assorted sexual crimes and assorted crimes related to assault and battery. Dressed as a woman, Horton had led an 11-year old boy to an abandoned warehouse where

Horton held a screwdriver to the child's neck and forced him to simulate sex acts. One of the quiet controversies was whether the boy had been whoring at the project.

Blaming the prosecutor for the presence of the media during the sentencing hearing, Lopez outburst at him. "You may sit down. You may sit down now or I'll get a court officer to make you sit down!" The clip of her outburst aired repeatedly on our local TV news shows. She referred to the crimes as "low-level" offenses, angering relatives of the boy, and paroled Horton to house arrest in the housing development where he lived, angering the residents who lived there.

A few years later, after a trial, the Massachusetts Commission on Judicial Conduct found that Lopez had abused her office and lied under oath and that she ought to apologize and serve a six-month suspension. Rather than apologize and accept a suspension, Lopez resigned in May 2003, having decided that the battle was not worth fighting. She had already become a lightning rod for both the media and public opinion.

After the Horton debacle, her husband took her to South America, India, and China for a change of pace. Shortly thereafter a new career emerged when a television agent selected her to be the Latina judge for whom he had been searching, one who was not afraid to speak her mind. At the time, Lopez said, "They want me to be controversial. They want conflict drama on television."

The situation was ironic. Her passion and brusqueness had become assets which worked to her advantage. "I should probably send thank-you notes," she was heard saying. "If not for all the things that happened to me, I wouldn't be here today." But her national prominence as a TV judge did not work out. Her show ran for two seasons until the show was canceled due to low ratings.

Bloggers riddled her with criticism. One was so captured by her beauty, he wrote that he was anxiously awaiting for the opportunity to bed her. Others found her behavior unconscionable. Many questioned her TV decisions: they were based on her guts rather than on the law.

Anecdote #4.

The insolence of Judge Dyanne Klein was revealed when she approved Magistrate/Clerk Henry Shultz's finding me in default after I notified Shultz that I was going to be an hour late for a status hearing in the clerk's office. There is no excuse to have made the client suffer by the dismissal of his case. The motive of Klein has not been revealed. Shultz, who has sat in his chair laughing for a few decades about his escapades with women, might finally have made headway with Klein.

Anecdote #5.

The insolence of Judge Christopher J. Muse was revealed when he struck a Notice of Appeal three times. (*See* Chapter 22.) He simply did not want his devastating ruling about a minor procedural matter to be scrutinized. Given his temperament, there must be many complaints against him at the Commission on Judicial Conduct. Secrecy of how many complaints there are enhances political and judicial corruption. The public has a right to know how their judges are performing.

Anecdote #6.

The insolence of Judge William Young, formerly Chief Judge of the United States District Court at Boston, was revealed when he held in one memorandum of decision that the Eleventh Amendment does not forbid cases for money damages against alleged governmental employees and then, when politically correct but corrupt agendas intruded, changed his mind four months later and found that the Eleventh Amendment does forbid cases for money damages against the same employees. I can only assume that he was pressured to change his earlier decision. A trusted federal court person averred, "Nothing happens in this court that is not political."

Anecdote #7.

The intimidation of Superior Court Judge Thomas P, Billings appeared before his insolence was revealed. I was suing the Board of Bar Overseers, Office of Bar Counsel, Daniel Crane (the Bar Counsel in his individual and professional capacities) and Susan Strauss-Weisberg (the Assistant Bar Counsel assigned to prosecute the disciplinary case against me) for defamation and emotional distress. All four entities were defending by saying they had immunity, meaning that they could not be sued because the law had made them *unaccountable* for their actions. I responded to their Motion to Dismiss by arguing that they did not have immunity and based my arguments on several theories. (The documents in which I argued why immunity was inapplicable to that case are on my website. Look for **Barb v. The Bar** in the Drano Series Table on my Home Page—*www.falseallegations.com*—and click the links.)

In his decision and memorandum, Judge Billings wrote at one point that my argument appeared to be correct, for the law did say what I wrote it said and at another point that I was correct, but given not that the law had changed but that society had changed, he did not feel comfortable finding in my favor on the defendants' Motion to Dismiss.

Billings opinion was a "friendly" one, but I had no choice but to appeal it. The Appeals Court, as I anticipated, rubber-stamped his decision, but not too much later, his rulings in a distinctly different case belied what had happened. I believe that he caught hell from the higher-ups in the judicial branch for agreeing with my legal conclusions. Enough hell to intimidate him.

That intimidation turned into insolence in the second case.

The insolence was revealed when he wrote in a footnote in that second case about my bar disciplinary proceedings. That second case had nothing to do with bar proceedings. There was only one purpose: to spread the word to other judges that I did something that was not politically correct and that should be countenanced by any court.

Anecdote #8.

The insolence of Federal Magistrate Judge Robert B. Collings was revealed when he, too, wrote in a footnote about my bar disciplinary proceeding when the case in which he put the footnote had nothing to do with bar proceedings; it was a client's case. There was only one purpose, the same as that as Billings had. What it told me, however, is that the judiciary had conspired to get a buzz out there amongst the judges that I was politically undesirable and that my arguments were not to be countenanced.

Anecdote #9.

The insolence of Worcester District Court Judge Ernest S. Hayeck was revealed during a motion hearing on a client's case dealing with a charge of "driving under the influence." The client had taken a breathalyzer test and I had filed a brief to suppress the results of it. The machine was used allegedly to measure the amount of alcohol consumed. It does not, of course; that is just another myth perpetuated by the manufacturers and the courts. The brief was technical . . . and as such included numbers.

Hayeck interrupted me in the middle of argument in front of a packed courtroom of lawyers and defendants, and asked, "Where do you come from?"

"Huh?" I reacted. He took me by surprise. What did he mean by the question in this context?

"Where do you come from?"

"Where do I come from?"

"Yes."

"Newton."

"Oh, now I know," he said with an enlightened look on his face. He paused for seconds and then said, "Sidebar." The assistant DA and I walked up to the side of the judge's bench. Hayeck looked at me smiling, "Counselor, your people still use letters. My people are the ones who invented numerals."

I have no recall of what I said. (This incident occurred in 1989. If I got a tape of it, it's got to be in storage.) I do recall being stunned. I did not expect to fight an Arab-Israeli war in the middle of Worcester District Court. By knowing, he meant he assumed I was Jewish. Newton was then often thought of as a "Jewish" city, although the population at that time was roughly divided evenly between Catholics, Protestants, and Jews—⅓, ⅓, ⅓. Of course, he denied the motion.

Fast forward to the trial. In the middle of the trial, I was demonstrating where the police car and my client's truck were, and I said, "I am the truck." Hayeck chimed in something about my husband being lucky or unlucky. He then began regularly interrupting my cross-examination of the policeofficers.

"What does '____' mean in English?" That was the first of a string of words in German or Yiddish that he wanted me to translate. Clearly he was trying to tell the jury, too, I was Jewish.

Astonished, I said, "May I, Your Honor, resume examining?'

He let me resume for a while, then suspended the trial briefly and called the ADA and me to his chamber neighboring the courtroom. Speaking directly to me, he said that he was Syrian and his wife was

Greek. So I spoke to him in Greek. It was his turn to be surprised. "I don't speak Greek," he said.

"I thought you might have learned."

"But we did buy a house in Monemvasia."

"Monemvasia is beautiful, but you have to be a billy-goat to live there."

After a while, he stopped talking. There was, of course, nothing related to his stories about his wife and Monemvasia and the "driving under" case being tried. There was only one reason for the suspension of the trial, and that was to interrupt the rhythm I and most attorneys develop during a properly prepared examination. Hayeck had used all the tools in his quiver against me because he believed I was Jewish. He wanted to get me! I was not a regular in his court but had already won two out of two jury cases there. He wanted that to stop. He didn't give a damn about my client, the defendant,\[649]/ who happened to have been a juror for my previous trial in Hayek's court.

Postscript #1.

I got back to my office and spoke to one of my friends, a lawyer I had known since high school. He told me to call Judge Samuel Zoll, who is now retired but used to be the Chief Judge of the district courts. Zoll wanted to know which offended me most, religious or gender discrimination. I could not select one over the other. Nevertheless, soon after that hearing with Zoll, Hayeck was moved from Worcester District Court to an outlying, smaller, less busy district court.

A year later, he was back in Worcester. Soon thereafter, in 1992, the year he retired, Hayeck was awarded the American Bar Association Franklin N. Flaschner Judicial Award for excelling in the courtroom. He has been and still is a faculty member of the National Judicial College.

Hypocrisy. Inanity.

Anecdote #10.

The insolence of U.S. District Court Judge Douglas P. Woodlock was revealed in an employment discrimination case based on race. Gregory was a handsome, young, black man who was hired by Brigham & Women's Hospital when he arrived in the North after graduating high school down South. His job was in the Emergency Operating Room, "a black man's job." He worked there 12 years. His first review was very good and made one recommendation: that he work hard on improving his grammar, spelling, and punctuation.

His second noted a great improvement of his grammar, spelling, and punctuation. Each successive review was better than the previous one. His attitude was excellent, he willingly helped others, he never complained about his 12-hour shifts, he filled in wherever needed, he was very sociable, and everyone liked him.

One of the later reviews said he was ready for promotion. So Gregory applied. The hospital claimed there were no openings for unskilled black labor except in the boiler room. Greg did not consider a job in the boiler room to be a promotion. Dark, hot, no people around . . . and he was a "people" person. He, therefore, did not get a promotion either in job or salary.

In the meantime, he had taken time to read the employee manual from cover to cover. He helped others use the internal complaint system. He, himself, had used it when appropriate, and he always prevailed. The Emergency Room staff over the years was changing from black to Hispanic. He taught the new arrivals how to protect themselves at the hospital. And he began dating a white nurse. Interracial relationships, if not yet fashionable, were not readily approved of by the general populace, including employers.

Someone must have secretly complained—possibly the Hispanic woman with whom he had three children and with whom he had lived those many years; she also worked in the hospital, but in a clerical position, not in the Emergency Room. The result, Gregory was fired.

His first employment attorney did obtain a two-page document on which there were 12 paragraphs, each a few lines long and each describing an alleged event of sexual harassment of an anonymous white nurse. Gregory said here and there a snippet of an alleged event sounded familiar but the events as described never happened. The first attorney, who had a very good reputation, could not get the hospital to identify the 12 nurses, the dates, or other necessary facts. Gregory came to me for representation.

Help! I took the case and brought it to federal court. It was assigned to Judge Woodlock. We were at our first hearing, when I spoke about the anonymity. "Your Honor, there is not one hospital record showing that there was even one oral complaint. There is not one hospital record showing that there was even one written complaint. More troublesome is that the hospital has revealed to us that the events as described on those two pieces of paper never occurred. The descriptions of the events are composites. Facts shuffled like a deck of cards, allegedly as the hospital's attempt to provide privacy to the nurses.

"The hospital must produce the name of these 12 anonymous nurses, these alleged complainants, in order for us to conduct discovery. Proper notice, of course, is an issue. Thus my motion to this court for an order commanding the hospital to produce the names of the 12 alleged complainants."

Woodlock said, Yes, he would order the hospital to produce the names. Well, he didn't!

I ordered the transcript of the hearing. The court replied, saying that there was neither a tape nor a court reporter who had been present at that hearing. Insolence, insolence, insolence.

Anecdote #11.

Jolie filed for divorce from Ryan about two years ago. Jolie, from a very wealthy family, has access to private jets, nannies, trust funds etc. She makes over $500,000 in interest and dividends alone. For that reason, the couple agreed that child support from Ryan was unnecessary. Ryan got very little in assets because of a prenuptial agreement he signed before they were married. Ryan was left with only his house, on which there is now a lot of debt. He has no meaningful cash.

The Rhode Island divorce judge said that he would not allow "no child support" at all and that Ryan should pay something, so he ordered the minimum for four kids: $200 a month.

Then another Judge, Jeremiah S. Jeremiah, Jr., Chief *Judge* of the *Rhode Island* Family Court, about a year ago quintupled Ryan's child-support obligation to $1000 a month . . . apparently for no reason. Nothing had changed. In fact, at the time, Ryan was without a job and was looking for work.

Ryan appealed the quintupling of child support to the Rhode Island Supreme Court and won!!! The supreme court read the transcripts and agreed with Ryan (who was acting *pro se*) that Judge

Jeremiah had no findings to justify the 400% increase in child support. The high court sent it back to the judge to re-do the findings and judgment.

Judge Jeremiah immediately stayed the child support pending the retrial. Then, without explanation, without the retrial even beginning or findings submitted to the Supreme Court as ordered, Jeremiah lifted the stay and ordered Ryan to pay the stayed child support, which was then $10,400 in arrears. Jeremiah also ordered Ryan to pay within 30 days $1500 to a GAL that Ryan had never wanted or thought necessary.

Ryan did not have the funds to pay the arrears.

Within the last month, Ryan walked into court for what he thought was a scheduled hearing and trial and was thrown into jail for failure to pay the ransom. He was ordered to sit there day after day until he comes up with the money . . . money he does not have. He cannot borrow against his house because there is too much debt on it and he is way behind on his mortgage payments.

Jolie now sits in her house with her maids and nannies and private jets while Ryan sits in jail needing to raise $11, 900 to get out. Jolie refuses to ask the judge to free him. She is holding the key and will not let him out.

Despite his having been voted "Judge of the Year" in 2005 by the National Council of Juvenile and Family Court Judges during the organization's 68th Annual Conference held in Pittsburgh, Pa., Jeremiah S. Jeremiah, Jr., a judge with frequent and numerous complaints against him, is the latest judge full of insolence.

Anecdote #12.

What has appeared to be insolence by family court justices when they ignored the statute mandating that the Commonwealth pay the fees of the guardians *ad litem* and ordered, instead, the parties to pay the GAL fees, was not insolence.

The judges were following orders of a Chief Judge, John Irwin, now retired, to put the burden of payment on the parties. His order, popularly known as Memo #14, ordered the justices to assess the ability of the parties to pay those fees, but the justices never do the financial assessments . . . and almost always put the burden of payment on the male. Some men who refused to pay have either been threatened with a decision adverse to them or have been handcuffed and thrown into a holding cell awaiting transportation to jail.

The willingness to follow an unconstitutional order, an order to justices to violate intentionally a duly ratified statute, constitutes the willingness to be a participant in an unlawful conspiracy. But there is nowhere to bring a complaint against a judge. Courts automatically dismiss cases against judges. There is no district attorney who will bring a complaint against a judge. There is no attorney-general who will bring a case against a judge. Attorney-generals give them free legal representation and immediately move to dismiss on the grounds of immunity.

The judges themselves have gladly accepted judge-made immunity to make themselves unaccountable. Therein lies the insolence. The judges know they break the law on a daily basis, yet are unwilling to accept any responsibility.

Anecdote #13.

When Meuse was charged with Parental Kidnapping, his defense was always the "necessity defense," namely the need to get the child to proper medical care. Literally a few minutes prior to trial, the ADA moved to preclude the necessity defense and Judge Allen Swan allowed the motion. Neither the motion nor the decision had any justification.

During my Opening Statement, I told the jury we had planned to tell them about the necessity to take the child, but as of a few minutes ago, the judge said I could not do that. I added that it was too late for me to change all the questions I had intended to ask, so every time they heard the assistant district attorney say, "Objection," and the judge say, "Sustained," think "Reasonable Doubt." And I waved my hand as if I were ringing a bell. I was trying to invoke an analogy to Jimmy Stewart's Christmas movie, "It's a Wonderful Life," with "Clarence." Every time a bell rings, an angel gets his wings.

The next day I brought in a bell. After ringing the bell twice, the judge ordered me to put the bell away. The next day, I removed a small almost-antique Scales of Justice from the window mantle in my kitchen and placed it on my desk in the courtroom. The judge ordered me to take the Scales of Justice off my desk. Forbidding the Scales of Justices to be displayed in a courtroom! The Scales lost that round, but we won the war. The jury found Reasonable Doubt and found Meuse Not Guilty.

Anecdote #14.

The insolence of Judge Jonathan J. Kaplan of Vernon Rockville GA#19 *Connecticut* Superior Court was remarked upon by Chris Kennedy of Ellington, Connecticut. "I have not seen my children in years— ALL as a direct result of Judge Jonathan Kaplan calling prosecuters, issuing blank restraining orders, fabricating document, tampering with court folders and withholding facts to have me arrested and prosecuted in all three cases and to remove my children. All as a direct result of my complaint against him and appealing his ruling."\[650]/

It all began when Kennedy's "wife stabbed him about 5 years ago. While Leanne Putnam was awaiting her days in court for felony assault, she was awarded sole custody of their three children, allegedly by Rockville Superior Court Judge Jonathan J. Kaplan in Connecticut."\[651]/

Kennedy then lodged complaints against Kaplan, and after he lodged them, the charges were dropped against his ex-wife. It was at that point that Kennedy became the target of Kaplan, who became, in turn, out of control.

Anecdote #15.

I had my own experience with Judge Kaplan in Rockville, Connecticut. I had filed the proper documents for requesting permission to appear *pro hac vice* in his court to represent a defendant who could not find a local attorney to represent him zealously. That was the last thing the district attorney wanted. The D.A. wanted another conviction to add to his belt so that when running for re-election, he would appear sufficiently competent to deat any appointment.

Normally a *pro hac v*ice hearing is a Q & A between the sitting judge and the out-of-state attorney. But not this one. Kaplan allowed the assistant district attorney to chime in. She had done her homework on the Internet and had learned that I challenged judges. So Kaplan resolved the issue immediately. He denied me permission to appear "because you might sue the judges." That I was the defendant's choice of counsel was of no consequence to Judge Jonathan Kaplan.

Anecdote #16.

One day I received a letter from a local jail. The man had been there 9 months and had never had a trial. I met him at his next hearing in court. He was well-educated, Nigerian, very black, and representing himself—he had attended law school for a while and wanted some day to return, but that did not happen when some judge had put him in jail and threw away the key.

At that time in Lawrence (MA) District Court, there was string of blankety-blank judges. I shall not dignify them by calling them law-and-order judges. Lawrence has a very high Latino population and miscellaneous large Asian communities. It was evident that most of the defendants were considered guilty even before they stood for their arraignment.

I made two unsuccessful attempts to get him released on his personal recognizance. The first judge was going our way until the assistant D.A. caught his attention. The second judge was Allen J. Jarasitis, whom I later dubbed "Judas to Justice" when he issued a **fourth** criminal complaint for allegedly violating—*while he was in jail . . . and her address was impounded*—a restraining order against the client. Jarasitis said he issued it because the client did not appear in court. I retorted that the client had to rely on the Sheriff's Department to bring him to court for a hearing. He could not walk out of the jail on his own. Jarasitis, of course, knew that. There are too many Jarasitis stories to include here. I'll have to make him a character in a legal genre whodunnit.

Jarasitis also always complained about the inadequate court budget—that was around 2002 or 2003—so when he refused to release my client, I told him never to complain about the budget again. He was wasting $3000 a month of taxpayer money by keeping my client in jail longer than any punishment he would receive had he been guilty after trial. Jarasitis retorted the monthly cost had risen to around $3600 a month. The response of a smart ass, not a competent judge who believed in the Constitution or the statutes.

Finally I did manage to get the Nigerian a probable cause hearing. Judge Stephen S. Ostrach presided. I put his wife on the stand. She admitted that he never had laid a hand on her, but she had bruises on her stomach.

I asked the logical question, "If he never laid a hand on you, how was he responsible for the bruising?"

"Because he believes in Voodoo. And my sister has them, too."

"Where is she?

"In Michigan."

"Was your husband in Michigan?"

"No, but his friends are."

I moved immediately for dismissal and the client's release.

The wife immediately interrupted and told Ostrach that she was living in a shelter and she would be made to leave the shelter if her husband was released and had not been found guilty.

Given that she might have to go out and work and provide for her own shelter was something Ostrach did not consider. He just as quickly denied the dismissal and the release.

Given also the woman's excuse was no reason to keep her husband in jail, and if I were to give the judge respect, I would have had also to conclude that the judge was not prejudiced against very black Nigerians and that he, too, believed in Voodoo.

When my client and I next appeared in court, we were headed for trial. The court had brought a new judge to conduct the trial. He had not yet absorbed the Black Robe Syndrome. My client was released . . . and the other criminal charges dismissed. The assistant D.A. blew a gasket. The judge said, "Take it up."

I was delighted that I did not have to put up with more Voodoo Justice.

But again the only relief from absolutely inexcusable injustice is the abolishment of absolute judicial immunity.

Chapter 24

The Bar v. Barb and
Barb v. The Bar et al

The Bar v. Barb

As I have mentioned throughout this book, I had disciplinary proceedings brought against me in Massachusetts. I sued a few judges, I
criticized a few of them on my website, and I ran in 2002 for governor
on a platform of court reform, that is, the need for judicial accountability, particularly in the family-law court, and the abolishment of judicial and quasi-judicial immunity.

Three weeks after the election, a prosecutor for the disciplinary
entity phoned me and said a Petition for Discipline would issue shortly.
It did, right after the holiday season, during the first week of January
2003. I fought them until I was disbarred in Massachusetts in August
2006, and have continued to fight them since then.\⁶⁵²/

The grounds upon which bar counsel may petition the single justice for disciplinary action against an attorney include:

- misuse or loss of client funds,
- neglect of client interests,
- fraudulent conduct,
- sanction in another jurisdiction,
- conviction of a crime and
- misrepresentation to the court.

None, none, none of those grounds is in the disciplinary case
against me. I was the exception to the rule. Criticism of judges is simply not an infraction for which any sanction may be imposed. In fact,
it is a lawyer's obligation to report wrongdoing when he or she sees it.

I also maintain a website, *www.falseallegations.com*, which has drawn
the attention of millions across our nation and on which I publish fun-

damental legal "how-to" and "what-is" information, some of my state and federal pleadings, and opinions—mine and occasionally some of diverse courts. A few dozen of my website files were the primary so-called "evidence" in the disciplinary action against me.

In my pleadings in the Bar fight, I have continuously argued that the BBO does not have jurisdiction over First Amendment matters. I also argued that the disciplinary action was in retaliation for exercising my right to political speech and free expression, to wit, for exercising both my right and my obligation to criticize the judicial system where I saw wrongdoing and those judges who intentionally deprived parties of their rights to constitutional due process and equal protection. The First Amendment issue was a recurring theme in the proceedings and pleadings below.

When I addressed the panel of justices at the Massachusetts Supreme Judicial Court, I said, *"Surprise me and reverse your predetermined judgment of disbarment."* Although disbarment seemed inevitable, I had naïvely held out hope that reason and justice would prevail. I was wrong.

"Your agent, the Board of Bar Overseers," I continued, *"violated my First Amendment rights, my right to constitutional due process, my right to constitutional equal protection, my right to a fair and impartial trial . . . and my right to a public trial, a right expressly given me under the rules created by this very Court.*

"On the day of the scheduled public trial, the hearing officer ordered the public out of the room. Because the hearing officer had previously ordered the stenographer to go off the record when I spoke and to go back on when he spoke, I feared that the BBO could put false words into my mouth and I would have no proof that I did not say them. So I left with the public.

"The so-called trial went on in my absence and in the absence of the public. The only persons present at the alleged or so-called trial was a special hearing officer, an assistant general counsel, and the prosecutor. The prosecutor produced no witnesses, no supporting documents, and only unauthenticated copies of my website files . . . but failed to identify where there was anything offending or unlawful in them. The prosecutor produced, in sum, no support either factually or legally for the accusations against me.

"In contrast, I had evidence, factual and legal support for my issues, but I was not allowed to present it. I was not allowed to have trial witnesses. Before I left that day of the hearing, the BBO had quashed all my trial subpoenas. I was not allowed to offer documents. Repeatedly before the trial, the BBO had ruled

it was precluding me from offering documents in my defense. In sum, I was willfully prevented from presenting my defense to the BBO accusations

"*I was entitled to a fair and impartial trial. I did not get even what amounts to the appearance of a fair trial. I was the victim of a kangaroo court.*

"*Where there was no evidence brought forward in a public trial, there is no right to disbar me.*"

Further, "*it is not only my right to criticize the judiciary when I see wrongdoing, it is my obligation to do so, particularly when the judiciary will not police itself.*

"*Disbarment will not accomplish what you hope it will. It will not keep me from using my knowledge, my spirit, and my speech to achieve court reform or the abolishment of judicial and quasi-judicial immunity, and to address judicial inequities. Disbarment will serve only to wrongfully punish me for exercising my constitutional right to free, political speech.*

"*So I can only hope that you will restore honor and integrity to this Court by reviewing all the facts and concluding rightfully that a travesty of justice has occurred.*

"*Surprise me, do your duty and make a fair and impartial decision to reverse your predetermined judgment.*" They didn't!

In fact, the judges sat mute during my "argument," except for Chief Judge Margaret Marshall, who interrupted telling me my time was over. Untrue. The light that warns you when your 15 minutes is over had been set for 10 minutes and had not yet come on. I brought that fact to her attention and continued. She looked grim. She had the image of an evil woman. I have been wondering why the identity of Marshall's first husband has remained hidden from public view . . . as well as from Google's. If anyone knows who or where the man—dead or alive—is or on which continent the marriage occurred, please write and inform me. I believe Marshall is currently married to Anthony Lewis, forever a columnist for the New York Times.

I also argued against the judgment of contempt, after which I was jailed:

"*The judgment of contempt and my subsequent imprisonment was more a punishment of my clients because they had me as their lawyer than a punishment against me . . . although it was that, too.*

"*By denying my Motion to Stay the Order to withdraw from my clients' cases, the single justice both deprived my clients of their right to have counsel of their choice and interfered with the orderly prosecution of their cases. The judge never considered the immediate and irreparable harm and damage his order would cause my clients.*

"The full Court did similarly when the clerk on this Court's behalf, so I've been told, summarily denied the Motion to Stay I filed here. Upon learning of the denial, I reasonably concluded that the Judgment of Disbarment was predetermined and that the single justice, too, knew that, . . . for were this Court neutral and the option to reverse Judge Spina's decision still open, he would have allowed me to continue, at the very least, to represent my then-existing clients.

"Each of my clients' cases was about to be horribly and needlessly prejudiced.

"I was less upset at that time about my own disbarred status than I was for my clients. Their cases were generally complex and at stages which made it unlikely that another lawyer could be effective. My clients would be left without their counsel of choice when they most needed counsel familiar with their cases. My duty to them and to their cases was my responsibility, and had priority.

"I thought the court would understand and would not exalt procedure over substance. And I was unwilling to defy justice by sacrificing substance for procedure.

"During the 30 days between the Judgment of Disbarment and the date it became effective, I had been working to tie up as many loose ends in my cases as possible.

"The disbarment was effective on September 8th, a Friday. Prior to that date, two of my clients had been ordered to court on the following Monday and Tuesday. Without adequate opportunity to find substitute counsel, my clients would be at a loss were I not there. So in one court, I appeared also to deliver what I had been ordered prior to the disbarment to write and produce on Monday. And in the second court, I appeared to inform the judge of my idea for a reasonable settlement—as well as to inform him that I had not heard from this Court regarding my Motion to Stay.

"Those appearances prompted the assistant bar counsel who was prosecuting the case against me to add an allegation of Unauthorized Practice of Law to the Complaint for Contempt she filed in the single-justice session.

"Given that I had already filed an appeal of the judgment of disbarment, the single justice no longer had jurisdiction to hear the contempt.

"At that hearing, I attempted to show that where an order had no pretense of validity when it issued, it is a transparently invalid order and cannot form the basis for a contempt citation.

"Nevertheless, because I had failed to withdraw from my cases as the judge ordered, he found me in contempt and imprisoned me to force my compliance.

Nothing Judge Spina wanted me to do, however, could be done from prison. I did not hold the key to my cell door. I was being punished.

"*The contempt was thus criminal in nature with the possibility of indefinite incarceration, and but for having friends, a few human angels, I would still be imprisoned. That gave me an entitlement to a jury trial, for which I asked but was denied.*

"*Further, where I did not hold the key to my cell door and the contempt charge brought against me was de facto criminal in nature, the County Court had no jurisdiction either to hear or to sentence me to any incarceration, definite or indefinite.*

"*Judge Spina did not declare it a criminal contempt because currently there is no statute or case law addressing the issue of incarceration for criminal contempt in the single-justice session. He would have had to treat me disparately and thus violate my right to equal protection. The denial of equal protection is, unfortunately, done in our courts daily. For instance, a defendant being tried for criminal contempt in family court is denied a jury trial, but a defendant being tried for criminal contempt in superior court is afforded a jury trial.*

"*Where the single justice acted intentionally and knowingly to deprive me of my constitutional rights, the judge was no longer acting as a judge, but as a 'minister' of his own prejudices.*

"*In sum, where I **did** appeal the Judgment of Disbarment on the grounds that it was transparently invalid or had only a frivolous pretense to validity, I could ignore the order until the appeal was resolved——and the appeal is still not resolved.\\[653]/ Therefore, the Order issuing simultaneously with the disbarment judgment was void ab initio; the finding of contempt, a clear error of law requiring reversal; the resulting incarceration, an egregious abuse of discretion and clear error of law.*

"*Where I was deprived of equal protection, the judge not only deprived me of the benefit of appealing the disbarment to the full Panel of this Court. It gives the appearance that the right to appeal his judgment is but a sham.*

"*The practice of law, allegedly a 'learned profession,' is a fundamental right. To have deliberately, recklessly, and with callous indifference deprived me of my fundamental rights to property and subsequently my liberty before I had had the benefit of an appeal as other members of the populace have, Judge Spina also violated both article IV, section 2, and the Fourteenth Amendment of the United States Constitution.*

"*I rest on my brief that Judge Spina's implicit or inferential finding that I was practicing law by my appearance in court one business day after the disbarment order became effective ('Axe Day') was clear error. A criminal charge must have elements so as not to be vague or overbroad. If the practice of law cannot be defined, neither can the unauthorized practice of law be, making §§41, 46A, 46B, 46C unconstitutionally vague."*

The nature of the cases that were damaged by my disbarment was

(1) a legal malpractice case;

(2) one contract and tort case regarding a transcript;

(3) the counterclaim on another transcript case (transcriber's case-in-chief had been dismissed;

(4) a case in which the primary defendant had filed for bankruptcy and which the bankruptcy eventually sent the case back to the state court, from which I had already been disbarred;

(5) a malicious prosecution which had been brought in federal court but from which the state pending claims had been sent to state court. That part of the federal case which had remained in federal court was stayed. That part which had been sent to state court was—after I won three appeals brought by the defendants—on the way to being won when I was disbarred, leaving my client without representation. When he could not find another lawyer, the winning case was dismissed;

(6) a child custody case;

(7) a rape case, which fortunately was dismissed when the client appeared in court with a new lawyer. The client said, since the new lawyer had not even spoken to him, the dismissal happened because of the discovery I had accomplished before I was disbarred. The client nevertheless lost the money the new lawyer took from him as a retainer for nothing;

(8) a federal collection case which had been settled and for which my client was still owed money;

(9) a contempt case for which the appeal had been written but not yet filed.

After winning three of the defendants' appeals in the Meuse case (#5 in the above list), I was disbarred and forced by incarceration to withdraw from the case. There went my retirement. Ditto with the contempt case before Judge Smoot (#9 in the above list). My client could have appealed Smoot's decision on his own, given that I had already written the appellate brief, but the client would have been vulnerable to sanctions, which he would not have been had I still been his attorney. That was a shame because the Smoot decision was so obviously discrimination, it could have altered the course of discrimination in Massachusetts' family courts. Cheated.

> Attorneys and counsellors . . . are officers of the court, . . . , upon evidence of their possessing sufficient legal learning and fair private character. It has been the general practice in this country to obtain this evidence by an examination of the parties.

Ex parte Garland, 1 U.S. (4 Wall.) 333, 378-79 (1866). There was no evidence, no proof whatsoever that I lacked sufficient legal learning—in fact, I received the Corpus Juris Secundum award upon graduation from law school, the first amongst firsts—and no evidence that my private character was less than fair.

Barb v. The Bar et al

After the Bar issued the Petition for Discipline against me, both the Bar Counsel, Daniel Crane, and the Assistant Bar Counsel, Susan Strauss Weisberg, went public in an effort to ruin my reputation and credibility. Only lies could do that, so that is what they did: lied.

I countered by suing them for defamation. They defended solely by saying they were immune from suit.

I argued that the BBO and OBC, not being enabled by the legislature, were private employers, and that Crane and Weisberg, not receiving paychecks from the Commonwealth, were private employees. As private entities, none was entitled to immunity.

I also argued that if the court deemed them to be public employers and employees, then Article V of the Massachusetts Constitution prevents them from being given immunity. Article V mandates that all the public officials of all three branches of government must be accountable to the people *at all times*. That article renders all immunities—whether all judge-made (common-law) or statutory immunity—unconstitutional in Massachusetts.

Judge Thomas Billings let them get away with it. He dismissed the case of the grounds of sovereign immunity, common-law immunity, and prosecutorial immunity. He and the judges on both appellate tiers ignored our Declaration of Rights. The Hell with their Oaths, they told us, in so many words. This is unacceptable. Should they be impeached forthwith or should they first be given a trial? If a trial, a civil or criminal one?

Immunity must go. It must be abolished. It prevents accountability. All of us must be accountable for our personal and professional conduct.

I fought each of the cases, **The Bar v Barb** and **Barb v. The Bar et al** all the way to the United States Supreme Court. I was not granted *certiorari*. That is, the High Court decided not to review those cases. I know not why.

Tainted Report Damages Court's Credibility

On February 11, 2009, *fitsnews*[654]/ wrote:

> . . . we never suspected that the ABA may have been complicit in a rigged review of the state's attorney discipline system—or at least as negligent as they were in performing their duties. . . .
>
> A South Carolina lawmaker investigating the Court has provided FITS with a copy of an explosive report that outlines serious ethical lapses on the part of both the Court and the ABA review team in the conduct and findings of the investigations.
>
> The report, excerpts of which are published here for the first time, pulls no punches.
>
> "Inaccurate descriptions and a deceptive analysis of the present South Carolina judicial and attorney discipline systems within this ABA consultation team's report represent a breach of the ABA team's duty to the Supreme Court of South Carolina, South Carolina Bar and public of South Carolina," the report states.
>
> Specifically, the ABA team is accused of intentionally neglecting relevant documents, ignoring key witnesses and omitting unflattering aspects of our state's attorney discipline system in order to reach the predefined conclusion that the Court should maintain its current corrupt hold over the profession.
>
> "In ratifying and endorsing an attorney discipline system based on the sole discretion of the South Carolina Chief

Justice and her four associate justices, void of any equitable discovery process or the U.S. Constitution protections of due process and equal protection, the six members of the ABA team have also breached their duties to the U.S. Constitution and the ABA Constitution," the report continues.

Given the worthlessness of the ABA report on the attorney discipline system in Massachusetts, I suspect an intelligent, vigorous, diligent investigative reporter would find the same corruption in the work of the ABA team in the Commonwealth of Massachusetts also.

Chapter 25

Court Reform

Order or chaos. Which do we want? Order, not chaos, of course. What do we get when we go to court today? Thoughts of revolution. Thoughts of tyranny. Impeach the bastard judge. Impeach the bitch judge. Do you know where he lives? Do you know where she lives? Nowadays one hears "Do you know where he or she lives?" more in person than online because the people fear moles or the government's technological ears online. Don't go near their homes! Why not, we can't sue the bastards because they have immunity? The courts are inefficient and heavily biased and make lawsuits too expensive.

In Massachusetts, there is fear. Judicial fear. The judges want protection. That creates a problem. There is little room for secure security either inside or outside the many, old courthouses across the Commonwealth. In Taunton, for instance, the judges have only reserved parking spaces next to the courthouse, which saves the judges the anxiety of walking across the street to a parking lot. In Boston, under the "new" courthouse named after Barbara Walter's former lover, the former senator, Edward Brooks, there is a secure parking garage with its own elevator. On the inside, the judges' chambers are behind a very thick glass, locked door behind which is a long hallway about 100 feet in length. On the wall next to the thick glass door is a voicebox and a coded number pad. At the end of the hallway, there appears to be another layer of security. I cannot tell you what it is because I never got past the first tier of security.

Their fear of violence would end, of course, if they conceded they are not entitled under state and federal statutes or constitutions to judicial immunity. For everyone's good, we must abolish judicial immunity.

People who have never been involved with a court have no idea what this is all about.

Well, as I have tried to illustrate throughout this book, the courts must be reformed. The question then becomes not only How? but also, given the present societal and economic ills of the country and pending and existing wars in both hemispheres, Will it be possible to get state and federal congresses to pay attention to a subject that appears to be no less critical and less dramatic than the problems requiring immediate congressional and presidential attention?

Only if we unite . . . and show how reforming the court will not require increasing budgets but will save billions of dollars and restore both stability to the American family and the faith of the public as a whole in our Constitution. Great benefits in return for the expenditure of primarily time rather than costs.

To begin with, we must not treat fathers differently than we treat mothers. We must, therefore, repeal or rewrite from scratch the laws that favor one gender over another, namely, the Violence Against Women Act (VAWA), Title IV-D awards.

We must eliminate programmatic mandatory reporting of alleged abuse that paints the innocent and the guilty with the same broad brush. The mandatory reporting structure needs to be revisited to better protect people legitimately at risk while not destroying lives and families. The courts are parentectomizing children while systematically ignoring fathers' and children's rights.

We must also rewrite the statutes that unconstitutionally imprison nonviolent prisoners, overwhelmingly, primarily fathers, for alleged arrearages so that they be immediately released from debtors prisons. This means the Bradley Amendment and all its state progenies must be immediately repealed.

Then, we must amend statutes that are poorly drafted, laws that generate needless litigation, increasing cost and legal fees to the parties, costs and legal fees that would not be incurred but for the poorly drafted legislation.

Next, we must review and amend our Rules of Civil Procedure. Many are poorly drafted, are not adhered to by the judiciary, and generate needless litigation, resulting in the increase of cost and legal fees to the parties. Specificity would go a long way to cure the arbitrary and capricious rulings by those sitting on the bench. Evidentiary errors are rarely, if ever, considered or cured on appeal. Rules are supposed to create order out of chaos. Our rules do not do that.

If we can get around the controversy surrounding codification, codification of the rules would go a long way to cure arbitrary and capricious rulings. Not only would legal costs and fees be cut dramatically, the intellectual burden on the sitting justices would be lessened enormously. Because many judges are not bright—many having become judges because they could not maintain a law practice and needed financial security—or do not like reading, there is considerable law they simply do not know. Codification would make more visible all that law they never have bothered learn.

Lastly, there should be a separate section in the court solely for discovery. Sitting justices do NOT want to hear about discovery problems even though they can make or break your case. They rarely enforce discovery and procedural rules, which, if the did, would result in both fewer court appearances for parties and more efficient use of court resources. And discovery problems, too, are rarely, if ever, considered or cured on appeal.

I am besieged daily—yes, before and after disbarment—by folks who want to appeal. Most appeals are a waste of time and money. The state court currently charges $350 to file an appeal. The First Circuit, $450. Boilerplate denials are like "scrod," the "fish of the day," the fish most abundant in the day's catch. Justice is thereby denied. Perhaps only 3 percent of the cases make it to the SJC. That means 97 percent of those who feel they were wronged have no remedy. (There's a lot more to say on this topic.)

Possible additional solutions

We need more judges, as well as more legislators so that the people have access to their legislators. (Michael Warnken of California has done considerable work on the issue of how many legislators his state should have. Search Google and YouTube for Michael Warnken . . and William J. "bj" Wagener.)

States that have not yet codified their law must do so.

We need intelligence tests for judges, both sitting judges and judicial candidates. Those with less than a predetermined quotient may not serve. We also need psychological testing, similar to the tests given or once-upon-a-time required by Harvard Law School when application for entry is made, for both sitting judges and judicial candidates.

The reasons for these measures are obvious, or should be: All too many of the judges were, at least in Massachusetts, merely political gophers, campaign workers, and campaign contributors. All too many of the judges applied because they could not cut it as practicing attorneys. All too many of them could not cut it because they were not people persons and were unable to develop a clientèle sufficient to support an independent law practice. All too many never practiced law, or at most a year or two before they went onto the public dole by working for the government in one small capacity or another.

Judges who, prior to being seated, practiced only criminal law—assistant district attorneys, district attorneys, criminal defense attorneys—must be limited to judging criminal matters. They are dangerous in civil cases. They simply do not have the requisite experience or knowledge to adjudicate civil cases.

I am less inclined to limit judges who, prior to being seated, practiced only civil law to civil cases. Why? Because criminal defendants are far better protected from judicial abuse than are civil defendants. For instance, a murderer is more likely to have his constitutional rights protected in a criminal session than an average working dad has his protected in a family-law courtroom.

Homosexual judges appointed to the family-law courts must be limited to handling only those cases between homosexuals. Lesbians to sit on lesbian cases. Gay males to sit on gay male cases. Why? Because we do not know whether or how much each of the lesbian judges resents or hates or wants to punish the opposite sex or even straight females. Because we do not know whether or how much each of the gay male judges resents or hates or wants to punish the opposite sex or straight males. I am as yet unaware of transvestite judges. I know only one transvestite, a wonderful, bright, talented person, but his/her psychological status is complex. I know only her female persona and think of her only as a woman. What she would be like on the judicial bench? I have not the slightest idea.

In Massachusetts, where judges are appointed and not elected, lesbians and gays are being appointed simply because the appointing governor wants to keep courting lesbian and gay constituent associations. Politics rather than meritorious professional performance prevails.

We need transparency. People complain about judges, but the commissions charged with investigating and resolving the complaints do nothing. Private and public scrutiny are rivals in this area. I suggest that the complaints be made public BUT with numbers substituted for the judges' names. If, after investigation of the alleged misconduct, there are public outcries and they are based on reasonable outrage, then the alleged wrongdoer's name should be revealed.

This is a precaution given that many, many complaints are frivolous, but certainly, once it has been determined by scrutinizing the facts that it is not a frivolous complaint, the public has a right to know.

We need strong committees to work with legislatures to amend or repeal ineffective or damaging statutes. Our legislators act according to *their* perception of the wishes of interest groups, when, in fact, the legislators should act according to the wishes of their entire constituency.

Adoption, Termination of Parental Rights, DSS, DCF, CPS, DFS *et al*

This area of law devastates the American family. A war against this devastation should be America's War Against Terrorism. Although the higher courts have required judges to prove by clear and convincing evidence that parents are unfit before removing a child from its parents, all too many judges do not provide an evidentiary hearing at which the parents can testify. The burden of proof should be on the governmental agency, but all too often the burden is put on the parents. The incredible psychological damage done to the children is irreversible. Then neither the parents nor the children have a remedy from any court. Why? Because the judges and the family service workers and so-called mental health workers are given immunity, which shelter them from suit and liability. Where the judges, family service workers, and so-called mental health workers are aware that what they do cannot be reviewed or criticized, their attitude changes from when they started the job: they get careless, they get bored, they get negligent, and they reach the point where they see so many children and parents, "they don't give a damn."

And that's where the tsunami that removes children from their parents takes on epic proportions. Women, mothers and grandmothers phone me crying at any time day or night. The family rights' groups are flooded. Children are taken from parents the moment they come out of the birth canal, literally, until they are teenagers. I had a case where one family's children had as many as 30 foster parents, have tried to commit suicide multiple times, and have ended up in mental institutions where they might or might not recover.

Splitting of the Attorney-General's Office

The Attorneys-General offices need to be divided in two. There is an inherent conflict of interest in the AGs powers. On one hand, the AG is the attorney for the *people*. On the other, the AG may sue on behalf of the State and defend it against you. I say "may" because the AG's choice is discretionary, but he never uses his powers for the people. He always uses it for the State. (In Massachusetts, the AG is now a "she.")

In consumer protection, for example, he acts for the folks from time to time, but he and his predecessors have done almost nothing in the area of civil rights. For instance, when John Doe sues the Commonwealth for violations of civil rights by the State and its agencies, departments, etc., the AG defends the state entities against John Doe.

Given the publicity, the AG knows or should know that many married or unmarried men should not be paying child support under the guidelines because the guidelines contemplate (1) that the couple have a traditional custody and visitation arrangement and (2) that the parents are to be sharing equally in the support of the child(ren).

Where has the AG been on this issue? Nowhere . . . because he is more interested in defending the Commonwealth: it is, after all, the political and powerful side of the conflict. He has chosen to let the people be damned. I want to see two offices with two different AGs at the helm. It is a must!!! He has boilerplate to defend all government employees on the grounds of immunity.

Immunity must go! All the flavors of immunity must go!

* * *

John Adams said that our government was designed for wise, tolerant, and virtuous people, and is wholly unsuited for the governance of any other kind. But if the people are not the above, then what they get is a sloppy government that is representative of what they really are.

And that is how we got to where we are.

Jefferson went one step further. He said revolution was essential for every generation to have in order to overcome the tyranny of the laws of the previous generation . . . since the next generation always faces a different reality than did the previous generation.

Jefferson was not necessarily thinking of a violent revolution, though he certainly was not opposed to it. But he certainly was thinking of a revolution in laws.

These kinds of revolutions often only seem to take place in the wake of some kind of catastrophic event, but before sweeping reform can occur, the current government system needs to fall, either from internal rot or by outside intervention.

Bets are on that the U.S. system will collapse after a severe energy shortage. If so, the rise of a strong man, possibly a temporary dictator, like Cincinnatus, or a Caesar, a Napoleon, will be necessary to restore order.

But given that the U.S. Constitution has no provision for temporary dictators, the only way to get court reform is via an Evolutionary, not Revolutionary, process—in other words, by working within the present system.

If we do nothing, the country will continue to drift slowly from bad to worse. Only continuing civil disobedience, demonstrations, including the recent much-laughed-at Tea Parties must first take place. When the voting public finally becomes active and educated as to what kind of person they should elect to governmental office, only then can the Evolutionary process begin.

ENDNOTES

Endnotes—Preface

1   Shays' Rebellion gave impetus to the pro-national-government people at the Federal Convention in 1787, out of which our Constitution arose. "Daniel Shays, a Revolutionary War veteran, who headed an 'army' of 1,000 men. They marched first for Worcester where they closed own the commonwealth's supreme court, then turned west to Springfield where they broke into the jail to free imprisoned debtors." Shays' Rebellion: Wars and Battles, 1786-1787, *http://www.u-s-history.com/pages/h363.html.*

2   42 United States Code §1983, abbreviated as 42 USC §1983.

3   The domestic violence laws began at the federal level. The federal government then instructed the States to draft their own state DV and child-support guidelines appropriate for their communities, some statewide, some local.

4   CAPTA, originally enacted in 1974, has been repeatedly amended and rescued for more than three decades. It may be found under 42 USC chapter 67; 42 USC §5101 *et seq;* 42 USC §5116 *et seq.*

5   My website for Campaign 2002 is still online: *http://www.barbforgovernor. com.*

6   To serve means to put in a U.S. Postal Service mailbox.

7   Rule 8(c) of the Massachusetts Rules of Civil Procedure lists the affirmative defenses. All other States that base their rules on the Federal Rules of Civil Procedure list the affirmative defenses in their rule 8(c).

8   "When a party has mistakenly designated a defense as a counterclaim or a counterclaim as a defense, the court on terms, if justice so requires, shall treat the pleading as if there had been a proper designation." Mass.R.Civ.P. 8(c).

9   That a contract was violated is **not** the ultimate question, but it might have been Sammy the Smithy who violated it, not you, so the ***ultimate*** question in your contract trial is **whether you** violated it or not.

10   Lizotte, Brian N., "Publish or Perish: The Electronic Availability of Summary Judgments by Eight District Courts," Wisconsin Law Review, p. 107 *et seq.* (June 19, 2007). Lizotte has a B.A. and M.S. from Yale University; an Ed.M. from Boston University; a J.D., from Yale Law School, and is an Associate at Bingham McCutchen LLP in Hartford, Connecticut.

Endnotes—Chapter 1

11   In 2001, I sued on behalf of a client in Hampshire County Superior Court at Northampton on the breach of promise to stay wed "until death do us part." The wife argued that given that most marriages end in divorce in our society, her husband was foolish to rely on that promise. A convoluted story, but at the end, she had to deed over to him her 50 percent of the real property in Hampshire County. He did not have to buy her out.

12   "Marriage is not a mere contract between two parties but a legal status from which certain rights and obligations arise."

13   1 Massachusetts Practice § 1:2.

14   *Goodridge v. Department of Public Health,* 440 Mass. 309, 321, 798 N.E.2d 941, 954 (2003) (allowing same-sex marriages).

15   1 Massachusetts Practice § 1:2.

16   Charles P. Kindregan, Jr., Monroe L. Inker, *Family Law and Practice,* 1 Massachusetts Practice § 1:5 n. 4.

17   1 Massachusetts Practice § 1:5.

18   1 Massachusetts Practice § 1:2.

> The founders of Massachusetts, influenced by the views of the Protestant Reformation, believed that absolute divorce was permissible. Since there were no ecclesiastical courts in the Massachusetts Bay Colony, the determination of marital status rested exclusively with the legislature, i.e. on the Court of Assistants and other judicial bodies which functioned under the authority of the General Court.

1 Massachusetts Practice § 1:5 (internal citations omitted).

19   *Id.* (internal citations omitted).

20   1 Massachusetts Practice § 1:2.

21   *Id.* Banns were already an established Canon Law (Catholic) practice.

22   *Id.* (internal citations omitted).

23   *Id.* n. 14 (internal citations omitted).

24   *Id.*

25   1 Massachusetts Practice § 1:5.

26   *Id.*

27   I. RESIDENCE AND DOMICILE DISTINGUISHED

The term "residence" is a common, everyday word that refers to "the place, esp. the house, in which a person lives or resides; dwelling place; home." (20) A person therefore resides in the state in which she lives. If the state in which a person resides is in controversy, i.e., homes in several states, then a court may determine residence by considering objective evidence such as the amount of time spent in each state, where the person pays taxes, where the person can vote, where the person sees the doctor, where the person registers her car, and the like.(21)

"Domicile," on the other hand, is a technical, legal term that often turns on the subjective intent of the person. Every person has a domicile of origin, assigned at birth, which derives from the domicile of one's parents.(22) Once. a person is legally capable of choosing a domicile of her own, she may do so by being physically present in the new state with the "inten[t] to make that place [her] home for the time at least."(23) According to the comments to the Restatement (Second) of Conflict of Laws, "[f]requently, this intention is expressed in terms of the durability of the intended stay, as, for example, that one must intend to reside indefinitely in the place place. . . ."(24) A person's "feelings toward the place" are also relevant in determining domicile.(25) If the state of a person's domicile is in controversy, then the outcome invariably turns on the requisite state of mind.(26) In such cases, a person's own testimony about her subjective intentions, and her formal and informal declarations, as well as her acts, will be considered as evidence.(27)

Rhonda Wasserman, "Divorce and domicile: time to sever the knot," William and Mary Law Review, Vol. 39, 1997.

28   *Kelley v. Snow,* 185 Mass. 288, 70 N.E. 89 (1904).

29   185 Mass. at 297-298, 70 N.E. at 94.

30   " 'Divorce' on grounds of incest or bigamy would have actually been an annulment in the light of the same statute declaring such marriages null and void. 1 Massachusetts Practice §1:7 n. 5.

31   Adultery is not enforced in Massachusetts, for it has fallen into "desue-
tude," said our State High Court.

> "Despite widespread official knowledge of such violations [of the
> adultery statute], prosecutions by law enforcement officials are
> essentially non-existent.... It seems beyond dispute that the [statute]
> defining or punishing the [crime] of ... adultery ... [has] fallen into
> a very comprehensive desuetude."

Com. v. Stowell, 389 Mass. 171, 175-176, 449 N.E.2d 357, 362 (1983) (affirmed
conviction under M.G.L. c. 272, § 14 for adultery). The penalty for the crime
"shall be punished by imprisonment in the state prison for not more than
three years or in jail for not more than two years or by a fine of not more than
five hundred dollars."

Notwithstanding the Court's opinion on adultery, from time to time,
divorces are granted on the grounds of adultery. In fact, about 25 years ago,
a divorce after one year of marriage on the grounds of adultery was settled
for over $100,000. Ironically the adulterer was a Harvard Law School profes-
sor who was seen regularly on ABC as its "legal expert." His then-wife later
became a client of mine; she came to me to bring a contempt action against
her first husband for nonpayment of child support. The case was quite complicated, but with proper preparation on my part, she walked out of court
with an award of $256,000, payable in $20,000 increments. The court allowed
only $4000 for my fees.

To this day, I have not collected the $4000. Given that statutory interest
in Massachusetts is 12 percent, making the principal double every six years,
her first husband owes me four times that amount.

Two years ago, I learned that she and Husband #1 were in court once
again. The judge, Christina Harms, now the First Justice of Norfolk County
Probate & Family Court, awarded her the back support but inadvertently (???)
did not include the money that was to come to me. I moved for an amended
judgment but have heard nothing from that court in the intervening years.
If you are reading this, it means that the book was published. With the bit
of notoriety that might come from publishing such a book, maybe the Clerk
of Court and Christina Harms will change their corrupt ways of ignoring the
rights of those who do not play politics with justice.

In Maine, the adultery, bigamy, and polygamy statutes have been repealed. The Texas LDS situation, in which over 400 children were taken by
the State, would never have happened in Maine.

32   1 Massachusetts Practice §1:7.

33 *Id..*

34 19 M.R.S.A. s 33 (1964).

35 *Lukich v. Lukich,* 379 S.C. 589, 666 S.E.2d 906 (S.C.,2008).

36 *State v. Fischer,* 199 P.3d 663, 2008 WL 2971520 (Ariz.App. Div. 1, 2008).

37 1 Massachusetts Practice § 1:8.

38 1 Massachusetts Practice §§ 1:6 and 1:8.

39 1 Massachusetts Practice § 1:8.

40 1 Massachusetts Practice § 1:6.

41 "In 1997 the domestic relations rules were amended to change the time standards for notice of a hearing on motions from 3 to 7 days, to improve discovery procedures, to introduce for the first time summary judgment in some post-divorce actions and to eliminate some archaic practices. The Supplemental Rules were also amended in 1997 to require for the first time that financial statements be exchanged between the parties within 45 days of the service of the summons, to mandate sanctions for failure to observe the rules governing such statements, to require the exchange of specific financial documents, and to introduce case management rules into domestic relations practice. In 1999, effective January 1, 2000, the rules were amended to provide for automatic restraining orders on assets in divorce and separate support actions." 1 Massachusetts Practice § 1:8 [footnoted citations omitted].

42 Title IV, United States Code.

43 The Violence Against Women Act (VAWA), the signature-banner of Senator Joseph Biden, D-Del, and the Department of Justice grant entitled "Grant to Encourage Arrest-Preferred Policies and the Enforcement of Protection Order Programs."

44 Title IV, United States Code.

45 See *DeMatteo v. DeMatteo,* 436 Mass. 18, 31, 762 N.E.2d 797 (2002).

46 *Smith v. Smith,* 171 Mass. 404, 409, 50 N.E. 933 (1898). See also *French v. McAnarney,* 290 Mass. 544, 546, 195 N.E. 714 (1935).

47 In a commonwealth, landowners do not possess mineral or oil rights to their land. People are the sovereigns in commonwealths. The Commonwealth of Massachusetts is a voluntary association of the people. Preamble to the Constitution and Massachusetts General Laws c. 4, §7.

48   When Gov. Ronald Reagan signed the legislation, California became the first State to have a No-Fault Divorce law. He later said that it was the worst legislation he signed, because of the devastation it caused to families, but particularly, the turmoil it caused in children. In *Twice Adopted,* his son Michael wrote, "Divorce is where two adults take everything that matters to a child—the child's home, family, security, and sense of being loved and protected—and they smash it all up, leave it in ruins on the floor, then walk out and leave the child to clean up the mess." *Id.* at 37.

49   On the Internet, opposition to No-Fault divorce is considerable. Some folks are liking it to the "takings doctrine," by which the government uses its power of eminent domain to take land from private citizens. "The similarity to no-fault divorce is that the state has the power to 'take' marriage through a court order. . . ." Judy Parejko, *Stolen Vows: The Illusion of No-Fault Divorce and the Rise of the American Divorce Industry.* There only has to be a desire by one spouse to get out of a marriage. Also under No-Fault, living apart for 6 months is sufficient reason to grant a divorce for childless couple or 12 months for a couple with minor children. Some ask, Why is 6 months' separation the magic number to conclude that a marriage is broken beyond repair? Others ask, Shouldn't the State be supporting marriages rather than granting easy-exit divorces?

50   Divorce is destroying 3,471 homes per day in the United States, and nothing is being to address the problem. If 3,471 children daily across our country were being murdered, both law enforcement and prosecution would actively pursue the murderers. (**Note**: Billy Miller provided the data and the analogy. Email, Thursday, May 22, 2008 8:19 A.M.)

51   The observer noted that the composition of a committee conducting a recent legislative study in Ohio is exactly as that stated above.

52   Familiarize yourself with the legal scheme in your State. To do that, read your State's statute or code on the subject of divorce. If you are familiar with the scheme, you will know where your legislature stands regarding divorce, for the scheme is a product of your legislature. The judicial scheme is something else. You will have to familiarize yourself with the case law, the decisions, to know whether the judges follow the legislative scheme or whether they have invented their own scheme. Much of divorce law is made by judges, not by legislatures.

53   *Cobble v. Commissioner of Dept. of Social Services,* 430 Mass. 385, 719 N.E.2d 500 (1999) (vacated affirmance of DSS' decision supporting a report of abuse by *minister father using, five or six times during preceding seven-month period, a belt*

to discipline nine-year-old child, Judah, with arthrogryposis, a congenital muscle condition, which requires him to wear braces on his back and legs and to undergo regular physical therapy, and remanded, holding that the evidence did not support the Department's finding of abuse or substantial risk of abuse). The Court found that the nine-year-old child's statements that spankings by father with belt left temporary red or pink marks on his buttocks that would fade after ten minutes or so did not establish abuse or substantial risk of abuse.

The father contended that DSS's action was unjustifiable interference with his fundamental rights to the free exercise of his religious beliefs and privacy in child rearing. The high court remanded the case because in 1993, the definition of "abuse" had changed: the "legislature had deleted the reference to 'serious' injury and expanded the definition of 'abuse' to encompass conduct 'which causes harm or substantial risk of harm to a child's health or welfare.' " *Id.,* 430 Mass. at 386, 719 N.E.2d at 502. Judah also had attention deficit disorder. After striking Judah, Rev, Cobble also read the Bible with him. The minister claimed that God approves of corporal punishment. "In the heart and mind of Woburn pastor Donald R. Cobble Jr., he has a God-given and biblically sanctioned right to punish his young son by spanking him with a leather belt." *http://www.apologeticsindex.org/an990430.html.*

54   In addition to or in lieu of a judgment to pay alimony, the court may assign to either husband or wife all or any part of the estate of the other, including but not limited to,

- all vested and nonvested benefits, rights and funds accrued during the marriage and which shall include, but not be limited to,
    - o   retirement benefits, military retirement benefits if qualified under and to the extent provided by federal law,
    - o   pension,
    - o   profit-sharing,
    - o   annuity,
    - o   deferred compensation and
    - o   insurance.

In determining the amount of alimony, if any, to be paid, or in fixing the nature and value of the property, if any, to be so assigned, the court, after hearing the witnesses, if any, of each party, shall consider

- the length of the marriage,
- the conduct of the parties during the marriage,
- the age,

- health,
- station,
- occupation,
- amount and sources of income,
- vocational skills,
- employability,
- estate,
- liabilities and
- needs of each of the parties and
- the opportunity of each for future acquisition of capital assets and income.

In fixing the nature and value of the property to be so assigned, the court shall also consider

- the present and future needs of the dependent children of the marriage.

The court may also consider

- the contribution of each of the parties in the
  - o acquisition,
  - o preservation or
  - o appreciation in value of their respective estates and
- the contribution of each of the parties as a homemaker to the family unit.

When the court makes an order for alimony on behalf of a spouse, said court shall determine

- whether the obligor under such order has health insurance or
- other health coverage available to him through an employer or organization or
- has health insurance or other health coverage available to him at reasonable cost that may be extended to cover the spouse for whom support is ordered.

When said court has determined that the obligor has such insurance or coverage available to him, said court shall include in the support order a requirement that the obligor do one of the following:

- exercise the option of additional coverage in favor of the spouse,
- obtain coverage for the spouse, or
- reimburse the spouse for the cost of health insurance.

In no event shall the order for alimony be reduced as a result of the obligor's cost for health insurance coverage for the spouse.

55 Guardians *ad litem* who out of 278 cases find for the mothers 270 times are *prima facie non*neutral. A court investigator, a recent British émigré who is likely a homosexual, who has been over 73 times and all but three times was appointed by the same judge is a *prima facie non*neutral; he is, instead, the judge's toy boy. A dyed in the wool lesbian who hates men is a *prima facie non*neutral mediator for a heterosexual couple.

56 Panelist judges were Cynthia J. Cohen, Peter C. DiGangi, Anne M. Geoffrion, Edward M. Ginsburg (ret.), Spencer M. Kagan, David H. Kopelman, Robert W. Langlois, Edward J. Lapointe, Denise L. Meagher, James V. Menno, Elizabeth O'Neill LaStaiti, Angela M. Ordonez, Robert A. Scandurra, Stephen C. Steinberg, Robert E. Terry, with more than a dozen lawyers.

Pricing: Judges (to cover cost of lunch): $25.00; Massachusetts Bar Association member recent admittees (05-06), member paralegals and law students: $100.00; Family Law Section members: $160.00; Barnstable County Bar Association members and Other MBA members: $180.00; Nonmembers: $220.00.

57 "Petticoat Judges" is a term coined by a former judge in a Western State.

58 "All the judges of the Superior Court have equal powers, and in most matters each is vested with all the powers of the court." *Peterson v. Hopson*, 306 Mass. 597, 603, 29 N.E.2d 140, 145 (1940) (internal cites omitted), and cases gathered. Clearly, where the Commonwealth retains jurisdiction over child support, there has not been a final judgment that would bar the power to undo the work of another judge.

59 Although a judge should not lightly undo the work of another judge, *Barbosa v. Hopper Feeds, Inc.*, 404 Mass. 610, 622, 537 N.E.2d 99, 106 (1989), the power to reconsider an issue remains in the court until final judgment. *Peterson v. Hopson*, 306 Mass. 597, 601, 29 N.E.2d 140, 145 (1940). 'Even without rehearing, a judge may modify a decision already announced, so long as the case has not passed beyond the power of the court.' Id. 306 Mass. at 602, 29 N.E.2d at 145.

Cataldo Ambulance Service, Inc. v. City of Chelsea, 43 Mass.App.Ct. 26, 27, 680 N.E.2d 937, 938 (1997).

A judge should . . . hesitate to undo the work of another judge. But until final judgment or decree there is no lack of power, and occasionally the power may properly be exercised.

Cataldo Ambulance Service, 43 Mass.App.Ct. at 27 n. 4, 680 N.E.2d at 938 n. 4 (internal citations omitted).

> Later cases in the Second Federal Circuit tend towards what we consider the sound rule, that another judge has all the powers that the judge who originally acted would have. . . . That rule is supported by the weight of authority generally, and in our opinion is the law of this Commonwealth....

Peterson v. Hopson, 306 Mass. 597, 604, 29 N.E.2d 140, 145 (1940) (cites omitted). *King v. Globe Newspaper Co.,* 400 Mass. 705 (1987) (until final judgment, there is no lack of power to undo the work of another judge).

Endnotes—Chapter 2

60   In Massachusetts, there is very little mentioned re children in the chapter containing the scheme for the dissolution of marriage, or divorce. Children are but a possible byproduct of a marriage. Children are, of course, mentioned in the chapter containing the scheme for actions involving out-of-wedlock relationships, for without children, there would be no need of the chapter. These children are euphemistically called "nonmarital children." The term "bastards" is a term of yesteryear kept pulsating in Charles Dickens' novels. Nonmarital children are to be treated the same as "marital children" are.

61   "Elaine Epstein, former president of the Massachusetts Women's Bar Association, admitted in 1993: 'Everyone knows that restraining orders and orders to vacate are granted to virtually all who apply . . . In many [divorce] cases, allegations of abuse are now used for tactical advantage.'" Phyllis Schlafly, "Time to Defund Feminist Pork—the Hate-Men Law," *http://www. eagleforum.org/psr/2005/oct05/psroct05.html.*

62   "Over 85% of contested custody suits end with mothers receiving sole custody over children. The remaining 15% divide children between other family members, agencies and fathers, so in fact fathers arrive at sole custody about 7% of the time." Barbara Kay, Keynote Speech at Conference, held in Ottawa on 20 September 2008, on the occasion of the 25th anniversary of REAL Women.

63   A list of the monies received by each State in 2006 from the feds is on the Internet at *http://www.ovw.usdoj.gov/grant_activities2006.htm* and "FY 2006 Office on Violence Against Women Grant Activity by State (with State Totals)."

64   Phyllis Schlafly wrote in "Time to Defund Feminist Pork—the Hate-Men Law," VAWA gives $75 million annually in grants to encourage arrest

and enforcement of protection orders, and $55 million annually to provide free legal assistance to victims (but not to the accused men)." By 2006, the federal government gave, in fact, $_____ to the 50 States and Puerto Rico. See Appendices A and B.

65   Department of Justice began the STOP (Services, Training, Officers, Prosecutors) Violence Against Women Grant Program through VAWA funding.

66   To obtain these lucrative funds and increase the dollars in their coffers, many States arbitrarily classify and discriminate against law-abiding and decent fathers by applying the child-support guidelines even when the guidelines are not appropriate. See Chapter 8 below.

67   Phyllis Schlafly, "Time to Defund Feminist Pork—the Hate-Men Law," *http://www.eagleforum.org/-psr/2005/oct05/psroct05.html* (October 5, 2005).

68   Phyllis Schlafly, "Federal Incentives Make Children Fatherless," *http://www.eagleforum.org/column/-2005/may05/05-05-11.html* (May 11, 2005).

69   The percentage of children under age 18 living with two married parents[3] fell from 77 percent in 1980 to 68 percent in 2007.[4] In 2007, 23 percent of children lived with only their mothers, 3 percent lived with only their fathers, 3 percent lived with two unmarried parents, and 4 percent lived with neither of their parents.

Federal Interagency Forum on Child and Family Statistics, citing U.S. Census Bureau, Current Population Survey, Annual Social and Economic Supplement (2007) at *http://www.childstats.gov/americaschildren/famsoc.asp#4.* |

70   "About three-quarters of the 28 million men who have children (under age 19) live with those children." Centers for Disease Control, *http://www.cdc.gov/nchs/pressroom/06facts/fatherhood.htm.*

71   "Judges Accused of Jailing Kids for Cash" by Michael Rubinkam and Maryclaire Dale, Associated Press, Feb. 11, 2009, *http://news.aol.com/article/juvenile-court-kickbacks/338834.*

72   "Among the offenders were teenagers who were locked up for months for stealing loose change from cars, writing a prank note and possessing drug paraphernalia. Many had never been in trouble before, and some were imprisoned even after probation officers recommended against it. Many of the youths didn't have attorneys."

"Plead Guilty To Fraud For Taking $2.6M In Kickbacks To Send Teens To Private Detention Centers," Associated Press, www.cbsnews.com, Feb. 13, 2009.

Another, a teenager lampooned her assistant principal on her webpage; she was sentenced to three months. Judges Accused of Jailing Kids for Cash" by Michael Rubinkam and Maryclaire Dale, Associated Press, Feb. 11, 2009, *http://news.aol.com/article/juvenile-court-kickbacks/338834.*

73   An *ex parte* hearing is a secret hearing between the judge and one of the parties. The other party does not know about it and therefore is not present to defend himself against any accusation.

74   That restraining order was ultimately extended indefinitely

75   In Massachusetts, the focus in a Care & Protection case is on the behavior of the parents; that is, the parents might be neglecting or abusing the child. In a CHINS (Child in Need of Services), the focus is on the behavior of the child; for intance, the child is acting out.

76   *Matter of John A. Markey*, 427 Mass. 797, 696 N.E.2d 523 (July 14, 1998) (NO. SJC-07740) (holding that the judge's misconduct, which consisted of an improper ex parte communication to another judge, Prudence McGregor, that led to dismissal of an abuse prevention order and a pattern of failing to engage in plea colloquies, warranted a public reprimand and a suspension for three months without pay, where he continued to deny, despite overwhelming contrary evidence, that the communication was intended to influence the latter judge's decision, notwithstanding many mitigating facts concerning his reputation, personal stress, and lack of financial gain. Suspending a judge without pay for three months as a disciplinary sanction would not be a *de facto* unconstitutional removal from office).

> The sanction imposed on Judge McGregor is relevant as both judges were involved in the misconduct, and Judge Markey's transgressions were substantially more serious than those of Judge McGregor. He initiated the ex parte communication with her, asked her to advance the hearing date as a favor to him, volunteered his personal observations with respect to the condition of the Macedos' apartment, and sought to influence her decision on the 209A order.
>
> > FN5. The Commission determined that Judge McGregor violated the Code of Judicial Conduct by permitting a private communication designed to influence her judicial action, and by permitting that communication to influence her judicial action. Judge McGregor agreed to a six-week suspension without pay and a two-week education program during her vacation time and at her own expense.

Markey, 427 Mass. at 807, 807 n. 5, 696 N.E.2d at 530, 530 n. 5.

77   Eagle Tribune.

78   This was confirmed a year later by Judge Allen Swan in a written opinion in 2001.

79   "Before shootings, fears for girls' safety: Family members say father wanted custody" by Michael Levenson, Boston Globe, August 29, 2007.

Endnotes—Chapter 3

80   When I sued four judges in the Fall of 2001, one of the issues was about the GALs. After filing, I uploaded the Complaint on my website. It caught considerable attention. I alerted the fathers groups. The chief judge of the family court then revisited the issue. All GALs were invited to Boston to a seminar about standards for the GALs. The men held a demonstration with signs outside the meeting place. Ultimately standards issued which the GALs were to follow for the first time.

81   *Delmolino v. Nance,* 14 Mass.App.Ct. 209, 213-214, 437 N.E.2d 578, 581(1982).

82   *Adoption of Paula,* 420 Mass 716, 724*ff.,* 651 N.E.2d 1222, 1229 (1995).

83   *Adoption of Arthur,* 34 Mass.App.Ct. 914, 916. 609 N.E.2d 486, 489 (1993). The *Quentin* case, the *Marro* case, the *Kirin* case. *Hale v. Hale, Yannas v. Frondistou-Yannas, Gilmore v. Gilmore.* There are cases after cases saying the same thing. They are consistent.

84   *Adoption of Sean,* 36 Mass.App.Ct. 261, 266, 630 N.E.2d 604, 607 (1994).

85   Attorney Monroe L. Inker, the recently-deceased granddaddy of divorce law, and Law Professor Charles P. Kindregan, Jr., in "Domestic Relations: Can Custodial Parents Dictate a Child's Home?" [25 M.L.W. 1307, February 24, 1997], wrote of "the many-fronted wars over the rights of noncustodial parents (usually fathers)" and essentially called today the age of "the feminist rebellion."

86   The scanned excerpt from Chouteau's bill may be seen on my website in Exhibit 247 at *http://www.falseallegations.com/drano95-court-commits-crimes. htm.*

87   *See Matter of Ford,* 404 Mass. 347, 535 N.E.2d 225 (1989) (NO. EO-059, S-4954), in which the Supreme Judicial Court censured Judge Ford for violating judicial canons by serving as chief executive officer of nonprofit corporation while serving as judge (in violation of Canon 5(c)(2)), exercised his

powers of appointment with favoritism (in violation of Canon 3(B)(4)), and swore to false information (in violation of Canon 2(A)):

> From 1979 through 1988, Judge Ford appointed Attorney J. Michael Roberts in 305 different Probate Court matters, from which Mr. Roberts received a total of $264,724.69 in fees.

> Sixty-four per cent of these 305 appointments were as guardian *ad litem* in Medicaid trusts, "Rogers cases," and medical treatment cases. Mr. Roberts had special competence in these types of cases. Of the other 36% of his appointments, most were as master in divorce and other cases, and as guardian *ad litem* in estates or trusts.

> Despite the marked redundancy of appointments to Mr. Roberts, we accept the premise that the above 64% of the cases were directed to Mr. Roberts for reasons consistent with impartiality on the part of the judge.[FN2]

>> FN2. We recognize that some redundancy of appointments may be justified by the special qualifications of an appointee, the needs of the court, and the unavailability of other persons having the required qualifications and a willingness to accept appointments.

Nevertheless, the records disclose that, for the remaining 36% of the appointments where no special expertise has been shown, Mr. Roberts received a total of $136,773.04 in fees. We conclude, from our common experience, that these total payments would not have occurred in any reasonable rotation of appointments among competent and available counsel. This was an inordinate diversion of fees to Mr. Roberts by Judge Ford, and favoritism in appointments has been thus shown, contrary to the mandate of Canon 3(B)(4).

Our conclusion that favoritism has been shown to Mr. Roberts in probate appointments is confirmed by the fact that Judge Ford hired Mr. Roberts as a staff person for NEAVS, and for the years 1981 through 1985, Mr. Roberts received $87,394 in salary from NEAVS. This simultaneous attention by Judge Ford to Mr. Roberts's interests, in court appointments and in disbursements from NEAVS, supports a clear inference that court appointments to Mr. Roberts were based on partiality and not on merit.

Partiality to Mr. Roberts is also shown by the fact that Mr. Roberts's sister, Lisa Roberts, who was first assistant register in the Norfolk Probate Court became, after Judge Ford assumed the presidency of NEAVS, a member of that organization's board of directors as well as its vice president and, as coordinator of NEAVS publications, received from NEAVS, from 1981 through 1986, $124,782 in salary. NEAVS's funds were also used to establish a pension fund for her, and to pay in part for a graduate program in tax law for her.

During Judge Ford's presidency, also, NEAVS employed three of Mr. Roberts's other relatives and two of his "in-laws," one of whom was elected to the board of directors. In short, if further proof were needed that Judge Ford's redundant probate appointments to Mr. Roberts were a palpable abuse of the judge's obligations under Canon 3(B)(4), that proof is found in the demonstrated support of the Roberts family members in the NEAVS context.

Ford, 404 Mass. at 349-350, 535 N.E.2d at 226-227. There were also other Ford recipients: his step-daughter, his brother, three relatives of Lisa Roberts, and two of J. Michael Roberts's "in-laws," real estate commissioners who were paid out of the sale proceeds of litigants' real estate, plus other lawyers and six other employees of the Probate & Family Court. *Ford*, 404 Mass. at 354-355, 535 N.E.2d at 230. Lisa Roberts "resigned her position as first assistant register of probate in 1988" [*Ford*, 404 Mass. at 357 n. 5, 535 N.E.2d at 231 n. 5], a year before the opinion issued. She then went to work for another of Ford's relatives and was finally nominated for a judgeship. As a reward for her honesty?

There are two attorneys named Robert M. Ford identified on the Board of Bar Overseers' website. The status on one of them is "Retired"; the status of the other is "Active." For each of them, the BBO declares on its website, "This attorney has no record of public discipline." Lying in the legal community is commonplace—even at the regulatory entities—if not universal.

88   And Mary McCauley Manzi, too, was implicated circumstantially in a scandal shortly before her appointment to a judgeship. Her husband was one of Judge Troy's favorite puppy dogs. *See In re Troy*, 364 Mass. 15, 72-73, 306 N.E.2d 203, 235-236 (1973) (judge disbarred from the practice of law in the courts of the Commonwealth, and enjoined from exercising any powers or duties as a judge). The former Judge Troy is not listed on the BBO website as being active, retired, or deceased. Other attorneys who are deceased are idenfified as being "deceased."

In reaching our ultimate decision in this case, we rely in major part upon the following six extremely serious charges which were proved before us against Judge Troy: (1) He lied under oath in answering interrogatories. . . . He repeated those lies before this court in the hearing of this case. He also lied to the Superior Court judge . . . , and he repeated some of that false testimony at the hearing before this court. . . . (6) He procured substantial legal services from Mr. Manzi and Mr. Carvin. He paid these lawyers nothing for their services. Further, he gave them numerous assignments as court-appointed counsel for indigent defendants for which the two lawyers were compensated at public expense. During the time when Mr. Manzi and Mr. Carvin were serving as his personal attorneys, he presided over cases in which they appeared as counsel for private litigants, and he made no disclosure of the relationship between judge and counsel. On one occasion, without disclosing his relationship to counsel, he presided over a tort case and made a substantial finding in favor of a plaintiff represented by Mr. Carvin.

[20] Any one of these six matters, standing alone, warrants severe disciplinary action against Judge Troy. Taken cumulatively, they clearly require the result we have reached.

Judge Troy is herewith disbarred from the practice of law in the courts of this Commonwealth, and he is enjoined from the exercise of duties and powers as a judge.

So it appears that one of the qualifications to be a judge in Massachusetts is to be involved in some nefarious affair first. And unfortunately, Massachusetts is one of two States in which judges are appointed for life or until the age of 70, and they have not developed dementia or Alzheimers, they mght be invited back as a "Recall Judge."

89   General Law c. 215, § 56A,

90   *See* note 1, *supra.*

Endnotes—Chapter 4

91   A search on Westlaw of all 50 States for "perquisite income" yields only four cases: two from California, one from New Jersey, and one from Massachusetts, the latter being the case cited in the note that follows.

92   *Crowe v. Fong,* 45 Mass.App.Ct. 673, 676, 701 N.E.2d 359, 362 (1998) (attributed to father "perquisite income" of $350 per week from his employer,

representing the fair rental value of father's rent-free occupancy of his parents' house, for purposes of calculating father's child support obligation, where father worked for his parents' dry cleaning business, and father's siblings who worked for business were also offered rent free occupancy in family home. Child Support Guidelines, Guideline I, subd. A.

A case "decided prior to the adoption of the guidelines [held] that certain benefits received by the father from family business were loans or gifts, dependent on the generosity of others and, therefore, subject to discontinuance at any time." *Crowe*, 45 Mass.App.Ct. 673, 681, 701 N.E.2d 359, 365 citing *Hlllery v. Hillery*, 342 Mass. at 373-374, 173 N.E.2d 269 (1961).

93   **A. Sources of Income.** For purposes of these guidelines, income is defined as gross income from whatever source regardless of whether that income is recognized by the Internal Revenue Code or reported to the Internal Revenue Service or state Department of Revenue or other taxing authority. Those sources include, but are not limited to, the following:

(1)   (a) salaries, wages, overtime and tips,
       (b) income from selfemployment;
(2)   commissions;
(3)   severance pay;
(4)   royalties;
(5)   bonuses;
(6)   interest and dividends;
(7)   income derived from businesses/partnerships;
(8)   social security excluding any benefit due to a child's own disability 1;
(9)   veterans' benefits;
(10)   military pay, allowances and allotments;
(11)   insurance benefits, including those received for disability and personal injury, but excluding reimbursements for property losses;
(12)   workers' compensation;
(13)   unemployment compensation;
(14)   pensions;
(15)   annuities;
(16)   distributions and income from trusts;
(17)   capital gains in real and personal property transactions to the extent that they represent a regular source of income;

(18) spousal support received from a person not a party to this order;

(19) contractual agreements;

(20) perquisites or in kind compensation to the extent that they represent a regular source of income;

(21) unearned income of children, in the Court's discretion;

(22) income from life insurance or endowment contracts;

(23) income from interest in an estate, either directly or through a trust;

(24) lottery or gambling winnings received either in a lump sum or in the form of an annuity;

(25) prizes or awards;

(26) net rental income;

(27) funds received from earned income credit; and

(28) any other form of income or compensation not specifically itemized above

94   *Richards v. Mason*, 54 Mass.App.Ct. 568, 767 N.E.2d 84 (2002). *O'Meara v. Doherty*, 53 Mass.App.Ct. 599, 602-605, 761 N.E.2d 965 (2002) ($180 weekly support ordered by judge was within guidelines, notwithstanding that under mother's guidelines worksheet calculations $335.15 might have been ordered). In *Croak v. Bergeron*, 67 Mass.App.Ct. 750, 751, 856 N.E.2d 900, 901-902 (2006), child support began at $240 per week, then in April 1999 to $510 a week by agreement of the parties, then in October 1999 to $969.54 per week by order of court.

95   Jean Hopfensperger, "New child support rules spark backlash," Star Tribune, September 6, 2008.

96   *Id.*

97   Under the old guideless most noncustodial parents paid 25 percent of their net income for one child and 30 percent for two children. Hopfensberger does not give us figures that we can use to compare with the old ones.

98   Jean Hopfensperger, "New child support rules spark backlash," Star Tribune, September 6, 2008.

99   *Id.*

100   42 U.S.C.A. § 651. The Public Health and Welfare Chapter 7. Social Security Subchapter IV. Grants to States for Aid and Services to Needy Families with Children and for Child-Welfare Services Part D. Child Support and

Establishment of Paternity § 651. Authorization of appropriations. *Id.* at § 654, State plan for child and spousal support. *Id.* at § 657, Distribution of collected support. *Id.* at § 666, Requirement of statutorily prescribed procedures to improve effectiveness of child support enforcement.

101   "[T]o capture conditional grants of Congress to promote child support collections under the Federal Family Support Act of 1988 (42 United States Code, Sections 654, 666, and 667, implemented by 45 Code of Federal Regulations, Sections 302.33, 302.55, and 302.56), all States of the Union adopted guidelines for the determination of child support for all obligators." John Remington Graham, Underlying Legal Principles for Sound Child Support Awards.

It will, therefore, be necessary to review the key provisions of the Federal Family Support Act of 1988. Two provisions are of key importance. The first is 42 United States Code, Section 667, which reads,

"(a) Each States, as a condition for having its State plan approved under this part, must establish guidelines for child support award amounts within the State. The guidelines may be established by law or by judicial or administrative action, and shall be reviewed at least once every four years to ensure that their application results in the determination of appropriate award amounts.

"(b)(1) The guidelines established pursuant to subsection (a) of this section shall be available to all judges or other officials who have the power to determine child support awards within the State.

"(b)(2) There shall be a rebuttable presumption, in any judicial proceeding for the award of child support, that the amount of the award which would result from the application of such guidelines is the correct amount of child support to be awarded. A written finding or a specific finding on the record that the application of the guidelines would be unjust or inappropriate in a particular case, as determined under the criteria established by the State, shall be sufficient to rebut the presumption in that case."

The other is 45 Code of Federal Regulations, Section 302.56(h), which reads as follows: "A State must consider economic data on the cost of raising children and analyze case data, gathered through sampling or other methods, on the application of, and deviations from the guidelines. The analysis must be used in the State's review of the guidelines to ensure that deviations are limited."

102   Phyllis Schlafly, "Federal Incentives Make Children Fatherless," *http://www.eagleforum.org/column/-2005/may05/05-05-11.html* (May 11, 2005).

103   *Id.*

104   "The stimulus program provided $600 checks for most individuals and $1,200 for couples filing jointly, with a $300 per-child credit added on." "Deadbeat parents' stimulus checks funneled to children," by Associated Press, Boston Globe, September 10, 2008.

105   "Deadbeat parents' stimulus checks funneled to children," by Associated Press, Boston Globe, September 10, 2008.

106   *Id.*

107   *Id.*

108   *Id.*

109   *Id.*

110   *Id.*

111   *Id.*

112   Stephen Baskerville, "Child Support and The Marriage Question," p. 21, at Symposium: Defining Marriage.

113   Jerry did prove, however, that his earnings never exceeded $25,000 per year over the past several years, that he is earning barely above the Federal Poverty Guidelines, and that his child-support obligation pushes him substantially below those guidelines (he has consistently paid $80 a week, which was all he could afford), making it impossible for him either to support himself or to purchase the medications necessary to treat his illness.

114   In *Joseph M.M. v. Mary Ellen C.M.*, 642 N.Y.S.2d 713, 714, 227 A.D.2d 561, 562 (N.Y.A.D. 2nd Dept. 1996) the court held that the father's lack of contact with his child was attributable to the mother's interference with visitation and that mother's interference, which caused the child to abandon the relationship with the father for over 8 years, resulted in the termination of child support.

115   *See Kershaw v. Kershaw*, 701 N.Y.S.2d 739, 741, 268 A.D.2d 829 (N.Y.A.D 3rd Dept. 2000).

116   The law is like an intimate love triangle, but instead of three people, it can be three States plus a uniform law or two, or two States and a foreign country (e.g., New York, Alaska, and Poland (Eastern Europe Poland). Then

add a little federal law as seasoning and a few judges who are motivated by federal incentives and a few lawyers who want to paid their fees. Desperately, desperately, the courts must be reformed. And legislatures and legislators are beyond the scope of this book!

117   42 U.S.C. §658a.

118   Ohio began preparations for the phased in federal changes to the calculation of incentive dollars to states. OCS will be restructuring the distribution of these to Ohio's 88 counties in SFY 03 with new formulas based on individual county performance. OCS will phase in the implementation of the incentive formula so that counties will not be adversely affected. The actual application of the formula will begin in January 2005. The roll out of county monthly monitoring has supported our preparations for the incentive change by providing counties with the tools with which to increase their compliance with federal regulations. Increasing incentive dollars to Ohio's county operations helps to maintain the level of service necessary to increase the number of families who will receive support and to assist children in establishing parentage that may result in financial, medical and social well-being.

Ohio Child Support continues to be a national leader in the collection of child support. Ohio consistently ranks second in the nation in collections distributed.

OCS Annual Report SFY 2002, pages 11-12, *jfs.ohio.gov/ocs/annualreportsfy 2002.pdf.*

In SFY 2002, Ohio collected $1.9 billion ($1,900,000,000.00).

Id. at 12, collection table.

119   Jerry speculates that the Support Magistrates are getting bonuses or promotions according to how much money they collect or how many unsuspecting litigants they are unconstitutionally imprisoning for a civil child support debt.

120   *Tumey v. Ohio,* 273 U.S. 510 (1927); *Ward v. Monroeville,* 409 U.S. 57 (1972); *Gibson v. Berryhill,* 411 U.S. 564, 579 (1973), *et al*), holding that judges cannot sit in judgment of cases where they have a financial interest in the outcomes of such cases; to do so creates an unconstitutional conflict of interest. *In re Murchison,* 349 U.S. 133, 75 S.Ct. 623 (1955). The High Court held that judges who do sit on cases where they have a pecuniary interest in the case

and who maliciously use their contempt powers to extract/extort more and more monies out of unsuspecting litigants that come before them (e.g., in child support award, modification and enforcement hearings).

121   Derron Darcy, Wed, 8 Oct 2008.

122   B.C.N., Wed, 8 Oct 2008

Endnotes—Chapter 5

123   Massachusetts Domestic Relations Special Rule 401, Reporter's Notes—1997.

124   Massachusetts Domestic Relations Special Rule 401(b).

125   Massachusetts Domestic Relations Special Rule 401(f).

126   Id.

127   Uniform Probate Court Practice XXX, Filing of Financial Statements.

128   A previously filed Financial Statement may be used if the party signs a sworn statement that no changes in the party's finances occurred since the last Statement was filed. Uniform Probate Court Practice XXX, Filing of Financial Statements.

129   That federal Complaint is still on my website as Drano #57, *http://www. falseallegations.com/drano57-complaint-against-judges.htm.*

130   In fact, I have never known a judge to charge a liar with perjury.

Endnotes—Chapter 6

131   Chouteau, pronounced "shoe-toe."

132   *Dickinson v. Cogswell,* 66 Mass.App.Ct. 442, 848 N.E.2d 800 (June 5, 2006), quoting from M.G.L. c. 208, § 30.

133   *Dickinson,* 66 Mass.App.Ct. at 447, 848 N.E.2d at 804, quoting from M.G.L. c. 208, § 30.

134   *Id.,* quoting *Yannas v. Frondistou-Yannas,* 395 Mass. 704, 711, 481 N.E.2d 1153 (1985) (*Yannas*).

135   *Dickinson,* 66 Mass.App.Ct. at 447, 848 N.E.2d at 804, quoting *Williams v. Pitney,* 409 Mass. 449, 453, 567 N.E.2d 894 (1991), quoting from *Yannas, supra* at 711, 481 N.E.2d 1153.

136   *Id.*

137   *Dickinson,* 66 Mass.App.Ct. at 447-448, 848 N.E.2d at 804-805, quoting *Williams,* 409 Mass. at 453, 567 N.E.2d 894 (1991), quoting from *Yannas, supra.*

138   *Id.,* 66 Mass.App.Ct. at 449, 848 N.E.2d at 805, quoting from *Yannas,* 395 Mass. at 711-712, 481 N.E.2d 1153, and *Rosenthal v. Maney,* 51 Mass.App. Ct. 257, 267-268, 745 N.E.2d 350 (2001).

139   *Id.,* quoting from *Yannas, supra* at 712, 481 N.E.2d 1153.

140   Judge William Cowin (husband of SJC Justice Judith Cowin), writing for the *Pizzino v. Miller* panel (Grasso, Cowin, & Kafker, JJ.).

141   *Pizzino v. Miller,* 67 Mass.App.Ct. 865, 873, 858 N.E.2d 1112, 1119 (2006).

142   *Id.,* 67 Mass.App.Ct. 865, 873, 858 N.E.2d 1112, 1119-1120 (December 26, 2006).

143   The charges that led to Judge Livingstone's resignation included:

- Making a false statement in an affidavit about his involvement in High Low Properties.

- Threatening a tenant with an illegal utility shutoff.

- Claiming personal expenses and business expenses.

- Running a commercial property at 261 Union St. that houses tenants who practice law in the Probate and Family Court.

- Failing to report that he was receiving law fees from another lawyer, Jane Warren, who took over his clients after he became a judge in 2002.

144   *Wakefield v. Hegarty,* 67 Mass.App.Ct. 772, 857 N.E.2d 32 (2006).

145   *Abbott v. Virusso,* 68 Mass.App.Ct. 326, 862 N.E.2d 52 (2007) (Duffly, Luke, & Kantrowitz, JJ.; Kantrowitz, dissenting), (vacating and remanding), 450 Mass. 1031, 881 N.E.2d 133 (2008).

146   In "*Luke v. Gloria,*" the children were 6½ years old when they were taped by Luke. That tape was not allowed into evidence, nor was the proposed testimony of the expert who had analyzed the tape.

147   *Abbott,* 68 Mass.App.Ct. at 339-340, 862 N.E.2d at 62, citing *Dickenson v. Cogswell,* 66 Mass.App.Ct. 442, 449, 848 N.E.2d 800 (2006); 848 N.E.2d 800 (2006); *Pizzino v. Miller,* 67 Mass.App.Ct. 865, 874, 858 N.E.2d 1112 (2006).

148   *Abbott,* 68 Mass.App.Ct., n. 2.

149   *Abbott,* 68 Mass.App.Ct. at 328-329, 862 N.E.2d at 55-56.

150   395 Mass. 704, 481 N.E.2d 1153 (1985).

151   *Mason v. Coleman,* 447 Mass. 177, 178, 850 N.E.2d 513 (2006).

152   *Id.* at 184.

153   *Baltzer v. Cleri,* 63 Mass.App.Ct. 1105, 2005 WL 549479, 823 N.E.2d 435, (unpublished), (March 08, 2005), No. 03-P-995. See also *Cleri v. Cleri,* 2002 WL 33945981 (Trial Order), Massachusetts Probate & Family Court (July 02, 2002).

154   *Cartledge v.* Evans, 67 Mass.App.Ct. 577, 855 N.E.2d 429 (2006).

155   *Cartledge,* 67 Mass.App.Ct. at 582-583, 855 N.E.2d at 434.

Endnotes—Chapter 7

156   See Special Report, "VAWA Programs Discriminate Against Male Victims," RADAR, Respecting Accuracy in Domestic Abuse Reporting (December 2007); Michael Burlingame, *The Inner World of Abraham Lincoln*; and Philip Cook, *Abused Men: The Hidden Side of Domestic Violence.*

157   Monica Karuturi. "Assessing the Implementation of Mandatory Arrest Policy for Intimate Partner Violence in the State of Rhode Island," page 31 (Dept. of Public Policy and American Institutions, Brown University, April 2001).

158   "A Culture of False Allegations: How VAWA Harms Families and Children" (RADAR, Rockville, MD 2007), http://www.mediaradar.org/docs/RADARreport-VAWA-A-Culture-of-False-Allegations.pdf, citing Miller N. What does research and evaluation say about domestic violence laws? A compendium of justice system laws and related research assessments. Alexandria, VA: Institute for Law and Justice, 2005, footnote 28.

http://www.ilj.org/publications/dv/DomesticViolenceLegislationEvaluation.pdf.

159   *http://www.mediaradar.org/alert20081020.php#sdendnote1anc;*
http://www.mediaradar.org/docs/RADARreport-VAWA-Restraining-Orders.pdf

160   R.A.D.A.R.—Respecting Accuracy in Domestic Abuse Reporting—is a non-profit, non-partisan organization of men and women working to im-

prove the effectiveness of our nation's approach to solving domestic violence. *http://www.mediaradar.org.*

161   "A Culture of False Allegations," citing Zorn E., "A seminar in divorce, Down-and-dirty style," *Chicago Tribune* (November 4, 1988), p. 1.

162   "A Culture of False Allegations," citing Leving J.M. and Sacks G., "Some progress for California fathers, but still a long way to go," *Ifeminists.net* (July 5, 2006), *http://www.ifeminists.net/introduction/editorials/2006/0705sacks.html.*

163   For a more detailed definition of "domestic violence," *see* http://www.ovw.usdoj.gov/domviolence.htm.

164   M.G.L. ch. 265, §13A.

165   M.G.L. ch. 209A.

166   *See* 42 U.S.C.A. § 3796hh, United States Code Annotated Title 42. The Public Health and Welfare Chapter 46. Justice System Improvement XII-I . Grants to Encourage Arrest Policies and Enforcement of Protection Orders § 3796hh.

> Grants (a) Purpose The purpose of this subchapter is to encourage States, Indian tribal governments, State and local courts (including juvenile courts), tribal courts, and units of local government to treat domestic violence, dating violence, sexual assault, and stalking as serious violations of criminal law. (b) Grant authority The Attorney General may make grants to eligible States, Indian tribal governments [FN1] State, tribal, territorial, and local courts (including juvenile courts),, [FN2] or units of...
>
> ...2) To develop policies, educational programs, protection order registries, and training in police departments to improve tracking of cases involving domestic violence, dating violence, sexual assault, and stalking. Policies, educational programs, protection order registries, and training described in this paragraph shall incorporate confidentiality, and privacy protections for victims of domestic violence, dating violence, sexual assault, and stalking. (3) To centralize and coordinate police enforcement, prosecution, or judicial responsibility for domestic violence, dating violence, sexual assault, and stalking cases in teams or units of police officers, prosecutors, parole and probation officers, or...

...parole and probation officers, and both criminal and family courts. (5) To strengthen legal advocacy service programs for victims of domestic violence, dating violence, sexual assault, and stalking, including strengthening assistance to such victims in immigration matters. (6) To educate judges in criminal and civil courts (including juvenile courts) about domestic violence, dating violence, sexual assault, and stalking and to improve judicial handling of such cases. (7) To provide technical assistance and computer and other equipment to police departments, prosecutors, courts, and tribal jurisdictions to facilitate the widespread enforcement of protection orders, including interstate enforcement, enforcement between States and tribal jurisdictions, and enforcement between tribal jurisdictions. (8) To develop or strengthen policies and training for police, prosecutors, and the judiciary in recognizing, investigating, and prosecuting instances of domestic violence and sexual assault against older individuals (as defined in section 3002 of this title) and individuals with disabilities (as defined...

167   *See* 42 U.S.C.A. § 3796gg, United States Code Annotated Title 42. The Public Health and Welfare Chapter 46. Justice System Improvement Subchapter XII-H. Grants to Combat Violent Crimes Against Women § 3796gg. Purpose of program and grants

Purpose of program and grants (a) General program purpose The purpose of this subchapter is to assist States, State and local courts (including juvenile courts), Indian tribal governments, tribal courts, and units of local government to develop and strengthen effective law enforcement and prosecution strategies to combat violent crimes against women, and to develop and strengthen victim services in cases involving violent crimes against women. (b) Purposes for which grants may be used Grants under this subchapter shall provide personnel, training, technical assistance, data collection and other equipment for the more widespread apprehension, prosecution, and adjudication of persons committing violent crimes against women, and specifically, for the purposes of— (1) training law enforcement officers, judges, other court personnel, and prosecutors to more effectively identify and respond to violent crimes against women, including the crimes of sexual assault, domestic violence, and dating violence; (2) developing, training, or expanding units of law enforcement officers,

judges, other court personnel, and prosecutors specifically targeting violent crimes against women, including the crimes of sexual
assault and <u>domestic violence</u>; (3) developing and implementing
more effective police, court, and prosecution policies, protocols,
orders, and services specifically devoted to preventing, identifying,
and responding to violent crimes against women, including the
crimes of sexual assault and <u>domestic violence</u>; (4) developing,
installing, or expanding data collection and communication systems, including computerized systems, linking police, prosecutors,
and courts or for the purpose of identifying and tracking <u>arrests</u>,
<u>protection orders</u>, violations of <u>protection orders</u>, prosecutions,
and convictions for violent crimes against women, including the
crimes of sexual assault and <u>domestic violence</u>; (5) developing,
enlarging, or strengthening victim services programs, including
sexual assault, <u>domestic violence</u> and dating violence programs,
developing or improving delivery of victim services to underserved
populations, providing specialized <u>domestic violence</u> court advocates in courts where a significant number of <u>protection orders</u>
are granted, and increasing reporting and reducing attrition rates
for cases involving violent crimes against women, including crimes
of sexual assault and <u>domestic violence</u>; (6) developing, enlarging, or strengthening programs addressing stalking; (7) developing, enlarging, or strengthening programs addressing the needs
and circumstances of Indian tribes in dealing with violent crimes
against women, including the crimes of sexual assault and <u>domes-
tic violence</u>; (8) supporting formal and informal statewide, multi-
disciplinary efforts, to the extent not supported by State funds, to
coordinate the response of State law <u>enforcement</u> agencies, prosecutors, courts, victim services agencies, and other State agencies
and departments, to violent crimes against women, including the
crimes of sexual assault, <u>domestic violence</u>, and dating violence;
(9) training of sexual assault forensic medical personnel examiners in the collection and preservation of evidence, analysis...

...providing expert testimony and treatment of trauma related to
sexual assault; (10) developing, enlarging, or strengthening programs to assist law <u>enforcement</u>, prosecutors, courts, and others
to address the needs and circumstances of older and disabled
women who are victims of domestic violence or sexual assault,
including recognizing, investigating, and prosecuting instances

of such violence or assault and targeting outreach and support, counseling, and other victim services to such older and disabled individuals; (11) providing assistance to victims of <u>domestic violence</u> and sexual assault in immigration matters; (12) maintaining core victim services and criminal justice initiatives, while supporting complementary new initiatives...

...families; (13) supporting the placement of special victim assistants (to be known as "Jessica Gonzales Victim Assistants") in local law <u>enforcement</u> agencies to serve as liaisons between victims of <u>domestic violence</u>, dating violence, sexual assault, and stalking and personnel in local law <u>enforcement</u> agencies in order to improve the <u>enforcement</u> of <u>protection orders</u>. Jessica Gonzales Victim Assistants shall have expertise in <u>domestic violence</u>, dating violence, sexual assault, or stalking and may undertake the following activities— (A) developing, in collaboration with prosecutors, courts, and victim service providers, standardized response policies for local law <u>enforcement</u> agencies, including triage protocols to ensure that dangerous or potentially lethal cases are identified and prioritized; (B) notifying persons seeking <u>enforcement</u> of <u>protection orders</u> as to what responses will be provided by the relevant law <u>enforcement</u> agency; (C) referring persons seeking <u>enforcement</u> of <u>protection orders</u> to supplementary services (such as emergency shelter programs, hotlines, or legal assistance services); and (D) taking other appropriate action to assist or secure the safety of the person seeking <u>enforcement</u> of a protection order; and (14) to provide funding to law <u>enforcement</u> agencies, nonprofit nongovernmental victim services providers, and State, tribal, territorial, and local governments, (which funding stream shall be known as the Crystal Judson <u>Domestic Violence</u> Protocol Program) to promote— (A) the development and implementation of training for local victim <u>domestic violence</u> service providers, and to fund victim services personnel, to be known as "Crystal Judson Victim Advocates," to provide supportive services and advocacy for victims of domestic <u>violence</u> committed by law <u>enforcement</u> personnel; (B) the implementation of protocols within law <u>enforcement</u> agencies to ensure consistent and effective responses to the commission of <u>domestic violence</u> by personnel within such agencies (such as the model policy promulgated by the International Association of Chiefs of Police ("<u>Domestic</u>

Violence by Police Officers: A Policy of the IACP, Police Response to Violence Against Women Project" July 2003)); (C) the development of such protocols in collaboration with State, tribal, territorial and local victim service providers and domestic violence coalitions. Any law enforcement, State, tribal, territorial, or local government agency receiving funding under the Crystal Judson Domestic Violence Protocol Program under paragraph (14) shall on an annual basis, receive additional training on the topic of incidents of domestic violence committed by law enforcement personnel from domestic violence and sexual assault nonprofit organizations and, after a period of 2 years, provide a report of the adopted protocol to the Department of Justice, including a summary of progress in implementing such protocol. **(c) State coalition grants (1) Purpose The Attorney General shall award grants to each State domestic violence coalition and sexual assault coalition for the purposes of coordinating State victim services activities, and collaborating and coordinating with Federal, State, and local entities engaged in violence against women activities. (2) Grants to State coalitions The Attorney General shall award grants to— (A) each State domestic violence coalition,** as determined by the Secretary of Health and Human Services through the Family Violence Prevention and Services Act (42...

168   *See also* 42 U.S.C.A. § 3796hh-1 United States Code Annotated Title 42. The Public Health and Welfare Chapter 46. Justice System Improvement Subchapter XII-I. Grants to Encourage Arrest Policies and Enforcement of Protection Orders § 3796hh-1. Applications.

See also 42 U.S.C.A. § 3796hh-4 United States Code Annotated Title 42. The Public Health and Welfare Chapter 46. Justice System Improvement Subchapter XII-I. Grants to Encourage Arrest Policies and Enforcement of Protection Orders § 3796hh-4. Definitions and grant conditions In this subchapter the definitions and grant conditions in section 13925 of this title shall apply.

See also 42 U.S.C.A. § 10410 United States Code Annotated Title 42. The Public Health and Welfare Chapter 110. Family Violence Prevention and Services § 10410. Grants for State domestic violence coalitions.

See also 42 U.S.C.A. § 14031 United States Code Annotated Title 42. The Public Health and Welfare Chapter 136. Violent Crime Control and Law Enforcement Subchapter III. Violence Against Women Part F. National Stalker and Domestic Violence Reduction § 14031. Grant program.

169   "A Culture of False Allegations." citing Miller N., Domestic violence: "A review of state legislation defining police and prosecution duties and powers." note 13 (Alexandria, VA: Institute for Law and Justice, 2004). *http://www.ilj.org/publications/DV_Legislation-3.pdf*

170   *See also* Monica Karuturi. "Assessing the Implementation of Mandatory Arrest Policy for Intimate Partner Violence in the State of Rhode Island," page 38 (Dept. of Public Policy and American Institutions, Brown University, April 2001), citing Kane, Robert J. "Police Responses to Restraining Orders in Domestic Violence Incidents: Identifying the Custody-Threshold Thesis," *Criminal Justice and Behavior* (2000: Sage Publications Inc.): Vol. 27, No. 5, 561-581.

171   *Id.*

172   Monica Karuturi. "Assessing the Implementation of Mandatory Arrest Policy for Intimate Partner Violence in the State of Rhode Island," page 39 (Dept. of Public Policy and American Institutions, Brown University, April 2001).

173   *Id.*

174   The arrest grant may be seen at *http://www.ovw.usdoj.gov/arrest_grant_desc.htm.*

175   Monica Karuturi. "Assessing the Implementation of Mandatory Arrest Policy for Intimate Partner Violence in the State of Rhode Island," page 37 (Dept. of Public Policy and American Institutions, Brown University, April 2001), citing Mills, Linda G. "Mandatory Arrest and Prosecution Policies for Domestic Violence," *Criminal Justice and Behavior.* (1998: Sage Publications Inc.): Vol. 25, No 3, 306-319.

176   Monica Karuturi. "Assessing the Implementation of Mandatory Arrest Policy for Intimate Partner Violence in the State of Rhode Island," page 48 (Dept. of Public Policy and American Institutions, Brown University, April 2001), citing Buzawa, Eve S., Austin, Tomas, "Determining Police Response to Domestic Violence Victims-The Role of Victim Preference," *American Behavioral Scientist.* (1993): Vol. 36, No. 5, 610-624.

177   "A Culture of False Allegations: How VAWA Harms Families and Children" (RADAR, Rockville, MD 2007), *http://www.mediaradar.org/docs/RADAR-report-VAWA-A-Culture-of-False-Allegations.pdf,* citing Durose MR et al. Table 5.9.

178   Monica Karuturi. "Assessing the Implementation of Mandatory Arrest Policy for Intimate Partner Violence in the State of Rhode Island," page 49

(Dept. of Public Policy and American Institutions, Brown University, April 2001), cites to sources not provided.

179   "A Culture of False Allegations," citing American Bar Association, "Custody decisions in cases with domestic violence allegations" (2004), *http:// www.abanet.org/legalservices/probono/childcustody/domestic_violence_chart1.pdf.*

180   "A Culture of False Allegations," citing RADAR: Bias in the judiciary: The case of domestic violence. Rockville, MD: Respecting Accuracy in Domestic Abuse Reporting, 2006. *http://www.mediaradar.org/docs/Bias-In-The-Judiciary.pdf.*

181   "A Culture of False Allegations," citing Bleemer R., "N.J. judges told to ignore rights in abuse TROs," *New Jersey Law Journal,* April 24, 1995. *http:// www.ancpr.org/amazing_nj_legal_journal_article.htm.*

182   According to the FBI National Incident-Based Reporting System, 106,962 persons (58,113 spouses and 48,849 boyfriends/girlfriends) were arrested for violent crimes in 2000 (as reported by Durose et al, 2005, Table 5.8). This number is an underestimate for two reasons: 1. It does not include divorced couples, which account for about 18% all intimate partner violence (as reported by Catalano S, 2006). 2. The NIBRS receives data from only one-quarter of law enforcement agencies in the United States, which collectively have jurisdiction over 13% of the crime. Therefore it is calculated that 1,003,392 persons are arrested each year for intimate partner violence: 106,962/0.82 = 130,441 persons from areas covered by reporting agencies; 130,441/0.13 = 1,003,392 total.

"A Culture of False Allegations: How VAWA Harms Families and Children" (RADAR, Rockville, MD 2007), *http://www.mediaradar.org/docs/RADARreport-VAWA-A-Culture-of-False-Allegations.pdf.*

183   "A Culture of False Allegations," citing Durose MR et al. Family Violence Statistics. Washington, DC: Department of Justice. NCJ 207846, 2005. *http://www.ojp.usdoj.gov/bjs/pub/pdf/fvs.pdf.*

184   "A Culture of False Allegations," citing RADAR, "Without restraint: The use and abuse of domestic restraining orders."

185   "A Culture of False Allegations," citing Eng P., "Safety and Justice for All" (New York: Ms. Foundation for Women, 2003), *http://www.ms.foundation. org/user-assets/PDF/Program/safety_justice.pdf.*

186   "A Culture of False Allegations," citing Suk J. Criminal law comes home," Yale Law Journal, Vol. 116, No. 2 (2006), *http://www.yalelawjournal. org/pdf/116-1/Suk.pdf.*

187   "A Culture of False Allegations: How VAWA Harms Families and Children," (RADAR, Rockville, MD 2007), *http://www.mediaradar.org/docs/RADAR-report-VAWA-A-Culture-of-False-Allegations.pdf.*

188   "A Culture of False Allegations," citing U.S. Census Bureau. Statistical Abstract of the United States, 1999. Tables 155, 159. Washington, DC: U.S. Government Printing Office, 2000.

189   "A Culture of False Allegations," citing Johnston J *et al.* "Allegations and substantiations of abuse in custody-disputing families," *Family Court Review,* Vol. 43, No. 2, April 2005.

190   "A Culture of False Allegations: How VAWA Harms Families and Children," page 8 (RADAR, Rockville, MD 2007), *http://www.mediaradar.org/docs/RADARreport-VAWA-A-Culture-of-False-Allegations.pdf*

191   "A Culture of False Allegations," citing Horn W.F. and Sylvester T., Father Facts, pp. 103–105.

192   Bob Parks, "Correct 'The Violence Against Women Act' Now," Friday, September 12, 2008, *http://www.canadafreepress.com/index.php/article/4969* and New Media Alliance - Bob Parks: Blogging for Truth and Liberty, *http://thenma.org/blogs/index.php/parks?skin=slamp_pink.*

193   FY 2006 Office on Violence Against Women Grant Activity by State (with State Totals) at in Appendix A in this book. The source: *http://www.ovw.usdoj.gov/grant_activities2006.htm#ma*

194   "Quill" was charged with the offense of violating in Massachusetts a restraining order issued in Maine. The statutory basis for charging him in Massachusetts is found in the first paragraph of G.L. c. 209A, §5A.**2**/ Section 5A has not yet been interpreted by the State High Court, which made Quill's case of first impression.**3**/

> **fn2** Paragraph 1 of §5A of G.L. c. 209A reads:
>
> > Any protection order issued by another jurisdiction, as defined in section one, shall be given full faith and credit throughout the commonwealth and enforced as if it were issued in the commonwealth for as long as the order is in effect in the issuing jurisdiction
>
> **fn3** Section 5A also does not appear on the Criminal Complaint against Quill—only §7 and §3B do – but §5A was argued by the assistant district attorney at the hearing on Quill's motion to dismiss and relied upon by the court.

Quill contends that the Commonwealth may not give, in accordance with the first paragraph, full faith and credit to the Maine order because that order was never filed in any court in Massachusetts with or without the affidavit required of Cobaka by the second paragraph of G.L. c. 209A, §5A.\4/ Clearly, the first paragraph is not mutually exclusive of the second one. There would be no purpose of including the second paragraph, if the first were not dependent upon it. Thus, the first paragraph is triggered only if the procedure in the second paragraph has been followed. Here, where the second paragraph was not followed, the first paragraph may not and cannot apply.

fn4 The relevant portion of ¶2 of §5A of G.L. c. 209A reads:

> A person entitled to protection under a protection order issued by another jurisdiction may file such order in the superior court department or the Boston municipal court department or any division of the probate and family or district court departments by filing with the court a certified copy of such order. . . . Such person shall swear under oath in an affidavit, to the best of such person's knowledge, that such order is presently in effect as written. Upon request by a law enforcement agency, the register or clerk of such court shall provide a certified copy of the protection order issued by the other jurisdiction.

For more details of this case, *see http://www.falseallegations.com/drano94-restraining-order-in-another-state.htm.* After Boston Municipal Court Justice Sally A. Kelly denied Quill's motion to dismiss, I sought to invoke the general superintendence of the High Court to to correct errors of law and abuses of discretion and reverse the interlocutory order. The High Court then dismissed Quill's petition on the grounds that he had to use the ordinary route of appeal. That would have meant more time of anxiety and more fees. Fortunately when we reached the day of trial, there was another judge presiding. He dismissed the case prior to selecting a jury.

195   According to law, it is the executive branch—of which the district attorney is a part—which must move for dismissal and not the judicial branch. Thus the trial judge acted *sua sponte*, on his own.

196   *See the* entire decision on my website at *http://www.falseallegations.com/crespo-v-crespo-nj-schultz-decision-61908.htm.*

197   *Kvarta v. Rego,* 2008 WL 5396651 (N.J.Super.A.D., 2008) (unpublished).

198   *http://www.mediaradar.org/docs/RADARwhitepaper-False-Allegations.pdf.*

Endnotes—Chapter 8

199   "Visitational Interference - A National Study."

200   Massachusetts Rules of Criminal Procedure 43 ["Mass.R.Crim.P."].

201   *Id.*

202   *Com. v. Diamond,* 46 Mass.App.Ct. 103, 103, 703 N.E.2d 1195, 1196 (1999).

203   *Id.,* 46 Mass.App.Ct. at 108, 703 N.E.2d at 1199 (Flannery, J., concurring).

204   *R.W. v. M.G.,* 64 Mass.App.Ct. 1105, 832 N.E.2d 705, (Table, Text in WESTLAW), 2005 WL 1924211 (August 11, 2005) (NO. 04-P-1205)(unpublished), citing *Furtado v. Furtado,* 380 Mass. 137, 141, 402 N.E.2d 1024, 1030 (1980).

205   *Parker v. United States,* 153 F.2d 66, 70 (1st Cir.1946) [citations omitted].

206   *Cf. Id.*

207   *Cf. The Superadio Ltd. Partnership v. Winstar Radio Productions, LLC,* 446 Mass. 330, 342, 844 N.E.2d 246, 255 (2006), citing *Godard v. Babson-Dow Mfg. Co.,* 319 Mass. 345, 347, 65 N.E.2d 555, 557 (1946).

208   *Vakalis v. Shawmut Corp.,* 925 F.2d 34, 37 (1st Cir. (Mass.) 1991).

209   This was my second incarceration for civil contempt, the excuse for isolating me in a "hospital" room. The authorities—not the warden but the court—did not want me giving legal advice to the criminal population.

Bed was a 2-foot wide metal slab built into the wall with a foam mattress a few inches thick, covered in plastic, and already flat in the middle. The sheets kept on slipping and the blanket was quite short. I was let out for 1 hour a day on those days I spoke to my counsel, and perhaps once or twice for 2 hours a day. The bed was significant because there was nowhere to sit or write, there being neither chair nor table.

The food was unrecognizable as food. It certainly was not in accordance with any accepted dietary laws or recommendations by nutrition professionals.

One kind officer did let me use a nonpay phone to call two friends, one an attorney.\a/,\b/ Each did a yeoman's work getting me information between 2:30 A.M. and 7:30 P.M. on Friday from the gentleman to whom I had given my bag and papers when handcuffed, from my home, and from the bank.

> **FNa** There were some decent officers, of both genders. My un-informed observations were that about one-third of the Correc-tion Officers had IQs hovering well under 100, a handful were borderline sadistic, and the remaining were of, at least, average intelligence.

> **FNb** After a few days, I was given a pin number to use for a phone, but the number did not work. "Unreasonable restrictions on prisoner's telephone access may violate First, Sixth, and Four-teenth Amendments." *Miller v. Comm'r of Correction*, 36 Mass.App. Ct. 114, 118 (1994) ("[c]ivilly committed patients … may be en-titled to greater privileges than prisoners"), citing *Tucker v. Ran-dall*, 948 F.2d 388, 390-391 (7th Cir. 1991). On the fourth day of her confinement, the pin number worked.

The attorney arrived in the morning, stayed with me inside the House of Correction, and helped me fill out some forms and envelopes. Two security people did not, however, let counsel stay with me to finish the tasks in Spina's order, or to leave with me the information I needed to comply with it.

Later Friday evening, a lawyer working at the House of Correction to help inmates appeared like an angel. Some other **_unknown_** angel had sent him to me Friday afternoon. He went over the notices with me and said he would copy them, and because I arrived without money, he would consider me indigent and charged the cost of the certified forms and green return receipts on the envelopes to the Suffolk County Sheriff.

He then prepared a Power of Attorney and after leaving the H/C Friday night, he generously and graciously delivered the document to my friend's home so that she could close the IOLTA account on Saturday. I wish I could recall his name and thank him.

My attorney friend arrived at the H/C on Sunday to deliver to me the bank document that confirmed that the IOLTA account had been closed, but thwarted on arrival, she had to try again on Monday to get it delivered to the H/C Records department.

I believe I was drugged—perhaps inadvertently—on Saturday after-noon. Then Attorney Dmitry Lev arrived. I believe it was Saturday evening. He stayed what seemed to be several hours. He had read the order with a fine-tooth comb. He took all the papers, in order to type and deliver the requested lists to the prosecutor, Susan Strauss-Weisberg, and the court on Monday. He apparently stayed with Weisberg while she reviewed them. Weisberg then wrote an assented-to motion for my release. Lev might also have written one. He delivered them that afternoon to the S.J.C for Suffolk County. At 4 P.M. on Monday the 23rd, I was released.

Thus, but for five human angels plus a handful of correction officers, I would not have been able to satisfy the order, and would still be incarcerated.

Clearly, nothing Judge Spina wanted me to do could be done from prison. I was being punished. I did not hold the key to any door. But for having friends, I would still be imprisoned. The contempt was criminal in nature with the possibility of indefinite incarceration. I had been entitled to a jury,\c/ for which I asked but was denied. The hearing afforded me was unconstitutional.

> **FNc** "When a judge acts intentionally and knowingly to deprive a person of his constitutional rights he exercises no discretion or individual judgment; he acts no longer as a judge, but as a 'minister' of his own prejudices". *Pierson v. Ray*, 386 U.S. 547, 567 n. 6 (1967) (Mr. Justice Douglas, dissenting).
>
> > [N]o tribunal is sacred in the eye of existing usurpation, and every character, however excellent, must go down under the baleful progress of despotic power. **Under the provisions of this section (section 1), every judge in the State court** and every other officer thereof, great or small **will enter upon and pursue the call of official duty with the sword of Damocles suspended over him** by a silken thread, and bent upon him the scowl of unbridled power, the forerunner of the impending wrath, which is gathering itself to burst upon its victims.
>
> Globe 42nd Congress, 1st Session. March 31, 1866, 365-366, from which the boldfaced and underlined words were excerpted and quoted in *Pierson* at 562 (dissent).

210 *Id.*

211 *Cf. The Superadio Ltd. Partnership v. Winstar Radio Productions, LLC,* 446 Mass. 330, 342, 844 N.E.2d 246, 255 (2006), citing *Godard v. Babson-Dow Mfg. Co.,* 319 Mass. 345, 347, 65 N.E.2d 555, 557 (1946).

212   *Edgar v. Edgar,* 403 Mass. 616, 618 n. 3, 531 N.E.2d 590, 592, n. 3 (1988).

213   *Id.,* 403 Mass. at 618, 531 N.E.2d at 592.

214   *Aroesty v. Cohen,* 62 Mass.App.Ct. 215, 219 n. 7, 815 N.E.2d 639, 643 n. 7 (2004), quoting *Edgar v. Edgar,* 403 Mass. 616, 618, 531 N.E.2d 590 (1988).

215   "Practice before the single justice is governed by the Massachusetts Rules of Civil Procedure, SJC Rule 2:01 et seq. and pertinent Standing Orders.

216   "Practice and Procedure Single Justice," published at *http://www.sjc-countyclerk.com/singjusprpr.html* (emphasis supplied).

217   *Furtado,* 380 Mass. at 143 n. 5, 402 N.E.2d at 1031 n.5.

218   Mass.R. Crim.P. 44(a), 378 Mass. 920 (1979).

219   *Edgar,* 403 Mass. at 618-619, 531 N.E.2d at 592.

220   Rule of Criminal Procedure 44(a):

> **(a) Nature of the Proceedings.** All criminal contempts not adjudicated pursuant to Rule 43 shall be prosecuted by means of complaint, unless the prosecutor elects to proceed by indictment. Except as otherwise provided by these rules, the case shall proceed as a criminal case in the court in which the contempt is alleged to have been committed.

Rule 43 sets out summary contempt proceedings, which are applicable to District Court and Superior Court.

221   *Edgar,* 403 Mass. at 618-619, 531 N.E.2d at 592.

222   *Id.*

223   "[An] equal protection analysis requires strict scrutiny of a legislative classification only when the classification impermissibly interferes with the exercise of a fundamental right FN3 or operates to the peculiar disadvantage of a suspect class.FN4" *Murgia,* 427 U.S. 307, 312, 96 S.Ct. 2562, 2566 (1976); *Izquierdo Prieto v. Mercado Rosa,* 894 F.2d 467, 471 (1st Cir. (Puerto Rico), 1990) (same); *Disabled American Veterans v. U.S. Dept. of Veterans Affairs,* 962 F.2d 136 (2d Cir. (N.Y.), 1992) (same).

224   *Goodridge v. Department of Public Health,* 440 Mass. 309 (2003).

225   Sections 41, 46, 46A, 46B of Massachusetts General Laws chapter 221.

226   Massachusetts General Laws, Part III (Courts, Judicial Officers and Proceedings in Civil Cases) of Title I (Courts and Judicial Officers), Chapter 221 (Clerks, Attorneys and Other Officers of Judicial Courts and Attorneys at Law, Section 41 (Unauthorized practice of law; solicitation of business; penalty).

227   When this case was active, I had not yet seen the Settlement Agreement referred to in the Complaint as "the order." I did not know whether that Settlement Agreement had merged into the judgment or had survived the divorce judgment and become an independent enforceable contract and retained independent legal significance. *DeCristofaro v. DeCristofaro*, 24 Mass. App.Ct. 231, 508 N.E.2d 104 (1987). *Bracci v. Chiccarelli*, 53 Mass.App.Ct. 318, 759 N.E.2d 330 (2001). The Complaint for Contempt did not have the Settlement Agreement or the relevant provisions of the Agreement attached to it and the divorce file was unavailable.

228   *Lafayette Place Associates v. Boston Redevelopment Authority et al*, 427 Mass. 509, 519-520, 694 N.E.2d 820, 827 (1998), citing *Leigh v. Rule*, 331 Mass. 664, 668, 121 N.E.2d 854; (1954) and other cases gathered there.

229   *Massachusetts Mun. Wholesale Elec. Co. v. Town of Danvers*, 411 Mass. 39, 45, 577 N.E.2d 283 (1991) ("A condition precedent defines an event which must occur before a contract becomes effective or before an obligation to perform arises under the contract"). "If the condition is not fulfilled, the contract, or the obligations attached to the condition, may not be enforced. *Id.*, citing 5 S. Williston, *Contracts*, sec. 663 (3d ed. 1961 & Supp. 1990); Restatement (Second) of *Contracts*, sec. 225 (12981). *Cf. Ng Brothers Const., Inc. v. Cranney*, 436 Mass. 638, 766 N.E.2d 864 (2002); *Nile v. Nile*, 432 Mass. 390, 401, 734 N.E.2d 1153 (2000) ("settlement agreement had as a condition precedent the approval of a Massachusetts probate judge").

230   *Fidelity Management & Research Co. v. Ostrander*, 40 Mass.App.Ct. 195, 201, 662 N.E.2d 699 (1996):

> "'[S]he who comes into equity must come with clean hands'....
> [T]hus 'the doors of equity' are closed 'to one tainted with inequitableness or bad faith relative to the matter in which [s]he seeks relief, however improper may have been the behavior of the' other party." *United States v. Perez-Torres*, 15 F.3d 403, 407 (5th Cir.1994), quoting from *Precision Instrument Mfg. Co. v. Automotive Maintenance Mach. Co.*, 324 U.S. 806, 814 (1945). "[W]hile

'equity does not demand that its suitors shall have led blameless lives' ... as to other matters, it does require that they shall have acted fairly and without fraud or deceit as to the controversy in issue." *Id.*, 324 U.S. at 814-815.

231 "In order to deny relief to a party because of inequitable conduct, the conduct at issue must directly affect the claim being brought." *Amerada Hess Corp. v. Garabedian*, 416 Mass. 149, 156, 617 N.E.2d 630 (1993) (internal cite omitted).

232 *Id.*

233 *Lima v. Lima*, 30 Mass.App.Ct. 479, 486, 570 N.E.2d 158 (1991).

234 *Edinburg v. Edinburg*, 22 Mass.App.Ct. 199, 208, 492 N.E.2d 1164 (1986) ("our conclusion is fortified by the principle that a court or equity will not look kindly on one who seeks to benefit be his own turpitude");

235 Massachusetts Child Support Guidelines, II(D)(1),

236 The total population in Massachusetts' prisons is expected to be 12,000 this year, 2009. Jonathan Saltzman, "MA: Prisoners to be double bunked due to sentencing/war on drugs." Boston Globe, November 16, 2008. "On Nov. 3, the state's 18 prisons held 11,380 inmates, putting them at 44 percent above capacity, Clarke said. The number is projected to grow by 5 to 7 percent next year, which would put the population at between 11,949 and 12,176."

"Prisoners are a major fiscal burden on the rest of society. It costs Massachusetts $43,000 a year to keep an inmate behind bars. " Daniel G. Meyer, "MA: Stopping the School to Prison Pipeline." Boston Globe, May 28, 2008.

According to State Rep. Elizabeth Poirier (R), "two years of incarceration for one prisoner alone costs between $75,000 and $100,000." Stephanie Ganias, "Local legislators weigh in on prison fee idea," Milford Daily News correspondent, Feb 08, 2009.

237 The sheer stupidity—there truly is no more appropriate adjective for the phenomenon—of keeping these men incarcerated cannot rationally be explained. In prison, they cannot earn money to give to the families. When they get out and still cannot pay, their driving licenses are revoked, thereby preventing most of them from (1) finding a job and (2) getting to it should they find an employer willing to take the chance on hiring someone who might be thrown back into jail for arrears. The courts continue to apply indiscriminately and inappropriately the child-support guidelines because the

400 BEHIND THE BLACK ROBES

states and the courts get annual bonuses from the federal government for applying the guidelines. Oversight, if any, is virtually worthless.

Bill Robinette, years ago, was divorced. As a result of an event, he found himself on probation. One day, he had a friend deliver a payment to the Probation Department. Apparently his payment was $28 short. One late Friday afternoon, he received notice that he owed $28. There was no time to get to the court. Okay, he'd bring the $28 to the court on Monday. Saturday morning, the police came and arrested him and then jailed him until Monday, when they took him to court, where he waited all day to be transferred to another court to "straighten" everything out. Two days in jail for $28 at a cost to the Commonwealth of $1500.

238   *Maryanne Panaro v. Dennis P. Grady*, 2002 WL 32116845, 31 M.L.W. 391, slip op. at 56 (Lawyers Weekly, No. 15-009-02 (88 pages) (Bristol Probate & Family Court) (Docket No. 01D-0186-DV1). It was appealed under a different name: *Mary Anne Panaro Grady v. Dennis Patrick Grady*, 2004 WL 1396264, 61 Mass.App.Ct. 1112, 810 N.E.2d 862 (2004) (Table), No. 03-P-1142 (unpublished).

239   *http://www.falseallegations.com/drano152-contempts--by-both-pocahontas-and-smith-92405.htm.*

Endnotes—Chapter 9

240   Put *"David Parker" lexington homosexual school* into Google and read about an ongoing struggle about early education in Lexington, Mass.

241   *Nolle prosequi.*

242   The Harvard College student handbook, including the guidelines, constituted a contract between the parties. *Berkowitz v. President and Follows of Harvard College*, No. 00-0956, 2001 WL 13239 (Mass.Super. 2001) (Brassard), J.) (January 4, 2001). The Brandeis University handbook constitutes a contract between the university and a student. *Schaer v. Brandeis University*, 432 Mass. 474, 476 (2000).

243   *See* "Avoiding Kids: How Men Cope with Being Cast as Predators," by Jeffrey Zaslow, Wall Street Journal, September 6, 2007. *jeffrey.zaslow@wsj.com.*

Endnotes—Chapter 10

244   Email: 10/30/2008 1:50 PM.

Endnotes—Chapter 11

245   Receiver appointed pursuant to divorce proceeding to sell couple's property and divide proceeds enjoyed immunity against former husband's § 1983 civil rights claim attacking receiver's authority to act as receiver. *Huszar v. Zeleny,* 269 F.Supp.2d 98 (E.D.N.Y.2003).

246   On 23 March 1994, GJ's previously filed Motion to Withdraw was allowed.

247   GJ was correct, in that the judgment was not entered into the docket by Spring 1994. I filed a motion to Correct the Docket, which was denied. Gordon was served my motion but gave no support for his alleged client.

248   M.G.L. c. 93, s. 102C.

249   In accordance with Dist./Mun.Cts.R.Civ.P. Rule 64.

250   The Board of Bar Overseers identifies him as a lawyer sworn into the Bar in 1963 and practicing law in Dedham, Norfolk County, MA. Martindale Hubbell has him as a District Court judge at Orleans District Court, Barnstable County, MA, but Martindale Hubbell, according to a letter from the company to me, Martindale Hubbell does not verify the information it receives. See *http://www.falseallegations.com/hubbell.htm.* Further discovery shows St. Cyr to have been a legal assistant to Attorney General Brooke between 1964 and 1966, was a Representative to the General Court between 1968 and 1972, and Town Counsel to Towns of Millis and Medfield between 1963 and 1976; was a Special Justice of Wrentham District Court between 1972 and 1983; and the Presiding Justice of Wrentham District Court between 1983 and 1996.

251   *People v. Zajic,* 88 Ill.App.3d 477, 410 N.E.2d 626 (1980).

252   *Bulloch v. United States,* 763 F.2d 1115, 1121 (10th Cir. 1985).

253   *Kenner v. C.I.R.,* 387 F.3d 689 (7th Cir, 1968); 7 Moore's Federal Practice, 2d ed., p. 512, ¶ 60.23.

254   *Id.*

255   *The People of the State of Illinois v. Fred E. Sterling,* 357 Ill. 354; 192 N.E. 229 (1934).

256   *Allen F. Moore v. Stanley F. Sievers,* 336 Ill. 316; 168 N.E. 259 (1929).

257   *In re Village of Willowbrook,* 37 Ill.App.2d 393 (1962); *Dunham v. Dunham,* 57 Ill.App. 475 (1894), affirmed 162 Ill. 589 (1896); *Skelly*

Oil Co. v. Universal Oil Products Co., 338 Ill.App. 79, 86 N.E.2d 875, 883-884 (1949); *Thomas Stasel v. The American Home Security Corporation*, 362 Ill. 350; 199 N.E. 798 (1935).

258   *Hazel-Atlas Glass Co. V. Hartford-Empire Co.*, 322 U.S. 238, 262 n.18, 64 S.Ct. 997, 1009 n.18 (1944).

259   *Id.*

260   *Id.*

261   *Id.*

262   *Hazel-Atlas Glass*, 322 U.S. at 260, 64 S.Ct. at 1008-1009.

Endnotes—Chapter 12

263   This section and the following subsections were written by RADAR, Respecting Accuracy in Domestic Abuse Reporting, P.O. Box 1404, Rockville, MD 20849, <info@mediaradar.org>, *http://www.mediaradar.org.*

264   Center for Immigration Studies: *http://cis.org/marriagefraud.*

265   RADAR Services. VAWA-funded immigration fraud costs American taxpayers $170 million a year. 2008. *www.mediaradar.org/docs/RADARreport-VAWA-Funded-Immigration-Fraud.pdf.*

266   *http://www.caso-carrascosa.com/pdfs/americaninjustice.pdf.*

267   *http://www.roydenhollander.com.*

268   Paragraph 225 of Hollander's Complaint at *http://www.roydenhollander.com/documents/AmnddComplaintFirst.pdf.*

269   Paragraph s 11 through 17 of Hollander's Complaint at *http://www.roydenhollander.com/documents/AmnddComplaintFirst.pdf.*

270   *http://www.roydenhollander.com/documents/SunopsisVAWA Complaint.doc.*

Endnotes—Chapter 13

271   I had only one case in which the plaintiff herself was the cause of the failure of the case. She had withheld from me important information, namely, that she filled out and lied on certain loan applications. The applications surfaced when the defense attorney cross-examined her. The applications had not been produced during the discovery phase of the case. I objected. Their

defense was that it was rebuttal evidence and did not have to be produced. The judge agreed with them. When the jury added the plaintiff's demeanor to the lie, they found against her. She might not have won her case, but I, who had taken the case on contingency, was, therefore, never compensated for the prodigious work I had put into the case. That work included having an aggressive colleague cross-examine her extensively to prepare her for testifying . . . particularly her demeanor while testifying. At trial, the plaintiff ignored everything we thought she had been taught, and decided to play the role of Greta Garbo, speaking slowly, silently, and sparsely. After she was on the witness stand for only a short while, I knew she had lost the case . . . even before the applications had surfaced.

272   The names used for the women and their husbands in this chapter are pseudonyms.

273   After so many years later, I forget the exact nature of his intended report to the IRS.

274   The judges' names throughout this book are real. Judges have judge-made immunity from suit. In Massachusetts, they are almost never sanctioned for wrongdoing. Complaints against judges are kept secret. The First Amendment is the only avenue to let the public know which judges bear watching.

275   Kozlowski used $2 million of company funds to host a charter jet to the island of Sardinia for his wife's birthday party. Amongst other things at the party, there was an ice sculpture modeled after Michaelangelo's King David. Just as the original Michaelangelo statue depicted a nude, well-endowed King David, so, too, did the ice sculpture, with the added distinction that the fabricator of the ice statue fitted King David's penis with a catheter from which vodka flowed, so that King David was peeing pure vodka!

276   Roxbury, near Boston's Franklin Park, was once famous for its zoo and home of the chicken-wire fenced-in victory gardens tended to by Italian POWs during WWII, who relished the Italian delicacies brought and passed through the fence to them by the local Italian residents. No one feared them. I recall playing alongside the fence in late Spring and Summer and listening to the jabber of Italian, which I did not understand but I loved to hear. It was, I thought, a musical language. My grandmother's best friend, Gracie Piscopo, used to bring me a bright yellow chick every Easter. My grandmother used to put it in a topless box beneath the window in the pantry. I have no memory

of what happened to those chicks every year after the Easter season passed. It hurts, now, to guess.

277   Sulesky, a fine man, wrote, **FILED IN COURT** and the date atop each of defense counsel's motions filed without advance notice throughout the Spring. Sulesky cared that O'Connor was seeking and getting an advantage by violating the rules. McGill didn't.

278   The excruciating details of this entire case are explained on my website at *http://www.falseallegations.com/drano90-part-iii-answer-bbo-count-three-lily.htm.*

279   The jury found Woodward guilty. Much to the consternation of some of the public, Judge Hiller Zobel changed the verdict to involuntary manslaughter and sentenced her to time served. Woodward returned to England and after a few years became a lawyer.

280   In all States except two, of which Massachusetts is one, judges are elected. In Massachusetts they are appointed and remain in office until the age of 70. They were originally appointed for life, but the constitutional provision was amended when a concern arose that dementia or Alzheimer's might impede their ability to perform judicial functions. If retired and believed not to be suffering from dementia or Alzheimer's, they are often "recalled" to sit when extra judges are needed.

Endnotes—Chapter 14

281   *Menici v. Orton Crane & Shovel Co.,* 285 Mass. 499, 189 N.E. 83 (1934).; *Rubin v. Town of Arlington,* 327 Mass. 382, 99 N.E.2d 30 (1951); *Cochrane v. Com.,* 175 Mass. 299, 56 N.E. 610 (1900).

282   *Northrup v. Brigham,* 63 Mass.App.Ct. 362, 826 N.E.2d 239, Mass.App. Ct., April 29, 2005 (NO. 04-P-87) (held that intestate's oral promise to make will leaving majority of assets to companion was unenforceable under Statute of Frauds.

283   *Green v. Richmond,* 369 Mass. 47, 49, 337 N.E.2d 691 (1975), and *Hastoupis v. Gargas,* 9 Mass.App.Ct. 27, 32, 398 N.E.2d 745 (1980).

284   *http://www.newsaic.com/ftvlojuryindex.html.*

Endnotes—Chapter 15

285   *http://news.bbc.co.uk/2/hi/29501.stm.*

286   According to Wikipedia, "a derivation from the Hebrew *Mephistoph*, meaning 'destroyer of the good.' Another possibility is a combination of the Hebrew words *mephiz* ('liar') and *tophel* ('destroyer')."

287   Massachusetts General Law c. 269, s. 13A.

288   *M.A.F. v. G.L.K.*, 573 So. 2d 862 (Fla. Dist. Ct. App. 1991). "Nevada is in the minority, finding this type of fraud to be extrinsic because it prevents the husband from knowing he has a claim or defense." *Parker v. Parker, infra* at **n. 3**, citing *Love v. Love*, 114 Nev. 572, 959 P.2d 523 (1998). "In *M.A.F.*, the First District found that because paternity is presumed when a child is born to a marriage due to the presumption of legitimacy, a father is under no obligation to contest or try the issue of paternity during the dissolution of marriage proceedings; and because the father in that case had no reason to contest paternity otherwise, the wife's misrepresentation concerning paternity constituted extrinsic fraud which may be attacked any time." *Parker v. Parker, infra* at n. 3.

289   *Parker v. Parker*, 950 So.2d 388, 32 Fla. L. Weekly S67, Fla., February 01, 2007 (NO. SC05-2346).

290   *Hazel-Atlas Glass Co. v. Hartford-Empire Co.*, 322 U.S. 238, 262 n. 18, 64 S.Ct. 997, 1009 n. 18 (1944).

291   *Id.*

292   *Id.* at 241-242.

293   *Batrouny v. Batrouny*, 13 Va. App. 441, 412 S.E.2d 721 (1991).

294   *In re Marriage of M.E.*, 622 N.E.2d 578 (Ind.App. 4 Dist., 1993).

295   *Id.*

296   *Id.*

297   *Id.*

Endnotes—Chapter 16

298   In my opinion, the formal commencement of a criminal proceeding is quintessentially this type of state action. The initiation of a criminal prosecution, regardless of whether it prompts an arrest, immediately produces "a wrenching disruption of everyday life." *Young v. United States ex rel. Vuitton et Fils*, 481 U.S. 787, 814 (1987). Every prosecution, like every arrest, "is a public act that may seriously interfere with the

defendant's liberty, whether he is free on bail or not, and that may disrupt his employment, drain his financial resources, curtail his associations, subject him to public obloquy, and create anxiety in him, his family and his friends." *United States v. Marion*, 404 U.S.307, 320 (1971). In short, an official accusation of serious crime has a direct impact on a range of identified liberty interests. That impact, moreover, is of sufficient magnitude to qualify as a deprivation of liberty meriting constitutional protection.*fn9

Albright v. Oliver, 510 U.S. 266, 295-296, 114 S.Ct. 807, 824-825,(1994) (Stevens, J., with whom Blackmun, J. joined, dissenting). The dissenting justices continued:

> I can think of few powers that the State possesses which, if arbitrarily imposed, can harm liberty as substantially as the filing of criminal charges.

Albright, 510 U.S. at 312, 114 S.Ct. at 833 (dissent).

> . . . the Due Process Clause of the Fourteenth Amendment constrains the power of state governments to accuse a citizen of an infamous crime.

Albright, 510 U.S. at 316, 114 S.Ct. at 835 (dissent).

299   There is no "respondeat superior" in a section 1983 action, therefore do not expect the police department to indemnify the police officer(s). "*Respondeat superior*" means the superior entity (the officer's boss) is not responsible for what the officer does in his individual capacity. For more details of that which you can sue the police department, go to *http://www.falseallegations.com/drano38-1983-fai-malicious-prosecution.htm.*

300   You may, though, sue the police department for (a) the failure to train, instruct, supervise, control, and discipline on a continuing basis, (b) the failure to prevent or aid in preventing the commission of said wrongs, when it could have done so by reasonable diligence, (c) knowingly, recklessly, or with gross negligence failing or refusing to do so, and (d) approved or ratified the unlawful, deliberate, malicious, reckless, and wanton conduct of Defendant police officers.

301   Defendants base their motion on the traditional *Younger\1/* abstention doctrine arguments. That reliance is misplaced. "[T]he equitable abstention doctrine does not deprive the federal court of jurisdiction; rather, it is a judicially imposed self-restraint based on principles of equity, comity, and federalism." *Brindley v. McCullen*, 61 F.3d 507, 507 (6th Cir. 1995) (remanded to stay

proceedings),\2/ citing *Younger v. Harris*, 401 U.S. at 43-44. "Comity is not a rule of law, but one of practice, convenience, and expediency." *Mast, Foos & Co. v. Stover Manufacturing Co.*, 177 U.S. 458, 488 (1900). "Comity persuades; but does not command." *Id.*

> FN1 *Younger v. Harris*, 401 U.S. 37 (1971).

> FN2 "Issuing a stay avoids the costs of refiling, allows the plaintiffs to retain their place on the court docket, and avoids placing plaintiffs in a sometimes difficult position of refiling their case before the statute of limitations expires." *Brindley*, 61 F.3d at 507.

302   *Ankenbrandt v. Richards*, 504 U.S. 689, 707 (U.S.La. 1992) (complaint sought monetary damages for alleged sexual and physical abuse of the children committed by the divorced father of the children and his female companion).

> Whether or not the domestic relations "exception" is properly grounded in principles of abstention or principles of jurisdiction, I do not believe this case falls within the exception. This case only peripherally involves the subject of "domestic relations." "Domestic relations" actions are loosely classifiable into four categories. The first, or "core," category involves declarations of status, e.g., marriage, annulment, divorce, custody, and paternity. The second, or "semicore," category involves declarations of rights or obligations arising from status (or former status), e.g., alimony, child support, and division of property. The third category consists of secondary suits to enforce declarations of status, rights, or obligations. The final, catchall category covers the suits not directly involving status or obligations arising from status but that nonetheless generally relate to domestic relations matters, e.g., tort suits between family or former family members for sexual abuse, battering, or intentional infliction of emotional distress. None of this Court's prior cases that consider the domestic relations "exception" involves the type of periphery domestic relations claim at issue here.

Ankenbrandt, at 713 (Blackmun, J., concurring in the judgment).

303   **Merita Hopkins was Piemonte's boss. At some point during the case in front of Collings, Piemonte went to work at Carpenter & Roach. When**

Carpenter died, Roach became a judge, Carpenter & Roach closed down, and Piemonte went to work for the Assistant U.S. Attorney in Boston, where the whole disgraceful affair described below began.

M. Ellen Carpenter died from a brain aneurysm at the age of 53 in December of 2005. She was in line for a judicial appointment. As a result of Carpenter's premature death, her partner, **Christine M. Roach**, was appointed to the Superior Court bench in Carpenter's stead. Both were unsuitable candidates. One of the members of the Governor's Council, **Mary Ellen Manning**, wrote a tell-all report re Christine Roach:

ON THE APPOINTMENT OF CHRISTINE M. ROACH TO THE SUPERIOR COURT

The process by which a nominee is selected my be transparent and open, the candidate candid and accessible only then can the public get what they seek: judges who are not only competent and objective, but also accountable to the public. We have had great tragedies of late that have highlighted the lack of accountability of our judges and the non-responsiveness of our elected officials to address the public's real concerns. There is no big ger day in a person's life than the day he or she steps into a courtroom seeking justice. People's lives and livelihoods are at stake every day in every court.

And we address the qualifications of Christine M. Roach for a judgeship to the Superior Court. Attorney Roach has no criminal experience, and her civil trial experience is limited, first-seating thee or four trials in the last 18 years. Under her watch, the City of Boston suffered significant losses, resulting in millions of taxpayer money lost. But courtroom experience alone is not determinative.

Attorney Roach served on the Judicial Nominating Commission, a sub rosa form of government, under Governor Romney for three years and resigned amid a furor over the JNC's failure to approve Judge Merita Hopkins. Once several members of the JNC were asked to resign by the administration, Judge Merita Hopkins was approved within a few weeks. When asked whether she recused herself from reviewing Judge Hopkins' application in her capacity as a member of the JNC, Attorney Roach refused to answer, citing "confidentiality." This is false, and it shows at the very least a misunderstanding of ethics, hard to believe given that Attorney Roach served for five years on the Ethics Commission. Sometimes not getting an answer is indeed an answer.

Here is what is not "confidential;" that Attorney Roach earned a nice living for several years as outside counsel for the City of Boston defending its discriminatory policies and procedures. She was hired by the Corporation Counsel Merita Hopkins. Hopkins was not only a municipal client, she was also a personal client of Attorney Roach— an anchor client. Hopkins' referrals did not stop there, however, Attorney Roach also billed the United States to represent a supervisor of FBI agents who were found to have conspired with notorious criminals to murder informants and then protected the murderers. Of course, the fact that Merita Hopkins's husband was also an FBI agent in the same FBI office might explain how she landed that case.

It is absolutely ridiculous that this Council is rebuffed when trying to assess whether Attorney Roach is the sort of person who will recuse herself from a case where, as in the Hopkins matter, she has a financial and personal relationship with the person before her. To be this ethically ambidextrous, using confidentiality as an artifice to deny the public its right to assess her ethics, is most troubling.

Unlike courtroom experience, a candidate's ethics are determinative. We cannot tolerate another Judge who will invent rules to hide from the public. Accountability common sense and decency must reign over resume-building, bill-churning and insiderism.

1/16/08

Merita Hopkins, now a judge in the Massachusetts Superior Court, was the chief of the City of Boston Law Department. **Eve Piemonte Stacey**, one of Hopkins' staff attorneys, was the opposing counsel representing the police officers in one of Lucas Stockdale's malicious prosecution actions. (His wife, like the Energizer bunny, had caused two criminal actions against, but both were dismissed prior to trial; hence the two malicious prosecution actions.)

Eve, in my opinion, acting on Hopkins' instructions, unlawfully withheld evidence and suborned perjury by the officers. One of the officers, William Toner, Area A-1, Boston, admitted on the stand that Stockdale was prosecuted on a criminal complaint with a forged complainant's signature and that the application for a criminal complaint was not the one that he——the complainant——had made out and caused to be filed in the criminal court. Toner's partner, Edward McMahon, too, in my opinion, testified falsely.

Magistrate-Judge Robert B. Collings did not give a damn. Later I learned that Collings was on a federal committee to defend federal judges against complaints of judicial wrongdoing. Given his professional demeanor, I was not suspicious of him until he refused to do "anything" after he heard the police officers' astonishing testimony.

The corruption throughout the judicial system is far deeper and widespread than you and I have imagined.

304   "Federal judge praises Connolly role," by Shelley Murphy, Boston Globe, October 15, 2008, *http://www.boston.com/news/local/articles/ 2008/10/15/federal_judge_praises_connolly_role/*

305   *Id.*

306   *Id.*

307   *Id.*

308   *See* "The Kennedy Connection – 'Chappaquiddick Revisited,'" *http:// www.qui-tam.net/chappaq.htm* :

> The question has come up "Why is this Federal Judge, Edward Harrington, going to such lengths to protect the lawyer John Hanify of Hanify & King in Boston, Massachusetts and his father Edward Hanify?"
>
> Here are the facts for you to discern:
>
> **EDWARD HARRINGTON**
> Federal Judge Edward F. Harrington failed to be recommended for a Massachusetts Superior Court appointment by Governor Dukakis' Judicial Nominating Council. Subsequently Senator Edward M. Kennedy recommended that he be put up for the Federal Bench. Edward Harrington was well-known to Ted Kennedy at the time of the Chappaquiddick affair and in the years that followed.
>
> Edward Harrington was the law partner of Paul Markham, one of the two individuals at Ted Kennedy's side the night Mary Jo Kopoechne died, drowning inside the car upside-down underwater beneath the Dyke Bridge on Chappaquiddick Island. Edward Harrington also served under Paul Markham on the Strike Force of the U.S. Attorney's office in Boston.
>
> **EDWARD HANIFY**

Edward B. Hanify is the father of John Hanify. Edward Hanify of Ropes & Gray in Boston was the lead attorney in Ted Kennedy's extensive defense team as stated in the book <u>Chappaquiddick Revealed</u>, "The Kennedy attorneys were brilliantly led by Edward B. Hanify, a Boston Brahmin if ever there was one. Hanify headed the venerable Boston law firm of Ropes & Gray...."(p105)

Edward Hanify was asked by Ted Kennedy to go to Washington, DC and speak on behalf of Edward Harrington's nomination before the Senate Judiciary's confirmation hearings because there were stiff objections to Edward Harrington being confirmed as a Federal Judge by many other prominent attorneys in the Boston legal community. [See link U.S. Senate *Judiciary*]

JOHN HANIFY

John Hanify is the son of Edward Hanify. Both he and his law firm Hanify & King represented ComFed Savings Bank before it failed and was taken over by the FDIC/RTC. John Hanify obstructed the pay back of the Sweeney loan while he was representing the bank and he helped develop the loan documents that ComFed Bank used to defraud the Sweeneys and many others doing business with ComFed. He was the personal Defense Attorney for the same ComFed Bank officers who committed "unfair and deceptive trade practices" against the Sweeneys and who were later charged with racketeering (RICO) by the FDIC/RTC. He and Edward Harrington have both worked together at the same time in the U.S. Attorneys office in Boston during the years 1978-1980. They know each other well.

STEPHEN BREYER

Stephen Breyer is an Associate Justice of the Supreme Court of the United States. He worked extensively with Ted Kennedy during his time as Chief Counsel to the Senate Judiciary Committee in Washington, DC from 1979-1980. He also served as the Chief Justice in the First Circuit Court of Appeals in Boston where **he affirmed the actions of Judge Harrington by changing the facts of the Sweeney case in his written opinion, overlooking the fact that to this day the FDIC has never substituted into the Sweeney action as a party.** Ted Kennedy asked President Clinton twice to nominate him to the Supreme Court of the United States.

COMMENT

When John Hanify removed the $4,000,000 state court judgment and hid it in the law offices of Hanify & King for 28 days he was desperate to get the entire case to his friend Judge Edward Harrington. The case was supposed to be "drawn" randomly in Federal Court. However it was conveniently "re-assigned" to Judge Harrington. Judge Harrington then proceeded to call a special hearing, and in less than one hour proceeded to completely ignore all of the work done in State Court over a nine-month period, and a three-week trial by the State Court Judge. He then ruled a "summary judgment" in favor of his friend and colleague John Hanify. Judge Harrington "expunged and nullified" the 45-page opinion of State Court Judge Catherine Liacos Izzo. He put everything under seal. No one has seen the original opinion written by Judge Izzo to this day.

An initialed true copy of that opinion was given to the Sweeney's attorneys by Judge Izzo herself when she learned that the original had been removed from state court. It is that precedent-setting document, the first United States "lender liability" victory against a bank, that is now up on the internet for the world to see. **Judge Harrington has at all times known of the fraud that was committed against the Sweeneys by ComFed Bank and its lawyers, one of which was his friend John Hanify. He has chosen, along with the FDIC, to cover up these crucial facts and insist that no 45-page opinion of "unfair and deceptive trade practices" exists or ever happened.**

The obvious question that needs to be answered by Judge Harrington, John Hanify, and the FDIC is..."WHY?"

309   *Aversa v. United States*, 99 F.3d 1200, 1208 (1st Cir. 1996), at ¶57, quoting Manual, ch. 7, §§ 1–7.001 (1988).

310   28 C.F.R. 50.2(b)(3).

311   *See* my website for the legal details:
- *www.falseallegations.com/drano1-meuseall.htm*
- *www.falseallegations.com/drano3-custody.htm*
- *www.falseallegations.com/drano4-ap-itrl.htm*
- *www.falseallegations.com/drano8-211-3-petition.htm*
- *www.falseallegations.com/drano10-sjc-app.htm*
- *www.falseallegations.com/drano11-dunphy.htm*
- *www.falseallegations.com/drano13-a-bf-sjc.htm*

- *www.falseallegations.com/drano16-o-cmpl-d.htm*
- *www.falseallegations.com/drano24-af-ms.htm*
- *www.falseallegations.com/drano30-ptj-rhrg.htm*
- *www.falseallegations.com/drano67-complaint-writ-certiorari-denial-dismissal.htm*
- *www.falseallegations.com/drano116-brian-meuse-federal-complaint-2-21-04.htm*
- *www.falseallegations.com/drano121-brian-meuse-opp-fox-dismiss-52404.htm*
- *www.falseallegations.com/drano123-opp-stf-dismiss-52404.htm*
- *www.falseallegations.com/drano124-opp-ncmec-dismiss-70904.htm*
- *www.falseallegations.com/drano126-m-reconsider-harrington-61704.htm*
- *www.falseallegations.com/drano127-replies-to-opps-by-stf-fox-71104.htm*

312   *Rogers v. Management Technology Inc.*, 123 F.3d 34, 37 (1st Cir. 1997). *See Day v. Massachusetts Air Nat'l Guard*, 167 F.3d 678, 685 (1st Cir. 1999); *Lyons v. Brown*, 158 F.3d 605, 610 (1st Cir. 1998); *Davric Maine Corp. v. United States Postal Service*, 238 F.3d 58, 66 (1st Cir (Me.) 2001).

313   *Schowengerdt v. General Dynamics Corp.*, 823 F.2d 1328, 1333 n. 3 (9th Cir. (CAL.) 1987) (internal citations omitted).

314   *Bivens v. Six Unknown Named Agents of the Fed. Bureau of Narcotics*, 403 U.S. 388, 396-397, 91 S.Ct. 1999, 2004-2005 (1971).

Endnotes—Chapter 17

315   The federal statute commonly known as the Westfall Act accords federal employees absolute immunity from tort claims arising out of acts undertaken in the course of their official duties, 28 U. S. C. §2679(b)(1), and empowers the Attorney General to certify that a federal employee sued for wrongful or negligent conduct "was acting within the scope of his office or employment at the time of the incident out of which the claim arose," §2679(d)(1), (2). Upon such certification, the United States is substituted as defendant in place of the employee, and the action is thereafter governed by the Federal Tort Claims Act. If the action commenced in state court, the Westfall Act calls for its removal to a federal district court, and renders the Attorney General's certification "conclusiv[e] ... for purposes of removal." §2679(d)(2)

Osborn v. Haley, (6th Cir. 2007)   No. 05-593

316   *Younger v. Harris*, 401 U.S. 37, 44 (1971). Compare *Fair Assessment in Real Estate Assn. v. McNary*, 454 U.S. 100 (1981), with <u>id</u>., 119-125 (Justice Brennan concurring, joined by three other Justices).

317   *http://www.law.cornell.edu/anncon/html/art3frag58_user.html*. The content of the CRS Annotated Constitution was prepared by the Congressional Research Service (CRS) at the Library of Congress, and published electronically in plain text and PDF by the Government Printing Office.

318   The fundamental interest in federalism that allows individual States to define crimes, punishments, rules of evidence, and rules of criminal and civil procedure in a variety of different ways——so long as they do not violate the Federal Constitution——is not otherwise limited by any general, undefined federal interest in uniformity. Nonuniformity is, in fact, an unavoidable reality in a federalist system of government. Any State could surely have adopted the rule of evidence defined in *Crawford* under state law even if that case had never been decided. It should be equally free to give its citizens the benefit of our rule in any fashion that does not offend federal law.

Danforth v. Minnesota [FN16]

> [T]he "end result [of this opinion] is startling" because "two criminal defendants, each of whom committed the same crime, at the same time, whose convictions became final on the same day, and each of whom raised an identical claim at the same time under the Federal Constitution" could obtain different results. *Post,* at 1047. This assertion ignores the fact that the two hypothetical criminal defendants did not actually commit the "same crime." They violated different state laws, were tried in and by different state sovereigns, and may——for many reasons——be subject to different penalties. As previously noted, such nonuniformity is a necessary consequence of a federalist system of government.

Danforth v. Minnesota,

319   The CRS Annotated Constitution citing *Mast, Foos & Co. v. Stover Manufacturing Co.*, 177 U.S. 458, 488 (1900).

320   E.g., *O'Shea v. Littleton*, 414 U.S. 488, 499-504 (1974); *Huffman v. Pursue, Ltd.*, 420 U.S. 592, 599-603 (1975); *Trainor v. Hernandez*, 431 U.S. 434, 441 (1977); *Moore v. Sims*, 442 U.S. 415, 430 (1979).

321   *Francis v. Henderson*, 425 U.S. 536, 541 and n. 31 (1976); *Wainwright v. Sykes*, 433 U.S. 72, 83, 88, 90 (1977); *Engle v. Isaac*, 456 U.S. 107, 128-129 (1982).

322   *See also Rosewell v. LaSalle National Bank*, 450 U.S. 503 (1981); *Fair Assessment in Real Estate Assn. v. McNary*, 454 U.S. 100 (1981). And see *Missouri v. Jenkins*, 495 U.S. 33 (1990).

323   "[T]he State's interest in protecting 'the authority of the judicial system, so that its orders and judgments are not rendered nugatory'" was deemed sufficient. *Id.*, 14 n. 12 (quoting *Judice v. Vail*, 430 U.S. 327, 336 n. 12 (1977)).

324   *Id.*, 14.

325   *Burford v. Sun Oil Co.*, 319 U.S. 315 (1943); *Alabama Pubic Service Comm. v. Southern Ry.*, 341 U.S. 341 (1951); *Great Lakes Dredge & Dock Co. v. Huffman*, 319 U.S. 293 (1943); *Martin v. Creasy*, 360 U.S. 219 (1959); *Moses H. Cone Hosp. v. Mercury Constr. Corp.*, 460 U.S. 1 (1983);

326   *Colorado River Water Conservation Dist. v. United States*, 424 U.S. 800 (1976); *Will v. Calvert Fire Insurance Co.*, 437 U.S. 655 (1978); *Arizona v. San Carlos Apache Tribe*, 463 U.S. 545 (1983).

327   *City of Chicago v. Atchison, T. & S.F.R. Co.*, 357 U.S. 77 (1958); *Zwickler v. Koota*, 389 U.S. 241, 249-251 (1967). *See Babbitt v. United Farm Workers Nat. Union*, 442 U.S. 289, 306 (1979) (quoting *Harman v. Forssenius*, 380 U.S. 528, 534-535 (1965)).

328   *Harman v. Forssenius*, 380 U.S. 528, 534-535 (1965); *Babbitt v. United Farm Workers*, 442 U.S. 289, 305-312 (1979).

329   *American Trial Lawyers Assn. v. New Jersey Supreme Court*, 409 U.S. 467, 469 (1973); *Harrison v. NAACP*, 360 U.S. 167 (1959). Dismissal may be necessary if the state court will not accept jurisdiction while the case is pending in federal court. *Harris County Comrs. v. Moore*, 420 U.S. 77, 88 n. 14 (1975).

330   E.g., *Spector Motor Service v. McLaughlin*, 323 U.S. 101 (1944); *Louisiana Power & Light Co. v. City of Thiobodaux*, 360 U.S. 25 (1959); *Harrison v. NAACP*, 360 U.S. 167 (1959).

331   *McNeese v. Board of Education*, 373 U.S. 668 (1963); *Griffin v. School Board*, 377 U.S. 218 (1964); *Hostetter v. Idlewild Bon Voyage Liquor Corp.*, 377

U.S. 324 (1964); *Baggett v. Bullitt,* 377 U.S. 360 (1964); *Davis v. Mann,* 377 U.S. 678 (1964); *Dombrowski v. Pfister,* 380 U.S. 479 (1965); *Harman v. Forssenius,* 380 U.S. 528 (1965); *Zwickler v. Koota,* 389 U.S. 241 (1967); *Wisconsin v. Constanineau,* 400 U.S. 433 (1971).

332   *England v. Louisiana State Bd. of Medical Examiners,* 375 U.S. 411, 426 (1964) (Justice Douglas concurring). See C. Wright, *Handbook of the Law of Federal Courts* (St. Paul: 4th ed. 1983), 305.

333   *Baggett v. Bullitt,* 377 U.S. 360, 378-379 (1964).

334   *Clay v. Sun Insurance Office Ltd.,* 363 U.S. 207 (1960); *Lehman Brothers v. Schein,* 416 U.S. 386 (1974); *Bellotti v. Baird,* 428 U.S. 132, 151 (1976).

335   Compare *Harrison v. NAACP,* 360 U.S. 167 (1959), with *McNeese v. Board of Education,* 373 U.S. 668 (1963).

336   Compare *Baggett v. Bullitt,* 377 U.S. 360 (1964), and *Dombrowski v. Pfister,* 380 U.S. 479 (1965), with *Younger v. Harris,* 401 U.S. 37 (1971), and *Samuels v. Mackell,* 401 U.S. 66 (1971). See *Babbitt v. United Farm Workers,* 442 U.S. 289, 305-312 (1979).

337   *Younger v. Harris,* 401 U.S. 37, 91 S.Ct. 746 (U.S. (Cal) 1971).

338   E.g., *Ankenbrandt v. Richards,* 112 S.Ct. 2206, 2215 (1992).

339   *Younger v. Harris,* 401 U.S. 37 (1971); *Rooker v. Fidelity Trust Co.,* 263 U.S. 413, 44 S.Ct. 149; *District of Columbia Court of Appeals v. Feldman,* 460 U.S. 462, 103 S.Ct. 1303; *Burford v.* Sun Oil Co., 319 U.S. 315 (1943); *Railroad Comm. v. Pullman Co.,* 312 U.S. 496 (1941).

340   The rule was formulated in *Prentis v. Atlantic Coast Line Co.,* 211 U.S. 210 (1908), and Bacon v. Rutland R. Co., 232 U.S. 134 (1914).

341   *City Bank Farmers' Trust Co. v. Schnader,* 291 U.S. 24 (1934); *Lane v. Wilson,* 307 U.S. 268 (1939). *But see Alabama Public Service Comm. v. Southern Ry. Co.,* 341 U.S. 341 (1951). Exhaustion of state court remedies is required in habeas corpus cases and usually in suits to restrain state court proceedings.

342   *Patsy v. Board of Regents,* 457 U.S. 496 (1982). Where there are pending administrative proceedings that fall within the Younger rule, a litigant must exhaust. *Younger v. Harris,* 401 U.S. 37 (1971), as explicated in *Ohio Civil Rights Comm. v. Dayton Christian School, Inc.,* 477 U.S. 619, 627 n. 2 (1986). Under title VII of the Civil Rights Act of 1964, barring employment discrimination on racial and other specified grounds, the EEOC may not consider a claim until a state agency having jurisdiction over employment discrimination

complaints has had at least 60 days to resolve the matter. 42 U.S.C. Sec. Sec. 2000e-5(c). See *Love v. Pullman Co.*, 404 U.S. 522 (1972). And under the Civil Rights of Institutionalized Persons Act, there is a requirement of exhaustion, where States have federally-approved procedures. See *Patsy, supra*, 507-513.

343   *Danforth v. Minnesota*, 128 S.Ct. 1029 (U.S.Minn., 2008).

344   Federal Civil Rights Act, 42 U.S.C. § 1983:

> Every person who, under color of any statute, ordinance, regulation, custom, or usage, of any State or Territory or the District of Columbia, subjects, or causes to be subjected, any citizen of the United States or other person within the jurisdiction thereof to the deprivation of any rights, privileges, or immunities secured by the Constitution and laws, shall be liable to the party injured in an action at law, suit in equity, or other proper proceeding for redress, except that in any action brought against a judicial officer for an act or omission taken in such officer's judicial capacity, injunctive relief shall not be granted unless a declaratory decree was violated or declaratory relief was unavailable. For the purposes of this section, any Act of Congress applicable exclusively to the District of Columbia shall be considered to be a statute of the District of Columbia.

In 1996, under President Bill Clinton, the immunity of judicial officers was enhanced by an amendment: "Pub.L. 104-317, § 309(c), inserted provisions relating to immunity of judicial officers from injunctive relief unless declaratory decree was violated or declaratory relief is unavailable."

345   *In re Ruffalo*, 390 U.S. 544, 88 S.Ct. 1222 (U.S. (Ohio), April 08, 1968) (NO. 73).

346   *Danforth v. Minnesota*, 128 S.Ct. 1029, 1047 (U.S.Minn., 2008).

347   *Danforth v. Minnesota*, 128 S.Ct. 1029, 1057 (U.S.Minn., 2008) (dissenting, Roberts, C.J.)

348   The test does not appear in *Younger* itself.

349   *Bettencourt v. Board of Registration in Medicine*, 904 F.2d 772 (1st Cir. 1990).

350   One might expect interlocutory review for "federal constitutional challenges." See *Gibson v. Berryhill*, 411 U.S. 564 (1973) and *Brooks v. New Hampshire Supreme Court*, 80 F.3d 633, 639 (1st Cir. 1996).

351   *Middlesex County Ethics Committee v. Garden State Bar Association*, 457 U.S. 423 (1982).

352   *Middlesex*, at 433-434.

353   *Middlesex*, at 433.

354   *Middlesex County Ethics Committee v. Garden State Bar Association*, 457 U.S. 423 (1982)

355   In the year prior to establishing the OBC and BBO, the SJC held that disbarment proceedings were civil in nature and the "'rules of evidence applicable to civil trials . . . (are) rightly enforced.'" *Matter of Troy*, 364 Mass. 15, 24-25, 306 N.E.2d 203, 208 (1973), quoting *Matter of Ulmer*, 268 Mass. 373, 392, 167 N.E. 749 (1929) and *Matter of Mayberry*, 295 Mass. 155, 166-167, 3 N.E.2d 248; and *Collins v. Godfrey*, 324 Mass. 574, 577-578, 87 N.E.2d 838.

356   *Butz v. Economou*, 438 U.S. 478, 512-513 (1978).

357   Paragraph 64 in *Rio Grande*.

358   *Bettencourt v. Board of Registration in Medicine*, 904 F.2d 772, 780 (1st Cir. 1990) (emphasis supplied).

359   *Brooks v. New Hampshire Supreme Court*, 80 F.3d 633, 639 (1st Cir. 1996).

360   *Bettencourt v. Board of Registration in Medicine*, 904 F.2d 772, 780 (1st Cir. 1990) (emphasis supplied).

361   *Middlesex*, at 427.

362   *Middlesex*, at 430-431.

363   *Middlesex*, at 429.

364   *Id.*

365   *Id.*

366   *Id.*

367   *Id.*

368   *Perez v. Ledesma*, 401 U.S 82, 85, 91 S.Ct. 674, 677 (1971).

369   *Younger*, 401 U.S. at 55, 91 S.Ct. 755. *See Gibson v. Berryhill*, 411 U.S. 564, 577 (1972).

370   The case was decided in 1973, not 1972 as asserted in *Bettencourt*.

371   *Bettencourt*, at 780, quoting *Younger* at 54.

372   *Bettencourt.*

373   *Bettencourt,* at 781.

374   In my Complaint (see Drano Series #114 on my website at *http://www. falseallegations.com/drano114-bbo-opp-dismiss-1-23-04.htm*), I was not asking the court to interfere with the State proceedings. It is true, however, that as a result of the defendants' deficient memorandum in support of their motion to dismiss, I reverted to seeking a temporary injunction. An injunction simply appeared to be more appropriate than ever. *See also* Plaintiff's Opposition to Motion to Dismiss Amended Complaint and Supporting Memorandum in the Drano Series on my website.

375   *Bettencourt,* at 781.

376   *Gibson,* 411 U.S. at 570.

377   *Gibson,* at 571.

378   *Gibson,* at 572.

379   *Brooks,* t80 F.3d 633 (1st Cir. 1996).

380   *Brooks,* at 64.

381   *Id.* (internal cites omitted).

382   For most plaintiffs, definitive proof of such wrongdoing would be virtually impossible to gather . . . and would cost the government millions of dollars and the appointment of special prosecutors.

383   *Brooks,* at 640 (internal cites omitted).

384   Paragraphs 48-55, 58-61, Addendum, Papers 20, 25, 28, 35, 43, 45-46, 53, 78, including my motions, OBC oppositions, BBO orders and letters, all from 6/21/03 through 9/16/03.

385   Paragraph 69, Addendum, Papers 50, 74 and 75.

386   Paragraph 146 of my Complaint, Addendum, Paper unnumbered but filed and denied 12/01/03.

387   Paragraph 146 of my Complaint, Addendum, Paper 95, filed 11/5/03 and denied 11/18/03.

388   Paragraph 37 of my Complaint, Paper 90 (11/04/03); denied.

389   Paragraph 194; denied on 12/12/03 by Phillips.

390   *Brooks v. New Hampshire Supreme Court,* 80 F.3d 633, 640 (1st Cir. 1996),

391　*Middlesex,* 457 U.S. at 435.

392　The words "bias" or "recuse" do not appear in the *Middlesex* opinion, making the reliance for this proposition somewhat curious.

393　*Bettencourt,* 904 F.2d at 780.

394　For this proposition, the court in *Bettencourt* cites *Standard Alaska, infra,* and *Peterson v. Sheran,* 635 F.2d 1335, 1341 (8th Cir. 1980) (similar).

395　*Standard Alaska Prod. Co. v. Schaible,* 874 F.2d 624, 629 (9th Cir. 1989), *cert. denied,* 495 U.S. 904 (1990) (bias exception inapplicable when plaintiffs fail to utilize state tribunal's disqualification procedures).

396　*Brooks v. New Hampshire Supreme Court,* 80 F.3d 633, 640 (1st Cir. 1996).

397　Compl. ¶111(a-d).

398　Compl. ¶45-47, 128, 131-133.

399　*See Brooks,* at 640.

400　*Brooks,* at 636.

401　*Brooks,* at 640.

402　*Brooks,* at 639.

403　*Id.*

404　That the NHSC justices "retain[ed] a strong interest in preserving the expectations of confidentiality created by the former regime" [*Brooks,* at 639 n. 6] . . . and did not dissent to amendments liberalizing the confidentiality rule . . . and were "not wed to secrecy" [*Brooks,* at 640 n. 9] was relegated to two footnotes

405　Compl. ¶134.

406　Compl. ¶179.

407　Compl. ¶182.

408　Compl. ¶186.

409　*Brooks,* at 640.

410　Defs. Mem., at 6: *Bettencourt v. Board of Registration in Medicine,* 904 F.2d 772,779 (1st Cir. 1990),

411　Defs. Mem., at 6: *Judge v. City of Lowell,* 160 F.3d 67 (1st Cir. 1998).

412   *Judge*, 160 F.3d at 72.

413   Paragraphs 41-47 of my Complaint.

414   Paragraph 92 of my Complaint.

415   Paragraphs 93(c-f) of my Complaint.

416   Paragraph 111 of my Complaint.

417   Footnote 18 on page 18 of my Complaint.

418   Paragraph 116 of my Complaint; *see* Figures 2(a-e).

419   Paragraph 151 of my Complaint.

420   Paragraphs 234 and 235 of my Complaint.

421   *Weitzel v. Division of Occupational and Professional Licensing of the Department of Commerce of the State of Utah*, D-Cr. No. 99-CV-670-K (10th Cir. 2001) (Tacha, C.J.), slip op. 7.

422   *Younger*, 401 U.S. at 53.

423   *See Younger*, 401 U.S. at 43.

424   The appellate route of the state disciplinary proceeding is clear: a review by the BBO, review by a single justice of the SJC, review by the SJC bench.

425   The *Younger* abstention doctrine does not apply, however, to my claims for money damages pursuant to Section 1983 or Section 1985, or to her defamation claim, since she will not have the opportunity to make these claims in the state proceeding. See *Deakins v. Monaghan*, 484 U.S. 193, 202 (1988) (stating that even if the *Younger* abstention applies, the district court has no discretion to dismiss rather than to stay claims for monetary relief that cannot be redressed in the state proceeding). Thus, while declaratory judgment Counts 1 through 6 were dismissed *in toto* in reliance on *Younger*, the civil rights Counts 7 through 9 were dismissed under *Younger* only to the extent that I sought equitable relief.

426   *Younger*, at 65.

427   *Lance v. Dennis*, 546 U.S. 459, 463, 126 S.Ct. 1198, 1200-1201 (U.S., 2006).

428   *Lance*, 546 U.S. 459, 126 S.Ct. 1198 (U.S., 2006).

429   *Lance*, 546 U.S. at 463, 126 S.Ct. at 1201, quoting *Rooker*, 263 U.S., at 416, 44 S.Ct. 149..

430   *Lance*, 546 U.S. at 463, 126 S.Ct. at 1201, quoting *Rooker,*, quoting 460 U.S., at 476, 103 S.Ct. 1303, citing 460 U.S., at 476, 103 S.Ct. 1303.

431   *See Lance*, 546 U.S. 459, 464-465, 126 S.Ct. 1198, 1201-1204 (U.S., 2006).

> *Rooker* and *Feldman* are strange bedfellows. *Rooker*, a unanimous, three-page opinion written by Justice Van Devanter in 1923, correctly applied the simple legal proposition that only this Court may exercise appellate jurisdiction over state-court judgments. See *Rooker v. Fidelity Trust Co.*, 263 U.S. 413, 416, 44 S.Ct. 149, 68 L.Ed. 362. *Feldman*, a nonunanimous, 25-page opinion written by Justice Brennan in 1983, was incorrectly decided and generated a plethora of confusion and debate among scholars and judges.[FN*] See *468 *District of Columbia Court of Appeals v. Feldman*, 460 U.S. 462, 103 S.Ct. 1303, 75 L.Ed.2d 206; *id.*, at 488, 103 S.Ct. 1303 (STEVENS, J., dissenting). Last Term, in Justice GINSBURG's lucid opinion in *Exxon Mobil Corp. v. Saudi Basic Industries Corp.*, 544 U.S. 280, 125 S.Ct. 1517, 161 L.Ed.2d 454 (2005), the Court finally interred the so-called " *Rooker-Feldman* doctrine." And today, the Court quite properly disapproves of the District Court's resuscitation of a doctrine that has **1204 produced nothing but mischief for 23 years.
>
> Even if the Court had good reason to doubt the Court of Appeals' determination of state law, it would, in my judgment, be a far wiser course to certify the question to the *777 Colorado Supreme Court.[FN3] Powerful considerations support certification in this case. First, principles of federalism and comity favor giving a State's high court the opportunity to answer important questions of state law, particularly when those questions implicate uniquely local matters such as law enforcement and might well require the weighing of policy considerations for their correct resolution.FN4 See *Elkins v. Moreno*, 435 U.S. 647, 662, n. 16, 98 S.Ct. 1338, 55 L.Ed.2d 614 (1978) (*sua sponte* certifying a question of state law because it is "one in which state governments have the highest interest"); cf. *Arizonans for Official English v. Arizona*, 520 U.S. 43, 77, 117 S.Ct. 1055, 137 L.Ed.2d 170 (1997) ("Through certification of novel or unsettled questions of state law for authoritative answers by a State's highest court, a federal court may save 'time, energy, and resources, and hel[p] build a cooperative

judicial federalism' " (brackets in original)).[FN5] *778 Second, by certifying**2816 a potentially dispositive state-law issue, the Court would adhere to its wise policy of avoiding the unnecessary adjudication of difficult questions of constitutional law. See *Elkins,* 435 U.S., at 661-662, 98 S.Ct. 1338 (citing constitutional avoidance as a factor supporting certification). Third, certification would promote both judicial economy and fairness to the parties. After all, the Colorado Supreme Court is the ultimate authority on the meaning of Colorado law, and if in later litigation it should disagree with this Court's provisional state-law holding, our efforts will have been wasted and respondent will have been deprived of the opportunity to have her claims heard under the authoritative view of Colorado law. The unique facts of this case only serve to emphasize the importance of employing a procedure that will provide the correct answer to the central question of state law. See *Brockett,* 472 U.S., at 510, 105 S.Ct. 2794 (O'CONNOR, J., concurring) ("Speculation by a federal court about the meaning of a state statute in the absence of a prior state court adjudication is particularly gratuitous when, as is the case here, the state courts stand willing to address questions of state law on certification from a federal court").[FN6]

FN3. See Colo. Rule App. Proc. 21.1(a) (Colorado Supreme Court may answer questions of law certified to it by the Supreme Court of the United States or another federal court if those questions "may be determinative of the cause" and "as to which it appears to the certifying court there is no controlling precedent in the decisions of the [Colorado] Supreme Court").

Town of Castle Rock, Colo. v. Gonzales, 545 U.S. 748, 776-778, 125 S.Ct. 2796, 2815-2817 (U.S., 2005).

In such cases, the purpose of abstention is not to afford state courts an opportunity to adjudicate an issue that is functionally identical to the federal question. To the contrary, the purpose of *Pullman* abstention in such cases is to avoid resolving the federal question by encouraging a state-law determination that may moot the federal controversy. *340 See 375 U.S., at 416-417, and n. 7, 84 S.Ct. 461. FN21 Additionally, **2503 our opinion made it perfectly clear that the effective reservation of a federal claim was dependent on the condition that plaintiffs take no action to broaden the scope of the state court's review beyond decision of the antecedent state-law issue.[FN22]

San Remo Hotel, L.P. v. City and County of San Francisco, Cal., 545 U.S. at 339-340, 125 S.Ct. at 2502-2503.

The *Rooker -Feldman* doctrine, at issue in this case, has been applied by this Court only twice, in *Rooker v. Fidelity Trust Co.*, 263 U.S. 413, 44 S.Ct. 149, 68 L.Ed. 362, and in ****1519** *District of Columbia Court of Appeals v. Feldman*, 460 U.S. 462, 103 S.Ct. 1303, 75 L.Ed.2d 206. In *Rooker*, plaintiffs previously defeated in state court filed suit in a Federal District Court alleging that the adverse state-court judgment was unconstitutional and asking that it be declared "null and void." 263 U.S., at 414-415, 44 S.Ct. 149. Noting preliminarily that the state court had acted within its jurisdiction, this Court explained that if the state-court decision was wrong, "that did not make the judgment void, but merely left it open to reversal or modification in an appropriate and timely appellate proceeding." *Id.*, at 415, 44 S.Ct. 149. Federal district courts, *Rooker* recognized, are empowered to exercise only original, not appellate, jurisdictions. *Id.*, at 416, 44 S.Ct. 149. Because Congress has empowered this Court alone to exercise appellate authority "to reverse or modify" a state-court judgment, *ibid.*, the Court affirmed a decree dismissing the federal suit for lack of jurisdiction, *id.*, at 415, 417, 44 S.Ct. 149. In *Feldman*, two plaintiffs brought federal-court actions after the District of Columbia's highest court denied their petitions to waive a court Rule requiring D.C. bar applicants to have graduated from an accredited law school. Recalling *Rooker*, this Court observed that the District Court lacked authority to review a final judicial determination of the D.C. high court because such review "can be obtained only in this Court." 460 U.S., at 476, 103 S.Ct. 1303. Concluding that the D.C. court's proceedings applying the accreditation Rule to the plaintiffs were "judicial in nature," *id.*, at 479-482, 103 S.Ct. 1303, this Court ruled that the Federal District Court lacked subject-matter jurisdiction, *id.*, at 482, 103 S.Ct. 1303. However, concluding also that, in promulgating the bar admission Rule, the D.C. court had acted legislatively, not judicially, *id.*, at 485-486, 103 S.Ct. 1303, this Court held that 28 U.S.C. § 1257 did not bar the District Court from addressing the validity of the Rule itself, so long as the plaintiffs did not seek review of the Rule's application in a particular case, 460 U.S., at 486, 103 S.Ct. 1303. Since *Feldman*, this Court has never applied *Rooker -Feldman* to dismiss an action for want of jurisdiction. However, the lower federal courts have variously interpreted the *Rooker -Feldman* doctrine to extend far beyond the contours of the *Rooker* and *Feldman* cases, overriding***281** Congress' conferral of federal-court jurisdiction concurrent with jurisdiction exercised by state courts, and superseding the ordinary application of preclusion law under 28 U.S.C. § 1738.

Exxon Mobil Corp. v. Saudi Basic Industries Corp., 544 U.S. 280, 280-281, 125 S.Ct. 1517. 1518-1519 (U.S., 2005).

****1520** *Held:* The *Rooker -Feldman* doctrine is confined to cases of the kind from which it acquired its name: cases brought by state-court losers complaining of injuries caused by state-court judgments rendered before the federal district court proceedings commenced and inviting district court review and rejection of those judgments. *Rooker -Feldman* does not otherwise override or supplant preclusion doctrine or augment the circumscribed doctrines allowing federal courts to stay or dismiss proceedings in deference to state-court actions. Pp. 1526-1528.

(a) *Rooker* and *Feldman* exhibit the limited circumstances in which this Court's appellate jurisdiction over state-court judgments, § 1257, precludes a federal district court from exercising subject-matter jurisdiction in an action it would otherwise be empowered to adjudicate under a congressional grant of authority. In both cases, the plaintiffs, alleging federal-question jurisdiction, called upon the District Court to overturn an injurious state-court judgment. Because § 1257, as long interpreted, vests authority to review a state-court judgment solely in this Court, *e.g., Feldman,* 460 U.S., at 476, 103 S.Ct. 1303, the District Courts lacked subject-matter jurisdiction, see, *e.g., Verizon Md., Inc. v. Public Serv. Comm'n of Md.,* 535 U.S. 635, 644, n. 3, 122 S.Ct. 1753, 152 L.Ed.2d 871. When there is parallel state and federal litigation, *Rooker -Feldman* is not triggered simply by the entry of judgment in state court. See, *e.g.,* ***282** *McClellan v. Carland,* 217 U.S. 268, 282, 30 S.Ct. 501, 54 L.Ed. 762. Comity or abstention doctrines may, in various circumstances, permit or require the federal court to stay or dismiss the federal action in favor of the state-court litigation. See, *e.g., Colorado River Water Conservation Dist. v. United States,* 424 U.S. 800, 96 S.Ct. 1236, 47 L.Ed.2d 483. **But neither *Rooker* nor *Feldman* supports the notion that properly invoked concurrent jurisdiction vanishes if a state court reaches judgment on the same or a related question while the case remains *sub judice* in a federal court.** Disposition of the federal action, once the state-court adjudication is complete, would be governed by preclusion law. Under 28 U.S.C. § 1738, federal courts must "give the same preclusive effect to a state-court judgment as another court of that State would give." *Parsons Steel, Inc. v. First Alabama Bank*, 474 U.S. 518, 523, 106 S.Ct. 768, 88 L.Ed.2d 877. Preclusion is not a jurisdictional matter. See Fed. Rule Civ. Proc. 8(c). **In parallel litigation, a federal court may be bound to recognize the claim- and issue-preclusive effects of a state-court judgment, but federal jurisdiction over an action does not terminate automatically on the entry of judgment in the state court. Nor does § 1257 stop a district court from exercising subject-matter jurisdiction simply because a party attempts to litigate in federal court a matter previously litigated in state court.** If a federal plaintiff presents an independent claim, even one that denies a state court's legal conclusion in a case to which the plaintiff was a party, there is jurisdiction, and state law determines whether the defendant prevails under preclusion principles. Pp. 1526-1527.

(b) **The *Rooker-Feldman* doctrine does not preclude the federal court from proceeding in this case. ExxonMobil has not repaired to federal court to undo the Delaware judgment in its favor, but appears to have filed its federal-court suit (only two weeks after SABIC filed in Delaware and well before any judgment in state court) to protect itself in the event it lost in state court on grounds (such as the state statute of limitations) that might not preclude relief in the federal venue.** *Rooker-Feldman* did not prevent the District Court from exercising jurisdiction ****1521** when ExxonMobil filed the federal action, and it did not emerge to vanquish jurisdiction after ExxonMobil prevailed in the Delaware courts. The Third Circuit misperceived the narrow ground occupied by *Rooker-Feldman*, and consequently erred in ordering the federal action dismissed. Pp. 1527-1528.

364 F.3d 102, reversed and remanded.

GINSBURG, J., delivered the opinion for a unanimous Court.

Exxon Mobil Corp. v. Saudi Basic Industries Corp., 544 U.S. at 281-282, 125 S.Ct. at 1520-1522.

See *Verizon Md. Inc. v. Public Serv. Comm'n of Md.*, 535 U.S. 635, 644, n. 3, 122 S.Ct. 1753, 152 L.Ed.2d 871 (2002) (*Rooker-Feldman* does not apply to a suit seeking review of state agency action); *Johnson v. De Grandy*, 512 U.S. 997, 1005-1006, 114 S.Ct. 2647, 129 L.Ed.2d

775 (1994) (*Rooker -Feldman* bars a losing party in state court "from seeking what in substance would be appellate review of the state judgment in a United States district court, based on the losing party's claim that the state judgment itself violates the loser's federal rights," but the doctrine has no application to a federal suit brought by a nonparty to the state suit.); **1524** *Howlett v. Rose*, 496 U.S. 356, 369-370, n. 16, 110 S.Ct. 2430, 110 L.Ed.2d 332 (1990) (citing *Rooker* and *Feldman* for "the rule that a federal district court cannot entertain an original action alleging that a state court violated the Constitution by giving effect to an unconstitutional state statute"); *ASARCO Inc. v. Kadish*, 490 U.S. 605, 622-623, 109 S.Ct. 2037, 104 L.Ed.2d 696 (1989) (If, instead of seeking review of an adverse state supreme court decision in the Supreme Court, petitioners sued in federal district court, the federal action would be an attempt to obtain direct review of the state supreme court decision and would "represent a partial inroad on *Rooker -Feldman's* construction of 28 U.S.C. § 1257.");[FN2] ***288** *Pennzoil Co. v. Texaco Inc.*, 481 U.S. 1, 6-10, 107 S.Ct. 1519, 95 L.Ed.2d 1 (1987) (abstaining under *Younger v. Harris*, 401 U.S. 37, 91 S.Ct. 746, 27 L.Ed.2d 669 (1971), rather than dismissing under *Rooker- Feldman*, in a suit that challenged Texas procedures for enforcing judgments); 481 U.S., at 18, 107 S.Ct. 1519 (SCALIA, J., concurring) (The "so-called Rooker-Feldman doctrine" does not deprive the Court of jurisdiction to decide Texaco's challenge to the Texas procedures); *id.*, at 21, 107 S.Ct. 1519 (Brennan, J., concurring in judgment) (*Rooker* and *Feldman* do not apply; Texaco filed its federal action to protect its "right to a meaningful opportunity for appellate review, not to challenge the merits of the Texas suit."). But cf. 481 U.S., at 25-26, 107 S.Ct. 1519 (Marshall, J., concurring in judgment) (*Rooker- Feldman* would apply because Texaco's claims necessarily called for review of the merits of its state appeal). See also *Martin v. Wilks*, 490 U.S. 755, 783-784, n. 21, 109 S.Ct. 2180, 104 L.Ed.2d 835 (1989) (STEVENS, J., dissenting) (it would be anomalous to allow courts to sit in review of judgments entered by courts of equal, or greater, authority (citing *Rooker* and *Feldman*)).[FN3]

Exxon Mobil Corp. v. Saudi Basic Industries Corp., 544 U.S. at 287-288, 125 S.Ct. at 1523-1524.

The Court of Appeals, on its own motion, raised the question whether "subject matter jurisdiction over this case fails under the *Rooker -Feldman* doctrine because ExxonMobil's claims have already been litigated in state court." *Id.*, at 104.[FN6] The court did not question the District Court's possession of subject-matter jurisdiction at the outset of the suit, but held that federal jurisdiction terminated when the Delaware Superior Court entered judgment on the jury verdict. *Id.*, at 104-105. The court rejected ExxonMobil's argument that *Rooker -Feldman* could not apply because ExxonMobil filed its federal complaint well before the state-court judgment. The only relevant consideration, the court stated, "is whether the state judgment precedes a federal judgment on the same claims." 364 F.3d, at 105. If *Rooker -Feldman* did not apply to federal actions filed prior to a **1526 state-court judgment, the Court of Appeals worried, "we would be encouraging parties to maintain federal actions as 'insurance policies' while their state court claims were pending." 364 F.3d, at 105. Once ExxonMobil's claims had been litigated to a judgment in state court, the Court of Appeals held, *Rooker -Feldman* "preclude[d] [the] federal district court *291 from proceeding." 364 F.3d, at 104 (internal quotation marks omitted).

> FN6. One day before argument, the Court of Appeals directed the parties to be prepared to address whether the *Rooker-Feldman* doctrine deprived the District Court of jurisdiction over the case.

Exxon Mobil Corp. v. Saudi Basic Industries Corp., 544 U.S. at 290-291, 125 S.Ct. at 1525-1526 (U.S., 2005)..

> But neither *Rooker* nor *Feldman* supports the notion that properly invoked concurrent jurisdiction vanishes if a state court reaches judgment on the same or related question while the case remains *sub judice* in a federal court.

Exxon Mobil Corp., 544 U.S. at 287-288, 125 S.Ct. at 1523-1524 (U.S., 2005).

432   See the Complaint against the judges in Drano Series #57 on my website at *http://www.falseallegations.com/drano57-complaint-against-judges.htm*.

433   The unconstitutionality arises out of the guardian *ad litem* statute, Massachusetts General Laws, chapter 215, section 56A, allowing justices to abrogate their judicial responsibilities by delegating them to untrained persons who are required to have no relevant credentials or knowledge and who work to no standards.

434   The child-removal statute is Massachusetts General Laws, chapter 208, section 30.

435   The MCCJA is Massachusetts General Laws, chapter 209B, section 5(a).

436   *Hill et al v. Town of Conway,* 193 F.3d 33 (1st Cir. 1999).

437   *Pennzoil Co. v. Texaco Inc.,* 481 U.S. 1, 18 (1987) (Scalia, J., Concurring, with whom Justice O'Connor joined). Justice Marshall agreed also with Justices Scalia and Brennan that the *Rooker-Feldman* doctrine did not apply in *Pennzoil.*

Justice Stevens agreed with Justices Brennan and Scalia that the *Rooker-Feldman* doctrine "[did not bar] the federal courts from considering Texaco's claims." *Pennzoil* at 31 n. 3 (concurring footnote 3). For like reasons, the *Rooker-Feldman* doctrine does not apply to the instant case.

Thus under *Pennzoil,* the *Rooker-Feldman* doctrine does not apply to the case at bar. "`The very purpose of sec. 1983 was to interpose the federal courts between the States and the people, as guardians of the people's federal rights.'" *Pennzoil,* at 19 (Brennan, J., Concurring), quoting *Juidice v. Vail,* 430 U.S. 327, 342 (1977) (Brennan, J.), Concurring) (quoting *Mitchum v. Foster,* 407 U.S. 225, 242 (1972).

"Only a state court adjudication that itself has preclusive effect can bring the *Rooker-Feldman* doctrine into play." *Cruz v. Melecio,* 204 F.3d 14, 21 (1st Cir. 2000), citing *Davis v. Bayless,* 70 F.3d 367, 376 (5th Cir. 1995). "*Rooker-Feldman* does not 'bar an action in federal court when that same action would be allowed in the state court of the rendering state.'" *Cruz,* at 21, quoting *Davis,* at 376. "[C]laims for declaratory and injunctive relief are general constitutional 'challenges to a state statute and hence not barred by the *Rooker-Feldman* doctrine.'" *Canty v. Larhette.* 201 F.3d 426, 426 (1st Cir. 1999), citing *Schneider v. Colegio do Abogodos de Puerto Rico,* 917 F.2d 620, 628 (1st Cir. 1900) (*Rooker-Feldman* doctrine does not bar facial challenges to state statutes).

438   [The *Rooker*] principle that federal appellate review of judgments rendered by state courts can occur in the Supreme Court on appeal or by writ of *certiorari* . . . applies only to review of the substance of state judgments, and that the federal action now before us involved solely a constitutional challenge to procedures for enforcement of the state judgment, totally apart from the merits of the state-court action itself.

Pennzoil, supra at 24-25 (Marshall, J., concurring), cite omitted.

439   M.G.L. 215:56A, 208:30, and 209B:5(a).

440   *N.H. Ins. Guar. Association v. Markem Corp.*, 424 Mass. 344, 352 (1997), quoting *Larson v. Domestic & Foreign Commerce Corp.*, 337 U.S. 682, 689-690 (1949), discussed at length in *Pennhurst, supra.*

441   *See Pennhurst* at 153.

> That the doctrine of sovereign immunity does not protect conduct which has been prohibited by the sovereign is clearly demonstrated by the case on which petitioners chiefly rely, *Larson v. Domestic & Foreign Commerce Corp.*, 337 U.S. 682 (1949). The <u>Larson</u> opinion teaches that the actions of state officials are not attributable to the State——are *ultra vires*—— in two different types of situations: **(1)** when the official is engaged in conduct that the sovereign has not authorized, and **(2)** when he has engaged in conduct that the sovereign has forbidden. A sovereign, like any other principal, cannot authorize its agent to violate the law. When an agent does so, his actions are considered *ultra vires* and he is liable for his own conduct under the law of agency. Both types of *ultra vires* conduct are clearly identified in <u>Larson.</u>

Pennhurst at 153 (Stevens, J., with whom Brennan, Marshall, Blackmun, JJ, join, dissenting).

442   *Rankin v. Howard.* 633 F.2d 844 (1980), *cert. denied sub nom.*, *Zeller v. Rankin*, 451 U.S. 939 (1980). *See further discussion below.* The rationale had been stated in *Pennhurst*: "Since the State [can] not authorize the action, the officer [is] `stripped of his official or representative character and subjected in his person to the consequences of his individual conduct."

443   *Pennhurst*, at 102, quoting *Young*, at 160. And it was restated in *Mireles v. Waco*, 502 U.S. 9, 12 (1991) ("judge is not immune for actions, though judicial in nature, taken in the absence of all jurisdiction").

444   "This rationale, of course, created the 'well-recognized irony' that an official's unconstitutional conduct constitutes state action under the Fourteenth Amendment but not the Eleventh Amendment." *Pennhurst* at 104-105, cite omitted.

445   *Crane v. Comm'r of Public Welfare*, 400 Mass. 46, 48 (1987).

446   *District of Columbia Court of Appeals v. Feldman*, 460 U.S. 462 (1983).

447   *Maymó-Meléndez v. Álvarez-/Ramírez*, 364 F.3d 27 (1st Cir. (P.R.) 2004), and *Van Arken v. City of Chicago*, 103 F.3d 1346 (7th Cir. 1997). My appeal to the First Circuit Court of Appeals may be seen in Drano Series #133 on

my website at *http://www.falseallegations.com/drano133-bbo-barbs-appellate-brief-x1804.htm* and my Petition for Writ of Certiorari filed in the United States Supreme Court may be seen in Drano Series #151 on my website at *http://www.falseallegations.com/drano151-bbo-barbs-ussct-petition-for-writ-cert-62705.htm.*

448   *Van Harken v. City of Chicago,* 103 F.3d 1346, 1348-1349 (7th Cir. 1997) (holding that *Rooker-Feldman* doctrine, precluding district court review of final judgment of state court in judicial proceedings, does not apply to administrative decisions). And where there had been no judgment against me in the state disciplinary proceeding, *Rooker-Feldman* was inapplicable. *Id.*

In *Maymó-Meléndez,* the court assumed that all administrative proceedings were judicial in nature. An oxymoron. In Massachusetts, bar disciplinary proceedings, like disciplinary proceedings for judges, are **non**judicial. *Matter of McKenney,* 384 Mass. 76, 88 (1981) (re discipline of judges). *Matter of London,* 427 Mass. 477, 482 (1998) (re discipline of lawyers), citing *Matter of Eisenhauer,* 426 Mass. at 454 (special protections afforded to criminal defendant are not applicable in bar discipline proceedings as they are **administrative in nature** and respondent is not entitled to full panoply of rights afforded criminal defendant) (emphasis supplied). *See also Matter of Jones,* 425 Mass. at 1007.

"*Younger,* even where it presumptively applies, is not implicated where the federal claims cannot be raised and resolved somewhere in the state process." *Maymó-Meléndez,* 364 F.3d 27, 36 (1st Cir. (P.R.) 2004), citing *Middlesex County Ethics Comm.,* 457 U.S. at 432.

"The scope and conditions of the various <u>Younger</u> exceptions remain uncertain. Underneath the surface is an unspoken policy debate as to how much should be done by federal courts and how far state courts are to be trusted." *Maymó-Meléndez,* 364 F.3d 27, 37 (1st Cir. (P.R.) 2004). "About all that is certain is that there is some reason for interim federal court intervention where core constitutional values are threatened during an ongoing state proceeding and there is a showing of irreparable harm that is both 'great and immediate.' *Id.,* citing *Younger,* 401 U.S. at 46.

Further, the *Rooker-Feldman* doctrine does not extended to administrative judgments. The *Feldman* decision illustrates the distinction. **It allowed the plaintiffs to challenge the constitutionality of the rule under which they had been denied admission to the bar, 460 U.S. at 487-88, but they were not allowed to challenge the denial itself.**

If they prevailed on their challenge to the rule, they might or might not be able to get a new hearing on the denial of their applications for admission, and to that extent the *Rooker-Feldman* doctrine does not prevent a form of collateral attack upon——or, better perhaps, an oblique swipe at——a state court judgment by a suit brought in a federal district court.

So when stating, "*Rooker-Feldman* does not insulate from federal challenge administrative rulings standing alone," the district court here committed a "Totem Pole reversible error." The first error was by the First Circuit: in *Maymó-Meléndez*, it misread *Van Harken*,103 F.3d at 1349, for there appears to be no language in *Van Harken* which supports the proposition set forth in *Maymó-Meléndez* regarding when *Rooker-Feldman* is applicable and when it is not. And the misreading by the appellate panel in Maymó-Meléndez of Van Harken caused Judge Young to err.

Notwithstanding the Totem Pole error, the district court also erred by stating that "My challenge emanates from the proceeding currently underway in the Massachusetts Board of Bar Overseers." That was not true. While there was a pending state disciplinary proceeding against me, I did not seek anything to be vacated or modified or amended. I sought declaratory judgments.

My collateral attack or oblique swipe at or challenge of the Bar rules, by seeking declaratory judgments, arises from my reading and learning the rules and seeing them in practice. It is clear that the rules I challenged are unconstitutional "**standing alone**." And my claims for money damages for the harm and damages I suffered as a result of the wrongful and/or unlawful application of those rules provide the controversy required to make claim to a declaratory judgment.

Lastly, the BBO does not have jurisdiction over civil rights claims pursuant to 42 U.S.C. §1983 and common-law or First Amendment claims.

In *Johnson v. Rodrigues (Orozco)*, 226 F.3d 1103, 1109 (C.A.10 (Utah) 2000), the *Rooker-Feldman* doctrine did not apply where the underlying claims presented a general challenge to the constitutionality of the Utah adoption statutory scheme and alleged a due process violation. Such claims were asserted under federal question jurisdiction, and constitutional claims do not require a federal court to make a custody determination. Id. at 1111. So, too, are My claims asserted under federal question jurisdiction, and constitutional claims do not require a federal court to make a determination of whether an attorney should be disciplined.

449   28 U.S.C. sec. 1332. *Ankenbrandt v. Richards,* 504 U.S. 689, 707 (U.S.La. 1992) (complaint sought monetary damages for alleged sexual and physical abuse of the children committed by the divorced father of the children and his female companion).

450   28 U.S.C. sec. 1332. *Ankenbrandt,* 504 U.S. at 705-706 (complaint sought monetary damages for alleged sexual and physical abuse of the children committed by the divorced father of the children and his female companion). *Younger v. Harris,* 401 U.S. 37 (1971). *Burford v. Sun Oil Co.,* 319 U.S. 315 (1943).

451   *Ankenbrandt,* 504 U.S. at 716 n. 9.

452   *Ankenbrandt,* 504 U.S. at 705.

453   *Id.* .

454   *Ankenbrandt,* 504 U.S. at 713 (Blackmun, J., concurring in the judgment).

455   *Id..*

456   *Dunn v. Cometa,* 238 F.3d 38, 41 (C.A.1 (Me.) 2001),

457   *Dunn,* 238 F.3d at 40-41.

458   *Ankenbrandt,* 504 U.S. at 704.

459   *Dunn,* 238 F.3d at 42.

460   *Ankenbrandt,* 504 U.S. at 717.

461   *Id.*

462   *Agg v. Flanagan,* 855 F.2d 336, 339 (C.A.6 (Ohio) 1988).

463   *Id.* at 339.

464   *Rubin v. Smith,* 817 F.Supp. 987, 991 (D.N.H. 1993).

465   The *Burford* abstention did not apply in *Johnson v. Rodrigues (Orozco),* 226 F.3d 1103, 1109 (C.A.10 (Utah) 2000), where the alleged father's constitutional and tort claims did not depend on the status of the parties. *Johnson,* at 1112. Instead, Johnson's claim required a determination whether Defendants' conduct was tortious. *See,* e.g., *Ankenbrandt,* 504 U.S. at 706 ("Where, as here, the status of the domestic relationship has been determined as a matter of state law, and in any event has no bearing on the underlying tort alleged, we have no difficulty concluding that *Burford* abstention is inappropriate in

this case."). Accordingly, abstention did not apply to Plaintiff Johnson's tort claim for intentional infliction of emotional distress. *Johnson*, at 1112.

And again, in *Thomas v. New York City*, 814 F.Supp. 1139 (E.D.N.Y.), the lower court concluded that the issue of "whether the state's procedure used to separate parent from child complie[d] with constitutional due-process requirements [was] squarely within [the] court's federal question jurisdiction," and the determination of the issue did "not entail any investigation into the fitness of the parent to care for child, or into the decree." *Id.* at 1147.

A similar disposition was reached in *Friedlander v. Friedlander*, 149 F.3d 739 (C.A.7 (Ill.) 1998). Where a case merely arises out a domestic relations dispute and does not seek any of the distinctive forms of relief typically associated with domestic relations jurisdiction, the domestic relations exception does not bar diversity jurisdiction. *Id.*, at 740, citing *Lloyd v. Loeffler*, 694 F.2d 489 (7th Cir.1982), which involved a suit for interference with custody; *McIntyre v. McIntyre*, 771 F.2d 1316 (9th Cir. 1985) (similar to *Lloyd*); *DiRuggiero v. Rodgers*, 743 F.2d 1009, 1018-20 (3d Cir.1984) (similar to *Lloyd*); and *Stone v. Wall*, 135 F.3d 1438 (11th Cir. (Fla.) 1998) (similar to *Lloyd*); "and better yet" [*Dunn* at 740] *Raftery v. Scott*, 756 F.2d 335, 337-38 (4th Cir.1985), and *Drewes v. Ilnicki*, 863 F.2d 469 (6th Cir. (Ohio) 1988), both cases like *Friedlander*, one of intentional infliction of emotional distress.

In *Stone*, the court held that the domestic relations exception to exercising diversity jurisdiction is to be read narrowly and ordinarily does not include third parties in its scope.

In <u>*Raftery*</u>, the court held that the exercise of diversity jurisdiction over former husband's action against former wife for intentional infliction of mental distress, arising out of former wife's effort to destroy and prevent rehabilitation of relationship between former husband and the parties' son, did not contravene domestic relations exception to federal diversity jurisdiction.

In *Drewes*, the court held that the domestic relations exception to diversity jurisdiction does not apply to suits that are actually tort or contract claims having only domestic relations overtones. 28 U.S.C. sec. 1332(a)(1).

Going one step further, the court in *Catz v. Chalker*, 142 F.3d 279 (C.A.6 (Ohio) 1998), held that former husband's action, seeking a declaration that the state divorce decree was void as a violation of due process, was not a core domestic relations case to which the domestic relations exception applied. The action did not seek declaration of marital or parental status, but instead presented a constitutional claim in which it was incidental that the underlying action involved a divorce. *Id.* Fourteenth Amendment. The domestic relations exception has no generally recognized application as a limitation on federal question jurisdiction; it applies only as a judicially implied limitation on diversity jurisdiction. *U.S. v. Johnson,* 114 F.3d 476 (C.A.4 (Va.) 1997).

In *Johnson v. Rodrigues (Orozco),* 226 F.3d 1103, 1109 (C.A.10 (Utah) 2000), where the father was not a party to the adoption proceeding, the *Rooker-Feldman* doctrine did not apply. Neither did the domestic relations exception apply, because the plaintiff's underlying claims general challenged the constitutionality of the Utah adoption statutory scheme and alleged a due process violation. Such claims were asserted under federal question jurisdiction, and constitutional claims do not require a federal court to make a custody determination. *Id.* at 1111.

In *Dunn, supra,* the remaining claims—which were dismissed, and which dismissals were vacated by the appeals court—asked "the court to decide [] a series of [] legal questions about the duties and privileges of parties to a then existing marriage." *Id.* at 42. "[T]he legal framework for those claims is not fully developed under state law (or at least we have found no like cases and Dunn has pointed us to none). If state law were clear, there would be no reason to abstain in this case." *Id.* at 43. (TB and JL did not ask this court to decide such questions.)

466   *Burford v. Sun Oil Co.,* 319 U.S. 315 (1943).

467   *Ankenbrandt,* 504 U.S. at 706.

468   "The domestic relations exception [] divests the federal courts of power to issue divorce, alimony, or child custody decrees." *Ankenbrandt,* 504 U.S. at 703.

469   *Hans v. Louisiana,* 134 U.S. 1 (1890)

470   CRS Annotated Constitution 1197. *Ex parte Young,* 209 U.S. 123, 28 S.Ct. 441 (1908). A seminal case is the first case which deals with a particular subject, like the first email of a particular thread on the Internet. For instance, SUBJECT: Corruption. The other emails read, SUBJECT: Re: Corruption.

471   CRS Annotated Constitution 1198. The fiction is that while the official is a state actor for purposes of suit against him, the claim that his action is unconstitutional removes the imprimatur of the State that would shield him under the Eleventh Amendment. *Ex parte Young,* 159-160.

472   CRS Annotated Constitution 1200. *Supra,* pp.798–800.

473   CRS Annotated Constitution 1201. The quoted phrase setting out the general principle is from the Judiciary Act of 1789, Sec. 16, 1 Stat. 82.

474   CRS Annotated Constitution 1202. The older cases are *Fenner v. Boykin* 271 U.S. 240 (1926); *Spielman Motor Sales Co. v. Dodge*, 295 U.S. 89 (1935); *Beal v. Missouri Pac. R. Co.*, 312 U.S. 45 (1941); *Watson v. Buck*, 313 U.S. 387 (1941); *Williams v. Miller*, 317 U.S. 599 (1942); *Douglas v. City of Jeannette*, 319 U.S. 157 (1943). There is a stricter rule against federal restraint of the use of evidence in state criminal trials. *Stefanelli v. Minard*, 342 U.S. 117 (1951); Pugach v. Dollinger, 365 U.S. 458 (1961). The Court reaffirmed the rule in *Perez v. Ledesma*, 401 U.S. 82 (1971). State officers may not be enjoined from testifying or using evidence gathered in violation of federal constitutional restrictions, *Cleary v. Bolger*, 371 U.S. 392 (1963), but the rule is unclear with regard to federal officers and state trials. Compare *Rea v. United States*, 350 U.S. 214 (1956), with *Wilson v. Schnettler*, 365 U.S. 381 (1961).

475   CRS Annotated Constitution 1203. E.g., *Douglas v. City of Jeannette*, 319 U.S. 157, 163-164 (1943); *Stefanelli v. Minard*, 342 U.S. 117, 122 (1951). *See also Terrace v. Thompson*, 263 U.S. 197, 214 (1923), Future criminal proceedings were sometimes enjoined. E.g., *Hague v. CIO*, 307 U.S. 496 (1939).

476   CRS Annotated Constitution 1204. *Dombrowski v. Pfister*, 380 U.S. 479 (1965). Grand jury indictments had been returned after the district court had dissolved a preliminary injunction, erroneously in the Supreme Court's view, so that it took the view that no state proceedings were pending as of the appropriate time. For a detailed analysis of the case, *see* Fiss, *Dombrowski*, 86 L. J.1103 (1977).

477   CRS Annotated Constitution 1205. "[T]he allegations in this complaint depict a situation in which defense of the State's criminal prosecution will not assure adequate vindication of constitutional rights. They suggest that a substantial loss of or impairment of freedoms of expression will occur if appellants must await the state court's disposition and ultimate review in this Court of any adverse determination. These allegations, if true, clearly show irreparable injury." Id., 380 U.S., 485–486.

478   CRS Annotated Constitution 1212. Maraist, Federal Injunctive Relief Against State Court Proceedings: The Significance of Dombrowski, 48 Tex. L. Rev. 535 (1970).

479   CRS Annotated Constitution 1213. *Younger v. Harris*, 401 U.S. 37 (1971); *Samuels v. Mackell*, 401 U.S. 66 (1971); *Boyle v. Landry*, 401 U.S. 77

(1971); *Perez v. Ledesma,* 401 U.S. 82 (1971); *Dyson v. Stein,* 401 U.S. 200 (1971); *Byrne v. Karalexis,* 401 U.S. 216 (1971).

480   CRS Annotated Constitution 1217. *Samuels v. Mackell,* 401 U.S. 66 (1971). The holding was in line with *Great Lakes Dredge & Dock Co. v. Huffman,* 319 U.S. 293 (1943).

481   28 U.S.C. Sec. 2283

482   CRS Annotated Constitution 1218. *Samuels v. Mackell,* 401 U.S. 66, 72 (1971).

483   CRS Annotated Constitution 1220. *Doran v. Salem Inn,* 422 U.S. 922 (1975) (preliminary injunction may issue to preserve status quo while court considers whether to grant declaratory relief); *Wooley v. Maynard,* 430 U.S. 705 (1977) (when declaratory relief is given, permanent injunction may be issued if necessary to protect constitutional rights). However, it may not be easy to discern when state proceedings will be deemed to have been instituted prior to the federal proceeding. E.g., *Hicks v. Miranda,* 422 U.S. 332 (1975); *Huffman v. Pursue. Ltd.,* 420 U.S. 592 (1975); see also *Hawaii Housing Authority v. Midkiff,* 467 U.S. 229, 238 (1984).

484   CRS Annotated Constitution 1221. *Huffman v. Pursue, Ltd.,* 420 U.S. 592 (1975); *Judice v. Vail,* 430 U.S. 327 (1977); *Trainor v. Hernandez,* 431 U.S. 434 (1977); *Moore v. Sims,* 442 U.S. 415 (1979); *Middlesex County Ethics Committee v. Garden State Bar Assn,* 457 U.S. 423 (1982).

Endnotes—Chapter 18

485   Nat Hentoff, "Orwellian Justice on Campus: Columbia University's Star Chamber," Village Voice (N.Y.: November 8-14, 2000), reminiscing on what Supreme Court Justice William O. Douglas taught him.

486   *Id.*

487   *The Encyclopaedia Britannica,* 11th ed. (1911), vol. XXV, p. 795.

488   The court of the Star Chamber developed from the judicial proceedings traditionally carried out by the king and his council, and was entirely separate from the common-law courts of the day. In the 15th century, under the Lancastrian and Yorkist kings, the role of the council as an equity and prerogative court in creased, and it extended its jurisdiction over criminal matters. Faster and less rigid than the common-law courts, its scope was extended by the Tudors.

Under Chancellor Wolsey's leadership (1515–29), the Court of Star Chamber became a political weapon, bringing actions against opponents to the decrees and edicts of Henry VIII. Wolsey also encouraged petitioners to use the Court of the Star Chamber as a court of original jurisdiction, not as a last resort after the common-law courts had failed. Depositions were taken from witnesses, but no jury was employed in the proceedings. Although its sentences included a wide variety of corporal punishments, including whipping, pillorying, and branding, those convicted were never sentenced to death.

The court remained active through the reigns of James I and Charles I.

The traditional hostility between equity and common law was aggravated by the use made of the Star Chamber by the Stuarts as a vehicle for exercising the royal prerogative, particularly over church matters, in defiance of Parliament. It was abolished by the Long Parliament in 1641. In its later period the court was so reviled that Star Chamber became a byword for unfair judicial proceedings. The court's harshness, however, has been exaggerated." *The Columbia Encyclopedia,* 6th ed. (Columbia University Press, 2003).

References cited by *The Encyclopedia Brittanica for the history of the Star Chamber: Sir Thomas Smith, Commonwealth of England* (1633); *Lord Bacon, History of Henry VII,* edited by J. R. Lumby (Cambridge, 1881); William Hudson, "Treatise of the Court of the Star Chamber," *Collectanea Juridica,* vol. ii; H. Hallam, *Constitutional History of England* (1876); W. S. Holdsworth, *History of English Law* (fol. 1902); G. W. Prothero, *Statutes and Constitutional Documents 1559-1625* (1894); W. Busch, *England under the Tudors* (1895); S. R. Gardiner, *History of England* 1603-1642 (1883-84); D. J. Medley, *English Constitutional History* (1907); and A. V. Dicey, *The Privy Council.*

489   *The Columbia Encyclopedia,* 6th ed. (Columbia University Press, 2003).

490   *Id.,* citing William Hudson, "Treatise of the Court of the Star Chamber," in vol. ii. of *Collectanea Juridica.*

491   *Encyc. Brit.* 11th ed., vol. XXV, p. 795.

492   *Id.*

493   By 1529, exercising jurisdiction in that court was a president, chancellor, treasurer, bishop, two chief justices, and two alternate justices. *Id.*

Although the court had been initially a court of appeal, Henry VIII, Chancellor Wolsey, and Archbishop of Canterbury Cranmer had encouraged plaintiffs to bring their cases directly to the Star Chamber, bypassing the lower courts entirely.

494   The role of Cardinal/Chancellor Wolsey was played by Orson Welles in that classic film, *Man for All Seasons*. In that same film, Cranmer, Archbishop of Canterbury, was brilliantly portrayed by Cyril Luckham.

495   *Id.*

496   *Id.*

497   *Id.*

498   *Faretta v. California*, 422 U.S. 806, 821 (1975).

499   *See Irwin v. Comm'r of Dept. of Youth Services*, 388 Mass. 810, 448 N.E.2d 721 (1983).

500   *Chisholm v. Georgia*, 2 U.S. (2 Dall.) 419 (1793). In consequence of the decision of *Chisholm*, which held that a state could be sued by a citizen of another state in *assumpsit*, the Eleventh Amendment was passed

501   *Pennhurst State School & Hosp. v. Halderman*, 465 U.S. 89, 97 (1984), quoting *Monaco v. Mississippi*, 292 U.S. 313, 325 (1934).

502   *Bradley v. Fisher*, 80 U.S. (13 Wall.) 335 (1871).

503   England's Court of the Exchequer, *Scott v. Stansfield*, 3 L.R. Ex. 220, 223 (1868).

504   … *Floyd* frequently is cited as the foundation of the American judicial immunity doctrine. The federal courts' lavish reliance on this Star Chamber decision is puzzling. While this immunity doctrine focuses exclusively on civil liability for judicical acts, *Floyd* is concerned not with liability but with the proper method of disciplining alleged misconduct of judges. Indeed, *Floyd's* central concern is not judicial immunity at all, but judicial independence from the executive branch of government. The American constitutional system largely has resolved the problem that preoccupied the judges who wrote *Floyd*.

Robert Craig Waters, "Judicial Immunity vs. Due Process: When should a Judge Be Subject to Suit." Cato Journal, vol. 7, no. 8 (Fall 1987), page 461.

505   *Bradley v. Fisher*, 80 U.S. (13 Wall.) 335, 351 (1871). "The Supreme Court first relied on Floyd as a precedent for judicial immunity in *Bradley v. Fisher*, 80 U.S. (13 Wall.) 335, 351 (1872)." Robert Craig Waters, "Judicial Immunity vs. Due Process: When should a Judge Be Subject to Suit." Cato Journal, vol. 7, no. 8 (Fall 1987), page 461.

506   *Bradley*, 80 U.S. at 349 n. 16.

507   Legislative immunity was confirmed in *Tenney v. Brandhove*, 341 U.S. 367 (1951).

508   *See Gildea v. Ellershaw*, 363 Mass. 800, 815*ff*, 298 N.E.2d 847, 855*ff* (1973). While Judge Learned Hand's argument, as summarized in *Gildea*, regarding immunity was impressive, the bottom line of it was, We must not sue ten public employees, of whom nine are angels, in hopes of catching the one devil amongst them. While admirable in the context of social morality—If ten allegedly starving people come to our door, we must feed them all even if one of them is not starving—it defeats the notion of fundamental fairness, the cornerstone of due process, when it is applied to the judicial system. The practical effect of giving immunity—particularly judicial and quasi-judicial immunity and, sometimes, qualified immunity—has been to wipe out accountability. With no allegedly legal requirement of accountability, gross negligence, incompetence, bad faith, ulterior motives, and the like, have been allowed to blossom and proliferate in abundance. The public has thereby only suffered a constitutional right to seek a remedy, by having recourse to the laws, for wrongs committed against them.

509   "*This Constitution, and the laws of the United States which shall be made in pursuance thereof...shall be <u>the supreme law of the land</u>; and the judges in every state shall be bound thereby, anything in the Constitution or laws of any state to the contrary notwithstanding.*" U.S. Constitution, art. 6 (emphasis supplied).

510   It may also not preclude a citizen either of Massachusetts or of a foreign State from suing Massachusetts in federal or in State court. This proposition rests on a similar interpretation of the Eleventh Amendment. The "real" or first prong of the Amendment, the one not allowing a State to be sued by a citizen from a foreign State in federal court, was ratified by Congress. The second prong, the one not allowing a citizen to sue his or her own State in federal court, arose by judicial fiat. "[I]t is not the proper province of a federal court to rewrite a statute under the guise of interpretation." *Aulson v. Blanchard*, 83 F.3d 1, 4 (1996) (Selya, J.).

511   *Hans v. Louisiana*, 134 U.S. 1, 10 S.Ct. 504 (1890).

512   While the constitutional principle of sovereign immunity does pose a bar to federal jurisdiction over suits against nonconsenting States, see, *e.g.*, *Principality of Monaco*, 292 U.S., at 322-323, 54 S.Ct. 745, this is not the only structural basis of sovereign immunity implicit in the constitutional design. Rather, "[t]here is also the postulate that States

of the Union, still possessing attributes of sovereignty, shall be immune from suits, without their consent, save where there has been 'a surrender of this immunity in the plan of the convention.' " *Ibid.* (quoting The Federalist No. 81); accord, *Blatchford, [v. Native Village of Noatak*, 501 U.S. 775,] 781, 111 S.Ct. 2578 (1991); *Seminole Tribe, supra*, at 68, 116 S.Ct. 1114. This separate and distinct structural principle is not directly related to the scope of the judicial power established by Article III, but inheres in the system of federalism established by the Constitution. In exercising its Article I powers Congress may subject the States to private suits in their own courts only if there is "compelling evidence" that the States were required to surrender this power to Congress pursuant to the constitutional design. *Blatchford*, 501 U.S., at 781, 111 S.Ct. 2578.

Alden v. Maine, 527 U.S. 706, 730-731, 119 S.Ct. 2240, 2255 (1999) [emphasis supplied].

513   See note 27, *supra.*

514   "The Ninth Amendment protection of other 'rights retained by the people.' As already discussed, this important provision, insisted upon by the Anti-Federalists in 1791, has been dead-lettered by a combination of judicial doctrines, maxims and sophistries that in essence leave the people with few or no reserved rights." Roger Roots, "Constitutional Dead Letters."

515   *Marbury v. Madison*, 5 U.S. (1 Cranch.) 103 (1803),

516   *Pennhurst State School & Hosp. v. Halderman*, 465 U.S. 89,166 n. 51 (1984) (Stevens, Dissent).

517   Antonin Scalia's address entitled "Historical Anomalies in Administrative Law," delivered the Supreme Court Historical Society's 1985 Annual Lecture on May 13, 1985 in the restored Supreme Court chamber of the U.S. Capitol. His remarks are preserved at http://www.supremecourthistory.org/04_library/subs_volumes/04_c19_i.html.

518   *Marbury v. Madison*, 5 U.S. (1 Cranch.) 103 (1803), that '[t]he very essence of civil liberty certainly consists in the right of every individual to claim the protection of the laws, whenever he receives an injury.'"

519   *Cf. Morris v. Mass.Maritime Academy*, 409 Mass. 179, 187, 565 N.E.2d 422, 428 (1991) (waiving immunity to admiralty claims under Mass. Tort Claims Act).

520   *"Every subject of the Commonwealth ought to find a certain remedy, by having recourse to the laws, for all injuries or wrongs which he may receive in his person, property, or character. . . ."* Article 11 of the Massachusetts Declaration of Rights. Note that there is no explicit exclusion of the Commonwealth in the article.

521   Massachusetts General Laws, chapter 258.

522   "Departures are, of course, occasionally required by changes in the fabric of our society." *Pennhurst* at 164.

> This is an especially odd context in which to repudiate settled law because changes in our social fabric favor limitation rather than expansion of sovereign immunity. The concept that the sovereign can do no wrong and that citizens should be remediless in the face of its abuses is more a relic of medieval thought than anything else.

Id. at 164 n. 48.

523   M.G.L. c. 258 contains the list of causes of actions explicitly excepted from the imagined sovereign immunity, already abrogated by Article V. That list diminishes the immunity which the Massachusetts Constitution never intended to allow the Commonwealth or its agents.

"At the time [the *Massachusetts Tort Claims Act*] was enacted [in 1978], the Commonwealth's common law sovereign immunity had been abrogated for nearly one century as to certain claims." *Irwin v. Commissioner of Dept. of Youth Services*, 388 Mass. 810, 813, 448 N.E.2d 721, 724 (1983).

In *Irwin*, the Massachusetts highest court reviewed in excruciating detail the history of the Tort Claims Act after two "significant decisions of this court" [*Id.* at 816]: in 1973, *Morash & Sons, Inc. v. Com.*, 363 Mass. 612, 618, 296 N.E.2d 461, 465 (1973) (holding that "municipal and sovereign immunity are logically indefensible"), and four years later, *Whitney v. Worcester*, 373 Mass. 208, 366 N.E.2d 1210 (1977). In *Whitney*, the high court announced its intention to abrogate the sovereign immunity doctrine, retroactively to the date of the decision in *Morash*, should the Legislature have failed to act by the conclusion of its 1978 session. *Whitney*.

So the Legislature effected some loosening of sovereign immunity in the Commonwealth.

Given the explicit displeasure of Massachusetts' highest court with the "logically indefensible" sovereign immunity doctrine, it would not likely be offensive to the Massachusetts' high-court jurists if this court were to use its discretion to invoke the supremacy clause to abrogate completely Massachusetts' sovereign immunity in the federal courts, if not also in the state courts.

Not included amongst the causes of action excepted from the waiver statute, M.G.L. c. 258, are civil rights actions. *See,* for example, *Bain v. Springfield,* 424 Mass. 758, 678 N.E.2d 155, (1997), where the Supreme Judicial Court held that the antidiscrimination statute waived the Commonwealth's sovereign immunity and that of its political subdivisions by including them in the statutory definition of persons and employers subject to the statute. In that same case, the Commonwealth and its subdivisions were also held to be liable for punitive damages. *Bain,* at 424 Mass. at 762-763, 678 N.E.2d at 158-159.

The consent of the Commonwealth to suit may be derived from the judiciary as well as from the legislature [*Morash,* 363 Mass. at 615-616, 296 N.E.2d at 464, but, as the Supreme Judicial Court emphasized, "the doctrine of sovereign immunity is 'logically indefensible.'" *Hallett v. Town of Wrentham,* 398 Mass. 550, 558, 499 N.E.2d 1189, at 1194 (1986), quoting *Morash,* 363 Mass. at 618-619, 296 N.E.2d at 465-465. "[W]e stress that abrogation of governmental immunity need not necessarily mean that governmental entities would be liable for all harm which results from the conduct of their activities." *Whitney v. Worcester,* 373 Mass. at 212, 366 N.E.2d at 1213 (1977).

524   Although by its terms the Amendment applies only to suits against a State by citizens of another State, our cases have extended the Amendment's applicability to suits by citizens against their own States.

Board of Trustees of the University of Alabama v. Garrett, No. 99-1240 (11th Cir. 2/21/2001) (cite omitted).

525   *Whitney,* 373 Mass. at 212, 366 N.E.2d at 1213 (treatises omitted).

526   *Id.,* cites omitted.

527   GiGi had a "constitutional right to a safe and appropriate environment and adequate medical care." *McNemar v. Department of Public Health,* 53 Mass.App.Ct. 1113, 761 N.E.2d 551 (2002) (unpublished). "This includes taking reasonable steps to prevent foreseeable suicides." Id.

528   It is elementary that "when a State decides to alleviate some of the hardships of poverty by providing medical care, the manner in which it dispenses benefits is subject to constitutional limitations." *Maher v. Roe,* 432 U.S. 464, 469-470 (1977). While the State retains wide latitude to decide the manner in which it will allocate benefits, it may

not use criteria which discriminatorily burden the exercise of a fundamental right. *Massachusetts Pub. Interest Research Group v. Secretary of the Commonwealth,* 375 Mass. 85, 93, 375 N.E.2d 1175, 1181 (1978). *Opinion of the Justices,* 375 Mass. 795, 806, 376 N.E.2d 810, 818 (1978), and cases cited.

Moe v. Secretary of Administration and Finance, 382 Mass. 629, 652, 417 N.E.2d 387, 401 (1981).

529   *Cf. Hopper v. Callahan,* 408 Mass. 621, 624-625, 562 N.E.2d 822, 824-825 (1990) (constitutional rights of involuntarily committed individuals clearly established at time of defendants' acts).

530   The Massachusetts Supreme Judicial Court has never analyzed the confluence of Article V, Mass. Declaration of Rights, and the Eleventh Amendment to the United States Constitution. *Cf.Attorney General v. Desilets,* 418 Mass 316, 321, 636 N.E.2d 233, 235 (1994) (SJC chose not to adopt reasoning of the United States Supreme Court under the First Amendment).

531   *Alden v. Maine,* 527 U.S. 706, 764-765, 119 S.Ct. 2240, 2271 (1999).

532   *Alden,* 527 U.S. at 730, 119 S.Ct. at 2254 (emphasis supplied), quoting 292 U.S., at 322-323, 54 S.Ct. 745 (quoting The Federalist No. 81) (footnote omitted).

533   John Adams, one of a committee of 30, drafted "'a Declaration of Rights, and the Form of a Constitution,' to be laid before the Convention at its second session." Mass. Constitutional Convention, 1779-1780), Jour., p. 26.

To waive that constitutional mandate for accountability in Massachusetts, the procedures for an initiative petition, described in Article LXXIV (ratified in 1944) of the Articles of Amendment to the Constitution of the Commonwealth of Massachusetts, must be followed.

Those procedures have never been invoked vis-à-vis Art. V, leaving in effect the unequivocal mandate memorialized by our forefathers in Art. V of the Declaration of Rights: to wit, the mandate that all three branches of government at all times must be accountable to the people. Thus the State's waiver of the doctrine of immunity for public employees has long been effectuated.

In sum, since its ratification almost 223 years ago, Art. V has never been repealed, altered, or amended by any Massachusetts legislature. With accountability mandated at the convention, it is impossible for agents of the sovereign Massachusetts or its branches of government to be afforded absolute judicial or quasi-judicial or qualified immunity,[9] for where the forefathers of Massachusetts memorialized in Art. V the belief unequivocally that "the several magistrates and officers" of all three branches of government at all times must be accountable to the people, the State's waiver has long been effectuated.

Notwithstanding Art. V, in *LaLonde v. Eissner*, 405 Mass. 207, 210, 539 N.E.2d 538, 540-541 (1989), a court-appointed psychiatrist performing an allegedly essential function by rendering services to the court was deemed a "quasi-judicial" officer involved in an integral part of the judicial process and therefore entitled to immunity in the performance of those services.

Waiver and/or consent as issues here are therefore inapplicable. Notwithstanding that conclusion, for waiver of a State's constitutional mandate may only be effectuated by a state statute or constitutional provision. *Atascadero State Hospital v. Scanlon*, 473 U.S. 234, 238 n. 1, 105 S.Ct. 3142, 3145 n. 1 (1985). Massachusetts needs not consent anew: its constitutional article has never been repealed, altered, or amended in the 221 years since its ratification on 14 October 1780.

534   L. H. Butterfield, ed., The Adams Paper: Diary and Autobiography of John Adams, vol. 2, p. 401 n. 1 (Cambridge, Mass. Belknap Press of Harvard University, 1962).

535   *Moody v. Daggett*, 429 U.S. 78, 92 n. 5, 97 S.Ct. 274, 281 n. 5 (U.S. 1976) (NO. 74-6632); *Klopfer v. State of N.C.*, 386 U.S. 213, 226 n. 21, 87 S.Ct. 988, 995 n. 21 (U.S.N.C. 1967).

536   *Id.* at 2293.

537   *Hafer v. Melo*, 502 U.S. 21, 29 (1991), citing <u>Burns v. Reed</u>, 500 U.S. 478, 486-487 (1991).

538   "No such employee or official shall be indemnified under this section for violation of any such civil rights if he acted in a grossly negligent, willful or malicious manner." M.G.L. c. 258, §9. *Breault v. Chairman of Bd. of Fire Com'rs of Springfield*, 401 Mass. 26, 35 (1987) (immunity does not protect public officials from liability for intentional torts while performing ministerial acts). M.G.L. c. 258, §10.

539   *Memorial Hosp. v. Maricopa County*, 415 U.S. 250 (1974).

540   *Anderson v. Creighton*, 483 U.S. 635, 638 (1987), quoting *Malley v. Briggs*, 475 U.S. 335, 341 (1986) (emphasis supplied).

541   *Harlow v. Fitzgerald*, 457 U.S. 800, 815, 102 S.Ct. 2727 (U.S.Dist.Col. 1982).

542   *Id. See also Harlow*, 457 U.S. at 805 n. 9, 102 S.Ct. at 2732 n. 9. .

543   Good faith or qualified immunity has two aspects, an objective and a subjective aspect. *Harlow*, at 815. "The objective element involves a presumptive knowledge of and respect for 'basic, unquestioned constitutional rights.'" Harlow, at 815, quoting *Wood v. Strickland*, 420 U.S. 308, 322 (1975). *See also Laubinger v. Department of Revenue*, 41 Mass.App.Ct. 598, 605, 672 N.E.2d 554. 559 (1996) ("Immunity does not follow from the good faith of the official; the test is objective, that is, 'whether a reasonable [official] would have known that the conduct violated established constitutional norms in the circumstances as they appeared to the defendant [official]'"), quoting *Pasqualone* v. Gately, 422 Mass. 398, 402-403, 662 N.E.2d 1034, 1038 (1996) and citing *Martino v. Hogan*, 37 Mass.App.Ct. 710, 718, 643 N.E.2d 53, 59 (1994).

544   *See* Erwin Chemerinsky, "Absolute Immunity for Judicial," *Federal Jurisdiction*, 3d ed. (Aspen Law & Business, Aspen Publishers), p. 502, n. 45, citing *Stump v. Sparkman, infra*, and two law review articles discussing it

545   *Sparkman v. McFarlin*, 552 F.2d 172 (7th Cir. 1977). *See also* Cherminsky, at 502, n. 45.

546   *Id.*

547   552 F.2d, at 176.

548   *Stump v. Sparkman*, 435 U.S. 349, 98 S.Ct. 1099, 55 L.Ed.2d 331 (1978). Chemerinsky, "Absolute Immunity for Judicial," at 502, nn. 46 amd 47. Unfortunately, Professor Chemerinsky's criticisms of absolute immunity for judges does not go far enough and his book *Federal Jurisdiction* is also absent any discussion or analysis of whether there is a constitutional basis for absolute immunity. *See Pulliam v. Allen*, 466 U.S. 522, 104 S.Ct. 1970 (1984).

549   Erwin Chemerinsky, "Absolute Immunity for Judicial," *Federal Jurisdiction*, 3d ed. (Aspen Law & Business, Aspen Publishers), p. 502, n. 45

550   The Court made this point clear in Bradley, 13 Wall., at 357, where it stated: "[T]his erroneous manner in which [the court's] jurisdiction was exercised, however it may have affected the validity of the act, did not make the act any less a judicial act; nor did it render the defendant liable to answer in damages for it at the suit of the plaintiff, as though the court had proceeded without having any jurisdiction whatever . . . ."

Stump v. Sparkman, 435 U.S. at 359, 98 S.Ct. at 1106.

551   *Id.*, at 502, n. 45

552   Attorney Gary Zerman in an email to me. If he has written it elsewhere, I know not where.

553   Robert Craig Waters, "Judicial Immunity vs. Due Process: When should a Judge Be Subject to Suit." Cato Journal, vol. 7, no. 8 (Fall 1987), page 461.

554   *Id.* at p. 461.

555   *Id.* at p. 462.

556   *Id.* at p. 469.

557   *Id.*.

558   *Id.* at p. 470.

559   *See* note 76, *infra.*

560   . . . To preserve the integrity of the judicial process, the courts always should presume that a trial court properly exercised its jurisdiction. But they should permit a plaintiff to overcome this presumption by showing that the judge acted with actual malice, consisting of a knowing or reckless disregard of due process. Specifically, if the court is to enjoy immunity, it must afford three things—notice, a chance to be heard, and a method of appeal. Then, and only then, would an irrebuttable presumption of immunity exist requiring dismissal of any subsequent suit against the judge.

Id. at p. 471. Never, never, never should there be an irrebuttable presumption of immunity allowed in our justice system. Never, never, never should there be immunity, p-e-r-i-o-d. Waters' plan is totally unacceptable. It is too open to too many abuses and misuses.

561   Professor Erwin Chemerinsky, "Criticism of Absolute Immunities," *Federal Jurisdiction*, 3rd ed. (Aspen Law & Business, Aspen Publishers), p. 501.

Endnotes—Chapter 19

562   To see the Complaint discussed in this anecdote, *see http://www.falseallegations.com/drano5-complaint-linn.htm.*

563   Around 2000, I filed on Dick's behalf a civil rights action in United Stated District Court at Boston against Christopher Salt and some others who involved themselves in the Juvenile Court case: Christopher Salt, Eileen Kern,

Sandra Fyfe, Jack McCarthy, Jr., and Eli Newberger, a malicious medical whore who scams the court by pretending to be an expert in sex abuse and in so do-ing, devastates the lives of innocent parents. (Read Boston University Profes-sor Margaret Hagen's *Whores of the Court.*) It is in that case that I learned many of the facts included here. Unfortunately, the case was dismissed by a federal judge finding that some of the defendants were protected by immunity and others were not "state actors" (a legal term used in federal civil rights cases). The Complaint of that suit is on my website, *http://www.falseallegations.com.* It is Drano Series #5. Because the Complaint was filed so long after the events, I was relying on two cases—one, a Massachusetts case, and the other, a federal case—to support the belated findings.

564   Over a decade later, I received a copy of an alleged docket sheet, but I had reason to believe it was fabricated. See Chapter 25.

565   *See* 'The Fatherphobia of Family Courts" by Phyllis Schlafly, February 2, 2005, *http://www.eagleforum.org/column/2005/feb05/05-02-02.html.*

566   *See Ankenbrandt v. Richards,* 504 U.S. 689, 703 (1992).

567   42 U.S.C. § 1983, the Federal Civil Rights Act. *See Will v. Michigan Dept. of State Police,* 491 U.S. 58 (1989).

568   *City of Chicago v. International College of Surgeons,* 522 U.S. 156, 118 S.Ct. 523 (U.S.Ill., 1997).

> The "Dictionary Act" provision that a "person" includes "bodies politic and corporate" fails to evidence such an intent. This Court's ruling in *Monell v. New York City Dept. of Social Services,* 436 U.S. 658, 98 S.Ct. 2018, 56 L.Ed.2d 611—which held that a municipality is a person under § 1983—is not to the contrary, since States are protected by the Eleventh Amendment while municipalities are not.

Will v. Michigan Dept. of State Police, 491 U.S. 58, 109 S.Ct. 2304, 2307-2311 (U.S.Mich., 1989).

Important to note is that the Eleventh Amendment mentioned in *Will* is not the original or real Eleventh Amendment, it is the Eleventh Amendment made by the Supreme Court justices in 1890. NOTE: The U.S. Supreme Court is part of the judicial branch of government *not* part of the legislative branch.

> "The injunctive relief provided by this subsection shall not restrict any right which any person (or class of persons) may have under any statute or common law to seek enforcement of any standard or limita-

tion or to seek any other relief (including relief against the Administrator, the Secretary, or a State agency)." 33 U.S.C. § 1415(g)(5).

Respondents' right to proceed under § 1983 in light of these statutory provisions could have been made more plain only had Congress substituted the citation "42 U.S.C. § 1983" for the words "any statute" in the saving clauses.

Middlesex County Sewerage Authority v. National Sea Clammers Ass'n, 453 U.S. 1, 101 S.Ct. 2615 (U.S.N.J., 1981).

Mr. Justice BRENNAN, with whom Mr. Justice MARSHALL joins as to Parts I, II, and III, concurring in the judgment.

For the reasons set forth in my dissent in *Edelman v. Jordan,* 415 U.S. 651, 687, 94 S.Ct. 1347, 1367 (1974), I concur in the judgment of the Court.[FN1]

> FN1. In *Edelman v. Jordan,* 415 U.S., at 687-688, 94 S.Ct., at 1367-1368, I stated: "This suit is brought by Illinois citizens against Illinois officials. In that circumstance, **Illinois may not invoke the Eleventh Amendment, since that Amendment bars only federal court suits against States by citizens of other States. [NOTE: Emphasis supplied.]** Rather, the question is whether Illinois may avail itself of the nonconstitutional but ancient doctrine of sovereign immunity as a bar to respondent's claim for retroactive AABD payments. **In my view Illinois may not assert sovereign immunity for the reason I expressed in dissent in *Employees v. Missouri Public Health Dept.,* 411 U.S. 279, 298, 93 S.Ct. 1614, 1625, 36 L.Ed.2d 251 (1973):** the States surrendered that immunity in Hamilton's words, 'in the plan of the Convention,' that formed the Union, at least insofar as the States granted Congress specifically enumerated powers." . . . *350 **1150 I

. . . This is sufficient to sustain the Court's holding that such notice is not barred by the Eleventh Amendment. But the Court goes on to conclude, in what is patently dicta, that a State is not a "person" for purposes of 42 U.S.C. § 1983, Rev.Stat. § 1979.[FN2]

> FN2. Section 1983 states: "Every **person** who, under color of any statute, ordinance, regulation, custom, or usage, of any State or Territory, subjects, or causes to be subjected, any citizen of the United States or other person within the jurisdiction thereof to

the deprivation of any rights, privileges, or immunities secured by the Constitution and laws, shall be liable to the party injured in an action at law, suit in equity, or other proper proceeding for redress."

This conclusion is significant because, only three Terms ago, *Fitzpatrick v. Bitzer*, **427 U.S. 445, 96 S.Ct. 2666, 49 L.Ed.2d 614 (1976), held that "Congress may, in determining what is 'appropriate legislation' for the purpose of enforcing the provisions of the Fourteenth Amendment, provide for private suits against States or state officials which are constitutionally impermissible in other contexts."** *Id.,* at 456, 96 S.Ct., at 2671. **If a State were a "person" for purposes of § 1983, therefore, its immunity under the Eleventh *351 Amendment would be abrogated by the statute.** [FN3] *Edelman v. Jordan, supra,* had held that § 1983 did not override state immunity, for the reason, as the Court later stated in *Fitzpatrick,* that **"[t]he Civil Rights Act of 1871, 42 U.S.C. § 1983, had been held in** *Monroe v. Pape,* **365 U.S. 167, 187-191, 81 S.Ct. 473, 484, 5 L.Ed.2d 492 (1961), to exclude cities and other municipal corporations from its ambit; that being the case, it could not have been intended to include States as parties defendant."** 427 U.S., at 452, 96 S.Ct., at 2669.[FN4] **The premise of this reasoning was undercut last Term, however, when** *Monell v. New York City Dept. of Social Services,* **436 U.S. 658, 98 S.Ct. 2018, 56 L.Ed.2d 611 (1978), upon re-examination of the legislative history of § 1983, held that a municipality was indeed a "person" for purposes of that statute.** [FN5] As I stated in my concurrence in *Hutto v. Finney,* 437 U.S. 678, 703, 98 S.Ct. 2565, 2581, 57 L.Ed.2d 522 (1978), *Monell* **made it "surely at least an open **1151 question whether § 1983 properly construed does not make the States liable for relief of all kinds, notwithstanding the Eleventh Amendment."**

FN3. There is no question but that § 1983 was enacted by Congress under § 5 of the Fourteenth Amendment. Section 1983 was originally the first section of an Act entitled "An Act to enforce the Provisions of the Fourteenth Amendment to the Constitution of the United States . . . ." 17 Stat. 13.

. . .

Thus, the Court today decides a question of major significance without ever having had the assistance of a considered presentation of the issue, either in briefs or in arguments. The result is pure judicial fiat.

II

This fiat is particularly disturbing because it is most likely incorrect. <u>Section 1983</u> was originally enacted as § 1 of the Civil Rights Act of 1871. The Act was enacted for the purpose of enforcing the provisions of the Fourteenth Amendment.[FN9] That Amendment exemplifies the "vast transformation" worked on the structure of federalism in this Nation by the Civil War. <u>Mitchum v. Foster, 407 U.S. 225, 242, 92 S.Ct. 2151, 2162, 32 L.Ed.2d 705 (1972)</u>. *355 The prohibitions of that Amendment "are directed to the States. . . . They have reference to actions of the political body denominated a State, by whatever instruments or in whatever modes that action may be taken." <u>Ex parte Virginia, 100 U.S. 339, 346-347, 25 L.Ed. 676 (1880)</u>.[FN10] The fifth section of the Amendment provides Congress with the power to enforce these prohibitions "by appropriate legislation." "Congress, by virtue of the fifth section . . ., may enforce the prohibitions whenever they are disregarded by either the Legislative, the Executive, or the Judicial Department of the State. The mode of enforcement is left to its discretion." <u>Virginia v. Rives, 100 U.S. 313, 318, 25 L.Ed. 667 (1880)</u>.

The prohibitions of the Fourteenth Amendment and Congress' power of enforcement**1153 are thus directed at the States themselves, not merely at state officers. It is logical to assume, therefore, that <u>§ 1983</u>, in effectuating the provisions of the Amendment by "interpos[ing] the federal courts between the States and the people, as guardians of the people's federal rights," <u>Mitchum v. Foster, supra, 407 U.S., at 242, 92 S.Ct., at 2162</u>, is also addressed to the States themselves. Certainly Congress made this intent plain enough on the face of the statute.

Section 1 of the Civil Rights Act of 1871 created a federal cause of action **against "any person" who,** "under color of any law, statute, ordinance, regulation, custom, or usage of any State," **deprived another of "any rights, privileges, or immunities secured by the Constitution of the United States."** On *356 February 25, 1871, less than two months before the enactment of the Civil Rights Act, **Congress provided that "in all acts hereafter passed . . . the word 'person' may extend and be applied to bodies politic and corporate . . . unless the context shows that such words were intended to be used in a more limited sense."** [FN11] **§ 2, 16 Stat. 431. *Monell,* held that "[s]ince there is nothing in the 'context' of the Civil Rights Act calling for a restricted interpretation** of the word 'person,' the language of that section should prima facie be construed to include 'bodies politic' among the entities that could be sued." 436 U.S., at 689-690 n. 53, 98 S.Ct., at 2035. Even the **Court's opinion today does not dispute the fact that in 1871 the phrase "bodies politic and corporate" would certainly have referred to the States.** [FN12] See *Heim v. McCall,* 239 U.S. 175, 188, 36 S.Ct. 78, 82, 60 L.Ed. 206 (1915); *McPherson v. Blacker,* 146 U.S. 1, 24, 13 S.Ct. 3, 6, 36 L.Ed. 869 (1892); *357 *Poindexter v. Greenhow,* 114 U.S. 270, 288, 5 S.Ct. 903, 912, 29 L.Ed. 185 (1885); *Cotton v. United States,* 11 How. 229, 231, 13 L.Ed. 675 (1851); *Chisholm v. Georgia,* 2 Dall. 419, 447, 1 L.Ed. 440 (Iredell, J.), 468 (Cushing, J.) (1793); *Utah State Building Comm'n v. Great American Indemnity Co.,* 105 Utah 11, 16, 140 P.2d 763, 766 (1943); *Board of Comm'rs of Hamilton County v. Noyes,* 3 Am.L.Rec. 745, 748 (Super. Ct.Cincinnati 1874); 1 J. Wilson, Works 305 (1804); cf. *Keith v. Clark,* 97 U.S. 454, 460-461, 24 L.Ed. 1071 (1877); *Munn v. Illinois,* 94 U.S. 113, 124, 24 L.Ed. 77 (1877); *Georgia v. Stanton,* 6 Wall. 50, 76-77, 18 L.Ed. 721 (1868); *Butler v. Pennsylvania,* 10 How. 402, 416-417, 13 L.Ed. 472 (1851); *Penhallow v. Doane's Administrators,* 3 Dall. 54, 92-93, 1 L.Ed. 507 (1795) (Iredell, J.); Mass. Const., Preamble. **Indeed, during the very debates surrounding the enactment of the Civil Rights Act, States were referred to as bodies politic and corporate.** See, *e. g.,* Cong. Globe, 42d **1154 Cong., 1st Sess., 661-662 (1871) (hereinafter Globe) (Sen. Vickers) ("What is a State? Is it not a body politic and corporate?"); cf. *id.,* at 696 (Sen. Edmunds). **Thus the expressed intent of Congress, manifested virtually simultaneously with the enactment of the Civil Rights Act of 1871, was that the States themselves, as bodies corporate and politic, should be embraced by the term "person" in § 1 of that Act.**

FN11. *Monell v. New York City Dept. of Social Services,* 436 U.S. 658, 98 S.Ct. 2018, 56 L.Ed.2d 611 (1978), **held that the word "may" in the Act was to be interpreted as the equivalent of "shall": "Such a mandatory use of the extended meanings of the words defined by the Act is . . . required for it to perform its intended function—to be a guide to 'rules of construction' of Acts of Congress.** See [Cong. Globe, 41st Cong., 3d Sess., 775 (1871)] (remarks of Sen. Trumbull)." *Id.,* at 689 n. 53, 98 S.Ct., at 2035.

FN12. The phrase would also have referred to the United States. As Mr. Chief Justice Marshall stated: "**The United States is a government, and, consequently, a body politic and corporate . . . ..**"

United States v. Maurice, 26 Fed.Cas. No. 15747, 2 Brock. 96, 109 (CC Va.1823). See *Van Brocklin v. Tennessee,* 117 U.S. 151, 154, 6 S.Ct. 670, 672, 29 L.Ed. 845 (1886); *Dugan v. United States,* 3 Wheat. 172, 178, 4 L.Ed. 362 (1818) (argument of Attorney General William Wirt). In construing the meaning of the term "person" in a Texas law creating a statute of limitations for suits to recover real estate "as against any person in peaceable and adverse possession thereof," this Court stated: **"Of course, the United States were not bound by the laws of the State, yet the word 'person' in the statute would include them as a body politic and corporate.** Sayles, Art. 3140; *Martin v. State,* 24 Texas, 61, 68." *Stanley v. Schwalby,* 147 U.S. 508, 514, 517, 13 S.Ct. 418, 422, 37 L.Ed. 259 (1893). See *United States v. Shirey,* 359 U.S. 255, 257 n. 2, 79 S.Ct. 746, 747 n. 2, 3 L.Ed.2d 789 (1959); *Ohio v. Helvering,* 292 U.S. 360, 370, 54 S.Ct. 725, 727, 78 L.Ed. 1307 (1934); cf. *Pfizer Inc. v. India,* 434 U.S. 308, 315-316 n. 15, 98 S.Ct. 584, 589 n. 15, 54 L.Ed.2d 563 (1978).

The legislative history of the Civil Rights Act of 1871 reinforces this conclusion. The Act was originally reported to the House as H.R. 320 by Representative Shellabarger. At that time Representative Shellabarger stated that the bill was meant to be remedial "in aid of the preservation of human liberty and human rights," and thus to be "liberally and beneficently construed." [FN13] Globe App. 68. **The bill *358 was meant to give "[f]ull force and effect . . . to section five" of the Fourteenth Amendment,** Globe 322 (Rep. Stoughton), [FN14] see *id.,* at 800 (Rep. Perry); *Monell,* 436 U.S., at 685 n. 45, 98 S.Ct., at 2033 n. 45, and therefore, like the prohibitions of that Amendment, to be addressed against the States themselves.[FN15] See, *e. g.,* *359 Globe 481-482 (Rep. Wilson); 696 (Sen. Edmunds).[FN16] It was, as Representative**1155 Kerr who opposed the bill instantly recognized, "against the rights of the States of this Union." *360 Globe App. 46. Representative Shellabarger, **in introducing the bill, made this explicit, stressing the need for "necessary affirmative legislation to enforce**1156 the personal rights which the *361 Constitution guaranties, as between persons in the State and the State itself."** *Id.,* at 70. See, *e. g., id.,* at 80 (Rep. Perry); Globe 375 (Rep. Lowe); 481-482 (Rep. Wilson); 568 (Sen. Edmunds). Representative Bingham elaborated the point:

> FN13. *Monell, supra,* stated that **"there can be no doubt that § 1 of the Civil Rights Act was intended . . . to be broadly construed . . . ."** 436 U.S., at 700, 98 S.Ct., at 2041. See *Lake Country Estates, Inc. v.*

Tahoe Regional Planning Agency, 440 U.S. 391, 399-400, and n. 17, 99 S.Ct. 1171, 1176-1177, and n. 17, 59 L.Ed.2d 401 (1979). Senator Thurman of Ohio, who opposed the Act, stated with respect to § 1 that "**there is no limitation whatsoever upon the terms that are employed, and** *they are as comprehensive as can be used.*" Cong. Globe, 42d Cong., 1st Sess., App. 217 (1871) (hereinafter Globe App.) (emphasis added).

FN14. **One of the reasons** given by the Court in *Hutto v. Finney,* 437 U.S. 678, 98 S.Ct. 2565, 57 L.Ed.2d 522 (1978), **for not requiring an "express statutory waiver of the State's immunity,"** *ante,* at 1147 n. 16, before applying to the States the Civil Rights Attorney's Fees Award Act of 1976, 42 U.S.C. § 1988, **was that the Act had been "enacted to enforce the Fourteenth Amendment."** 437 U.S., at 698 n. 31, 98 S.Ct., at 2578.

FN15. . . . It was common ground, at least after the Fourteenth Amendment, that Congress could "dea[l] with States and with citizens." Globe 777 (Sen. Frelinghuysen). See *id., at 793 (Rep. Poland).* Representative Willard of Vermont, for example, who voted for H.R. 320, opposed the Sherman amendment, which would have held a municipal corporation liable for damages to its inhabitants by private persons " 'riotously and tumultuously assembled,' " *Monell, supra,* **at 664, 98 S.Ct., at 2022, on the grounds that the Fourteenth Amendment imposed liability directly on the States and not on such municipal corporations: "I hold that this duty of protection, if it rests anywhere, rests on the State, and that if there is to be any liability visited upon anybody for a failure to perform that duty, such liability should be brought home to the State. Hence, in my judgment, this section would be liable to very much less objection, both in regard to its justice and its constitutionality, if it provided that if in any State the offenses named in this section were committed, suit might be brought against the State, judgment obtained, and payment of the judgment might be enforced upon the treasury of the State."** Globe 791.See *id.,* at 756-757 (Sen. Edmunds). There was general agreement, however, that just as Congress could not impose affirmative obligations on municipalities, *Monell, supra,* at 681 n. 40, 98 S.Ct., at 2031, n. 40, so it could not "command a State officer to do any duty whatever, as such." Globe 795 (Rep. Blair). See *id.,* at 799 (Rep. Farnsworth); *Collector v. Day,* 11 Wall. 113 (1871); *Kentucky v. Dennison,* 24 How.

66, 16 L.Ed. 717 (1861); *Prigg v. Pennsylvania*, 16 Pet. 539, 10 L.Ed. 1060 (1842). Contrary to the suggestion of the Court, *ante*, at 1146 n. 14, however, the *Prigg-Dennison-Day* line of cases, which stands for the principle that "the Federal Government . . . has no power to impose on a State officer, as such, any duty whatever," 24 How., at 107, **no more "militate[s] against" the conclusion that States are "persons" for purposes of § 1983, than it militates against the conclusion that municipalities are such persons. Everyone agreed, after all, that state officers, as such, would be subject to liability for violations of § 1983. The doctrine of coordinate sovereignty, relied on in the *Prigg-Dennison-Day* line of cases, would not have distinguished between such liability and the liability of the State itself.** See *Monell*, 436 U.S., at 682, 98 S.Ct., at 2031.

FN16. . . . **State violations of the Fourteenth Amendment could most effectively be reached through imposing liability on the state officials through whom States acted.** . . . For the neglect or refusal of a State to perform a constitutional duty, the remedies and power of enforcement given to the General Government are few and restricted. It cannot perform the duty the Constitution enjoins upon the State. If a State fails to appoint presidential electors, or its Legislature to choose Senators, or its people to elect Representatives, Congress cannot act for them. Nor do prohibitions upon States authorize Congress to exercise the forbidden power. **It may doubtless require State officers to discharge duties imposed upon them as such officers by the Constitution of the United States.** A State office must be assumed with such limitations and burdens, such duties and obligations, as the Constitution of the United States attaches to it. The General Government cannot punish the State, **but the officer who violates his official constitutional duty can be punished under Federal law. What more appropriate legislation for enforcing a constitutional prohibition upon a State than to compel State officers to observe it?** Its violation by the State can only be consummated through the officers by whom it acts." Globe App. 314. **It is noteworthy that, even under this view, § 1983 would abrogate the Eleventh Amendment immunity of States to the extent necessary to provide full relief for any plaintiff suing a state officer.** Cf. Globe 365-366 (Rep. Arthur); 385 (Rep. Lewis); Globe App. 217 (Sen. Thurman). **Thus, even if this limited approach had emerged out of concern for the Eleventh**

Amendment immunity of States, the distinction "between pro-spective relief on one hand and retrospective relief on the other," *ante*, at 1143, which was drawn by *Edelman v. Jordan,* 415 U.S. 651, 94 S.Ct. 1347, 39 L.Ed.2d 662 (1974), would be eliminated by the congressional enactment of § 1983. **"The powers of the States have been limited and the powers of Congress extended by the last three amendments of the Constitution. These last amendments—thirteen, fourteen, and fifteen—do, in my judgment, vest in Congress a power to *protect the rights of citizens against States,* and individuals in States, never before granted.**

Quern v. Jordan, **440 U.S. 332, 99 S.Ct. 1139 (U.S.Ill., 1979).**

569　U.S.C.A. Const.Amend. 11. *Mangual v. Toledo,* 536 F.Supp.2d 127 (D.Puerto Rico, 2008); *Gutierrez v. Joy* 502 F.Supp.2d 352 (S.D.N.Y., 2007); *Lumbreras v. Roberts,* 319 F.Supp.2d 1191 (D.Or., 2004); *Allen v. College of William & Mary,* 245 F.Supp.2d 777 (E.D.Va., 2003); *Stack v. City of Hartford,* 170 F.Supp.2d 288 (D.Conn., 2001); *U.S. ex rel. McVey v. Board of Regents of University of California,* 165 F.Supp.2d 1052 (N.D.Cal., 2001), citing *Hafer v. Melo,* 502 U.S. 21, 30-31, 112 S.Ct. 358, 364, 116 L.Ed.2d 301 (holding "the Eleventh Amendment does not erect a barrier against suits to impose individual and personal liability on state officials under § 1983"). "The Eleventh Amendment, however, provides no immunity for state officials sued in their personal capacities." *Woods v. Goord,* 1998 WL 740782. citing *Dube v. State Univ. of N.Y.,* 900 F.2d 587, 595 (2d Cir.1990); *Farid v. Smith,* 850 F.2d 917, 920-923 (2d Cir.1988).

570　*Edelman v. Jordan,* 415 U.S. 651, 662-63 (1974).

571　*Alabama v. Pugh,* 438 U.S. 781 (1978).

572　*See Ex parte Young,* 209 U.S. 123 (1908),

573　"Thus, to the extent that plaintiffs would wish this court to grant some other injunctive relief (such as an order to the Trial Court or DSS to return plaintiffs' children to the custody of plaintiffs, as I infer from plaintiffs' complaint that plaintiffs are requesting), such an order issued by this court would be inappropriate because it would interfere with ongoing state probate and family law proceedings. As explained . . . above, to make an order interfering with ongoing state probate and family law proceedings would be inappropriate even if plaintiffs had met the pleading requirements for prospective injunctive relief, which they have not. Plaintiffs' claims against the Trial Court and DSS under Count 2 of the Complaint are dismissed in the order below."

574   Because there are no ongoing state probate and family law proceedings, plaintiffs had no need to plead for prospective injunctive relief.

575   *Seminole Tribe of Florida v. Florida*, 5 17 U.S. 44, 56 (1996).

576   *Pennhurst State School and Hospital v. Halderman*, 465 1J.S. 89 (1984).

577   *See* M.G.L. c. 258.

578   M.G.L. c. 258.

579   *See Irwin v. Commissioner of Dep't of Youth Servs.*, 3SS Mass. 810, 811,448 N.E.2d 721 (1983).

580   M.G.L. c. 258.

581   *Baker v. Carr*, 369 U.S. 186, 82 S.Ct. 691 (U.S.Tenn. 1962).

582   *See* M.G.L. c. 119, ss. 21 and 24.

583   *See Cleavinper v. Saxner*, 474 U.S. 193, 201 (1985) ("'Our cases clearly indicate that immunity analysis re-sts on functional categories, not on the status of the defendant.'").

584   *Cok v. Cosentino*, 876 F.2d 1, 2 (1st Cir. 1989) (internal citations omitted).

585   *Clcavingcr v. Saxner*, 474 U.S. 193, 199 (1985).

586   *Cok*, 876 F.2d at 3 (citing *Cleavinger*, 474 U.S. at 200).

587   *See Cok*, 876 F.2d at 3-4 (guardian ad litem); *LaLonde v. Eissner*, 405 Mass. 207, 210-21 2 (1989) (psychiatrist in custody proceedings).

588   151 F.3d 1, 10 (1st Cir. (Puerto Rico) 1998) (Selya, J.)

589   *Id.*

590   *See Gonzales-Morales v. Hernandez-Arencibia*, 221 F.3d 45, 48-49 (1 st Cir. 2000).

591   *Cleavinger*, 474 U.S. at 199.

592   151 F.3d 1, 10 (1st Cir. 1998),

593   *See Lugar v. Edmondson Oil Co.*, 457 U.S. 922, 939 (1982).

594   *Rodriguez-Garcia v. Davila*, 904 F.2d 90, 97 (1st Cir. 1990).

595   *Id.*, quoting *Blum v. Yaretskv*, 457 U.S. 991, 1004 (1982).

596   *Rodripuez-Garcia,* 904 F.2d at 98, quoting *Rendell-Baker v. Kohn,* 457 U.S. 830, 842 (1982).

597   *Rodriguez-Garcia,* 904 F.2d at 97-98.

598   *Rodriguez-Garcia,* 904 F.2d at 96, quoting *Ponce v. Basketball Federation of the Commonwealth of Puerto Rico,* 760 F.2d 375, 377 (1st Cir. 1985).

599   *Rodriguez-Garcia,* 904 F.2d at 98.

600   *Id.*

601   *Id.*

602   151 F.3d 1, 10 (1st Cir. 1998).

603   *Id.*

604   Indeed, . . . there is case law to the effect that people who are solely complainants to, or witnesses for, the police in connection with a prosecution are not deemed to be state actors as a result. See, e.g., *Grow v. Fisher,* 523 F.2d 875, 879 (7th Cir., 1975). **That having been said, however, there is also case law supporting the proposition that to act under color of state law for §1983 purposes does not require that the defendant be an officer of the State. It is enough that he is a willful participant in joint action with the State or its agents. Private persons, jointly engaged with state officials in the challenged action, are acting see "under color" of law for purposes of §1983 actions.** *Adickes v. S. H. Kress & Co.,* 398 U.S. 144, 152, 90 S.Ct. 1598, 1605, 26 LEd.2d 142 (1970); *United States v. Price,* 383 U.S. 787, 794, 86 S.Ct. 1152, 1156, 16 L.Ed.2d 267 (1966).

Dennis v. Sparks, 449 U.S. 24, 27 (1980) (footnote omitted) (emphasis supplied). The First Circuit has reiterated the concept:

> A private party's conduct is attributable to the state if the state "has so far insinuated itself into a position of interdependence with [the private party] that it must be recognized as a joint participant in the challenged activity." *Barrios-Velazquez v. Asociacion De Empleados Del Estado LibreAsociado,* 84 F.3d 487, 494 (1st Cir.1996) (citation and internal quotation marks omitted; alteration in the original).

Camilo-Robles v. Hoyos, 151 F.3d 1, 10 (1st Cir., 1998).

605   *Cok,* 876 F.2d at 3.

606   *Rodriguez-Garcia v. Davila,* 904 F.2d at 96, quoting *Ponce,* 760 F.2d, at 377.

607   *Id.* at 11 104, 105, 108 and 112.

608   M.G.L. c. 119, § 51A.

609   *See Rivet-a-Ramos v. Roman*, 156 F.3d 276, 282 (1st Cir. 1998) ("citizens can furnish information to the police without automatically becoming responsible for what the police then do with the information."); *Roche v. John Hancock Mut. Life Ins. Co.*, 81 F.3d 249, 254 n.2 (1st Cir. 1996) (to the extent that the appellant's thesis implies that a private citizen who articulates his suspicions to the police may, without more, be held liable as a state actor under § 1983 for an ensuing arrest and prosecution if probable cause is lacking, we unequivocally reject it.").

610   *Rodriguez-Garcia*, 904 F.2d at 97.

611   *Id.*, quoting *Blum v. Yaretskv*, 457 U.S. 991, 1004 (1982).

612   26 F.3d 254, 257-258 (1st Cir. 1994).

613   *Blum*, 457 U.S. at 1008.

614   *Barrios-Velazquez v. Asociacion De Empleados De Estado Libre Asociado De Puerto Rico*, 84 F.3d 487,493 (1st Cir. 1996).

615   See, e.g., *Thomas v. Beth Israel Hosp. Inc.*, 710 F.Supp. 935, 940 (S.D.N.Y. 1989) ("The fact that Beth Israel was complying with the New York State Child Protective Services Act (Social Services Law Title 6, § 411 et seq.) by reporting suspected child abuse does not mean it acted under color of state law."); *Haag v. Cuvahoga County*, 619 F.Supp. 262, 283 (N.D.Ohio 1985), *affd*, 798 F.2d 1414 (6th Cir.1986) (mandatory state child abuse reporting statute did not transform private individual into state actor); *Benavidez v. Gunnell*, 722 F.2d 615, 618 (10th Cir.1983) (same).

616   *Imbler v. Pachtman*, 424 U.S. 409, 430 (1976) (certain administrative or investigative conduct might warrant only qualified immunity).

> ... Out of concern for the integrity of the judicial system, the Supreme Court in *Imbler* thus extended absolute immunity to those prosecutorial activities "intimately associated with the judicial phase of the criminal process," such as initiating a prosecution or presenting the State's case. [*Imbler*], at 430, 96 S.Ct. at 994. It specifically left unanswered the question whether prosecutorial activity which is not closely associated with the trial process, **such as certain administrative or investigative conduct**, might warrant only a qualified immunity.

Chicopee Lions Club v. District Atty. for Hampden Dist., 396 Mass. 244, 248 (1985) (emphasis supplied).

A ministerial role does not suffice to trigger protection under the umbrella of generic immunity. *Breault v. Chairman of the Bd. of Fire Commrs. of Springfield*, 401 Mass. 26, 38 (1987), *cert. denied sub nom. Forastiere v. Breault*, 485 U.S. 906 (1988) (holding, "where intentional ministerial acts of public officials are involved, there is no basis to conclude, under the relevant statutes and case law, that immunity from suit should be granted").

> The doctrine of **qualified immunity** shields public officials who are performing discretionary functions, not ministerial in nature, from civil liability in §1983 actions if at the time of the performance of the discretionary act, the constitutional or statutory right allegedly infringed was not "clearly established."

Laubinger v. Department of Rev., 41 Mass.App.Ct. 598, 603 (1996), quoting from *Harlow v. Fitzgerald*, 457 U.S. 800, 818 (1982) (emphasis supplied).

Endnotes—Chapter 20

617   Massachusetts General Law, c. 93A.

618   Massachusetts General Law, c. 231, s. 102C.

619   "The Big Picture," Massachusetts Lawyers Weekly, August 01, 2005.

620   Monroe L. Inker, "Power of GALs in High-Conflict Cases," Massachusetts Lawyers Weekly, 25 November 2002.

621   *See*, e.g., the studies summarized in Wallerstein and Tanke, "To Move or Not to Move," 30 Family Law Q. 305 (1996). The Wallerstein research appears to have had considerable influence on the thinking of several courts in recent years. Monroe L. Inker and Charles P. Kindregan, Jr., "Domestic Relations: Can Custodial Parents Dictate A Child's Home?" 25 M.L.W. 1307, February 24, 1997.

622   Massachusetts General Law, c. 215, §56A.

623   The telephone calls counted do NOT include those telephone calls which were not the first task in an entry and thus were not subject to the SORT program. So the calculated percentages in this letter are smaller than what they really are.

624   In *Stanford v. President and Fellows of Harvard College.* 2001 WL 716834 * 2, 2 n. 3 (Mass.Super. 2001) (Cratsley, J.), citing *McMillan v. Massachusetts Society for the Prevention of Cruelty to Animals,* (Lawyers Weekly No. 02-266-96, (Civil Action No. 92-11178-RGS) (Stearns, J.), the court wrote, "costs for items that should be absorbed as overhead in an attorney's hourly rate are not compensable. Thus all costs for photocopying, postage, telephone charges, faxes, legal research, travel, expedited delivery are excluded."

Here, SAF billed $4,391.35 for expenses, depending on whether the expenses are identified as "work" or "expenses." Given the billing system, it appears that something went inadvertently awry when committed to the bill.

Please note that the time spent by CLC doing legal research is not included in this file. Only those payments to third parties are included in the file.

In any event, the superior court agreed with the court in *McMillan* and did not award costs.

In note 18 of *McMillan v. Massachusetts Society for the Prevention of Cruelty to Animals,* 140 F.3d 288 (1st Cir. 3/18/98), the court denied the requested fees for time one counsel spent counseling with another about the case. Significantly, lots of time billed in Emory's case was for one attorney or staffer talking with another. For instance, there is very little SAM did without first speaking to or consulting with AEE, and then speaking to AEE after SAM finished whatever it was she had been doing.

Endnotes—Chapter 21

625   *http://www.falseallegations.com/drano95-court-commits-crimes.htm.*

626   My client's money had also been frozen by the family court, and despite the law in his favor, his motion for the release of some of it to pay transcribers had been denied.

627   Between the years 1997 and 2001, Armos Eyal brought 78 collection cases. He brought them in the name of "Eyal Court Reporting, Inc." 67 times; in the name of Amos Eyal one time; in his own name "Eyal, Armos, Rpr" 4 times; and in the name of "Eyral Court Reporting" 3 times. Prior to filing my client's appeal, I did not learn the number of cases brought by Eyal between 2002 and 2005.

628   *Electronic Case Filing CM/ECF, User's Manual,* United States District Court for the District of Massachusetts (October 16, 2003), p. 4.

629   *Lipman v. Commonwealth of Massachusetts,* 475 F.2d 505,] 568 [(1st Cir. 1973) (since transcription is by definition a verbatim recording of other persons' statements, there can be no originality in the reporter's product).

630   *Linnen v. A.H. Robins Co., Inc.,* 1999 WL 317434 *2, No. 97-2307 (Mass. Super. 1999) (Brassard, J.).

631   Oft heard is the argument from transcription companies that they own the copyright. They do not. The law of *Lipman, supra,* is correct.

Endnotes—Chapter 22

632   In *Rudders v. Building Com'r of Barnstable,* 51 Mass.App.Ct. 108, 744 N.E.2d 83 (2001), the Appeals Court held that the lower court erred in striking the Notice of Appeal from the court's judgment.

633   As the Barnstable committee correctly argues, while the lower court may annul a notice of appeal for certain procedural reasons, (FN7) there is no basis for annulling a Notice of Appeal filed by a party to the action for the reason that, in the lower court's view, the appeal would be without merit, whether for the appellant's lack of aggrievement, or for any other ground of substance. Questions going to the merits of the claimed appeal are for the appellate court to decide.

Rudders, 51 Mass.App.Ct. at 110-111, 744 N.E.2d at 84-85,

634   Pursuant to Massachusetts General Law, c. 211, sec. 3.

635   *Zieminski v. Berkshire Div. of Probate and Family Court Dept.,* 408 Mass. 1008, 563 N.E.2d 690 (1990),

636   The single justice of the Supreme Judicial Court denied relief, and the husband appealed. The Supreme Judicial Court held that husband could have sought relief in Appeals Court from judge's action dismissing appeals, and thus denial of relief by single justice was in accord with Court's practice of not exercising its extraordinary power of review unless appellate review is otherwise unavailable. *Id*

637   *Id.*

638   *Id. See also Associated Chiropractic Services, Inc. v. Travelers Ins. Co.*, 1998
Mass.App.Div. 189, 1998 WL 695957 at 3 (1998), citing *Zieminski*, 408 Mass.
at 1008, and *Catalano v. First Essex Sav. Bank*, 37 Mass.App.Ct. 377, 384, 639
N.E.2d 1113, 1118 (1994), for the same proposition.

639   Other cases in which an allowance of a motion to strike an appeal was
reversed are *Novicki v. Morin*, 48 Mass.App.Ct. 1122 (2000) ("Order allowing motion to strike the notice of appeal dated March 7, 1997, reversed").
AFA Protective Systems, Inc. v. Security Club of America, Inc., 45 Mass.App.Ct. 1111
(1998), *cert. denied*, 428 Mass. 1104 (1998) ("The order allowing the motion
to strike the November 28, 1995, notice of appeal is reversed"). *Tompkins v.
Dugan*, 39 Mass.App.Ct. 1115 (1995) ("Order allowing motion to strike notice
of appeal and to issue execution reversed").

640   *Catalano v. First Essex Sav. Bank*, 37 Mass.App.Ct. 377, 384, ___ N.E.2d
(1994), for the same proposition.

641   *Id.* at 383, citing *Robinson v. Planning Bd. of Wayland*, 23 Mass.App.Ct.
920, 921 (1986).

642   2008 Year-End Report on the Federal Judiciary, Appendix, p. 10.

643   *Id.*

Endnotes—Chapter 23

644   The case was what we called a "remand" case, which is a case brought
in a superior court and sent to a local district court for adjudication. If a party
is unhappy with the decision, one can appeal to the superior court. If unhappy with the superior court decision, one can appeal to the Appeals Court.
This case was originally filed in superior court, was remanded to district, was
appealed to superior court, then appealed to the Appeals Court, which returned it to superior court for further hearing and then back down to district
court. Northwest then filed for bankruptcy. The Bankruptcy Court then sent
it back to the Commonwealth. I had been disbarred by the time the case was
returned to the State court. When I was disbarred and ordered off my cases,
it was Peter's wife's interests—as well as mine—which were interfered with.
I am now unsure where its resting place is. Northwest's defense has not yet
been heard. Meehan is well over 80 and has retired. No final judgment has
issued. I have to find a way to exhume it and get a final judgment for Peter's
wife. The case is almost 22 years old.

645   See note 1, *supra.*

646   Strapped by funding and staff cuts, the Massachusetts Civil Service Commission may have to turn away hundreds of grievances brought by public service employees.

> "The budget of the current year reduced our staff of two to a staff of one and required that we lay off our only professional employee – our general counsel," said Alexander Macmillan, chairman of the commission.. . .

> "That means that we will have to concentrate on merit violations, patronage abuses and other grievances relating to new hires and promotions in municipal and state service jobs," said Macmillan. "It also means that everyone else – and this includes employees with wrongful hiring and suspension cases – will have to rely on their unions to protect them," he said. "We just cannot do it all." . . .

> "This is a situation where the board is holding hearings, but it's not rendering any decisions because there is no legal counsel," said Grace. "The budget is too tight." . . .

> The agency announces Civil Service examinations and tests and acts as an informal court for state employees, who can appeal everything from a firing to a two-day suspension.

Diane E. Lewis, "Budget cuts hamper Mass. Civil Service grievance process," Boston Globe, October 18. 1995.

647   Salvatore "Sal" DiMasi (D) (September 28, 2004–January 27, 2009), resigned from both Speaker position and seat in House after a Federal Grand Jury probe had been launched investigating the charges that he and three associates received large payments related to multimillion dollar contracts. Thomas Finneran (D) (April 9, 1996–September 28, 2004), resigned and subsequently charged with three counts of perjury, but pled guilty in federal court to the obstruction of justice for misrepresenting his participation in the redistricting process. Charles Flaherty (D) (1991–April 9, 1996) was forced from office under a cloud after pleading guilty to a federal felony tax charge and admitting state ethics violations. .

For the pat year, two legislators have been hoping to fill DiMasi's position. One, Robert DeLeo, still appears to be clean. The other, majority leader John H. Rogers, "has been dogged by his own ethics scandal: He has been accused of paying a consultant with campaign funds, who in turn made mortgage payments on Rogers's Cape Cod vacation home." **Matt Viser,** "Despite investigations, DiMasi reelected House speaker," **Boston Globe,** January 7, 2009. As of January 28, 2009, DeLeo, still appearing to be clean, was chosen to be the New Speaker. I am curious as to whether he is related to Judge DeLeo . . . and what network connectivity he has!

648   Lopez and Bellotti were an item, frequently dining out together and with friends. Details can be seen in the Special Hearing Officer's Hearing Report at *http://www.mass.gov/obcbbo/ccd.pdf,* authored by M. Ellen Carpenter, Special Hearing Officer, May 11, 2005.

649   The first case was a young man. The second was for that young man's sister.

650   *http://www.fathersunite.org/Fathers%20Stories%20and%20Fatherlessness/ FathersStory_chris_kennedy.html.*

651   *http://www.opednews.com/maxwrite/diarypage.php?did=11309.*

Endnotes—Chapter 24

652   All the pleadings I wrote in this fight may be seen on my website, *http:// www.falseallegations.com.* Look for **The Bar v. Barb**, as well as **Barb v. The Bar**, when I sued them. You will find all the links to them in the Drano Series Table on my Home Page. You'll want to see Drano ##102 and 106 and all the appellate pleadings, including those filed in the U.S. Supreme Court. My last appeal was filed in 2008 and has not yet been uploaded to my website.

653   The appeal was resolved on December 5, 2007, and, as anticipated, was unsuccessful. It was a political decision. Justice was never considered.

654   *http://www.fitsnews.com/2009/02/11/tainted-report-damages-courts-credibility/.*

4222892

Made in the USA
Lexington, KY
07 January 2010